Medieval Crime Fiction

D1297245

Medieval Crime Fiction

A Critical Overview

ANNE MCKENDRY

McFarland & Company, Inc., Publishers
Jefferson, North Carolina

LIBRARY OF CONGRESS CATALOGUING-IN-PUBLICATION DATA

Names: McKendry, Anne (Anne Louise), author.
Title: Medieval crime fiction : a critical overview / Anne McKendry.
Description: Jefferson, North Carolina : McFarland & Company, Inc.,
    2019 | Includes bibliographical references and index.
Identifiers: LCCN 2019008918 | ISBN 9781476666716 (paperback : acid
    free paper) ∞
Subjects: LCSH: Detective and mystery stories—History and criticism. |
    Historical fiction—History and criticism. | Medievalism in literature.
Classification: LCC PN3448.D4 M38 2019 | DDC 809.3/872—dc23
LC record available at https://lccn.loc.gov/2019008918

BRITISH LIBRARY CATALOGUING DATA ARE AVAILABLE

ISBN (print) 978-1-4766-6671-6
ISBN (ebook) 978-1-4766-3625-2

Front cover: Derek Jacobi and Sean Pertwee in *Cadfael*, 1994
(ITV/Shutterstock)

Printed in the United States of America

McFarland & Company, Inc., Publishers
  Box 611, Jefferson, North Carolina 28640
  www.mcfarlandpub.com

For Jase, Josh and Hamish

Table of Contents

Acknowledgments

I very much thank Stephen Knight, who has encouraged this project from the beginning, discussed many aspects of it over several years, read through the manuscript (more than once), and offered invaluable advice at every stage.

I am, as ever, grateful to Stephanie Trigg for her unwavering support, generous mentorship and crucial suggestions in the book's final stages.

I have had the opportunity to present material at several seminars and conferences and I thank, in particular, John Ganim, Bruce Holsinger, Helen Young and the members of Melbourne University's Medieval Round Table for helpful and productive discussions.

Helen Hickey has worked alongside me and this book for a long time and I acknowledge her wonderful and supportive collegiality.

During a tea break at a symposium, Jenny Spinks suggested an appendix and this has helped to alleviate guilt about unavoidable omissions, for which I thank her.

Thanks go to Layla Milholen for helpful and sympathetic editorial support. I would also like to acknowledge and thank the two anonymous readers for their positive responses and constructive feedback.

The University of Melbourne's School of Culture and Communication Publication Support Scheme provided financial assistance for which I am grateful.

Finally, my husband Jason has provided unconditional encouragement and continued sustenance. He avows he is going to write his own medieval crime fiction series, featuring Scandinavian "Thorsten Tungsten," and I look forward to this very much indeed.

Introduction

Whenever I am asked why I am so fascinated with medieval crime fiction, I invariably find myself recounting an early scene from Ellis Peters' first novel featuring Brother Cadfael, *A Morbid Taste for Bones* (1977).[1] Upon viewing the body of a Welsh landowner who had objected to the bones of Saint Winifred being taken from her local burial site to the Benedictine monastery in nearby Shrewsbury, Prior Robert diagnoses divine intervention: "'Behold the saint's vengeance! Did I not say her wrath would be wreaked upon all those who stood in the way of her desire? ... Saint Winifred has shown her power and her displeasure'" (Peters, *Morbid Taste* 93). But one of the onlookers objects to Robert's assessment:

> "I don't believe it! ... What, a gentle virgin saint, to take such vengeance on a good man? ... If she had been so pitiless as to want to slay—and I do not believe it of her!— what need would she have of arrows and bows? Fire from heaven would have done her will just as well, and shown her power better. You are looking at a murdered man, Father Prior" [Peters, *Morbid Taste* 94].

Brother Cadfael agrees and diplomatically offers his observations through the same otherworldly frame: "'And the young man's right. This arrow never was shot from heaven. Look at the angle of it, up from under his ribs into the heart. Out of the earth, rather! A man with a short bow, on his knee among the bushes? True, the ground slopes...'" (Peters, *Morbid Taste* 94). Cadfael's tacit acceptance of divine intervention is crucial here: he does not deny that Saint Winifred *could* strike down a man who had displeased her; she simply was not responsible in this particular case.

This is a wonderful example of the complex intertwining of modernity and premodernity that medieval detectives constantly encounter throughout their investigations across the varied landscapes of the European Middle Ages. Brother Cadfael risks a charge of heresy should he deny the possibility that Saint Winifred intervened into earthly matters that displeased her. Rather than dismissing the potential for saintly intervention, however, Cadfael instead offers a logical explanation for the landowner's death-by-arrow that does not preclude the saint's ability to wreak vengeance from heaven, but carefully excludes this possibility on the grounds of the monk's assessment of the empirical evidence. Following the familiar procedure of many a literary detective before and after him, Cadfael perceives the solution that best fits the circumstances of the crime. And doing so successfully within the context of the Middle Ages renders Cadfael an exemplar of medieval crime fiction detectives.

The aim of this book is to explore the popular genre of medieval crime fiction: narratives featuring a crime or mystery that is solved by a "detective" and set during the European Middle Ages. These novels sit at the intersection of the historical novel, crime fiction and medievalism, harnessing the immense appeal of each to contemporary popular culture. The historical novel has consistently beguiled readers since at least Sir Walter Scott's *Ivanhoe* (1819), while detective fiction emerged in the mid-nineteenth century in such works as Edgar Allan Poe's short stories featuring Auguste Dupin (1841) and Wilkie Collins's *The Moonstone* (1868). The popularity of detective fiction rose exponentially between the two world wars of the twentieth century with the advent of the English clue-puzzle mysteries and the simultaneous development of the American hardboiled or private-eye model. Combining a detective narrative and a historical novel is not a particularly innovative generic move, but nor had it been particularly successful or widespread. However, the separate (although remarkably concurrent) decisions by Ellis Peters and Umberto Eco in the late 1970s to situate a detective story within a medieval setting propelled these novels into an unexpected realm of popularity.

Considering the precise conventions that structure this unprepossessing genre, it may surprise some to learn that there are hundreds of these novels, most collected into series, written by variously skilled authors. Today, detective narratives located in the European Middle Ages account for a disproportionate number of historical crime novels.[2] This book delves deeply into the previously unexamined genre of medieval crime fiction in an effort to uncover what generates this popularity. Is it simply a case of three popular culture genres magnifying each other to become more than the sum of their parts? Or is it the result of cultural, political or social forces that demand a gentle form of escapism from postmodernity? Or both?

Crime fiction is a vast and enormously popular literary field that, most critics conditionally accept, grew out of Edgar Allan Poe's short stories written in the mid-nineteenth century. Today, crime saturates our bookshelves, television screens and podcast feeds. For a genre that adheres securely to a recognizable and (relatively) stable set of conventions, crime fiction has succeeded in adapting and appropriating popular culture trends across multiple media platforms for almost two centuries. From the traditional narratives of the clue puzzle, hardboiled and police procedural novels, crime fiction has embraced literature's engagement with race, gender, sexuality and postcolonialism, among other social and political debates. Crime fiction has also generated innovative scholarship from both literary and cultural critics. Chapter One examines the crime fiction genre in more detail, outlining the generic framework within which medieval crime fiction flourishes.

Contemporary medievalism often reveals more about the culture that produces it than the medieval world it depicts. For example, nineteenth-century medievalism reached back nostalgically to a simpler, feudal world in which adherents could escape the fast-paced development of the Industrial Revolution and the modern cities. On the other hand, late-twentieth and early-twenty-first century medievalist incarnations tend more towards an ironic recreation of the Middle Ages, in which the nostalgia of the nineteenth century is replaced by postmodernity's critical distance. Postmodern culture reimagines the Middle Ages in order to address contemporary concerns: it understands that the medieval world was not comprised simply of castles, knights and princesses. The enormous success of Mel Gibson's epic, *Braveheart* (1995), for example, was generated in part by a burgeoning interest in Scottish devolution in the mid–1990s. In 2010, Russell Crowe and Ridley Scott produced yet another film version of Robin Hood, feeling that "the time seemed right" for a "reboot" of the famous English outlaw. Unspoken, but unavoidably present in this decision is the underlying influence of the Global Financial Crisis and its aftermath, in which the perpetrators of the crisis—large banks and corporations—appeared to be emerging unscathed thanks to government bail-outs across the world. Crowe and Scott offered a timely reminder that economic independence should be a fundamental human right and not reserved for the powerful alone; and they inscribed their message upon the landscape of the Middle Ages. More recently, Kazuo Ishiguro's *The Buried Giant* (2015) has beautifully reimagined an Arthurian landscape, disintegrating under the pressure of the Anglo-Saxon incursion, in order to explore contemporary issues surrounding collective identity and nationalist memory. Medieval crime fiction enacts both of these forms of medievalism: a nostalgic recreation of an idealized, simpler past; and a postmodern, ironic revisitation of a turbulent and fascinating historical period. Its popularity suggests that contemporary popular culture has once again marshaled the Middle Ages in order to create a safe space in which to address social, political or cultural concerns. This book endeavors to identify and account for those concerns.

It is, of course, not possible to describe, let alone comprehensively analyze, the vast body of work that comprises medieval crime fiction and so this book applies certain parameters to the following chapters. Firstly, I take seriously the modern or postmodern literary detective's primary function as the seeker of a rational, secular and, above all, human explanation for whatever crime or mystery he or she must solve. As any cursory glance at medievalist fiction, television, film or gaming will reveal, contemporary popular culture's love affair with the Middle Ages often involves sorcery (dark or benign), supernatural creatures such as dragons or giants or elves, and direct intervention by divine or diabolical forces. Novels set in the Middle Ages that feature these and related tropes, more appropriately termed "medievalist fantasy," are thus precluded, even if many of them also feature a mystery to be solved, an injustice to be corrected, and a main character that functions in a detective-like manner. Having denied entry to these novels, I must immediately append a tiny caveat: some of the novels *do* offer glimpses of unexplained or magical happenings, but these are either extraneous to the detective narrative or represent an author's dalliance with medieval mysticism in one or two novels within a longer series that privileges detective fiction conventions. These exceptions also illustrate a common medievalist practice by highlighting the irresistible lure of recreating an otherworldly and fantastical Middle Ages.

For similar reasons, novels that involve any form of time travel have no place in this book. Connie Willis's *Doomsday Book* (1992), despite its beguilingly authentic depiction of England ravaged by the Black Plague in the 1340s, is generically closer to science fiction than crime fiction.[3] There are also numerous examples of investigators in the twentieth or twenty-first centuries who discover an ancient text or artifact that represents some sort of puzzle to be solved. These novels either offer parallel narratives taking place in the present and the past or allow the contemporary detective access to the earlier period through some mysterious portal. Julia Kristeva's masterful postmodernist novel, *Murder in Byzantium* (2006), describes the actions of a serial killer in the present day, informed by the chaos of the first crusade in the eleventh century and its impact on the Byzantine Empire. More recently, Julie Christine Johnson's debut novel, *In Another Life* (2016), features Cathar historian Lia Carrer, who returns to Languedoc after her husband's death. Lia researches the thirteenth-century murder of a papal envoy attributed to the Cathars and resulting in the pope's declaration of a crusade against the heretical sect. Lia's investigation uncovers reincarnation and miraculous occurrences, both past and present, that she must force her rational mind to accept in order to succeed in her quest to resolve a medieval injustice. Most of these novels feature an academic, or academically minded, protagonist in what seems to be a not-so-subtle aligning of the scholar's and the detective's roles. There is doubtless some wish-fulfillment, too, for every researcher's dream is to discover that forgotten, unique, life-changing object, fragment or remnant from the past.

For reasons of space, I have also excluded novels that do not fall within the conventional temporal range of the Middle Ages; that is, the years between about 500 CE and 1500 CE While this arbitrary periodization—historically based upon defining the period between the "fall" of Rome and the European "discovery" of the Americas—has been productively problematized by historians and literary critics, it is nevertheless useful in this case as an exclusionary frame. However, imposing these temporal limits necessitates the omission of historical crime novels set in the ancient world, as well as the early modern period and beyond. There is even a short story set in the Australian Dreamtime, approximately 35,000 BCE, "Death in the Dawntime" by F. Gwynplaine MacIntyre, which features a "locked-cave" murder. The editor of the collection in which it appears, Mike Ashley, is "sure that makes it the earliest setting ever used for a detective story" (Ashley 3). Since Ashley's 1995 assertion, however, Kaye George in 2013 began a mystery series set in the time of the Neanderthals ("between about 230,000 and 30,000 years ago"), featuring a tribe struggling to survive as the climate teeters on the brink of an ice age (5). Agatha Christie's *Death Comes as the End* (1944) was her only novel set outside of the twentieth century (in Egypt in 2000 BCE), and is probably the earliest full-length historical mystery, narrowly preceding Robert van Gulik's first Judge Dee book, based on an eighteenth-century Chinese manuscript, published in 1949.[4] Lindsey Davis writes two well-received series set in the Roman world of the first century CE: twenty novels feature her detective, Marcus Didius Falco, while more recently, Davis has cast Falco's adopted daughter, Flavia Albia, as a detective in her own right. Prolific historical crime author Paul C. Doherty has written several series set in ancient Egypt, ancient Rome and ancient Greece that are not discussed here, although he does appear frequently throughout this book thanks to his medieval crime novels. C.J. Sansom's acclaimed novels featuring lawyer Matthew Shardlake are set during the reign of Henry VIII. Shardlake practices law at Lincoln's Inn and, in the first two novels, is reluctantly dispatched to investigate suspicious circumstances by Henry's chief minister, Thomas Cromwell. After Cromwell's demise, Shardlake finds himself in the service of (and a little bit in love with) Henry's sixth wife, Catherine Parr. While Sansom's Shardlake series is too Tudor-oriented to be included here, the author nevertheless makes an appearance in Chapter Three, as part of the collaborative writing effort undertaken by the so-called "Medieval Murderers."

This book also limits its geographical scope to western Europe, precluding novels such as Mary Reed and Eric Mayer's John the Eunuch series, set in sixth-century Constantinople. While this series just scrapes into the temporal limit of 500 CE, the continuation of the eastern Roman and Greek empire until well into the fifteenth century means that John—who serves the emperor Justinian—is more eastern European than western. This geographical constraint similarly excludes series set in medieval Asia, such as I.J. Parker's seventeen-book series set in Japan in the eleventh century, featuring Sugawara Akitada, and Robert van Gulik's Judge Dee series, noted above. Appearing originally in 1949, Judge Dee featured in numerous novels and short stories until the first full-length novel, *Poets and Murder*, published in 1968. The novels continue to be adapted into television series in the United States and China (most recently in the Chinese series *Young Sherlock* [2014]), as well as numerous films. Several other authors still write Judge Dee stories in English, French and Chinese.[5]

The decision to focus on the European Middle Ages has the effect of rendering this book rather western-oriented. However, in addition to the methodological necessity of restricting the number of qualifying novels to somewhere close to a manageable number, it is also true that the overwhelming majority of historical crime fiction novels—written in or translated into English—are set in the western European medieval period.[6] The greatest number are more precisely located in what is now the United Kingdom and Ireland. Despite the stratospheric rise in popularity that Scandinavian crime fiction has enjoyed over the past two or three decades, very few of these are set in the Middle Ages. There is Indrek Hargla's "Apothecary Melchior" series, located in early fifteenth-century Estonia, comprising six novels, the first two of which have been translated into English. Martin Jensen's "King Knud" series comes close: written in Danish, it features the investigative team of Halfdan (half Danish and half Saxon) and the Saxon former monk Winston, who now makes a living as an illustrator. The series takes place in England during the Viking reign of Cnut in the early eleventh century. Of the six books currently in the series, the first three have been translated into English.

The appeal of premodern England, Scotland, Wales, Ireland and, to a lesser extent, France and Italy, to contemporary authors of crime fiction is something that this book endeavors to comprehend, in addition to deciphering why a large proportion of these authors are based outside of Europe, particularly in North America. There seems to be two layers of nostalgia operating here: the deep (and often problematic) attachment to the fantasy of a medieval past by postcolonial societies; and a yearning for golden-age crime fiction in which the detective's role has not been superseded by the advances of forensic science.

This book is structured around the identity and generic type of its detectives rather than their geographical or temporal location. In other words, here genre supersedes history and so there is some blurring of periods that are usually separated, such as the early and late Middle Ages. As with all crime fiction, the character of the detective is fundamental to these novels, particularly when they form a series, and I have therefore grouped secular male detectives together in Chapter Two, religious male investigators in Chapter Three, female sleuths in Chapter Four, and so on. These character types interact with their medieval landscapes in very different ways: a cloistered nun, for example, has markedly less freedom of movement than a knight-coroner in charge of investigating suspicious deaths across an entire county. It seems more useful, then, to compare detectives in similar positions and facing analogous experiences in order to draw conclusions about the cultural work that medieval crime fiction undertakes. While all of the novels do conform to one or more of the familiar crime fiction subgenres such as the clue puzzle, spy thriller, or private eye, they invariably privilege the character of the medieval detective and the meticulously recreated Middle Ages: it is not uncommon that the crime narrative is not well executed and exists solely to allow the author to showcase his or her deep knowledge of medieval history and culture.

Chapter One constructs an academic framework for medieval crime fiction. It briefly discusses the scholarship that has productively investigated crime fiction over the past several decades, as well as exploring the excellent criticism emerging from medievalism studies. While neither of these fields has considered medieval crime fiction in any great depth, they nevertheless illuminate the cultural work that medieval crime fiction undertakes in reflecting and refracting contemporary popular culture. But, as will become clear as this book progresses, medieval crime fiction also intervenes into the crime fiction genre more broadly, troubling the pervasive "scientist is king [or queen]" trope that has dominated crime fiction over the past two or three decades. In other words, medieval crime fiction challenges the frenetic pace of advanced forensic techniques and recalls—often nostalgically—the ratiocinative processes of earlier detective traditions.

In terms of medievalism, the Middle Ages of western Europe continues to cast its spell over contemporary popular culture; in this case, it is happily complicit in crime fiction's appropriation of its irresistible characters, castles and cruelties to enable the latter's generic conventions to impose order and justice upon what many modern readers perceive to be an unruly premodern world. The detectives of medieval crime fiction translate the Middle Ages for a postmodern audience, demystifying this "foreign country" through the literary detective's ongoing search for a secular and rational solution to crime. However, this translation is not without risk: the detective necessarily imposes a distinctly modern form of justice upon Europe's premodern streets and this threatens to undermine the authenticity of the carefully constructed landscape of the Middle Ages. In this way, medievalism both scaffolds and destabilizes these historical crime novels. On the one hand, it offers the allure of a premodern crime scene that is mercifully free from the intervention of police tape and forensic teams, leaving the detective free to deploy his or her own observational and deductive powers in the service of solving the crime. On the other hand, this ratiocinative approach may undermine the authenticity of the medieval world that these authors meticulously recreate.

The second part of Chapter One considers the origins of medieval crime fiction and revisits the significant amount of scholarship written about Umberto Eco and, to a lesser extent, Ellis Peters. Peters is widely recognized as the first author to locate murder mysteries in the Middle Ages with her Brother Cadfael series, the first of which was published in 1977. Umberto Eco's *Il Nome della Rosa* was published in 1980, with the English translation released in 1983 (*The Name of the Rose*). These two contrasting writers remain among the most popular and successful of medieval crime fiction authors. There are two or three other authors who did, in fact, experiment with crime in the Middle Ages before Peters and two obscure texts will be examined, with a brief assessment of Jeremy Potter's *Death in the Forest* (1977) and Edward Frankland's *Murders at Crossby* (1955).[7]

In Chapter Two, the secular male investigators almost all conform to the conventions of "private eye" or "hardboiled" detective fiction. This is perhaps not surprising given that many of these characters are knights, former knights, ex-crusaders or bailiffs: they are handy with a sword and not afraid to use violence in the course of their investigations. But there are also doctors, scribes, clerks and booksellers, among others, and these less physically minded characters nevertheless inhabit narratives with distinctly hardboiled overtones. Chapter Two discusses, among others, Bernard Knight's twelfth-century coroner (or crowner) Sir John de Wolfe; Paul C. Doherty's Hugh Corbett, clerk and eventual spy for Edward III; Crispin Guest, Jeri Westerson's disgraced knight who scratches a living as a "tracker" on the mean streets of fourteenth-century London; and Susanna Gregory's fourteenth-century Cambridge physician, Matthew Bartholomew.

Chapter Three focuses on male detectives who are members of religious orders (excluding Ellis Peters' Brother Cadfael and Umberto Eco's William of Baskerville), considering in detail the restraints that a monastic life imposes upon a premodern detective, particularly with regard to the inherent medieval belief in divine and diabolical intervention. The literary detective must conform to the rules of "ratiocination," established by Poe's Auguste Dupin and entrenched in the crime fiction formula by Sherlock Holmes, Hercule Poirot and many characters since. However, as illustrated by the example that opened this introduction, medieval detectives—and religious ones especially—must cautiously navigate strongly held beliefs that God, Christ, the saints and Satan all actively intervene into earthly affairs. The manner in which these characters negotiate such contradictions is at times wonderful to behold. Religious detectives who undertake this delicate balancing act include Paul C. Doherty's egalitarian Brother Athelstan, based in a Southwark parish in the years leading up to and following the Great Uprising of 1381, an event that significantly informs the series. Maureen Ash's Bascot de Marins, a member of the Templar Order, is one of the very few medieval religious detectives to overcome a crisis of faith and return to the religious life after what might be termed an existential sabbatical. Of particular interest in this chapter are the two examples of medieval crime fiction that have received nominations for the UK's Booker Prize: John Fuller's *Flying to Nowhere* (1983) and Barry Unsworth's *Morality Play* (1995). Fuller's novel has received little critical attention and deserves more sustained examination for its provocatively complex metaphysical and allegorical medieval landscape. *Morality Play* was well-received by reviewers and adapted into a 2003 film called *The Reckoning* (directed by Paul McGuigan), which did not enjoy similar acclaim.

Chapter Four features the female detectives of medieval crime fiction, religious and secular. Women in the Middle Ages faced more restrictions than their male relations, although they were perhaps not as constrained as is popularly believed. Recent scholarship has recovered female voices from the medieval past, constructing a more complex account of their lives, occupations and agency. While both crime fiction and the Middle Ages have traditionally been viewed as privileging a patriarchal culture, feminist crime fiction and feminist medieval studies have productively challenged both of these positions. Chapter Four's medieval female investigators embrace the individual agency of the detective as a challenge to the entrenched patriarchy of the Middle Ages and, indeed, crime fiction more broadly. While there are a number of female medieval detectives in secular roles, many of them are members (or former members) of religious orders; these nuns, prioresses and abbesses demonstrate ingenious methods for obtaining information and evidence while ostensibly enclosed by the walls of a priory or abbey. Undermining the feminist project that many authors appear to promote, however, is the inevitable male companion, mentor, servant or partner whose presence is necessary to penetrate spaces or situations from which a woman is excluded.

Sister Fidelma, created by Peter Tremayne, is probably the most popular of these female medieval detectives, while Margaret Frazer's Dame Frevisse and Ariana Franklin's Adelia Aguilar also enjoy a devoted following.

Discussion of race in the Middle Ages is another area where medieval studies is attempting to recalibrate longstanding assumptions about the interaction among different ethnicities in the premodern world. Chapter Five considers medieval crime fiction's depiction of racial, religious and cultural conflict by exploring how these novels represent Jewish communities in medieval Europe. After Edward I's 1290 expulsion edicts, there was (theoretically) no Jewish presence in England for three hundred and sixty-odd years, until Oliver Cromwell overturned the edicts in 1657. A surprising number of medieval crime fiction authors have embraced the likely possibility that some Jewish people remained resident in England despite the expulsion orders, while others maintained trade links through secret journeys to London and elsewhere at considerable risk to themselves. Medieval crime fiction authors invariably portray these characters as sympathetic, intelligent and moral, harshly treated and undeserving of their arbitrary banishment. These authors similarly represent the non–Jewish characters who continued to trade with them and keep their secrets as performing a moral duty despite breaching the law. Notably, most medieval crime fiction series include at least one novel that features a Jewish character at the center of the narrative, while Jewish people make cameo appearances in a substantial proportion of all medieval crime fiction novels. This chapter explores the work of a range of medieval crime fiction novels, including those by Margaret Frazer, Tim Shaw and Jeri Westerson. While these authors confront the challenge of bringing Jewish characters into England during the interdict, Chapter Five will also consider the depiction of Jewish communities in thirteenth-century France by Sharan Newman, as well as Caroline Roe's Jewish detective, Isaac of Girona.

A recent trend in historical crime fiction casts famous authors or other well-known personages as detectives. Examples include Jane Austen, Arthur Conan Doyle, Charles Dickens, Benjamin Franklin, Elizabeth I, Oscar Wilde, Sigmund Freud, and many others. Medieval crime fiction also participates in this movement, with Geoffrey Chaucer, John Gower, Leonardo da Vinci, Dante Alighieri, Hildegard of Bingen, and Niccolò Machiavelli among the famous medieval figures that authors have pressed into service as investigators of crime. While every medieval crime novel portrays some historical figures, creating a revisionist biography of an author as canonical as Chaucer, for example, brings with it significant cultural baggage. Readers of medieval crime fiction—like readers of historical fiction generally—derive pleasure from identifying the inconsistencies and anachronisms contained in the narratives. Casting a historical figure in the main role greatly increases the chance of inaccuracies and thereby threatens the authenticity of the medieval landscape that the author constructs. For this reason, authors look for poorly documented periods in the biographies of figures such as Chaucer: for example, the poet's several trips to Italy and France on shadowy business for the crown. Chapter Six examines the consequences of casting a historical figure as a detective, especially one familiar to most readers. While the authenticity effect is important, these authors can also benefit from their readers' familiarity with the life and literary work of famous figures: Chaucer's *Canterbury Tales* is particularly appealing and structures the novels by Gertrude and Joseph Clancy and Mary Devlin, for example. Even Chaucer's scribe, Adam Scriven, becomes a detective who investigates Chaucer's alleged rape of Cecilia Champaigne in Garry O'Connor's *Chaucer's Triumph* (2007). Another popular figure is Leonardo da Vinci, whose unquestionable expertise with art, mechanics and anatomy provides him with unrivalled qualifications as a medieval detective: Martin Woodhouse, Robert Ross, Javier Sierra and Diane A.S. Stuckart approach their depictions of the historical Leonardo in remarkably different ways, indicating the malleability of the fifteenth-century inventor and artist.

As the following chapters demonstrate, medieval crime fiction is a varied, complex and appealing form of contemporary medievalism that not only recreates the European Middle Ages with an affectionate and rigorous approach to historical authenticity, it also makes intriguing interventions into crime fiction more broadly. By investigating medieval crime fiction's location at the intersection of the historical novel, medievalism and crime fiction, this book seeks to reveal the formula behind its consistent and widespread appeal.

Chapter One

Genres and Origins

Most people immediately comprehend the phrase "medieval crime fiction" through reference to the genre's famous novel, Umberto Eco's *The Name of the Rose*, published in 1980 and translated into English in 1983. When prompted further, fewer people recognize the names "Ellis Peters" and "Brother Cadfael," although enough do to suggest that they, too, retain some measure of cultural traction. At the very least, mention of these two authors and their novels addresses the question of what is meant by "medieval crime fiction": a contemporary crime novel that is set in the Middle Ages; not, as might be thought, crime narratives written during the medieval period.[1]

Medieval crime fiction combines the historical novel, medievalism and the conventions of detective fiction. This structure generates an unavoidable, productive and entertaining incongruity by allowing an essentially secular, (post)modern literary detective to operate in a religious, premodern context. Few medieval crime fiction authors acknowledge this incongruity as overtly as Eco, who explores how the postmodern literary detective fails to operate successfully within a medievalist world. Most other authors, including Ellis Peters, attempt to suppress this incongruity by invoking layers of nostalgia, both for the Middle Ages and for conventional detective forms. Medieval crime fiction fluctuates between this nostalgia and the irony inherent in creating a medievalist world for the purpose of portraying a modern, or postmodern, detective narrative, producing a complicated entanglement of nostalgic recreation and ironic revisitation of the Middle Ages. This structure also offers an intriguing and positive response to postmodernism's suspicion of historical authenticity and its call to revisit the past with a critical awareness of the present.

The Historical Novel and Postmodernism

According to Georg Lukács's influential 1937 study of the historical novel,[2] the originator and master of the form was Sir Walter Scott.[3] Lukács asserts

13

that the success of the historical novel is judged not by its faithful portrayal of the historical setting, but by the accurate depiction of the social and psychological behavior of its characters according to the mores of the time in which the novel is placed (42). Fredric Jameson has more recently described the historical novel as traditionally forming a "contract" between the author and reader "whereby we agree to tolerate a certain number of fictional characters and actions within a framework equally agreed to be factual" (298).

Today's postmodern interests call into question the ability to achieve this accuracy and even Lukács admits to the need for "necessary anachronism" in order to "translate" the language and manners of the past for the sake of clarity (62–63). Following Scott and his successors such as Hugo, Pushkin and Tolstoy, the historical novel suffered a certain marginalization and "feminization" during the late nineteenth- and early twentieth-century, often more frequently associated with romance and "light reading" (Wallace 76). However, the realization that the historical novel perfectly suited the postmodern project of questioning historical authenticity led to the appropriation of the form by writers such as Umberto Eco, John Fowles and A.S. Byatt. These novelists distinguished themselves from traditional historical fiction by their "recognition of the subjectivity, the uncertainty, the multiplicity of truths inherent in any account of past events" (Rozett 145). Postmodernist literature is, according to historian Hayden White, "the most 'historically-obsessed' literary movement in the history of the West" and the literary devices employed in historical fiction allow the "truth" to be subjected to what *could* have happened as well as what *did* happen (148–49).

Linda Hutcheon describes the link between history and literature as "the parodically doubled discourse of postmodernist intertextuality" (*Poetics* 128). Hutcheon defines parody as the "ironic use of intertextual references" ("Power" 41), and notes that the reprise of the past that parody performs is not nostalgic, but always critical (*Politics* 93): it is irony that gives parody its power ("Power" 39). For example, Eco's *The Name of the Rose* retells stories of both literature (Conan Doyle, Voltaire, etc.) and history (medieval religious tracts, chronicles, etc.) in an ironic manner that is designed to question modes of historical representation (Hutcheon, *Poetics* 128). For Hutcheon, "postmodern irony is the structural recognition that discourse today cannot avoid acknowledging its situation in the world it represents" ("Power" 36). Furthermore, postmodernism aims

> To make us look to the past from the acknowledged distance of the present, a distance which inevitably conditions our ability to know that past. The ironies produced by that distancing are what prevent the postmodern from being nostalgic: there is no desire to return to the past as a time of simpler or more worthy values [Hutcheon, *Poetics* 230].

Postmodernism exhorts authors to revisit the past critically, rather than nostalgically. While most medieval crime fiction novels generally do not pursue the ironic intertextuality of Hutcheon's postmodern parody, they cannot avoid some engagement with postmodern irony or issues of authenticity because they construct a medievalist space that ironizes itself through the critical distance of the modern detective who operates there. In medieval crime fiction nostalgia and irony can co-exist, although one or the other is generally ascendant. While certain authors operate with a self-conscious awareness of their ironic purpose, and others attempt to undermine this irony by invoking layers of nostalgia, it seems impossible for authors of medieval crime fiction to eliminate postmodern irony completely.

One well-known early example of the medieval historical novel is Scott's *Ivanhoe* (1819).[4] Set in twelfth-century England, it concerns the conflict between the Saxon nobility and their Norman conquerors, as well as tension between the Christian population and the Jewish minority.[5] While Lukács claims that Scott's "understanding for the problems of the present is not sufficiently deep for him to portray the problems of declassing as it affects the present" (34), more recent analyses of Scott's novels suggest a greater understanding of contemporary issues than Lukács admits. John Morillo and Wade Newhouse point to a rare "narrative gaffe" in Scott's description of the crowd (gathering to watch Ivanhoe and the Norman Templar knight Bois-Guilbert fight to determine the guilt or innocence of the Jewish heroine, Rebecca) as "a riot, or a meeting of radical reformers" (267). This characterization of the crowd is not medieval, or even medievalist, but instead reflects the conservative Scott's unease at the rising popularity of parliamentary reform and the examples of mob violence being experienced in post–Napoleonic Britain (Morillo and Newhouse 268).

In another example, the enthusiasm for the Middle Ages that existed in Scott's time was tarnished by examples of decidedly unchivalric behavior by rogues such as Abraham Thornton. Thornton was generally assumed to have escaped justice for murdering Mary Ashford in 1817 (two years before the publication of *Ivanhoe*) by evoking the ancient remedy of "trial by battel." Gary R. Dyer uses this case to argue that one of Scott's objectives in *Ivanhoe* is "to reclaim the name of chivalry for those men who embrace the chivalric values Thornton cynically exploited" (400). Scott's resuscitation of the chivalric code and his anachronistic reference to a medieval crowd as "radical reformers" are examples of how he uses the Middle Ages to reinforce the ideology of the conservative political and class structures of Hanoverian Britain (Dyer 398).

Today's historical novel bears a heavy weight of expectation. Along with recreating the past in order to "re-experience the social and human motives which led men [*sic*] to think, feel and act just as they did in historical reality" (Lukács 42), the historical novel both employs a nostalgic frame within which to address contemporary issues and engages with postmodernist demands for irony in order to question the authenticity of the past it recreates. Indeed, Jameson has recently claimed that "the historical novel of the future" will prompt a reconsideration of the "Western grand narratives" of history and he suggests that what is needed is "not so much a new theory or system, as precisely a new image of time" (298). He finds one in the film *Inception* (2010, directed by Christopher Nolan), in "its massive central elevator, which rises and falls to the levels of the various worlds, its portals opening on past or future indifferently" (301). For Jameson, the "historical novel today must be seen as an immense elevator that moves us up and down in time, its sickening lifts and dips corresponding to the euphoric or dystopian mood in which we wait for the doors to open" (301).

If he had been aware of Jameson's analogy, Eco would no doubt argue that the elevator of historical fiction retains the trace of the Middle Ages as it travels up and down through different temporal periods, inserting medieval tropes, aesthetics and worldviews into the social, political and scientific culture of each as the doors open. And what Jameson calls the "material leitmotif" is the figure of the detective itself, the embodiment of a sign "whose presence is enough to reassure us that history has a meaning after all" (302). In medieval crime fiction, the detective travels with us in the elevator to the past.

Medievalism

Medieval crime fiction is a contemporary example of medievalism, which is consistently defined as "the reception, interpretation or recreation of the European Middle Ages in post-medieval cultures" (D'Arcens, *Cambridge Companion* 1). In the early nineteenth century, Scott's medievalism nostalgically revisited the Middle Ages in order to reclaim chivalric values and a society that reflected his own politics—patriarchal and conservative. By the end of the nineteenth century, however, medievalism had been appropriated by ostensibly more progressive proponents. William Morris, in the *Preface* to his 1893 publication of Robert Steele's *Medieval Lore*, outlines the changing attitude to the Middle Ages. At the beginning of the century, he notes, medieval enthusiasts had been looking back for a simpler age, while by his time, those who studied the Middle Ages were more concerned with the "forward movement of modern life" (qtd. in Faulkner 144). Morris belonged to what Clare A. Simmons has described as the "socialist and aesthetic Medievalism" of the later nineteenth century, in which artists such as Dante Gabriel Rossetti and publishers such as Morris and Frederick J. Furnivall created the concept of "an idealized socialist medieval past" in order to promote a new vision of ideal labor relationships (9). As socially conscious as Morris and his contemporaries no doubt were, the medievalism they exhibited was still more a nostalgic recreation of the past than a force for social change. The textiles and wallpaper Morris produced reflected beautiful and unthreatening medieval art and the illustrations accompanying his medieval publications became progressively more sanitized (Simmons 9). The ineffectiveness of this form of medievalism is demonstrated by the fact that much of the medievalist, "socialist" art produced by the pre–Raphaelite Brotherhood was purchased by wealthy industrialists (Simmons 8–9).

Medievalism continues to flood contemporary culture, particularly in cinema and television. Scholars such as William D. Paden, Verlyn Flieger, Colin McArthur, Arthur Lindley and Nickolas Haydock have all argued that the presentation of the Middle Ages in films has more to do with contemporary concerns than with historical accuracy. As Paden points out, it is futile to criticize a "medieval movie" for its anachronisms, since by definition the entire film is an anachronism (92). A famous example of a medieval film that flagrantly misconstrues the past in order to promote contemporary ideological concerns is *Braveheart* (1995, directed by Mel Gibson). The rearrangement of time and historical facts by the filmmakers contributes to the "nationalist fairy-tale" presented by the film (Lindley 6), five hundred years before the concept of nationalism existed as a unifying force (McArthur 171). The film's presentation of English "abuse" and Celtic "resistance" reflects contemporary concerns with British devolution and the ongoing nationalistic tension in Northern Ireland and, to a lesser extent, Scotland. But while medieval cinema's primary focus is to use medievalism as a way of addressing contemporary ideological issues, medieval crime fiction rarely assumes this objective. Its concern with authentically recreating the Middle Ages means that it will strongly resist rearranging historical facts in order to make an ideological point in the manner of *Braveheart*, although it is impossible to excise every trace of the contemporary context in which the novels have been written, as noted throughout this book.

Academic scrutiny of medievalism has slowly built momentum, thanks in large part to the pioneering work by Leslie J. Workman in establishing *Studies in Medievalism*, as well increasingly sustained interest from medieval studies scholars. As David Matthews points out, "practitioners of medievalism studies generally began (and, in many cases, continue) their careers as medievalists" (8). Notable medieval scholars such as Stephanie Trigg, Thomas A. Prendergast, Carolyn Dinshaw, Louise D'Arcens, Laurie A. Finke, Martin B. Shichtman and Matthews himself, among many others, have pressed for an equal consideration of medievalism studies alongside medieval studies within traditional scholarship. Trigg has observed how medievalism imbues the culture of successive centuries in her brilliant study of Chaucerian reception, *Congenial Souls* (2002). Dinshaw has more recently demonstrated that the meeting of medieval and postmedieval moments creates space for both scholars and "amateurs" to embrace the culture of the Middle Ages in *How Soon Is Now?* (2012). Some excellent criticism of medievalism has emerged in the past few years, including Tison Pugh and Angela Weisl's *Medievalisms: Making the Past in the Present* (2013), D'Arcens's *Comic Medievalisms* (2014), Nickolas A. Haydock's *Movie Medievalism* (2008), Finke and Shichtman's *Cinematic Illuminations* (2010), and Kathleen Forni's concise but comprehensive volume, *Chaucer's Afterlife* (2013). Of particular note for the growing academic status of medievalism studies are *The Cambridge Companion to Medievalism* (2016), edited by Louise D'Arcens; Elizabeth Emery and Richard Utz's *Medievalism: Key Critical Terms*; and Matthews' important study, *Medievalism: A Critical History* (2015). In the latter's assessment, "medievalism today seems to have achieved acceptance" (8).

The sheer volume of recent critical analysis devoted to medievalism has not only propelled the field towards incisive and thoughtful scholarship that eschews the early habit of simply pointing out what made a particular cultural product "medieval," it also suggests the increasingly blurred line between medieval studies and medievalism studies. Gail Ashton and Daniel T. Kline hint at this convergence without explicitly situating their edited collection, *Medieval Afterlives in Popular Culture* (2012), within "medieval studies": "Contemporary explorations of how and why medievalism as a discipline is increasingly pivotal to medieval studies as a whole, and indeed beyond, both begin and end at the diverse intersections of cultures..." (2). Richard Utz, another foundational scholar of medievalism studies, argues that medievalism should shake off the role of "nonacademic sibling of medieval studies" and acknowledge that it is "a resurgent discipline in its own right, one supple enough to dismantle inter-disciplinary boundaries and the elephant-in-the-room of periodization" (qtd. in Ashton and Kline 10). However, rather than separate these two disciplines, Matthews argues for "an altered landscape with a conjoined medieval-medievalism studies" and he gives the example of Arthurian studies as one way this landscape could look (345). Earlier, Trigg invoked the concept of convergence culture as a framework through which to examine examples of medievalist film and novels, arguing that this concept is a very productive one for medievalism studies, when we come to consider the circulation of knowledge, ideas, and impressions about the medieval period across a variety of media, from conventional forms such as poetry and fiction, film and television; to community-based forms such as online games, social networking sites, fan fiction and discussion groups devoted to, or drawing on medievalism. Pedagogical and institutional contexts also make an important contribution to this convergence ["Medievalism" 100].

The proliferation of information and its accessibility means that scholarly "'research' ... is no longer the exclusive preserve of academic historians or literary critics" (Trigg, "Medievalism" 118). Consequently, popular culture products of medievalism often seem unaware of their status as either "professional" or "amateur": the meticulous research that authors undertake to create their own medievalist landscapes is intrinsic to the modern narrative they then overlay.

Finke and Shichtman note that "most people 'increasingly receive their ideas about the past from motion pictures and television, from feature films, docudramas, mini-series, and network documentaries'" (3). In a compelling analysis, they apply the Lacanian concept of the "anamorphic blot" to medievalist film in order to reveal the fantasy that imbues these reimaginings of the Middle Ages (9). As the authors argue,

> History does more than record "matters of fact." It also records our fantasies, and our methods of deploying history both in and out of the academy often speak as much to those fantasies as to "what really happened." As medievalists we have a stake in understanding the collective fantasies we call the Middle Ages [7].

As the following exploration of medieval crime fiction will show, these novels similarly deploy history in the form of an "authentic" Middles Ages that nevertheless conceals the fantasy of an idealized medieval justice system. Medieval crime fiction not only produces the convergence that Matthews and Trigg suggest through its comingling of medieval studies and medievalism, it also blurs the line between "professional" and "amateur" engagement with the Middle Ages in a manner welcomed by scholars such as Dinshaw.

Crime Fiction

Crime fiction has an established tradition of critical scholarship, including sustained analyses from Marxist, psychoanalytic, (post)structuralist, formalist and, more recently, postmodernist and feminist theorists.[6] An excellent, older collection that illustrates this point is *The Poetics of Murder* (1983), edited by Glenn W. Most and William W. Stowe. Most and Stowe gathered together "some of the most important studies of detective fiction to have been published" between 1940 and 1980 (xii). The essays showcase many of the eminent literary theorists of the mid-twentieth century and evince their interest in this ostensibly "popular" genre; these critics include Roger Caillois, Jacques Lacan, Umberto Eco, Roland Barthes, Fredric Jameson and Frank Kermode. Crime fiction, it seems, is able to withstand sustained, rigorous analysis even as it adapts to reflect the changing political, social and economic contexts in which it is produced.

In a particularly useful essay for this consideration of medieval crime fiction, Michael Holquist describes the "new" metaphysical detective story embraced by postmodernism. In drawing an unlikely connection between "kitsch" and "avant-garde" culture, Holquist argues that "what ... myth and depth psychology were to modernism (Mann, Joyce, Woolf, and so forth), the detective story is to postmodernism (Robbe-Grillet, Borges, Nabokov, and so on)" (150). In other words, the detective story adapts to its postmodernist context in the hands of authors who wish to fight "against the modernist attempt to fill the void of the world with rediscovered mythical symbols" (Holquist 173). These authors eschew traditional detective fiction's concern with restoring the status quo disturbed by the criminal act. Instead of a comforting familiarity, metaphysical detective fiction delights in strangeness, attacking its readers by dramatizing the void of the world: "If, in the detective story, death must be solved, in the new metaphysical story it is *life* which must be solved" (Holquist 173, emphasis in original). Holquist's description of the evolution of postmodern crime fiction uncovers a useful frame for analyzing its medievalist subgenre: "the kaleidoscope of popular and high culture constantly rearranges their patterns of relationship to each other" (173). This book hopes to demonstrate that medieval crime fiction is one such example of the increasingly blurred barrier between popular and "high" culture that Holquist and others predicted; moreover, the subgenre boasts several "metaphysical" detective novels, including Umberto Eco's *The Name of the Rose*, John Fuller's *Flying to Nowhere*, and Barry Unsworth's *Morality Play*.

Following Holquist, John Scaggs explains that these novels are called "metaphysical detective fiction" in preference to "anti-detective" fiction because they do not provide an opposition to the detective story; rather, they appropriate familiar and stable conventions in order to subvert them (141). Argentinian author, Jorge Luis Borges, pioneered this form of crime fiction; for example, in his short story, "Death and the Compass," the detective solves the elaborate puzzle laid out by his criminal counterpart, only to cause his own death at the novel's dénouement. In Alain Robbe-Grillet's *The Erasers*, the detective ends up shooting the man whose murder he is investigating

(Marcus 255). Walter Moseley appropriates "notoriously conservative" hard-boiled detective fiction by using postmodern strategies to insert his African American detective, Easy Rawlins, into Philip Marlowe's 1940s Los Angeles (Scaggs 139). Paul Auster's *The New York Trilogy* and Thomas Pynchon's *The Crying of Lot 49* are rightly acclaimed as exemplars of postmodern, metaphysical crime fiction.

Another early theorist of the field is Stephen Knight. Knight's *Form and Ideology in Crime Fiction* (1980) remains influential and he continues to contribute important scholarship to crime fiction.[7] Knight's expertise in both crime fiction and medieval studies informs much of this book. The following year, Dennis Porter published a similarly Marxist interpretation of the genre with *The Pursuit of Crime: Art and Ideology in Detective Fiction* (both of these scholars contribute essays to Most and Stowe's collection).

Heta Pyrhönen's insightful analyses situate detective fiction within an academic framework informed by postmodernist theory. Pyrhönen offers a review of the critical discussions of detective fiction throughout the twentieth century, beginning with G.K. Chesterton's 1902 essay, "A Defence of Detective Stories," which, Pyrhönen points out, "is among the first serious discussions of the detective narrative" (*Murder* 2). Pyrhönen maintains an awareness of the cultural context in which both detective fiction and its critics operate. This enables her not only to connect the nineteenth-century origins of the genre with the "reform of the legal and penal systems and the establishment of the modern police force" (*Murder* 94), but also to recognize the ideologies—Marxist, Foucauldian, Althusserian, among others—that influenced the critics who interpret the social, political and cultural work that detective fiction undertakes. In discussing Holquist's assessment of the critique that metaphysical detective fiction directs towards "the discourse of modernity," Pyrhönen reminds her readers that this postmodern genre also targets hard-boiled fiction and not just the "whodunit" style (*Murder* 42).

Pyrhönen also highlights the crucial relationship that crime fiction detectives develop with their readers: "As characters who provide answers to the mystery of crime posed at the beginning, detectives are portrayed in the genre as textually embedded *model readers* whose readerly and interpretive activities mirror the reader's own activity" (*Mayhem and Murder* 5, emphasis in original). Pyrhönen here suggests an explanation for the almost universal production of series in crime fiction, where the detective transcends the generic confines of the narrative to enter into a personal relationship with readers. More recently, Alison Joseph has supported this view by arguing that the detective is more than just a character in a story:

In a genre of storytelling that depends on clues, on facts, on tell-tale signs, the detective is the epistemological lynch-pin.... We do not simply read the story, but we accompany the detective on his or her journey, and in return, the detective holds us, supports us, allows us to suspend our disbelief, to inhabit the truth of the tale.... The detective enables us to stare death in the face, and, when we reach the end of the story, to close the book and find that after all, *we are still here* [190–91, emphasis in original].

In the case of medieval crime fiction, the reader not only stares death in the face, but also accompanies the detective to another time, doubling the sense of relief that occurs when the book is closed and the realization dawns that not only are "we ... still here" physically, but also temporally.

Indicating the sustained interest that crime fiction holds for literary critics, the turn of the millennium brought with it several critical surveys: Cambridge University Press issued *The Cambridge Companion to Crime Fiction* in 2003 (edited by Martin Priestman); Knight released another influential study, *Crime Fiction, 1800–2000: Detection, Death, Diversity* in 2004; while Lee Horsley, Charles J. Rzepka and John Scaggs all published general overviews in 2005. There continues to be a wealth of criticism concerning crime fiction, with an Oxford University Press "Short Introduction" published in 2013, while more specific studies have focused on the multitudinous subgenres that make up this vast literary field.[8]

One of the underlying paradoxes that haunts medieval crime fiction is the potential conflict between the literary detective's obligation to follow the process of ratiocination and the medieval setting that accepts the possibility of divine or diabolical intervention. The irony generated by this paradox is explored more fully in Chapter Three, with its focus on religious detectives. Charles J. Rzepka offers a possible explanation for the exclusion of religion from the literary detective by tracing the work of the "natural philosophers"— beginning with Sir Francis Bacon in 1620, Isaac Newton in 1687 and Pierre-Simon Laplace in 1786—that ultimately eliminated "the hand of God" from physical science hypotheses, including astronomy, physics and chemistry (34). Rzepka's point is that it took until the early nineteenth century before scientific study significantly eroded faith in what had previously been broadly accepted as historically factual by the European Christian world; that is, the Bible was the "Word of God" and a record of "His" miraculous deeds on behalf of "His" chosen peoples (33). Rzepka concludes that

At some point during this transition from sacred to secular explanations of the past the increasing tempo of the West's reiterated crises of historical explanation began to change people's understanding of the relative priority and weight to be given to material evidence, to what we might call the physical "clues" of history, as opposed to the "testimony," the oral or written accounts of past events, including God's, cited to explain those "clues" [35].

Rzepka points to another characteristic that the literary detective has appropriated from the development of scientific practices when he links the anthropological classification of the human species on the basis of its racial characteristics with Edgar Allan Poe's short story "The Man of the Crowd" (1840), in which the narrator follows an "old and decrepit wanderer" through the streets but cannot reconstruct the man's history (39). As Rzepka notes, Walter Benjamin famously compares Poe's "natural historian" narrator with the nineteenth-century Parisian *flâneur*, described by Baudelaire as a wanderer of the streets and arcades "reading" the "physiognomy of the crowd" like a botanist (Rzepka 40; Benjamin, 174). Rzepka suggests that the observational sleuthing by Poe's narrator anticipates "Sherlock Holmes's repeated trick of discerning the personalities and occupations of perfect strangers from their details of dress or the pattern of 'callosities' on their hands, much to Watson's repeated amazement" (40–41). This taxonomic scrutiny of the detective's suspects, clients and witnesses has further developed into crime fiction's overarching concern with social and cultural intervention. As Barry Forshaw points out in a recent study of police detectives, crime fiction has maintained its "tradition of social commentary ... which was always a key element in the genre" ("Editor's Introduction" 8). The detectives of medieval crime fiction embrace their metaphysical, social and scientific heritage, working hard to maintain the integrity of the postmodern literary detective within the context of their medieval worlds.

These overviews of the historical novel, medievalism and crime fiction are notable for the surprisingly small intersections among the three fields. What these academic disciplines do share, however, is an ostensible lack of interest in the popular genre that constructs itself out of all three. The preeminent exception to this puzzling lacuna is Umberto Eco's *The Name of the Rose*, a novel that garners attention from critics in all fields; a *tour de force* that may be accurately (if laboriously) described as medievalist postmodern "historiographic metafiction."[9] Eco's novel and his scholarship are critical for any study of medieval crime fiction and the second half of this chapter begins with a consideration of both.

Postmodern Medievalism: Umberto Eco and The Name of the Rose

Eco's *The Name of the Rose* remains the most cited example of the powerful combination of postmodern irony and medievalist recreation. Although the plot of *The Name of the Rose* is well-known, a brief synopsis serves as a reminder of its complexity.[10]

Set in a northern Italian abbey in 1327, the novel relates the events of one week in late November in which heresy, secular and religious politics, and murder intersect to challenge the diplomatic and interpretative skills of the Franciscan friar, William of Baskerville. The novel is narrated by Adso, a novice Benedictine monk who is accompanying William as his apprentice and who, at the end of his life, feels a compulsion to record the events of this visit. William and Adso arrive at the abbey a few days before a delegation from the Pope and the head of the Franciscan order, Michael of Cesena, are scheduled to meet to negotiate the terms of Michael's proposed visit to Avignon to resolve tensions surrounding the issue of Christ's poverty. William is representing the interests of the German Emperor, Louis, but is clearly sympathetic to the Franciscan cause. Upon their arrival at the abbey, however, William and Adso are prevailed upon by the abbot to investigate the death of a young monk found fallen from the windows of the abbey's famous library. More suspicious deaths occur and William is convinced that the perpetrator is imitating the sequence of signs of the Apocalypse as described in John's *Book of Revelation*. William also concludes that the reason behind the murders concerns the rediscovery of Aristotle's treatise on comedy, presumed lost.

The scheduled debate takes place between the papal delegation and the Franciscans, but it is interrupted by the discovery of the heretical past of two of the abbey's monks who are then subjected to interrogation by the Grand Inquisitor, Bernard Gui. William and Adso eventually unlock the code to the library's labyrinthine layout, only to find the villain, Jorge of Burgos, consuming the poisoned pages of the famous Aristotelian treatise while informing William of his mistaken interpretation of the pattern of the murders. In the ensuing chase, the library is set alight by an oil lamp snatched out of Adso's hands by Jorge, and the entire abbey is consumed. Although the cause of each death is explained, William is convinced he has failed as a detective because he was interpreting signs that were random and coincidental and not following the apocalyptic pattern he had deduced.

As he notes in "Reflections," Eco believes there are three ways of narrating the past. Firstly, the romance, in which the past is purely scenery, enabling the construction of an "elsewhere." Secondly, the "swashbuckling" novels, in which real events and people are depicted but the fictional characters demonstrate feelings and attitudes that could belong to any or all other periods. Finally, the historical novel, in which the fictional characters act and speak in a way that makes historical events more comprehensible (18). The last definition conforms to Lukács's characterization of Scott's success in depicting the past. For Eco, the historical novel must not simply repeat the actions and words of the people who really existed, but also ensure that "the fictitious characters like William say [what] *ought* to have been said in that period" ("Reflections" 18, emphasis in original).

Like Scott, Eco encounters the issue of authenticity; however, unlike Scott, Eco operates with a self-conscious awareness of this problem and confronts it overtly. The preface to *The Name of the Rose* tells the story of the discovery of Adso's manuscript and, after many diversions and distractions, the author claims to present an "Italian version of an obscure, neo-Gothic French version of a seventeenth-century Latin edition of a work written in Latin by a German monk toward the end of the fourteenth century" (4). The narrator questions the liberties taken by the translator of the Latin into the neo-Gothic French and admits to his own editing: "I have eliminated excesses, but I have retained a certain amount" (*Name of the Rose* 5). Adso's story is presented as unavoidably corrupted by transcriptions and translations over the centuries, highlighting the practical difficulties of achieving historical authenticity. The translation of the novel from Italian creates another layer between Adso and the English-speaking reader. Judy Ann Ford believes that by using this structure Eco is denouncing historical scholarship, claiming that any attempt to interpret the past accurately is open to error and is therefore arrogant and dangerous (108), while David H. Richter notes that Eco will never allow readers to lose themselves in a historical novel, as they are always reminded that what is being presented is a construction of history (262–63).

The treatment of the detective narrative in *The Name of the Rose* admirably conforms to its postmodernist purpose. Eco acknowledges the incongruity of placing a modern, secular detective into a premodern, religious setting and he explores how this incongruity eventually leads to William's failure and the destruction of his medievalist environment. William of Baskerville, as his name suggests, displays conventional detective characteristics such as acute observation and interrogation skills, logical reasoning and up-to-date scientific knowledge. He restricts his investigation to "things of nature," refusing to countenance the idea of supernatural intervention in Adelmo's death, despite the abbot's puzzlement at William's insistence "on speaking of criminal acts without referring to their diabolical cause" (*Name of the Rose* 30).

William's tendency to question first appearances and seek out alternative solutions unsettles his medievalist world of absolute truths. Adso expresses concern for William's attitude: "I had the impression that William was not at all interested in the truth, which is nothing but the adjustment between the thing and the intellect. On the contrary, he amused himself by imagining how many possibilities were possible" (*Name of the Rose* 306). While William's religious order alludes to the skepticism of the English Franciscans, particularly Roger Bacon and William Occam, Eco also makes him (post)modern. Richter describes William's inherent contradiction: "To be a detective at all … William of Baskerville must be essentially a modern man, but he must also be placed within a medieval setting that is as authentic as possible" (263).

William's investigative method involves abduction, the search for a theory into which all the known facts are fitted, which is also the preferred method of Sherlock Holmes. If a fact cannot be made to fit, then that theory is discarded and a new one developed until finally arriving at a theory that incorporates all the facts. The oft-quoted example of William's prowess at abduction is his description (including the name) of the abbot's horse without having seen it, based upon hoof-prints, broken branches, and his knowledge of the monastic mind. This abductive description of the horse has a distinct literary history, based on Voltaire's *Zadig* (1747) (M. Cohen 65; DelFattore 80), which in turn can be traced back to ancient Middle Eastern folklore (Bondanella 110). Carl Ginzburg has characterized this reasoning as reminiscent of "the oldest, perhaps, of the intellectual history of the human race: the hunter crouched in the mud, examining a quarry's tracks" (qtd. in Bondanella 110).

William's villainous opponent is Jorge of Burgos, the elderly blind monk who fears the distracting and secular influence of Aristotle's lost treatise on comedy and so is determined not only to punish those monks who inadvertently discover the manuscript (by poisoning the book's pages), but also to manipulate William's investigation towards the erroneous apocalyptic pattern he follows. Jorge represents the total authority of the medieval church, believing "that truth was not only knowable but known" (Hallissy 280). This truth is to be found in a select number of sacred texts, interpreted by a church hierarchy that alone has the power to arbitrate between truth and deception. There is therefore no need to engage in any more learning and Jorge believes it is dangerous to encourage impressionable young monks to expand their minds.

While Jorge is William's criminal opponent, the Grand Inquisitor, Bernard Gui, is his methodological counterpart. Characterized as the "official force" in the novel (Martín 156), Bernard recalls the incompetent policeman of traditional detective stories, continually misinterpreting clues and jumping to erroneous conclusions, although with far more sinister consequences. The Inquisitor searches for truth, like William, but his truth is confined to the absolutism of the fight between good and evil that exists in every human. His version of events is a parody of William's investigation, as shown by Jorge Hernández Martín:

the murders are mixed with heresy, and the manuscript sought by the murdered monks must be the letters from a leader of a heretical sect that have been entrusted to the librarian for safekeeping, and which Gui produces as irrefutable proof of his conjectures [156].

Bernard's discovery of the heretical past of Remigio and Salvatore, and his subsequent investigation, sabotage the primary purpose of William's presence at the abbey, to negotiate the terms of Michael of Cesena's safe passage to Avignon to meet the Pope. As William concedes: "Bernard has defeated us.... John wants you alone in Avignon, Michael, and this meeting hasn't given you the guarantees we were looking for" (*Name of the Rose* 391). William returns to the investigation of the murders, only to be defeated again, this time by his criminal opponent, Jorge.

While William is successful in his epistemological quest to solve the murders, it is the failure of his ontological quest that leads to William's famous despair at the end of the novel:

> What I did not understand was the relation among signs. I arrived at Jorge through an apocalyptic pattern that seemed to underlie all the crimes, and yet it was accidental. I arrived at Jorge seeking one criminal for all the crimes and we discovered that each crime was committed by a different person, or by no one.... Where is all my wisdom, then? I behaved stubbornly, pursuing a semblance of order, when I should have known well that there is no order in the universe [*Name of the Rose* 492].

In terms of detective fiction, then, *The Name of the Rose* offers a contradictory conclusion. All aspects of the murders are clarified and the people or the events responsible are revealed. In this sense, Eco conforms to the conventions of detective fiction. However, William's abductive reasoning as to the connection between the crimes proves to be woefully incorrect and he reaches the solution by following a pattern comprised of coincidences which did not exist.

The paradox between the empirical nature of William's investigation and the law of universals that underlies the medieval church's teachings means that William's methodology amounts to a questioning of his faith (M. Cohen 72; DelFattore 82). As Cristina Farronato points out, an assertion that there is no order in the universe would not have been possible for a Franciscan Friar in the Middle Ages (141), even one exposed to the "modern" thoughts of Roger Bacon and William Occam. William's dilemma is one that confronts all religious medieval detectives: they look for secular solutions in a world that has absolute faith in divine (and diabolical) intervention, causing internal conflict between knowledge and faith. However, it is only William who is self-aware enough to be conscious of this postmodern dilemma, enabling him to transcend and question the traditional detective conventions within which other medieval detectives remain firmly entrenched.

William's critical perspective contributes to the postmodernism of *The Name of the Rose*, an aspect of the novel that has captivated many critics. Teresa de Lauretis describes the novel as a "historiographic metatext" (245), while Richter characterizes it as an "intricate postmodern metafiction" (256). Hutcheon highlights the intertextual parody in *The Name of the Rose*, claiming that Eco's use of irony prevents an "infinite regress into textuality"; rather, it calls "our attention [to] the entire representational process ... and the impossibility of finding any totalizing model to resolve the resulting postmodern contradictions" (*Politics* 95). For Michael Cohen, the novel's postmodernism lies in William's deductive "failure" at every turn, making him less like traditional detectives and closer to the "futile and enigmatic" detectives of Jorge Luis Borges (72), the namesake of Eco's criminal monk. Farronato agrees, likening William's epistemological crisis at the end of the novel to Lyotard's characterization of the postmodern condition; that is, "an 'internal erosion of the legitimacy principle of knowledge'" (144). De Lauretis similarly believes Sherlock Holmes's rational path of deduction leads William to the library, "at which point Eco leaves Conan Doyle and steps into the postmodern condition" (245). For other critics, the novel's treatment of the reader is important. Peter Bondanella asserts that Eco is consciously postmodern in his attempt to appeal to a wide variety of audiences, including both popular and cultured readers (99). Rocco Capozzi highlights the novel's awareness of the different types of reader who will engage with the text according to the extent of their "encyclopaedic knowledge" (421). Farronato believes Eco has constructed a trap in order to doom the reader "to the attempt to reconstruct the past, to getting lost in the rhyzomic labyrinth of the mind" (84).

Eco's concern with historical authenticity and his comprehension of postmodernism's call to be suspicious of any such claim does not preclude him from allowing his own historical moment to intervene into his novel. Bondanella has made the connection between the date Eco claims to have started writing *The Name of the Rose* (March 1978) and the kidnap of the President of the Christian Democratic Party, Aldo Moro, by the Red Brigade on the sixteenth day of that month (96), pointing out the profound shock felt by Eco and other Italian intellectuals at Moro's assassination a few months later. He goes on to compare the novel's political opposition between the Pope and the German Emperor to the ideological struggle of the Cold War. Lois Parkinson Zamora similarly analyzes the imagery of the apocalypse throughout the novel and equates the "modern" sense of doom expressed by Adso with contemporary anxiety generated by political upheaval (32). Richter applies Barbara Tuchman's "Distant Mirror" motif to Eco's novel and finds compelling parallels between the twentieth and fourteenth centuries. He equates the "cold war between Louis the Bavarian and John XXII on the one hand, and the one that ran from 1949 to 1989 on the other between capitalism and communism, America and the Soviet Union, NATO and the Warsaw Pact" (267). Richter places the Franciscans in the position of the European socialist movements, with whom Eco sympathized (267). Eco, more than most, revisits the past with a self-conscious awareness of his present.

Along with Ellis Peters and Barry Unsworth, Eco is one of very few authors to have had his medieval crime fiction novel adapted for the screen. Finke and Shichtman compare *The Name of the Rose* with Jean-Jacques Annaud's 1986 film, analyzing the latter in terms of Bakhtin's chronotope; that is, the representation of time and space in language and discourse. In the novel, "time and space are rationalized, precisely counted off by the days of the week, the liturgical hours, and the apportioning of space in the monastery" (Finke and Shichtman 40). This rationalization is necessary for the detective narrative, Finke and Shichtman point out, but Annaud's film instead conveys a doubled sense of time by contrasting daytime and nighttime. This reflects the opposition between the public activities of the monks and the secret goings on in private spaces such as the cells and hidden library.

More recently, Louise D'Arcens has pointed out that "as long as there has been medievalism, people have been encouraged to laugh *at*, *with* and *in* the Middle Ages" (*Comic Medievalism* 5, emphasis in original). For D'Arcens, *The Name of the Rose* exemplifies the ironic place that humor occupies in modern ideas about the Middle Ages. In this "resolutely non-comic text," Eco "portrays a society riven by zealous opposition over the nature of laughter and the purpose and value of humour" (*Comic Medievalism* 9). D'Arcens perceives three parallel representations of the Middle Ages in the characters of Jorge of Burgos, William of Baskerville and the Dolcinite heretic, Salvatore. Together, these embodiments combine to "encapsulate the most widely disseminated post-medieval perceptions of humour in the medieval period" (*Comic Medievalism* 9). These three distinct formulations form the framework through which she considers a wonderfully wide-ranging selection of comic medievalisms. Like Finke and Shichtman, D'Arcens has extended her discussion of Eco's novel to encompass Jean-Jacques Annaud's film adaptation and other late-twentieth-century medievalist films, analyzing them through their depiction of what she terms the "mirthful face" ("Mirthful Faces" 51–66).

For Eco, the Middle Ages were his "day-to-day fantasy" and he has written much about the continuous return to what he believed are the origins of modern society ("Reflections" 9). He is convinced that "looking at the Middle Ages means looking at our infancy" (*Travels* 65), which is the same sentiment expressed by early-nineteenth-century commentators such as Scott. Eco differs in one major aspect, however, in that he revisits the Middle Ages with irony rather than with the nostalgia common to nineteenth-century medievalist reimaginings; indeed, he is one of the first authors to overlay his affection for the medieval period with the recognition that returning to the past is both unnecessary and, doubtless, uncomfortable. Instead, Eco's medievalism takes the form of a *longue durée* which has not yet come to a close.

In other words, society has no need to return to the Middle Ages for the simple reason that the Middle Ages has never gone away. In what has become a foundational essay for medievalism studies, and a well-worn taxonomy, Eco lists ten forms that medievalism assumes in contemporary society, including the Middle Ages as pretext (Eco's example of the "swashbuckling" narration of the past); as ironic revisitation; as a moment of national identity; and others (*Travels* 68–72).[11] All of Eco's Middle Ages are present in *The Name of the Rose*, although not necessarily positively portrayed (Bondanella 98). Eco is so entrenched in his medievalism that he explains anachronisms that occur in the novel by asserting:

> when I disguised quotations from later authors (such as Wittgenstein), passing them off as quotations from the period … I knew very well that it was not my medieval men who were being modern; if anything, it was the moderns who were thinking medievally ["Reflections" 18].

This is a telling comment from Eco that signals the important intervention that medievalism makes into crime fiction.

Authors of medieval crime fiction largely conform to Eco's conviction that the Middle Ages has never retreated from contemporary periodization (whether modern or postmodern) and, as every author would no doubt concede, *The Name of the Rose* haunts each iteration of crime novels set in the European Middle Ages. In Jameson's terms, Eco's medievalism has a permanent place in the elevator that transports audiences through time via historical fiction in all its forms.

Golden-Age Medievalism: Ellis Peters and Brother Cadfael

Umberto Eco has received vastly more critical attention than Ellis Peters and, consequently, the significant influence she has had on crime fiction, historical fiction and, in particular, medieval crime fiction has often gone unremarked. In spite of this, the debt that most medieval crime fiction authors owe to Peters is at least as meaningful as to Eco. Peters herself was well aware of the tendency to revere Eco's single novel above her own series: in interviews she "appeared miffed when her books were described as being 'in the tradition of *The Names of the Rose*'"; and "Comparisons with Eco rankled her" because not only had several of her books been published before Eco's, she also "dislikes *The Name of the Rose* because it is 'very dark, and very hopeless…. It doesn't give much consolation to any reader'" (Fichte 54).

Edith Pargeter (Ellis Peters) was born in Shropshire in 1913, the youngest of three children in a working-class family.[12] During the Second World War, she joined the WRENs, achieving the rank of Petty Officer and, in 1944, she was awarded the British Empire Medal. While Pargeter never attended university, she became adept at teaching herself history, the Czech language and other areas of interest to her. Pargeter became an eminent translator of Czech authors such as Bohmil Hrabal and Jan Neruda. In 1968, she was awarded the gold medal of the Czechoslovak Society for International Relations for her services to literature, although the Soviet invasion immediately afterwards and subsequent closure of the Czech borders significantly curtailed her interaction with both the country and the friends she had there (Vaughan).

Pargeter had written stories since she was a young girl and published her first novel in 1936. She turned out to be a prolific author, proud of her ability to make a living from her writing and remaining in Shropshire for most of her life. She wrote several historical novels concerning life in medieval Wales and England, as well as a successful series of contemporary detective mysteries featuring police inspector George Felse, the first of which was published in 1959. She combined her passion for the medieval history of her own region with the enjoyment she found in composing mysteries when she produced the first novel featuring Brother Cadfael, *A Morbid Taste for Bones* (1977). Before her death in 1995 at the age of 82, Pargeter, under the pseudonym Ellis Peters, had published twenty *Brother Cadfael* novels, set in the period between 1137 and 1145, as well as three short stories. She received an OBE in 1994.

Brother Cadfael is a Welsh monk attached to the Benedictine Abbey of Saint Peter and Saint Paul in Shrewsbury. Cadfael discovered his vocation later in life, entering the abbey in his forties after a varied career as a crusader, a Mediterranean ship's captain and a man-at-arms. He has had relationships with several women, one of which produced a half-Syrian son of whose existence Cadfael is made aware in *The Virgin in the Ice* (1982). These experiences distinguish Cadfael from most other cloistered monks and afford him an insight into human nature, as well as practical abilities such as an extensive knowledge of medicinal herbs, healing techniques and wounds. Cadfael is pragmatic, compassionate and observant, tolerant of human foibles and dedicated to ensuring innocent people overcome unjust accusations.

Reviewers and critics all note the innate compassion that Cadfael demonstrates and this means that, as Anne K. Kaler suggests, Cadfael "frequently obeys his own internal law of conscience rather than the Higher Law, or its legalistic dictates" (3). In this way, Peters indicates her strong penchant for following golden-age detective fiction conventions where, at times, seeking justice is assigned a higher priority than following the letter of the law. For example, in *Dead Man's Ransom* (1984), Cadfael assists in the escape of a young man across the Welsh border to avoid hanging for a murder he committed. The murdered man was probably dying anyway and, moreover, was causing significant harm to other characters by his recalcitrant behavior. It is difficult not to recall Agatha Christie's detectives, in particular, Hercule Poirot, who possess a similarly strong sense of natural justice.

Edwin Ernest Christian and Blake Lindsay claim that the Brother Cadfael series constituted "one of the most interesting and popular manifestations of medievalism today" (276). Their study is primarily concerned with Peters' medievalism, describing one of her conventions as the imposition of modern concerns and conceptions onto the medieval world (276). The authors note that each of the novels depicts strong women and they link these women with Cadfael's own innate androgyny and feminine traits (282).

In 1997, students participating in an Ellis Peters seminar combined under the name "The Germersheim Group" to examine the intersection of genre, time, place and gender in three of the early Brother Cadfael narratives. The Group interprets Cadfael's main role as a translator of events for his modern readers and criticizes Christian and Lindsay's praise of the historical context for many of Peters' murders, claiming that they are confusing "trappings with substance": while "The story woven around the crime may be called medieval; … the crime itself is not" (3–4). However, the medievalist context plays a more significant role than the Group allows. For example, the monk who commits murder in *A Morbid Taste for Bones* does so in order to remove the most influential objector to the transfer of Saint Winifred's bones from her Welsh burial place to the Shrewsbury abbey. The perceived importance of the acquisition of the relics motivates the monk's action and it is difficult to imagine this motive operating outside these specifically medieval conditions.

More recently, Alan T. Gaylord has offered a thoughtful consideration of the thematic trajectory of the Brother Cadfael series, noting in particular the strong influence of Saint Winifred. Gaylord emphasizes the inevitability of the Shropshire setting to all of Peters' novels, not just the Cadfael books, quoting the author: "I did not set out deliberately to make use of my origins. Shropshire is simply in my blood, and in the course of creation the blood gets into the ink, and sets in motion a heartbeat and a circulation that brings the land to life" (131). Gaylord goes on to describe the series as "a curious but curiously popular succession of twenty novels that may be said to fall between two Rules—one coming out of ancient and medieval ecclesiastical history, and the other out of contemporary popular literary genres (which had nothing inherently medieval about them)" (132). The tension between these two "Rules" is precisely what structures all medieval crime fiction, and the success or otherwise of each novel depends greatly upon its author's management of this tension. As Gaylord points out, Peters allows her "Benedictine Rule" to subsume the "rule of murder" (132). Consequently, the detective narrative often operates on the periphery of Peters' novels, functioning as a kind of *memento mori* upon the landscape of what Gaylord calls her "Arcadian mysteries" (132); in other words, Peters is mainly concerned with putting the investigation of murder to work in the service of "a larger process of accommodation, reconciliation, and resignation" of life (134).

Examples of medievalism consistently offer a commentary—to a greater or lesser extent—upon the political, social and cultural context in which they are created. For the Brother Cadfael series, there are notable traces of the second-wave feminist movement of the 1970s that was slowly intervening into traditionally masculinist popular genres such as crime fiction. In 1972, P.D. James created the first professional British female detective, Cordelia Gray, in *An Unsuitable Job for a Woman*. James's character signaled a move towards the appropriation of the overwhelmingly male private detective by the feminist movement. In the same year as the first Cadfael novel appeared, Marcia Muller published what Knight has described as the "first real feminist detective novel," *Edwin of the Iron Shoes* (1977), featuring Sharon McCone (*Crime Fiction* 214).

As far as this context influenced Peters, she appropriates the medieval for feminist concerns both in her characterization of Cadfael and in the presentation of her female characters. Christian and Lindsay describe Cadfael "as close to being a feminist as a medieval monk could be" (282), and he treats the women he encounters with an unusual sensitivity and insightfulness that confirms his feminist outlook, as indicated from the beginning of the series:

> Both men and women partake of the same human nature, Huw. We both bleed when we're wounded. That's a poor, silly woman, true, but we can show plenty of poor, silly men. There are women as strong as any of us, and as able [*Morbid Taste for Bones* 197].

Each novel contains examples of Cadfael's "strong" and capable women who are often able to make their own choices and determine their own futures. The Germersheim Group, however, claims that while strong women are portrayed in the novels, they generally act on behalf of a man's interests (8). Furthermore, the Group argues that the association of women with Wales and men with England represents the marginalization of Wales in terms of the "Anglocentric discourse" that "forms part of a much more widespread subordination-through-feminization of peripheral cultures" (9). While this assertion has interesting postcolonial implications, the Group does not elaborate upon how Cadfael's own Welsh heritage fits into this claim for marginalization.

In *A Morbid Taste for Bones*, the daughter of the murdered man, Sioned, inherits and continues to run his estate while at the same time helping Cadfael with his investigation. Sioned refused her father's choice of husband, preferring the attentions of a young English "outlander," Englehard, who works in the region and who is suspected of the murder. With Cadfael's assistance, Sioned confronts the real murderer in the guise of Saint Winifred, placing herself in considerable danger. Sioned is then apparently "used" by Saint Winifred to make clear her desire to remain buried in Wales; the saint pointedly choosing a woman for her voice rather than the male monks who have presumed to determine her fate up until now. The murderer is accidentally killed in his attempt to flee and in an ironic twist, Cadfael, Sioned and Engelard replace the saint's bones with the murderer's body, leaving Winifred at peace in Wales and taking the other remains back to Shrewsbury to be venerated as relics. In a postmodernist comment about authenticity, miracles occur in both locations, causing Cadfael to conclude wryly that "Evidently the body of a calculating murderer does almost as well as the real thing, given faith enough" (250).

The same feminist influence cannot be said of Eco's *The Name of the Rose*, of course, as the novel is striking for its lack of a female voice, as several critics have noted. Diane Elam, perhaps unjustly, argues that Eco's portrayal of romance (she describes the novel as "historical romance") "attempts to do more to erase the position of woman than it does to reinforce her role in the manner of traditional romance" (192). De Lauretis also argues that Eco has omitted the "problem" of women in his characterization of the Middle Ages as the root "of all our contemporary 'hot' problems" (254). Bondanella opposes this criticism of Eco's novel, claiming that such accounts of Eco's apparently "sexist approach to gender" are "certainly an exaggeration and an ideological distortion of Eco's perspective" (122–23). Bondanella rather rashly dismisses feminist concerns in a footnote, stating that "*The Name of the Rose* is simply not concerned with issues of gender in the strict constructionist sense applied by some feminist critics to literary texts" (123).

Nevertheless, the feminine is present in *The Name of the Rose* through the incursions of the peasant girl into Adso's investigation and dreams, and through the notable influence on William's old friend, the monk Ubertino, of three strong and independent women of faith: Clare of Montefalco, Angela of Foligno and Margaret of Città di Castello. Furthermore, William of Baskerville articulates a sentiment regarding women that is not unlike Brother Cadfael's views concerning equality, albeit more graphically expressed to Ubertino:

> That girl will soon be under torture, then on the pyre. She will become exactly as you say, mucus, blood, humors, and bile. But it will be men like us who dig from beneath her skin that which the Lord wanted to be protected and adorned by that skin. And when it comes to prime matter, you are no better than she [*Name of the Rose* 331].

Across time and place, William and Cadfael share a humanism that reveals itself through feminist remarks such as this one; a humanism it is not unreasonable to suggest that their creators also shared.

As Gaylord intimates, the murder plot becomes increasingly sidelined as the Brother Cadfael series progresses. By the final novel, *Brother Cadfael's Penance* (1994), "Peters has ... broken the rules of her genre—none of [Cadfael's actions have] anything to do with a murder, its mystery, or its investigation, nor does it demonstrate in Cadfael any of the usual attributes of detective" (Gaylord 142–43). While there is murder in the novel, and the perpetrator is revealed, Cadfael's primary purpose is to undertake a personal quest to seek out and rescue his son, taken captive during the ongoing conflict between King Stephen and the Empress Maud. Cadfael feels the familial bond deeply enough to breach his vow of obedience and defy his abbot in order to leave the monastery to search for Olivier. The sacrifice is an enormous one for Cadfael, who believes that, through his desertion, he is apostate and has forfeited his salvation:

> The ease of being loose in the world came first, and only gradually did the horror of release enter and overwhelm him. For he was recreant, he had exiled himself, knowing well what he was doing. And now his only justification must be the redemption of ... Olivier. If he failed in that he had squandered even his apostasy [*Brother Cadfael's Penance* 91].

It is here that Peters' medievalism is at its most poignant. Despite being, in essence, a modern character, Cadfael inhabits a premodern world that he loves and understands as much as his creator. Cadfael has just recently discovered Olivier's existence—and they have only met on two occasions. Indeed, at the time of Cadfael's search for Olivier, the young man remains unaware that Cadfael is his father. These circumstances, combined with Cadfael's genuine commitment to his faith and the Benedictine order, raise serious doubts as to whether a "historical" medieval monk would have undertaken this journey. However, Peters' sensitive handling of the conflict between religious obedience and parental obligation allows the reader to believe that

Cadfael not only perfectly suits his medieval context, but also transcends history to depict a moral dilemma that is relevant to any age. Moreover, there is a tangible sense of completeness in this, Peters' last novel, in which the news that Olivier will soon become a father himself establishes generational renewal. In her account, Marcia J. Songer suggests that "there are indications in the book that Peters herself may have felt it was the last Cadfael tale that she would create" (63).

The success of Peters' series has generated a significant number of complementary cultural products. For example, Robin Whiteman published an illustrated companion to medieval plants and their uses called *Brother Cadfael's Herb Garden* (1996). Whiteman also published *The Cadfael Companion: The World of Brother Cadfael* (1991), containing an introduction by Peters. A revised edition, published in 1995, was nominated for an Agatha Award for Best Nonfiction Literature. Furthermore, in 2000 Whiteman compiled a collection of Cadfael's sayings, using a medieval Book of Hours format and pointedly invoking the ever-present potential for conflict between Cadfael's dual occupations: *Brother Cadfael's Book of Days: The Material and Spiritual Wisdom of a Medieval Crusader-Monk*. In 1994, the British television production company, ITV Central, produced the first of four series of *Cadfael*, comprising thirteen episodes over the next four years. Brother Cadfael, played by Sir Derek Jacobi, and the series were warmly received by both critics and viewers (with the notable exception of the *New York Times*'s reviewer, who described it [and Jacobi] as "flat and lifeless" [J. O'Connor]).[13] Peters belongs to the extremely small group of medieval crime fiction authors whose fiction has been transferred to film. Finally, in a lasting acknowledgment of the influence of her Brother Cadfael series, for a time the British Crime Writers' Association named "the most prestigious UK prize in the field" after Peters.[14]

Eco and Peters—A Postscript

The journal *postmedieval* recently issued a special edition, "After Eco: Novel Medievalisms" (2016), indicating the enduring relevance of Eco's seminal work. The issue features a range of essays that examine medievalist historical fiction, three of which focus on what may be termed medieval crime fiction. However, the editors of the special edition, Bruce Holsinger (himself an author of medieval crime fiction, as discussed in Chapter Six) and Stephanie Trigg, are interested in the interaction of medievalism and historical fiction generally and therefore do not consider in any great detail Eco's contribution not only to crime fiction, but also to the surge in popularity of medieval crime fiction. Holsinger and Trigg's brief acknowledgment of Eco's decision "to combine the genres of detective fiction and the Middle Ages" is limited to what they term a "delightful historical paradox": it is, apparently, "a common error to believe that Ellis Peters' Brother Cadfael series must take its inspiration from Eco"; an error Holsinger and Trigg attribute to the fact that Peters' novels comprise an "ostensibly lightweight series" (177). The editors then reveal that, in fact, the first of Ellis Peters' novels appeared in 1977, three years before Eco's original Italian novel was published.

Despite this statement's revelatory tone, it is not at all clear who actually makes this "common error." Devotees of medieval crime fiction are astute and canny readers of both the period and the genre, as indicated by online discussion forums, speedy corrections to perceived errors in the depiction of the Middle Ages, and their habit of reading widely across the field. Although it is difficult, of course, to obtain evidence on this point one way or the other, it is nevertheless unlikely that these readers presume that Eco influenced Peters because they are fully aware of Peters' temporal precedence—after all, by the time Eco's English language version of *The Name of the Rose* was published in 1983, there were eight Brother Cadfael novels in Peters' well-established series. Moreover, Peters' first Cadfael novel did not emerge out of a vacuum: under her real name, Edith Pargeter, Peters had written several series of both historical and crime fiction.

But this belief in the supposed ignorance of popular fiction consumers is unfortunately widespread. In 2009 Bidisha SK Mamata reminded her *Guardian* readers that while the "literary world woke up to" the medieval murder mystery with Eco's "turgid riddler, … Eco was no pioneer, and neither is Sansom [*sic*[15]]. Their precursor and (I believe) their superior is Edith Pargeter, aka Ellis Peters, creator of the Cadfael mysteries" (Bidisha). Like the *postmedieval* editors, Bidisha clearly believes it is necessary to inform her audience that the medieval mystery form did not originate with Eco. Similarly, H. Wendell Howard opens his 2008 essay describing Cadfael's "world" with an acknowledgment that "readers outside the realm of mystery fiction" may be unfamiliar with Ellis Peters. However, Howard continues, for aficionados of mystery fiction, "this author of the Brother Cadfael Chronicles is reputed to be *the* literary find of the last thirty years"; indeed, "Some people argue that P.D. James might rival her for that designation, and yet even those present-day Jacobites admit that Ellis Peters in most ways is the equal of their preferred writer" (149). Howard locates Peters within the vastly broader context of all crime fiction through comparison with one of the foremost practitioners of the police procedural novel. He identifies a similarity in the appeal to readers of the two detectives—Brother Cadfael and Commander Adam

Dalgleish—both of who demonstrate a sympathetic insight into human behavior that transcends the centuries that separate their investigations.

Holsinger and Trigg, then, are presumably referring to a set of readers more concerned with literary intertextuality; in other words, with the historical relationship between texts, their contexts and their authors (that is, "professional" readers). This stance is further reinforced by their reframing of the question of influence: "The more curious question, then, might be about the conjunction of two such radically different novelists, each choosing to combine the genres of detective fiction and the Middle Ages at around the same time" (177). The editors seemingly discount the possibility that Eco might have read and been influenced by Peters—and why not?—in an example of the ongoing privileging of so-called "canonical" texts within the ostensibly popular cultural concerns of medievalism studies. It is not at all surprising that Edith Pargeter conceived of a detective novel set in the Middle Ages because she was already an award-winning novelist of both crime fiction and medieval historical fiction. And while Eco of course added "impetus" to the historical mystery genre (Knight, *Secrets* 176), the more "curious" question about medieval crime fiction is its sustained popularity and entrenched position within contemporary popular culture, a question this book seeks to address.

Before the Originators: Edward Frankland, The Murders at Crossby, and Jeremy Potter, Death in the Forest

Both Eco and Peters are correctly considered to be the establishing forces behind medieval crime fiction and are credited with creating many of the tropes that continue to characterize the genre. However, earlier in the twentieth century, two other novels were written that are intriguing, suggestive and deserving of brief acknowledgment.[16]

Professor of chemistry, Edward Percy Frankland, initially appears an unlikely candidate for the role of historical fiction author. Frankland's grandfather, Sir Edward Frankland, was one of the nineteenth century's eminent scientists, and his father, Percy Faraday Frankland (named for his godfather, the famous physicist Michael Faraday), also obtained a doctorate in chemistry and worked at Birmingham University. However, as Edward Frankland's daughter, Dr. Helga Frankland (a biologist), notes,

> Scandinavia held a strong fascination for my great grandfather, grandfather and my father. By skillful placing of relatively small, coniferous woods [on his Westmorland

farm], my father managed to create a landscape that looks more wooded than it actually is and therefore, has echoes of Scandinavia. This is entirely appropriate since Viking blood runs strongly in Dalesmen and Westmorland dialect and place names also show lasting affinities with Scandinavian language [H. Frankland].

This affinity with Scandinavian culture, language and landscape emerges throughout Frankland's novels, most obviously in what could very well be the first example of medieval crime fiction, *The Murders at Crossby* (1955), in which the characters are, indeed, Vikings. Frankland's unusual combination of crime narrative and a medieval setting was evident at the time the book was released, as indicated by its inside-front-cover blurb: "This is a highly original departure from the usual line of the 'historical' novel—a murder mystery which happens to be set, with great verisimilitude, among the Norse settlers of Westmorland in the tenth century" (E. Frankland, dust jacket).

The novel opens with a prologue set in western Norway in 915 and describes the exile of two good friends, Ulf Haklang and Egil the Slim after they are outlawed for killing one of their neighbors. The two friends spend some years raiding the Hebridean Islands and the Isle of Man, becoming famous as great warriors and skilled sailors, before amassing enough wealth to settle in "Westmoringaland" (now Westmorland) in the lands of a Welsh-speaking king, Owen. In 937, Ulf and Egil are killed fighting in what is now known as the Battle of Brunanburh, described in the *Anglo-Saxon Chronicle*. The novel then opens by continuing the story of their children, Thora, Grim, Haldor and Ketil.

Frankland's characters are formed through a combination of truly unpleasant traits, reflecting what appears to be the author's assessment of the innate brutality endemic to the Norse settlers. Frankland introduces Thora, Egil's only child, as a great beauty but an indifferent housekeeper, preferring "to be out of doors, in the woods, among the animals, or talking to the Brettas [local Welsh speakers]" (E. Frankland 9). Later, after Haldor's murder, Ketil and Grim are both cowed by Thora's ruthlessness, "thinking that she was a very beautiful, desirable, but dangerous woman. She was also indisputably the owner of Crossby" (E. Frankland 98–99). Ulf's three sons are similarly cast in dubious terms: Grim is "a handsome boy, unruly, boastful, and untruthful"; "Haldor was quarrelsome and conceited"; while "Ketil might seem more cautious and reasonable, but men said he was as bad-hearted as Haldor and a great deal cleverer" (E. Frankland 10). Due to the close bond between their fathers, Thora and the three men's lives are inextricably intertwined, not least because, as owner of Crossby, Thora becomes the object of each man's ambitions.

Frankland explores the complexity of sibling rivalry through the framework of a premodern Scandinavian morality that has little in common with the detective narratives familiar to readers in the mid-twentieth century. In

The Murders at Crossby, it is perfectly acceptable for the murderer to visit his victim's house and admit to the killing because "That is the custom among the Northmen when a man of birth has been killed" (95). Ketil's wife, Gunvor, believes that a neighboring Dane, Finn, killed her brothers-in-law (Haldor and Grim), but Finn's behavior undermines her confidence because he has not come forward: "On the whole her guess would be that Finn had been the murderer in both cases, but then why had he not admitted it? No one would think it particularly discreditable to murder a troublesome neighbour; on the contrary it would raise a man's prestige, especially if he could avoid paying compensation to kinsfolk" (E. Frankland 149). There is a desire to discover the perpetrator only in so far as it will make social relations run more smoothly. There is scant interest in justice for the dead.

Frankland's depiction of Thora occupies a liminal space between a tacit disapproval of her sexuality and a grudging sympathy for her position in a harshly patriarchal society. She is unrepentantly brazen in satisfying her desire with not only her husband, Haldor, who knew her to be "seductive when she chose, greedy for love-making" (E. Frankland 16), but also his half-brother Grim (the unacknowledged father of her children), her childhood friend and steward Rhodri, and, in the most unlikely scenario, Gunnar, a Viking whom she randomly encounters amongst the hills. Frankland seems to suggest that Thora's promiscuity contributes to her strength of character, casting her as a Scandinavian *femme fatale*. But he finally denies Thora death on her own terms. She is instead severely burnt in a fire Ketil starts; she survives to become the wife of Gunnar—that Viking from the hills. Thora has, however, lost the greatest source of her power (after her ownership of Crossby)—her extraordinary beauty. With the dubious comfort that she believes Gunnar to be a better husband for her, Thora is nevertheless condemned to replicate the life she had with Haldor.

Frankland's novel is an unusual example of medieval crime fiction in several ways. It is almost certainly the earliest example of this form; it is similarly unique in its concern with Scandinavian settlements in northeast England; it is starkly unemotional in its style; it refuses to sympathize with, let alone idealize, the local Celtic people whose land has been appropriated; and it portrays its characters as self-aware, but not willing to circumvent deeply immoral thoughts and actions. Redemption—a crucial component of crime fiction—is not permitted within Frankland's bleak and unforgiving Anglo-Viking landscape.

In 1977, Ellis Peters was not the only author to explore the premise of combining a medieval setting with a detective narrative. In the same year,

Jeremy Potter published *Death in the Forest*, set in England in the years following the Norman Conquest. The novel concerns Edith, a young princess of Scotland, who has been sent south to England. Her mother, Margaret of Scotland, is a descendant of Alfred the Great's and her brother, Edgar the Atheling (in Edith's opinion the rightful king of England), is in exile in Hungary. Edith is installed in the abbey of Romsey between the New Forest and Winchester, where her aunt is prioress. The young princess is aghast at the decision of her parents to confine her to a nunnery: she dreams of uniting Scotland and England and had accepted that the only way to achieve this ambition is to marry. However, she is instead forced to remain at Romsey and embark upon the life of a novice.

If Edith's parents had hoped to protect their daughter from the harshness of the outside world, then that plan is shattered when William the Conqueror's sons, intent on hunting in the New Forest, noisily invade the abbey and insist upon seeing Edith, whose beauty was legendary (she became known as the "Rose of Romsey"). When one of the princes is killed, Edith throws herself into the task of discovering the murderer, much to the horror of the nuns. Through her endeavors, an internecine crisis is averted and Edith, better known to history as Matilda of Scotland, eventually has her wish: she marries the future King Henry I and becomes a popular and capable queen. Although her dream of uniting Scotland and England never materialized, Matilda nevertheless contributed significantly to English politics. In particular, during Henry's dispute with Anselm, the Archbishop of Canterbury, over the granting of church offices, Matilda corresponded with Anselm while he was in exile awaiting a resolution, inserting her own voice into the debate.

Death in the Forest is not Potter's only foray into historical fiction. His primary interest was in Richard III and his reign, serving as Chair of the Richard III Society from 1971 to 1989. Most of his novels attempt to rehabilitate Richard's reputation and include *A Trail of Blood* (1971), in which Potter imagines Henry VIII attempting to discover the descendants of the princes in the Tower, who had escaped rather than be murdered by their uncle. Potter was a staunch advocate of the so-called "revisionist movement" for Richard III, which, according to Potter, was founded in 1924 with The Fellowship of the White Boar. It was revived in 1956 in the wake of Josephine Tey's enormously popular *The Daughter of Time* (1951) and its membership rose remarkably between 1960 and 1985 from 200 to 4,500 (Potter, "Richard III's Historians"). Richard III's rehabilitation project is arguably complete now that the king's remains have been discovered underneath a Leicester car park thanks to the extraordinary and tenacious research by the Society, historians and archaeologists. Unfortunately, Potter did not live to see the affectionate, worldwide response to Richard's ceremonial reburial in Leicester Cathedral in 2015, as "the last medieval king" (Rowley). Potter's lifelong ambition to recuperate Richard's reputation has also been embraced by medieval crime fiction authors (as noted throughout this book), who, generally speaking, consider Richard to have been grossly maligned by history in general and Shakespeare in particular as part of his support for Tudor ideology.

Medieval crime fiction is a compelling combination of medievalism, the historical novel and crime fiction. Epitomized by its most famous novel, Eco's *The Name of the Rose*, medieval crime fiction warrants further scrutiny for the complexity of its purposes that are belied by its unassuming, yet extensive, presence across the literary landscape. Eco's single novel not only established the standard against which all subsequent forms of medieval crime fiction are judged, it also demonstrates the powerful combination of medievalism and postmodernism that characterizes so much of contemporary popular culture. The other originator of medieval crime fiction, Ellis Peters, wrote the genre's first and enduringly popular series, creating a character, Brother Cadfael, that remains beloved. Eco and Peters are still consistently cited by other authors, reviewers and publishers as illustrative and appealing exemplars that continue to define medieval crime fiction.

There is a distinct lack of critical appraisal of this enormously popular genre, although the gradual emergence of analyses such as those contained in *postmedieval* and the recent work by critics such as Kathleen Forni and David Matthews suggest a developing interest from medievalism scholars. Traditionally viewed as a subgenre of crime fiction, within the overarching category of historical crime or mystery fiction, these novels may just as productively be considered through the framework of medievalism. In other words, medieval crime fiction novels are almost universally listed in taxonomies, anthologies and studies of crime fiction, while they are rarely even mentioned in commensurate academic studies of medievalism. For example, while Matthews' recent treatment of the history of medievalism—an important and comprehensive book that endeavors to define and map the field—limits its discussion of medieval crime fiction to a couple of paragraphs, the subgenre is, at least, noted.

The effect of this generic situatedness is that medieval crime fiction has mainly been critiqued in terms of crime fiction conventions and judged upon how successful its detective or mystery narratives may be. What little critical attention it draws is usually framed in terms of what effect crime fiction conventions have upon the landscape of the Middle Ages. For example, Fichte concludes that "Although some of these novels provide us with insights into the material culture of medieval England, the new [*sic*] hybrid (a combination of historical and detective novel) draws its strength from the mystery plot" (67). One aim of this book is to contest and reverse this focus and instead consider medieval crime fiction through the apparatus of medievalism studies. While the mechanics of crime fiction are, of course, inextricably woven throughout (for example, Chapter Two relies upon the conventions of the hardboiled fiction of early-twentieth-century America for its discussion of secular medieval detectives), up until now the question has often been, what does crime fiction contribute to medievalism? In addition, this book asks, what effects, interventions, or contributions does medievalism afford crime fiction? In order to answer these questions, the following chapters delve deeply into the array of medieval detectives that populate the reimagined European Middle Ages created by the many and varied authors who venture there.

Chapter Two

Soiled Knights and Medieval Mean Streets

In the opening to Raymond Chandler's *The Big Sleep* (1939), private investigator Philip Marlowe contemplates the stained-glass window above the entrance doors to the Sternwood mansion. The window depicts a knight in dark armor, rescuing a naked lady tied to a tree. Marlowe has the impression that the knight "didn't seem to be really trying" and muses that if he lived in the house, he would "sooner or later have to climb up there and help him" (*The Big Sleep* 4). As Charles J. Rzepka points out, while missing the irony of the soiled knight trope, "Chandler … wanted to return to a legendary past … to rescue a personal code of honour made pointless by the Great War's impersonal violence and the vulgar self-interest of the succeeding years" (202). But more than simply retrieving a set of ethics from the questing knight, Chandler infuses this reimagining of medieval chivalric culture with the innately American compulsion for self-improvement. As Marlowe's response to the stained-glass window suggests, whatever a medieval knight could do, he can do better.

In medieval romances, as Helen Cooper notes, "the quest places the focus of the story squarely on the knight as an individual" (50). The knight not only overcomes the physical challenges the quest requires, he also undertakes an ontological journey that is often both a personal challenge and a prerequisite to a successful outcome. *Sir Gawain and the Green Knight*, the late-fourteenth-century poem that recounts Gawain's quest to find the Green Chapel and face the return blow of the Green Knight's axe, is a well-known example of this dynamic. Gawain taints his success in withstanding Lord Bertilak's strike with the failure to overcome the "couardise and couetyse" he displayed in accepting Lady Bertilak's green girdle (*Sir Gawain* line 2508). For Gawain, the tarnishing of his chivalric honor by what he perceives to be his cowardice and covetousness negates the joy expressed by the court at Camelot when he unexpectedly returns from his quest.

In the private eye, or hardboiled,[1] crime fiction tradition, the investigative quest directs a similar level of scrutiny towards the detective, as Dennis Porter explains: "In brief, the private eye is held up to be the stubbornly democratic hero of a post-heroic age, righting wrongs in a fallen urban world in which the traditional institutions and guardians of the law, whether out of incompetence, cynicism or corruption, are no longer up to the task…" (97). Porter's description easily applies to this chapter's secular medieval detectives, who often behave in the manner of the jaded private eye made famous by American authors Dashiell Hammett and Chandler in the 1930s and '40s. Indeed, Chandler's memorable and oft-quoted statement remains apposite: "down these mean streets a man must go who is not himself mean, … He is the hero, … He must be, to use a rather weathered phrase, a man of honor" ("Simple Art"). Chandler's Marlowe exemplifies the "knight" of the streets that hardboiled detective fiction celebrates. However, this knight is tarnished by the city he traverses in a futile, single-handed fight against the encroaching decay of corruption. The private eye occupies the liminal space between criminal networks and the systems of authority set up to fight them: in much the same way the heroes of medieval romance have an obligation to demonstrate chivalric prowess, which triggers the pursuit of individual quests that anticipate the one-detective-against-the-world structure of early hardboiled detective fiction.

Marlowe thus assumes the mantle of the American-hero tradition in a manner heavily coded by the knights of medieval chivalric romance. Critics such as Philip Durham and Jonathan Holden quickly identified this turn to the Middle Ages, while more recently, Stephen Knight has revisited the medievalist opening to *The Big Sleep*.[2] John Scaggs, too, describes the combination of "tough-talking cynicism and romantic sensibility" that ironically identifies Marlowe with the heroes of medieval romances (61). Chandler certainly inculcates his private eye with the essence of the chivalric knight: alone on a quest for justice, he protects the weak, (mostly) saves the innocent, and punishes the guilty. Moreover, like many a questing knight, Marlowe also seeks "to maintain his personal integrity in the face of repeated temptations and deceptions" (Rzepka 180). Chandler deploys the chivalric culture of the Middle Ages in order to retrieve an ethical framework that supports his lone detective as Marlowe combats the corruption of the modern city. However, while Chandler repackages the medieval in order to develop his own distinctly modern private investigator, medieval crime fiction authors harness this modern construction of the hardboiled detective and reinsert it into the landscape of the Middle Ages.

This chapter explores the many examples of medieval crime fiction whose detectives engage in a seemingly hopeless fight against social and institutional malfeasance. Unlike Marlowe, however, they are rarely aware of the futility of their efforts and so are able, for the most part, to avoid his cynicism. These detectives inhabit a range of different places and occupations. They may be ex-crusaders or ex-Templar knights, traversing the unpaved streets of medieval London, Exeter or Ludlow, seeking ways to demonstrate their martial prowess through occupations that enable them to continue their fight for justice. They could also be lawyers, surgeons, scribes, bookmakers, peddlers and bailiffs; these medieval professions similarly dovetail with the demands of a literary detective. The modern hardboiled character type is a firm favorite among medieval crime fiction authors. Consequently, there are many examples contained in this chapter, which aims to provide a sense of breadth without descending into a tedious succession of synopses.

Notably, there is a distinct absence of sheriffs performing the detective's role. A corrupt or antagonistic local sheriff often opposes the medieval detective, invariably resenting the latter's intrusion into his jurisdiction. If sheriffs do undertake investigative work, it is usually as an assistant to the main detective: for example, Hugh Beringar, sheriff of Shrewsbury, ably assists Ellis Peters' Brother Cadfael. Most commonly, however, sheriffs in medieval crime fiction represent the institutional corruption that the modern hardboiled detective combats on his quest for justice. The reputation of the medieval sheriff, it seems, has not survived the taint of dishonesty bequeathed by the nefarious Sheriff of Nottingham.

The landscape that medieval detectives negotiate is as tough, uncompromising and resilient as they are. That landscape frequently conforms to Umberto Eco's description of the "barbaric" Middle Ages (*Travels* 68–72), allowing authors to revel in the depiction of filthy streets, cruel torments and deadly diseases. Most of the detectives in this chapter conduct their investigations in a variety of locations, one of which is always a city or major township; even Muirteach MacPhee, Susan McDuffie's scribe-sleuth from the remote Inner Hebrides, travels to the dangerous streets of Oxford in *The Study of Murder* (2013). London is the most popular city, although Paris, Florence, Exeter, York and Edinburgh also feature in an effort to exploit one of the key features of hardboiled detective fiction: the mean streets of the corrupt city.

Crusaders and Knights Make Excellent Crowners

The three medieval detectives considered in this section share a profession that provides a regular supply of suspicious deaths. As "crowners," or coroners, they are the first to be called to view a body, whether the loss of life has come about by another's malevolence or through misadventure.

Bernard Knight carefully constructs his medieval landscape, describing in detail the poverty, squalor and violence that tarnish Exeter and its surrounding villages: his depiction of the Middle Ages is one of (literally) soiled streets and survival in a harsh and unscrupulous environment. Knight's concern with anatomical precision also reflects his long career as a forensic pathologist. His medieval detective, Sir John de Wolfe, spent years fighting for Richard I in campaigns across France, Ireland and on crusade. He has returned home to Exeter in 1194 and accepted the position of coroner, recently created by Richard both to counterbalance the often-corrupt sheriffs of the counties, and to generate more funds for the king through the collection of fines. Sir John is scrupulous at performing his duties and each procedure is explained in detail, from the witnessing of executions and state-sanctioned torture, to the evidence of the "first finder" of a corpse, and the appropriation of any "royal" fish that may be found (whale or sturgeon). Sir John is ably assisted by his Cornish man-at-arms, Gwyn of Polruan, and Thomas de Peyne, an intelligent and self-effacing defrocked priest, falsely accused of rape and desperate to return to the church. John is illiterate, so Thomas provides an invaluable service in recording the details about the deaths they investigate, as well as undertaking the laborious and thankless task of teaching John to read and write. Gwyn offers his physical skills and gleans important information from playing dice and drinking with castle guards.

Sir John de Wolfe is experienced and a little worn from his long years on campaign and crusade. He now faces a domestic quest to seek justice and combat the corruption embedded in the feudal hierarchies that surround him. He growls his way through his investigations using a combination of intimidation and bravado, and is quick to resort to physical force to extract information. Like many hardboiled detectives, John stumbles upon much of his evidence by chance rather than through the ratiocination process favored by golden-age amateurs. In one example of optimism overcoming practicality, John wanders around the enormous Exeter fair accompanied by the surviving victim of a murder-robbery in the hope that the traumatized man will recognize his attacker. The victim and John do indeed spot and apprehend the perpetrator during a pause to watch a morality play performed by one of Exeter's guilds, in a scene that simultaneously depicts an important part of medieval cultural life and advances the detective narrative (B. Knight, *Figure of Hate* 111–12). Crowner John's investigative procedures evince Heta Pyrhönen's observation that hardboiled detectives "often spend the major part of the investigation simply trying to understand what is going on" (qtd. in Rzepka 180).

Sir John is honorable, chivalrous and fanatically loyal to the absent King Richard. While lacking the chastity of the knightly ideal (he has frequent affairs and keeps a permanent mistress), de Wolfe still champions the weak and defenseless in a manner that modern "knights" are unable to replicate. In *Crowner's Quest* (1999), Sir John challenges Sir Jocelin de Braose to a trial by battle on behalf of the young son whose father de Braose has murdered, vanquishing his opponent in a jousting contest (*Crowner's Quest* 325). However, Knight takes care to temper the glamor of these chivalric episodes, allowing the acknowledgment of the brutal side of medieval life to co-exist with his depiction of knightly honor. In *Figure of Hate* (2005), participation in the medieval tournament circuit is presented as dangerous and expensive and is used on at least one occasion as an opportunity for murder.

The systematic and institutionalized corruption faced by Chandler's Marlowe and other conventional hardboiled detectives informs Knight's recreation of late-twelfth-century Exeter. In many of his investigations, Sir John de Wolfe's brother-in-law, Sir Richard de Revelle, sheriff of Devon, impedes his progress. Like most sheriffs of the period, Sir Richard resents the threat that the new office of coroner represents to his monopoly on law enforcement. Sir Richard is not only crooked, but also a traitor, having supported Prince John's uprising against King Richard and only narrowly escaped punishment. He has no desire to uncover truth or to administer justice, consistently opposing John in order to promote his own financial and political interests. John is the outsider to Sir Richard's tainted system of authority in a construction that mirrors the conventional hardboiled detective's futile fight against the modern city's decay.

In the same year, 1194, in the northwest of England, another ex-crusader, Sir Faucon de Ramis, finds himself similarly grappling with the demands of the newly created position of Keeper of the Pleas, or *coronarius* (shortened to "crowner"), on behalf of his great-uncle, the Bishop of Hereford. Denise Domning's foray into medieval crime fiction stems from her successful medieval romance novels and she includes some of those characters as peripheral, although impactful, figures in her detective series. Rannulf, Lord Graistan, and Bishop William assign Faucon the revenue from both the village of Blacklea and the Priory of St. Radegund so that he may serve as coroner in Lord Graistan's stead.[3] While grateful for this income, Faucon is nevertheless a little annoyed to have been burdened with a largely administrative role, suited to his literacy skills, diplomacy and calm nature, instead of exploiting his military prowess. However, Domning's hardboiled framework ensures that Faucon experiences plenty of violence during the course of his investigations.

The Bishop also assigns a Benedictine monk from the Priory, Brother Edmund, to serve as Sir Faucon's clerk in what turns out to be a form of penance for Edmund's high-handed and overbearing attitude towards his fellow monks. Brother Edmund, in turn, becomes a trial for Faucon, thanks to the former's officious interference at every opportunity in order to explain the correct legal procedure in tedious detail. Edmund's narrative function is to educate the novel's audience and through this pedantic, annoying monk, Domning conveys a meticulous catalogue of medieval coronial practices such as identifying the first finder of a body, raising the hue and cry, and summoning an inquest jury.

In Sir Faucon and Brother Edmund's first case, recounted in *Season of the Raven* (2014), they attend the scene of a recently deceased miller. The general assumption by the local villagers is that the miller—known for his heavy drinking—fell into the mill's race and drowned when he became caught by the wheel. Brother Edmund immediately claims the wheel as "deodand"—an object that has caused the death of a person and is either forfeit to the crown or, if possible, dedicated to the Church and "cleansed" of its sin of murder (*Season of the Raven* 43). The miller's son protests that the family will starve without the means to pursue their livelihood and, to Faucon's frustration, Brother Edmund's insistence on sticking scrupulously to the letter of the law goads the son into rashly accusing his father's new young wife of his murder.

Meanwhile, one of the Priory's lay brothers, the herbalist Colin, had accompanied Brother Edmund to the village in order to collect some plants and is inspecting the scene. As Domning's version of Peters' Brother Cadfael, Colin discovers that, in fact, "the miller did not drown, but was dead when the one who killed him put him into the water" (*Season of the Raven* 56). Over the next several pages, Brother Colin shows Faucon physical evidence from the mill wheel and the body that proves the miller was murdered: the lack of marks on his hands to indicate he tried to save himself from the water (56); a similar lack of foam in his mouth or nose to suggest drowning (58); the dryness of the miller's eyes, signifying that he was killed on land (59). On the cover of Domning's novel is a quotation from author Christina Skye that describes the book as "CSI 12th century style." While this description seems at first to be comically anachronistic, Brother Colin's close and detailed examination of the murdered man's body and the manner of his presentation to the detective investigating the case certainly replicates the now familiar privileging of forensic science that characterizes contemporary crime novels and television dramas. In this way, Domning reframes modern forensic techniques into a form that can be reinserted into her medieval landscape.

Domning's Sir Faucon also confronts an incumbent and resentful sheriff, Sir Alain (who seems to lack a surname). Arriving at the scene of the drowned miller, Faucon encounters Sir Alain for the first time: "it was the flatness of his expression that held Faucon's eye. He'd seen that same look on the faces of old warriors, soldiers who'd dealt out so much hurt in their lives that their hearts had turned to stone" (*Season of the Raven* 40). Sir Alain's contempt for Faucon's youth and inexperience is magnified by his deep anger at what Faucon's position as crowner represents, that is, a substantial curtailing of a lucrative trade in corruption. In Domning's second novel, *Season of the Fox* (2015), Faucon's intervention into another murder investigation infuriates Sir Alain because the crowner's presence deprives the sheriff of the large bribe that the perpetrator had thoughtfully left for him to collect. Consequently, towards the end of the novel, Sir Alain sends a band of ruffians to dispatch Faucon— only the latter's fighting skills and the timely arrival of another of Domning's romance characters, Temric FitzHenry, ensure that the assassination attempt fails.

This episode illustrates Faucon's combat credentials, underscoring his belief that he deserves a more martial appointment than an administrative coroner. It also demonstrates the fragility of justice in Domning's medieval world. Faucon, in answer to Temric's question about raising the hue and cry to chase the men who had escaped, replies, "As this shire's Crowner I pronounce their killings justified.... I would just as well throw these two into the nearest cesspit. I'd rather they weren't identified" (Domning, *Season of the Fox* 149). Temric obliges Faucon by offering to take care of the bodies, since he knows a couple of characters in the nearby tavern he can pay to dispose of the evidence. Faucon thus ignores his procedural obligations in order to pursue his own form of retribution; an ignorance made easier by the fact that Faucon's pedantic assistant, Brother Edmund, is not present to voice his inevitable concerns.

The medieval detective's dilemma here converges with those of his modern counterparts: does the quest for justice justify undertaking morally ambivalent means to an end? Such scenarios are common to hardboiled detective fiction, of course, and serve both to reinforce and to undermine the genre's depiction of justice. As Chandler pointed out in "The Simple Art of Murder," one of the characteristics that casts this kind of detective as a loner is an innately superior morality that separates him or her from society, particularly from the corruption of the legal and police institutions. Faucon considers himself exempt from the legal processes that he imposes upon others because, quite simply, he is the "good guy" who defeats the "bad guy" sheriff's gang of assassins. Moreover, Temric conceives, discusses and (presumably) executes his plan to dispose of the bodies with a clinical and cool professionalism that recalls twentieth-century organized crime practices. These tropes trouble Domning's concern with detailing the medieval coronial process and problematize her representation of justice in late-twelfth-century England. But Domning also makes such mafia-esque activities acceptable because the medieval world she has created is one in which the conventions of modern hardboiled detective fiction are not only recognizable, but also embraced and absorbed.

In a notable contrast, Jason Vail's knight-turned-(assistant) coroner, Sir Stephen Attebrook, finds his ability to enact his morally superior form of justice repeatedly curtailed by the medieval legal system. In the mid-thirteenth century, Sir Stephen returns to the small Shropshire town of Ludlow, close to the Welsh border, recovering from battle wounds obtained in Spain that have left him crippled. Desperately poor, he accepts the position of deputy coroner, a post that comes with the familiar figure of an assistant clerk. Gilbert Wistwode is an ex-monk who runs a local tavern under the strict and capable direction of his formidable wife, Edith.

Stephen resides in the tavern because he cannot afford his own house. He still possesses, however, his cherished war horses, a valuable stallion and two mares. Selling the former alone would enable Stephen to purchase a small manor house but he resists this action both because he is loath to relinquish the last link to his fighting past, and because he retains the innate snobbery of his birth: "Rich merchants bought manors all the time and thereby entered the gentry. Yet he could not bring himself to take this step. He could not put words to why. It just felt like going down rather than up, and he was too far down already" (Vail, *Saint Milburga's Bones* 70). Stephen's missing half foot excludes him from the conventional exploits of a knight and recalls the physical perfection that is required of the heroes of medieval romance: his infirmity precludes his inclusion in the army that Prince Edward is amassing in Ludlow in order to quell the Welsh and he is acutely aware of the stares he receives due to his limping gait. Eventually, however, Harry—an acerbic, legless beggar who is an entertaining foil for Stephen throughout the series—modifies the knight's stirrup so that his foot remains firmly encased and his ability to fight on horseback is restored.

In contrast to Sir Faucon's experience with the ruffians that he summarily dispatches with no apparent consequence, Stephen's encounter with a group of criminals similarly intent upon killing him is far messier. In *Saint Milburga's Bones* (2015), Stephen is seeking stolen emeralds that had adorned the saint's relics. Having identified the perpetrators and where the precious stones are buried, Stephen and Gilbert arrive at the location to discover some of the culprits in the process of retrieving the gems. They attack Stephen, who kills two of them in a fight that is described at length, as is typical of Vail's novels.[4] Where other medieval crime fiction detectives—indeed most hardboiled detectives generally—would clean their sword and accept the grateful thanks owed to them, Stephen is instead arrested for homicide, despite his actions having clearly been in self-defense. More usually, the medieval detective escapes legal consequences through aristocratic discretion or a finessing of the law. Stephen is held for three weeks, awaiting trial and a sentence of death, until Prince Edward arrives to pardon him for the price of his beloved stallion, a truly wrenching cost. Nevertheless, Stephen does have his stallion returned to him and is also promoted to coroner at the end of the next novel (*Bad Money* [2016]).

Stephen conforms to the medieval crime fiction convention of the reluctant coroner: he has taken the position only out of desperation; he is generally disregarded by his superior, Sir Geoffrey Randall; and he must navigate the animosity of not one, but two hostile sheriffs. He recalls Sir Faucon in his disappointment that circumstances have conspired to force him to accept this lowly position, and, like Crowner John, he stumbles upon solutions to his cases more through good luck than any discernible investigative process. Stephen is inept at following even basic detective procedures, as he himself acknowledges. In *Bad Money* (2016), when Stephen is called into Mistress Bartelot's home, across from the inn, to look into the theft of her most precious items, he forgets to examine the floor for evidence of trespassers:

> He should have done this before, but he had not thought of it until now. He was always forgetting obvious measures of this sort, and just bungled along. It was a wonder he ever found out anything at all. It was a good thing people had not seen through his facade of competence, or his reputation, little as it was, would be even lower. And like all people, he treasured his reputation more than the contents of his purse [21].

There are many episodes such as this throughout the six books of the series (so far) and it is both amusing and frustrating that Stephen never seems to learn nor improve as a detective. As noted above, Stephen is also very proud, prone to frequent bouts of introspection at the course his life has taken, usually while he is hiding, incapacitated or held in prison.

These three coroners reveal certain aspects of the cultural work that medieval crime fiction undertakes. In particular, the role of "crowner" allows these authors to interpolate what are recognizably modern forensic and scientific methods into a medieval landscape. All three knights are reluctant investigators of crime, assuming the coronial mantle through a sense of duty, familial obligation or financial need. The productive tension between the coroners and their antagonistic sheriffs, moreover, realizes the institutional corruption that is a feature of hardboiled detective fiction. None of these coroners can function without the assistance of his clerk, who not only occupies the "side-kick" role, but also acts as translator of medieval legal processes for modern readers. Despite these companions, however, these medieval coroners are resolute loners, given to introspection and assuming sole responsibility for their actions as they undertake their quests for justice within a deliberately corrupt premodern context.

Medieval London's Mean Streets and a Modern Detective: Hugh Corbett

Paul C. Doherty is a prolific British author, having published over one hundred titles since the mid–1980s. While he has written several series of historical mysteries across different periods and locations, including Tudor England, ancient Egypt, ancient Rome, and ancient Greece, his most numerous and popular novels are set in the Middle Ages. Doherty began his Hugh Corbett series in 1986 and published its nineteenth novel in 2018. Corbett starts as a clerk from the Court of the King's Bench in London during the reign of Edward I and progresses from that rather lowly post to become Sir Hugh Corbett, spymaster and Keeper of the King's Seal. Corbett combines the education and intelligence of a clerk with the physical bravery of a knight as he constantly combats serial killers, traitors and spies for his king. Like many medieval detectives of knightly rank, Corbett is unswervingly loyal to King Edward and undertakes his assignments out of a sense of duty, despite frequent misgivings about the morality of both the king and certain tasks. Corbett also has an assistant he rescued from Newgate Prison, aptly named Ranulf atte Newgate. Ranulf and Corbett have a prickly relationship; while each is loyal to the other, it is unclear whether they feel more than a grudging mutual affection. Ranulf spends a significant amount of time drinking in taverns, attempting to seduce other men's wives and he also performs the role of bodyguard and enforcer in a complementary pairing of brawn to Corbett's brains.

Corbett operates mainly as a problem-solver and spy for Edward I and Doherty relies upon a standard set of contemporary mystery devices to illustrate Corbett's expertise as a medieval detective. The locked-room scenario is a particular favorite, as is Corbett's tendency to reveal the solution to a gathering of suspects, "usually at a sumptuous dinner" (Meek et al. 77), in order to achieve maximum drama. Doherty also deploys his historical expertise to good effect in this series, with several novels engaging with recorded events or conundrums. The first book, *Satan in St. Mary's* (1986), set in 1284, describes Edward's suppression of supporters of the late rebel baron, Simon de Montfort, who died at the battle of Evesham in 1258. In *The Song of a Dark Angel* (1994), Corbett discovers part of King John's treasure, lost in 1216, while investigating a series of murders along the Norfolk coast in 1302. In *Crown in Darkness* (1988), Doherty sets Corbett the task of investigating the mysterious death of King Alexander III of Scotland, which leaves the throne vacant and leads to a chaotic struggle for power within the Scottish court. Doherty also engages with figures of medieval legend, such as the reputed return of Robin Hood in *The Assassin in the Greenwood* (1993).

However, Corbett's primary function is to act as a guide for his readers' ventures to the mean streets of the Middle Ages. Corbett's assignments from the king inaugurate his quests for justice and he frequently combines his solitary wanderings through London with contemplative musings on the morality of the tasks he undertakes in the custom of both contemporary hardboiled detectives and many of his medieval companions. While Doherty's depth of historical knowledge emerges in his detailed descriptions of the landscapes, punishments, streetscapes, rituals and spectacles that Corbett encounters, the detective often surveys these experiences through the anachronistic sensibilities of a modern reader. He remains aloof from the surrounding chaos of the streets, generating the critical distance through which a contemporary audience may experience medieval London.

This experience includes a number of pitiful sights, often encountered in quick succession on the same day: a line of prisoners, including children, forced to march barefoot through the snow from Newgate to the King's Bench at Westminster; a corpse lying in the street, covered with an awning and surrounded by the coroner and a jury of twelve men; a monk leading a horse and cart upon which a coffin rested; "a bare-headed and bare-footed sanctuary man who had agreed to abjure the kingdom, his legs and ankles purple with the cold"; a death crier asking people to pray for a recently departed man (Doherty, *Angel of Death* 58, 104, 105). Corbett similarly reveals his modernity in his reaction to the standard of food that is available to him. This sensibility recurs throughout the series, with frequent observations such as these:

> He felt hungry and bought a pie from a baker but, after two bites, tossed it away, for he could taste the rancid meat beneath the spices. He went into the tavern on the

corner of Bread Street and sat near the fire warming himself with a bowl of soup. He tried to ignore the globules of fat bobbing about amongst the pieces of meat and vegetable by drinking three tankards of London ale ... [Doherty, *Angel of Death* 140].

These are, of course, sights and tastes that did occur on London's thirteenth-century streets, but Doherty's deliberate conflation of multiple shocking scenes into a tick-box list of medieval horrors emphasizes the touristy experience he is creating for his readers.

Doherty's privileging of the detailed recreation of medieval London's mean streets often undermines his detective narrative. *The Angel of Death* (1989) concerns the sudden collapse and death of the Dean of St. Paul's, Walter de Montfort, in the middle of celebrating mass in front of the Archbishop of Canterbury and King Edward. De Montfort's co-celebrants, five canons of the cathedral, are the main suspects in the murder, which was enacted by poisoning a chalice of wine that was, it turns out, intended for the king to drink. However, the characterization in Doherty's novel is woefully inadequate and renders the suspects so indistinguishable that the evidence Corbett uncovers could point to any one of them. For Doherty, the murderer's identity is clearly secondary to his motive: Edward's ruthless sacking of the Scottish border town of Berwick prompts one of the canons to seek revenge upon the king for the slaughter of his family.

Doherty's purpose is not to present an engrossing mystery, but rather to contribute to his meticulous recreation of the messy Middle Ages that so admirably suits his hardboiled detective. His detective narratives frequently fall into well-worn formulas that offer little innovation or intervention into crime fiction more broadly. However, this formulaic approach allows Doherty to demonstrate his unquestioned expertise in the history of the English Middle Ages. Doherty reverses Eco's construction of the Middle Ages as pretext, whereby the medieval forms a background for a modern story; here, crime fiction is used as pretext for Doherty's medievalism and the device of the detective acts as a cipher for the author's own desire to conduct a tour of the Middle Ages for his readers.

Knights Behaving Badly: Crispin Guest and Benedict Palmer

Jeri Westerson broadcasts her generic intentions by including the strapline, "A Medieval Noir," on the cover of each of her medieval crime fiction novels. Consequently, readers are prepared for the hardboiled mise-en-scène that suffuses her gritty depiction of the streets of fourteenth-century

London and the characters that ply their shady trades there. Westerson's hard-boiled detective is a disgraced knight called Crispin Guest, who plots against Richard II and subsequently forfeits his title, rank, and wealthy fiancée. Crispin escapes with his life thanks to John of Gaunt's intervention, in whose household Crispin worked as a squire and companion for Gaunt's son, Henry.

With no other income, Crispin embarks upon a hand-to-mouth existence selling his wits and sword. He builds a small reputation as the "Tracker," able to seek out and retrieve objects, people and secrets that have proved elusive. Westerson revels in the conventions of hardboiled detective fiction: Crispin is a hard-drinking, womanizing, smart-talking knight of the streets, regularly in trouble with the authorities and frequently beaten up by the Sheriff of London's serjeants. The cast of characters that surrounds Crispin contributes to Westerson's medieval noir landscape and includes young Jack Tucker, an orphan living alone on the streets of London and scratching out a precarious living as a cutpurse. Jack attaches himself to the markedly unenthusiastic Crispin, making himself useful as a servant and apprentice. Each novel also has at least one *femme fatale* who seduces Crispin at regular intervals, including his ex-fiancée, Rosamunde.

Medieval crime fiction detectives, male and female, are almost universally heteronormative. Queer characters occasionally appear, such as the cross-dressing, bisexual prostitute John/Eleanor Rykener (discussed below) and Priscilla Royal's gay Brother Thomas (discussed in Chapter Four), among others. Most authors, however, seem to subscribe to the perception of an entrenched suspicion of the homosexual other throughout the Middle Ages. In this way, medieval crime fiction lags behind crime fiction more broadly and while there is no evidence to suggest that this subgenre offers a platform for anti–LGBTQI+ sentiments, this lack of sexual and gender diversity nevertheless hints at a pattern of conservatism.

Westerson is one author who occasionally dabbles with the heteronormativity of the noir conventions she invokes, but she ultimately forecloses the productive possibilities of Crispin's queerness. In *The Demon's Parchment* (2010), Crispin must overcome his innate suspicion and distaste for the Jewish physician, Jacob, whom Richard II has invited to London to solve his queen's infertility. Jacob's son, Julian, accompanies him to London and demonstrates an equal animosity towards Crispin. Crispin accuses Julian of being involved in the murders of several young boys and the pair argue about the truth or otherwise of the so-called "blood libel" against medieval Jewish communities (discussed in more detail in Chapter Five). In the middle of their confrontation, something unexpected occurs: just as Crispin grudgingly admits to himself—"'God's blood! Was he in danger of *liking* this youth?'" (Westerson,

Demon's Parchment 202)—Julian suddenly grabs Crispin and kisses him forcefully on the lips. Crispin's confused response is unusual for medieval crime fiction detectives: "But for a fleeting moment, the tiniest of flickers that lasted only the blink of an eye... Crispin had liked it" (Westerson, *Demon's Parchment* 203).

Westerson imposes upon Crispin a minor crisis that troubles the former knight for the remainder of the novel. Up to this point in the series, Crispin's heterosexuality is unchallenged and his womanizing is a prominent feature of his particular mélange of hardboiled detective conventions. Crispin's reaction to the unexpected and unwelcome feelings that Julian's kiss has awakened in him propels him to seek relief in the stews of Southwark. With convenient irony, the first person Crispin encounters after he leaves the dock is John Rykener, a transvestite prostitute who goes by the name "Eleanor" when in female garb and whom Crispin has briefly encountered in previous novels. John/Eleanor Rykener is a historical figure who appeared before London's mayor and aldermen in 1394, charged with prostitution. Rykener had been arrested with a man named John Britby, from York, who had propositioned him/her along Cheapside and, having agreed a price, they went to a stall in Soper's Lane, where they were discovered (McCarthy 126).

At the time, prostitution was only permitted in legitimate brothels in the three English towns of Sandwich, Southampton and Southwark (McCarthy 126), so Rykener and Britby would probably have avoided these legal difficulties had they not been in London. The court closely questions Rykener about his/her history as a "whore" and his/her experiences with both men and women. Rykener confessed that s/he "often had sex as a man with many nuns...S/he] further confessed that many priests had committed that vice with him [*sic*] as with a woman, ..." (Text of the court records in McCarthy 127–28). The case suggests that transvestism was not unknown in the Middle Ages, although Conor McCarthy notes it is "a unique record" of this particular sexual practice and that "the court seems to have all sorts of difficulties in categorizing John/Eleanor" (126). Carolyn Dinshaw has analyzed the court transcript concerning John/Eleanor, noting the "fabliau-like" episodes in his/her past. She remarks that "John/Eleanor Rykener's existence has something of a textual nature" that enables its comparison with Chaucer's poetry and his characters (such as the Cook and the "queer" Pardoner). Furthermore, Dinshaw locates John/Eleanor's story within "a queer history" in which "stark gender binaries of heterosexual relations ... do not preclude more complex—queerer—desires" (*Getting Medieval* 103, 108). In *The Demon's Parchment*, Westerson adds her own touch of queer history to her hardboiled narrative. Crispin visits Rykener's lodgings in Southwark—having inadvertently scared off Rykener's client—and reluctantly listens to some of his/her history that Westerson appears to have gleaned from the medieval court record.

Crispin admits his confusion to Rykener, who suggests that the former knight enjoyed Julian's embrace because, among other things, "Perhaps he reminded you a bit of a woman" (Westerson, *Demon's Parchment* 215). This is the prompt Crispin needs to realize that "Julian" is, in fact, Jacob's daughter Julianne, enacting her own transvestism so that she could more easily learn the arts of the physician from her father. Jacob, for his part, believed the deception would protect his daughter from "Gentiles" on their travels (Westerson, *Demon's Parchment* 234). In this way, Westerson suppresses the impulse to explore further Crispin's own physical response to the "boy" and instead reasserts the heteronormativity of the hardboiled detective. This experience does, however, broaden Crispin's mind a little: John Rykener features more frequently throughout the remainder of the series and Crispin gradually acquires greater tolerance for those who pursue a different lifestyle to his own. This subsidiary narrative strand is effective in its demonstration of how a historical case of medieval queerness may intervene into contemporary crime fiction, challenging entrenched generic tropes from an unexpected direction, and participating in the "queer history" that Dinshaw identifies (*Getting Medieval* 142).

E.M. Powell begins her series featuring Sir Benedict Palmer with the intriguing premise that there was a fifth knight present during the assassination of Thomas à Becket in 1170. Powell introduces Sir Benedict (whom she irritatingly insists upon calling "Sir Palmer") in the middle of a stormy crossing of the English Channel whereupon Benedict demonstrates his strength and skill by securing the ship's broken mast and saving the boat's occupants from a watery grave. Powell relates how the seven-year-old Benedict was sent off to be a squire by his mother, who is not able to provide for him (and four small daughters) after the death of his father. Benedict demonstrates exceptional fighting skills and is knighted on the battle field, a year earlier than anticipated. However, with no land to provide income, Benedict resorts to fighting as a mercenary, and he is hired to participate in this expedition to Canterbury in order to arrest the recalcitrant archbishop.

Benedict is full of anticipation both for the huge reward for his services and for his future reputation as one of King Henry II's most faithful servants and greatest knights. The events in the cathedral, however, do not involve the arrest, but rather the murder of Becket, as well as the abduction of a young anchoress, Theodosia, who witnesses the killing blow by the leader of the knights, Sir Reginald Fitzurse. Benedict is shocked at what has transpired, but nevertheless follows Fitzurse's command to take Theodosia on his horse as the group flees to the castle of one of the other knights. Theodosia is imprisoned in the castle dungeon and Benedict's conscience is finally sufficiently pricked when he overhears Fitzurse and castle-owner De Morville's plans for the excruciating torture of Theodosia before she is killed. Benedict escapes with the young anchoress and the pair embarks upon a frantic race to find, firstly, Theodosia's mother in a distant priory, and then to travel to France to explain the whole catastrophe to Henry II. All the while, Benedict and Theodosia must avoid the dogged pursuit of Fitzurse who, in cartoonesque fashion, has a death-defying ability to survive wolf attacks and landslides, inexorably appearing whenever the young fugitives are confident that he is dead. While Benedict is an extremely skillful knight, Theodosia is also remarkably capable—considering she has spent most of her life in an anchorhold—saving Benedict's life on more than one occasion through her quick-wittedness and tree-branch-wielding skill.

Theodosia and Benedict are similar in their combination of ingenuity, capability and naivety. Benedict is dangerously credulous; he is easily manipulated by arch-criminal Fitzurse and continues to quaff wine that the devious Brother Edward plies him with when it is more than obvious that the rogue monk is attempting to render him incapacitated with a drink that may also be poisoned. Theodosia insists upon returning to check on a local man, Gilbert, who had helped them only to be betrayed by his wife, so risking their lives and allowing Fitzurse to pick up their trail. Benedict also conforms to the type of medieval detective that owes much to the floundering of Crowner John: eventually arriving at the correct solution through a combination of luck and an ability to avoid deadly threats through physical prowess.

Powell's medievalism owes a generic debt to historical romance, and the burgeoning relationship between Theodosia and Benedict seems to be her main narrative concern. Henry II appears at the end of the first novel and is delightfully depicted as having a quick and monumental temper, as well as an unusual comprehension of, and sympathy with, the impossible situation Theodosia and Benedict face, deciding to aid them as much as he can. With the support of the king, the young couple retreats into the obscurity of farming life in England and Benedict ostensibly renounces his knighthood and his martial aspirations.

However, Benedict is not permitted to enjoy this rural peace for long. Over the next two novels in Powell's series, Henry calls upon Benedict's loyalty to assist him when his mistress is threatened with assassination (*The Blood of the Fifth Knight* [2015]) and to monitor his unpredictable youngest son, John, as he embarks upon his appointment as overseer of Ireland (*The Lord of Ireland* [2016]). Benedict gradually becomes Henry's "right-hand man," in a manner that recalls Sharon Penman's Justin de Quincy, "the Queen's Man" (discussed below). Benedict combines the physical toughness of the private eye with the fighting skills of the medieval knight to form a convincing hard-boiled hero of medieval crime fiction. After his marriage to Theodosia, he also demonstrates a reluctance to deploy those skills, only grudgingly conceding to King Henry's appeal to the innate and finally irresistible sense of justice that he also shares with both medieval and modern detectives.

Overcoming Physical and Psychological Injuries: Owen Archer and Sir Baldwin Furnshill

Medieval detectives frequently harbor both physical and psychological scars from injuries sustained prior to their embarkation upon their investigative profession. These scars often represent a significant turning point in the character's life that prompts a voluntary or enforced change in occupation. Sir Stephen Attebrook's loss of half a foot affects both his personal pride as well as hampering his ability to perform his duties as a knight, as discussed earlier in this chapter. Bascot de Marins, Maureen Ash's Knight Templar, suffers from severe post-traumatic shock disorder and finds that the role of medieval detective aids his recovery while on enforced leave from his order, as discussed in Chapter Three. Owen Archer and Sir Baldwin Furnshill must overcome similar afflictions: the loss of an eye that engenders instant redundancy; and the ongoing emotional trauma of having witnessed the destruction of his knightly order.

In 1993, Candace Robb, a recognized medievalist, published *The Apothecary Rose*, the first in her successful Owen Archer series. From Wales, Owen is captain of the Duke of Lancaster's archers in France when he loses one eye in a skirmish, ending his archery career. Owen is despondent, but the Duke surprises him by insisting that he can continue to serve by becoming a spy. Two years later, the old Duke is dead and Owen distrusts the motives of his successor, John of Gaunt: "Gaunt was dangerous, noted for his treachery. Owen could well imagine the sort of work Gaunt would give him. To serve him would be an honour, but it would not be honourable. Not to Owen" (Robb, *Apothecary Rose* 32). Instead, Owen chooses to serve John Thoresby, Lord Chancellor of England and the Archbishop of York. In 1363, Thoresby tasks Archer with investigating the mysterious deaths of two noblemen in the same abbey in York. Owen meets Lucie Wilton, apprentice and soon-to-be widow of the local apothecary. They marry, settling down in York to run Lucie's apothecary business together, although Thoresby continues to summon Owen to investigate crime and uncover intrigues. There are currently ten books in the Owen Archer series; the last one, *A Vigil of Spies*, was published in 2008, while a short story, "The Bone Jar," was released in 2016. Most of the novels are set in York, although Owen does travel south to Windsor, further into the north of England and, memorably, in *A Gift of Sanctuary* (1998) undertakes a pilgrimage to his homeland of Wales in the company of his dying father-in-law and his friend, Geoffrey Chaucer (see Chapter Six).

Robb is an enthusiastic scholar of the Middle Ages, often referring to her ongoing engagement with the academic world of medieval studies.[5] This continuing relationship seems important and she regularly attends academic conferences such as the annual International Congress on Medieval Studies, hosted by the University of Western Michigan (M. Evans). There are several authors of medieval crime fiction in a similar situation to Robb, that is, academic medievalists who redirect their considerable expertise towards writing this very specific type of fiction. In Chapter Six, an examination of medieval studies professor Bruce Holsinger's novels considers the appeal of this "crossover" for academics. For Robb, historical fiction interacts with scholarship either by using a piece of academic research as inspiration (Robb notes that her Owen Archer series emerged out of her contemplation of an article about the longbow), or by speculating about a particular gap in the historical record (M. Evans). Robb's meticulous research enables her to create a believable medieval landscape for her fictional characters.[6] Owen, archer-turned-spy-turned-apothecary-turned-detective, struggles with the ethics of some of his assignments and he is credibly concerned with discerning and following God's purpose for him.

Archer is consistently described as a "spy" throughout the series, but he behaves more like a private investigator. He is rarely secretive about the tasks he undertakes for his superiors, such as Archbishop Thoresby or the Duke of Lancaster. Moreover, Archer frequently accepts assistance from his family and close friends, including his wife Lucie, his adopted son Jasper and his neighbor and tavern-owner, Bess Merchet, among others. This willingness to share the burden of his investigations reframes Robb's novels as premodern police procedurals, with Owen acting as the Inspector in charge of directing the enquiry and absorbing the information that his team has collected.

Notwithstanding her impressive historical context and Owen's rounded-out characterization, Robb's medieval world sometimes struggles to absorb the disruption of her detective's modernity as he prosecutes his investigations.

It is not simply Owen's superior sense of justice—this is necessarily shared by all medieval detectives—but the combination of world-weariness and resignation that Owen often displays towards his life and circumstances, suggesting that the Middle Ages is, at times, simply too exhausting to navigate. Lucie Archer also seems always to be tired, compounding the sense of an underlying unease with the medieval landscape Robb meticulously describes. While Owen and Lucie love each other and their children deeply, there is surprisingly little joy in their lives. Whether or not Robb deliberately depicts her main characters' exhaustion with the Middle Ages, it nevertheless evinces medievalism's effective deployment of postmodern irony: no matter how affectionately, accurately and frequently contemporary popular culture recreates the European Middle Ages, underlying all of these medievalist cultural products is the unspoken awareness that we would prefer not to be there.

Michael Jecks's medieval detective is the disillusioned ex-Templar knight Sir Baldwin Furnshill, who has returned to his family's landholding in Devon after witnessing the destruction of the Order of Templar Knights in Paris in the first decade of the fourteenth century. Traumatized by his experiences—particularly watching the leaders of the Order burnt at the stake—Sir Baldwin forges a new life in Furnshill Manor, on the edge of Dartmoor, which he inherits after the death of his brother. When in Devon, Baldwin meets the bailiff of the local castle, Simon Puttock, and the pair develops into an effective investigative team over the course of the series. But the ex-Templar finds it difficult to relinquish the past: he is clearly suffering from what Jecks depicts as post-traumatic stress disorder. In one example, Sir Baldwin overreacts to Simon's suggestion that suspects should be tortured:

> "The only way to get the truth out of most of them would be to put them on the rack!"
> *"Don't!"* Baldwin's short, anguished cry made Simon stop in horror, shocked at his friend's pained expression…. After a moment, the knight's fingers relaxed, but Simon was shocked at the way that the misery and depression remained in the dark eye [Jecks, *Last Templar* 99].

Baldwin struggles to control his breathing enough to explain to Simon his seemingly anachronistic assessment of the efficacy of torture:

> "My friend," he murmured, "don't think that the rack or other tortures would help. I have seen them, and the effect of them. They do not work; all they do is destroy a man. They cannot force him to tell the truth, but they can force him to tell a lie, just to stop the pain. They do not help us to find the truth, all tortures can achieve is the breaking of a man so that he is destroyed, ruined" [Jecks, *Last Templar* 100].

After receiving Simon's assurance that they will not use any torture in the course of their investigation, Baldwin admits to himself the weakness of his mental state: "There was no denying it, the knight knew he was still too badly affected by his experiences in France. To have erupted like that! … It was ridiculous" (Jecks, *Last Templar* 100). In this way, Baldwin resembles Maureen Ash's traumatized ex-crusader, Bascot de Marins (see Chapter Three), who must confront and resolve the lingering aftereffects of war and capture.

Jecks, like Ash, is engaged in an attempt not only to speculate about the psychological damage that the often idealized and sanitized chivalric past doubtlessly inflicted upon its participants, but also to endow Baldwin with a broader world perspective that aids him in his performance as a detective. Moreover, Baldwin's tormented mind recalls the hardboiled detective's conventional wrestling with past demons, as well as the ontological journey that many heroes of medieval romance undertake alongside their quests for feats of arms and honor. Jecks's medievalism combines these two characteristics in his troubled knight, who eventually embarks upon a pilgrimage to Santiago di Compostela (accompanied by Simon), which Jecks recounts in *The Templar's Penance* (2003).

Jecks is a prolific author and his Templar series exceeds thirty books. He is also a founding member of the Medieval Murderers writing group, discussed in Chapter Three, and is an active participant in associations such as the Royal Literary Fund, the Detection Club and Britain's Crime Writers' Association, as well as a frequent giver of talks and workshops (Jecks, "Who"). An avowed enthusiast for medieval history, he notes in an interview that what he values most about his writing is its ability to engender a similar delight in that history among his readers, especially if they "have come to [him] without any interest in Medieval English history at first" (Brodey). In the same interview, Jecks demonstrates an admirable awareness of the intermingling between premodern and modern that his books depict: "I write modern thrillers, effectively, which happen to be based in the past," while avowing that he "deliberately do[es] not make the books hard going" (Brodey). Jecks also has a strong aversion to being judged as a "literary writer" because he "think[s] of literary writers as pretentious" (Brodey). This defensive stance often appears among authors of genre fiction to circumvent criticism about their writing before it can be made. Jecks has a similar attitude towards reviews, suggesting that "if you really dislike a work, don't give it a miserable score—just don't review it" (Brodey). As well-meaning as Jecks's intentions are, his Templar series does suffer from both limited writing and contextual heavy-handedness. Many historical details are over-explained or repeated unnecessarily in overly long footnotes, while most of his narratives have a disjointed tendency to leap from character to place, to different character, different place or temporal period.

At the risk of sounding too much like the negative reviews that Jecks finds unproductive, he is an example of the amateurs who embrace medieval crime fiction from an undeniable place of affection and impressive research that does not necessarily translate into high-quality novels.[7]

Bastard Sons of Clergymen and the Loss of Innocence: Justin de Quincy and Muirteach MacPhee

Justin de Quincy was raised in the household of the Bishop of Chester, Aubrey de Quincy, after his mother died in childbirth. In the opening of the first book of Sharon Penman's series, *The Queen's Man* (1996), Justin discovers that he is the bishop's illegitimate son, a fact kept secret by the bishop for twenty years. Distraught, Justin leaves his employment as a squire, wishing to repudiate the past and make his own way in the world—although he does, in a moment of spite, adopt his father's name.

Wandering around at a loss, he encounters two thieves in the process of attacking a goldsmith and his groom in the woods outside Winchester. Justin is too late to save the goldsmith, but before the man dies he compels Justin to promise to deliver the letter he was carrying to the queen, Eleanor of Aquitaine. It is 1193 and Richard the Lionheart has disappeared on his way back from the Holy Land. Eleanor is desperately trying to find her son, while simultaneously ensuring that England does not descend into chaos and keeping a tight rein on the ambitions of her youngest child, John. Justin delivers the dying man's letter to Eleanor, which contains the welcome news that Richard is still alive, although a prisoner of Henry, the Holy Roman Emperor.

Eleanor, in her seventy-first year, is still a captivating and commanding figure:

> As he knelt, Justin caught the faintest hint of summer, a fragrance as intriguing as it was subtle, one sure to linger in a man's memory.... But what drew and held his gaze were her extraordinary eyes, gold flecked with green, candle-lit and luminous and quite inscrutable [Penman, *Queen's Man* 25].

Justin becomes "the Queen's man," with responsibility for undertaking whatever task Eleanor requires. The first of these is to discover who killed the goldsmith, which Justin does so by applying the conventions of a contemporary hardboiled detective. Over the course of this and the other three novels in the series, Justin becomes further entrenched into the service of Eleanor. In addition to investigating several mysterious deaths, he is caught up in royal intrigues such as thwarting John's attempts to prevent Richard's return to England and uncovering a Breton conspiracy.

Penman's depiction of medieval London is particularly detailed and evocative and, like Paul C. Doherty, she allows her medieval detective to become the translator of London's streets for her postmodern audience. Justin shares his first encounter with the capital city with the reader in a manner that casts them both as outsiders who have banded together to witness the astonishing sight, which is further magnified once Justin starts to navigate the streets:

> Reining in on Old Bourn Hill, Justin gazed down at the city below. Never had he seen so many rooftops, so many church steeples, such a tangled maze of streets and alleys.... Justin sat on his horse as the daylight began to fade, awed by his first glimpse of London.
>   Up close, the city was even more daunting, exciting and crowded and chaotic. The streets were narrow, unpaved, and shadowed by overhanging timbered houses painted in vivid shades of red and blue and black.... Weaving his way along the Cheapside, Justin had to check his stallion frequently, for the street was thronged with pedestrians, darting between lumbering carts and swearing horsemen with the aplomb of the true city dweller.... Marvelling at this urban insouciance, Justin rode on [Penman, *Queen's Man* 17–18].

Like many of her fellow historical novelists, Penman cannot resist describing the sordid, distasteful and cruel aspects of life in the late twelfth century that contrast sharply with her readers' contemporary experience. In one unpleasant episode, Justin finds himself carried along by a crowd going to watch two prisoners undergo an ordeal to determine their guilt or innocence by plunging their arms into a cauldron of boiling water. Justin anticipates the reaction of Penman's readers, as he "was not sure this was something he wanted to watch" (Penman, *Queen's Man* 121).

Justin's modernity similarly emerges in his attitude towards medieval medical practices such as bloodletting. Like all hardboiled detectives, Justin endures beatings by the criminals he is attempting to thwart and, after one particularly brutal encounter, he is laid up in bed for a week. Queen Eleanor is concerned and Justin confesses he has had a falling out with his doctor:

> "He wanted to bleed me and I thought I'd been bled more than enough already. In truth, my lady, I've never understood the logic behind bloodletting. How does losing blood make a man stronger? It seems to go against common sense does it not?" [Penman, *Queen's Man* 172].

Eleanor shares Justin's skepticism, remarking, "'I always thought it fortunate that doctors are barred from the birthing chamber, else mankind [*sic*] might have died out centuries ago'" (Penman, *Queen's Man* 172).

However, Penman is able to contain these occasional touches of modernity so they do not undermine the authenticity of her medieval world. She does this by surrounding these moments with a greater number of episodes that comprise a laudable attempt to interpret and describe medieval emotional practices. For example, Penman demonstrates an insightful presumption of the grief that suffused medieval daily life. Nell, the owner of Justin's closest tavern, explains to him that Gunter, the local farrier and Justin's landlord, has become a recluse after the loss of his thirteen-year-old son and wife: "Nell had related the farrier's sorrows as matter-of-factly as she'd recounted her own. She accepted grief as she accepted January's cold or July's parched heat" (Penman, *Queen's Man* 164). This pragmatic acceptance of the precariousness of life in the Middle Ages has led to erroneous depictions of the "emotionless" medieval family in cultural histories of the emotions.[8] While this privileging of early modern sensibilities has more recently been problematized and largely overcome,[9] the high mortality rate that was an inevitable part of medieval life is often challenging for today's readers. While helpless against the onslaught of disease and accidental death, medieval crime fiction nevertheless attempts to buttress this starkly harsh reality for a modern audience by at least insisting upon bringing the perpetrator of unnatural death to justice.

Throughout his adventures, Justin works hard to avoid the contemporary hardboiled detective's cynicism and to ensure that his experiences of royal intrigue and crisis do not impinge upon his sense of justice. At the end of the fourth book in the series, Prince John's sinister henchman Durand scoffs at Justin's naivety in thinking that a trial would be the most effective way of establishing the truth. Justin's response remains idealistic, despite his fast-growing experience with the corruption of the world:

> Justin had never thought of himself as an innocent, certainly not after more than a year as the queen's man. But he'd still clung to a few illusions about royal justice, illusions he was loath to surrender. As he glanced from Durand to John, he found himself hoping that he'd never become as jaded and distrustful as they were. The price of something and its value were not always one and the same [Penman, *Prince of Darkness* 293].

Justin here finds himself floating in the liminality so familiar to private eyes: tarnished by the constant exposure to corruption and crime and struggling to accept the fact that the complexity of human nature means that good people perform dark deeds. Justin's epistemological journey traces this gradual loss of naivety and the concomitant acquisition of knowledge that his experiences give him. For Justin, finally, the pursuit of justice entails a sacrifice of innocence that resembles the experiences of the questing knight of medieval romance.

Like Penman's Justin de Quincy, Susan McDuffie's medieval crime fiction series also concerns a clergyman's bastard. Muirteach MacPhee is the illegitimate son of Crispinus, head of Oronsay Priory, located in the Inner Hebrides off the coast of Scotland. In the prologue to McDuffie's first novel, *A Mass for*

the Dead (2006), set in 1373, Crispinus's body is found on the beach below the priory and Muirteach must discover the murderer in order to prove his own innocence.

Muirteach is a rather angry young man, nursing a lingering resentment with regard to his upbringing in the priory and a hatred for his father, but he suppresses these memories through a recurrent state of inebriation, much to the frustration of his neighbors and relatives. So far, so hardboiled. However, because of a childhood fever, Muirteach is lame in one leg and, while he can walk, he cannot move quickly. Fortunately, the islands of the Inner Hebrides rely upon the sea for most of their travel and industry. Moreover, thanks to his priory upbringing, Muirteach is an accomplished scribe and earns an income working for his uncle, "the MacPhee," brother to the murdered prior and a wealthy landowner on Oronsay. Muirteach is an outsider well-suited to the role of private eye, as he muses to himself:

> I had not been the son he'd hoped for, and he had made no secret of it. A cripple, good for nothing, except scriving, and hating that. And being a cripple, I had not even had the grace to settle quietly into the life of the Priory, as would have been only proper and seemly. Neither a fish nor a fowl. The spray touched my cheek like a benediction but I pulled hard at the oars, trying to row out my thoughts [McDuffie, *Mass for the Dead* ch. 1, loc. 122].

Muirteach tries to overcome this sense of disappointment throughout his investigation into the murder, in the process discovering his father's mistress and his own half-siblings. Assisting a reluctant Muirteach is Fearchar Beaton, a physician from a family respected all over the Isles for its knowledge. Beaton has a daughter, Mariota, whom he has trained as a doctor, a remarkably common practice in medieval crime fiction. McDuffie allows Muirteach to indulge in a conventionally hardboiled reaction to Mariota's presence—"For myself, I was wishing the Beaton had never brought his daughter with him, for all the opinions she had and the complications she was causing" (*Mass for the Dead* ch. 4, loc. 564)—before the inevitable romance between the two.

In McDuffie's third novel, *The Study of Murder* (2013), Muirteach is compelled to leave his islands in order to accompany thirteen-year-old Donald, son of the Lord of the Isles, to Oxford and to ensure he is settled into lodgings and study. Muirteach is extremely reluctant to accept this directive to be nursemaid to a spoilt, belligerent, entitled young lord, but his wife, the aforementioned Mariota (whom Muirteach marries at the end of the second novel, *The Faerie Hills* [2011]), is in favor of the plan because of the opportunity to sample the bookshops and, perhaps, the lectures that Oxford offers.

Muirteach is a little overwhelmed by the bustling city, being inexperienced with urban life, although he understands that "Oxford is not as crowded now as it was before the Plague days" (McDuffie, *Study of Murder* ch. 2, loc. 286). As a country detective, more used to the expanses of the remote Isles and a water-based transport system, this excursion to the mean streets of Oxford is "altogether new" to Muirteach. This does not, of course, prevent him from almost immediately becoming involved in the disappearance of a local tavern owner's daughter, Jonetta. Young lord Donald had taken a predictable shine to Jonetta and graciously offers the services of his "man" Muirteach to assist the undersheriff, Walter Grymbaud, in his investigation, much to Muirteach's disgust at both the boy's manner and the suggestion: "My man, Muirteach here, has a good head for solving mysteries. He has helped my father, who is a great lord in Scotland. The Lord of the Isles…. He can be of assistance to you, I am sure. You are welcome to his services" (McDuffie, *Study of Murder* ch. 2, loc. 394). McDuffie deftly captures Donald's immature sense of *noblesse oblige* and identifies a realistic opening that allows Grymbaud to accept Muirteach's help. Jonetta's father, the tavern-keeper, had earlier told the Scottish visitors about the St. Scholastica's Day riots, twenty years previously, in which many students and townspeople were killed during a three-day rampage. Relations between the university and the town are still strained, so Grymbaud asks Muirteach to keep an eye on one of the scholars who, they suspect, saw Jonetta last. "Townsfolk," it seems, "are [still] not overly welcome in the schools" (McDuffie, *Study of Murder* ch. 2, loc. 394).

Mariota, as is typical of most wives of medieval detectives, is educated, capable and an invaluable aid to Muirteach's investigations. A skilled and knowledgeable healer, taught by her father, Mariota is incensed that she is forbidden from attending the lectures on medicine in the many Oxford colleges because she is a woman. Her frustration is magnified by her observation that her father's reputation counts for nothing in Oxford, and neither does she, "While these great louts of students spend all their time in the taverns, and care nothing for their books!" (McDuffie, *Study of Murder* ch. 3, loc. 474). Mariota laments the gender of her birth in a proto-feminist manner that is typical of the women who populate medieval crime fiction: "'Och, I wish I was a man!' … It's all well for you to sympathize, Muirteach, but you've never had to forgo something due to the mischance of being born a woman'" (McDuffie, *Study of Murder* ch. 3, loc. 483).

Muirteach, hoping to appease Mariota, accompanies her to a bookseller, where "Master Bookman" suggests "A romance for the lady," *The Book of the Duchess*, only just written by "A man named Chaucer" (McDuffie, *Study of Murder* ch. 3, loc. 498). Mariota is more interested in the bookseller's texts on Galen and other medical treatises, but Muirteach purchases a copy of *Sir Gawain and the Green Knight* because "The tale had captured my fancy, and

I justified the purchase thinking that reading it would improve my English" (McDuffie, *Study of Murder* ch. 3, loc. 524). Authors of medieval crime fiction often include allusions to the medieval romances that their detectives may have encountered in a largely successful effort to construct a credible medieval landscape. Moreover, as is the case here, these allusions tighten the close literary connections between medieval romance tropes and contemporary hardboiled detective conventions.

Medieval Medicine, Premodern Forensic Investigators and Autopsies

A compelling aspect of the Middle Ages for many people is the ostensible barbarity of medieval medical practices. This perception forms an integral part of contemporary popular culture's fascination with authentically recreating the medieval past combined with the recognition that life in the Middle Ages was often deeply uncomfortable. The following section considers medieval medicine and how such anatomical knowledge not only assists the medieval detective, but also generates its own danger as the procedures are viewed with, at best, suspicion and, at worst, fear of heresy. Premodern medicine is an area that reveals a more overt discordance between crime fiction and medievalism than is usually discernible. This is because autopsy and other forensic practices are so fundamental to the modern detective's arsenal that they are not dispensable, even in a premodern context that frequently precludes such practices. In a fascinating juxtaposition, the medieval detective would appear more out of place by *not* employing some (inevitably modified) modern forensic techniques than by ignoring the evidence that can be gleaned from a wound or a corpse.

Susanna Gregory's series of twenty-one novels (and counting) features Doctor Matthew Bartholomew, a master of medicine at Michaelhouse, one of Cambridge University's first colleges. "Susanna Gregory" is one of the pen names used by Elizabeth Cruwys, a former forensic police officer who has experience working in the English coroner's office, as well as a doctorate that examined mammalian teeth and bones (Coakley 85). In this past experience, she resembles Bernard Knight, author of the Crowner John series, who, before retirement and full-time writing, enjoyed a thirty-year career as a Home Office pathologist and Professor of Forensic Pathology at the University of Wales, Cardiff. Both authors share a concern with anatomy and premodern forensic practices; the description of the corpses in these novels is subsequently authentic and often queasily graphic.

In Gregory's first novel, the anachronistically titled *A Plague on Both Your Houses* (1996), Bartholomew's fellow college master, Brother Michael, transforms from murder suspect into joint investigator and the monk has an increasingly important role throughout the rest of the series. Michael (described by Joan Coakley as "An academic Friar Tuck" [89]) is ambitious and eventually becomes Senior Proctor of the university, responsible for maintaining order and investigating crimes that concern the scholars. Brother Michael prosecutes criminal investigations in a more enthusiastic manner than Bartholomew does, whose prevailing concern remains his other fight against the ravages of disease. Gregory relies heavily upon the hardboiled convention of the detective as lone crusader against the onslaught of corruption and decay. Indeed, Coakley describes Bartholomew in terms that could easily apply to Philip Marlowe: the doctor is "above all a good man trying to lead a virtuous life while determining where he stands" (85). In Gregory's series, this corruption manifests most clearly in the illness and disease that Bartholomew combats every day.

In his mid-fourteenth-century context, Bartholomew is unorthodox in his belief that traditional medical practices such as composing astrology charts and applying leeches are poor substitutes for a close examination of the patient and an understanding of the causes of disease. However, like other medieval detectives, Bartholomew has a convincing history that attempts to explain his proto-modern attitude. He was educated at the Benedictine Abbey in Peterborough, at Oxford University and at the University of Paris. While at the latter, he studied under an innovative Arab physician, Ibn Ibrahim, who had a passion for cleanliness and investigated the links between sepsis, causality and contagion (Coakley 87). Despite the accuracy of this history, Bartholomew's progressive approach unsettles his Cambridge milieu and he must tread a careful path between deploying the latest scientific knowledge to treat his patients and countering the fear and superstition this knowledge generates among his colleagues. For example, Bartholomew "had risked the wrath of the clerics by refusing to allow the students to consider 'struck down by God' as a determinant for contagious disease...For Bartholomew], 'struck down by God' was a convenient excuse for not working out the real causes" (Gregory, *Plague on Both Your Houses* 127). However, the medieval university apparatus constrains Bartholomew with its demand that his students learn astrology in order to pass their examinations, even though Bartholomew clearly does not believe that the stars have any effect on a patient's wellbeing:

So Bartholomew had learned his traditional medicine, and answered questions about poorly aligned constellations in his disputations. But he had also learned Ibn Ibrahim's unorthodox theories on hygiene and contagion, and so his patients had the benefit of both worlds [Gregory, *Bone of Contention* 136].

Gregory here (perhaps unconsciously) illustrates the inherent instability of medieval crime fiction generated by the underlying conflict between premodern and modern that always threatens to emerge: Bartholomew does not believe in the efficacy of astrology and yet, because he was forced to learn it, "his patients had the benefit of both worlds." The slipperiness between Bartholomew's conflicting practices contributes to his alienation from his medieval landscape, which Coakley also identifies: "Compounding Bartholomew's dilemma about his teaching and practice of medicine is his loneliness: there is literally no one with whom he can share his innermost doubts and concerns" (89). It is this isolation that also inevitably recalls the alienated loner of the contemporary private eye.

The series opens in 1348, at the time when the Black Plague was moving inexorably towards England. Bartholomew knows the scourge is coming and that there will be little he can do to help its victims. In the meantime, he also contends with the suspicious deaths of scholars connected with Michaelhouse, receiving death threats himself. Morosely, he concludes "evil is afoot and will corrupt us all" (Gregory, *Plague on Both Your Houses* 60). In the soiled, diseased and shady streets of medieval Cambridge, this evil adopts both a human face and a vermin body. The strength of this novel lies in its depiction of the ravages that the Black Death unleashes upon medieval Cambridge, through Gregory's powerful descriptions of the destruction of entire communities, while doctors like Bartholomew can do little to save the plague's victims. Watching in horror as the bodies pile up in the streets, Bartholomew struggles to organize their removal before other diseases compound the disaster. This plague narrative, though compelling, overshadows the detective plot and there is not much investigative work undertaken by Bartholomew. Instead, Bartholomew's role is one that is commonly concomitant to the primary function of the medieval detective, although Gregory magnifies it in this case. Bartholomew is the mediator between the medieval landscape and the modern reader and his perspective translates the horrors of the Black Plague into a comprehensible balance between historical reality and contemporary hindsight.

Hugh de Singleton is another detective operating as a medieval surgeon in fourteenth-century England. This time, however, the location is Oxford and its environs; specifically, a little village called Bampton. Author Mel

(Melvin) Starr chose Bampton because, after visiting some friends who lived there, he "saw immediately the town's potential for the novel [he] intended to write" (*Unquiet Bones* 5). Hugh is "fourth and last son of a minor knight from the county of Lancashire" and, as the youngest son, he must find a profession of his own (Starr, *Unquiet Bones* 13). As he displays "a scholar's aptitude," his father sends him to Oxford University with the intention of training to be a clerk and, eventually, a lawyer or a priest (Starr, *Unquiet Bones* 13). Like Bartholomew, Hugh experiences the suffering of the plague, watching several members of his family perish, as well as close friends in Oxford.

One of these friends leaves his three books to Hugh and he becomes entranced by *Surgery*, written in 1312 by Henri de Mondeville, surgeon to Philippe Le Bel and Louis X. Hugh decides upon a career as a surgeon after seeking advice from none other than Master John Wyclif: "There is, [Hugh] thinks, no wiser man in Oxford" (Starr, *Unquiet Bones* 18). Wyclif appears occasionally throughout the rest of the series, acting as a mentor to Hugh, and in *A Trail of Ink* (2010) Wyclif himself requires Hugh's services to investigate the theft of some books. Hugh travels to Paris to study for one year and then returns to Oxford in 1363 to establish himself as a surgeon. Lord Gilbert Talbot of Bampton installs him as the town's surgeon and eventually appoints him bailiff of his castle. This role gives Hugh the authority (and the responsibility) to investigate crime, while his medical experience grants him forensic insights into the manner of the many deaths he encounters.

Hugh de Singleton's surgical knowledge dominates his investigations and he therefore has more in common with contemporary pathologists such as Patricia Cornwell's Kay Scarpetta or Kathy Reichs's Temperance Brennan than with detectives of the conventional hardboiled type. Hugh is often reluctant to be drawn into an investigation; in *The Abbot's Agreement* (2014), Hugh and his sometime assistant, the groom Arthur, are on their way from Bampton to Oxford in order to purchase a bible. The suspicious behavior of some crows distracts them and they discover the body of a Benedictine novice from the nearby abbey. Hugh would prefer not to be involved, but the abbot persuades him to stay and investigate the boy's death in exchange for a particular bible Hugh has long coveted. Starr's depiction of premodern medical practices is well-researched and convincing overall, despite the improbably successful outcome of Hugh's markedly modern surgical techniques.

British-born, Spanish-residing author David Penny's medieval physician is Thomas Berrington, an unlikely resident of the town of Gharnatah. This is the ancient name for Granada and at this time, 1482, it is the last stronghold of Muslim rule on the Iberian Peninsula. In just ten years, the last Muslim leader, Muhammed XII (son of the present Sultan), will surrender the city to Isabella of Castile and her husband, Ferdinand of Aragon. Thomas claims to have been born in "Mercia," although it is unlikely that name was still in usage in the late fifteenth century, and has ended up in Granada after witnessing the death of his father on a French battlefield in 1453. Only thirteen at the time, Thomas recognized that his father needed relief from his wounds and consequently "eased" his passing. He believes the lingering effect from that experience is the reason he now feels compelled to help men on the battlefield, either to attend to their wounds or to shorten their suffering.

In the first novel in Penny's series, *The Red Hill* (2014), Thomas finds himself in the unenviable position of having to investigate the murders of several women in the Sultan's harem, including a favored wife, Safya. While the trope of the reluctant detective is a common one in medieval crime fiction, Thomas elevates his distaste for his task to an unfeasible level of questioning his ruler's authority. Although he knows he cannot refuse, Thomas continually suggests to the Sultan that someone else—anyone else—would be more suitable:

> "I told you last night, I know nothing of investigating such things, Malik."
> The Sultan cast a cold gaze at Thomas. "You are the cleverest man I know. ...."
> "There must be others you trust." Thomas experienced a shiver of unease at the thought he might be the only one.
> "Trust—who can a Sultan trust?
> "..."
> "You will catch this man for me, Thomas?"
> "Because I am the only man in al-Andalus you trust?"
> The Sultan glanced at him. "And I'm not entirely sure I should trust you—an *ajami* [foreigner]." He softened his words with a brief smile.
> "Then ask Olaf Torvaldsson [the Sultan's Scandinavian general], as you meant to. He has skills I don't possess."
> "He is *ajmai*, too."
> "He is your man."
> "And you are not?"
> "You know the answer to that, Malik" [Penny 69].

This tediously circular conversation is an example of the repetition that suffuses Penny's narrative. Information is repeated, exchanges are full of rhetorical questions and innuendo. Even at the end of the novel, Thomas is resisting his role as detective, while reinforcing his suitability in a display of false humility: "Thomas wondered why he felt such an obligation to complete the task, to find the killer and whoever guided him, and all he could come up with was duty. That sense of duty made him a good surgeon. That same sense of duty wouldn't let him turn away from the quest, however ill-equipped he might be" (Penny 160).

While constantly second-guessing his investigative abilities, Thomas has no such doubts about his competence as a doctor. He is clearly a gifted physician (because he "had always possessed acute hearing," he is able to detect the fetal heartbeat within Safya's womb [Penny 39]) and has made a critical impact with his technique for castrating the boys destined to become eunuchs for the Sultan's harem:

> He [Jorge] had been one of Thomas's first surgeries, and he meant what he said, that Jorge would likely have died if someone else had carried it out. The making of eunuchs was not a subtle art, not then, involving much blood, hot coals and searing agony. Before Thomas's time less than one in nine survived. Since then he had not lost a single patient, using gentler techniques to unman each boy that was sent to him. It wasn't something he was proud of. He would have preferred not to perform the procedure at all, but knew the alternative was worse. Far worse [Penny 36].

"Jorge" is the eunuch assigned to Thomas to assist with the investigation. The fact that Thomas is responsible for his castration adds an interesting complexity to their relationship that is rarely glimpsed in other "Holmes-Watson" pairings. There is an underlying tension between the two that constantly threatens to erupt despite their complementary skills and burgeoning friendship.

The most spectacular performance of Thomas's distinctly modern medical abilities is to save the Sultan's unborn child (significantly, a son) by slicing open the body of Safya in the moments after she has been ambushed and murdered while taking a bath. Despite the horrified protests of the onlookers—already in shock from confronting a scene "like some distorted battlefield" (Penny 51)—and the punches Jorge is landing between his shoulder blades, Thomas calmly recommends that they look away and proceeds with an impressive Caesarian section. Thomas transfers this medical modernity into his detective persona, insisting upon viewing the body of the murdered bathing attendant, overruling Jorge's strong objections, although he is not able to penetrate the layers of medieval mores enough to examine Safya's corpse. Similarly, when he returns to the bathing chamber, he is frustrated that it "had already been cleaned," so that "They've destroyed any chance of us finding whatever spoor he [the assassin] had left behind" (Penny 73). Clearly, no one thought to inform the Sultan or his Vizier about securing a crime scene for forensic analysis.

Penny's Berrington reflects a modern desire to render the Middle Ages a little less painful and horrific as contemporary society imagines—at least, from a medieval medical point of view. Thomas is an English Christian living in Muslim al-Andalus, and his innate superiority is at times uncomfortably parochial. However, Penny endeavors to temper this westernized, Christian elitism by peppering the narrative with observations that Thomas has embraced this culture and would no longer be at home in England. More uncomfortably, Penny trots out the modern masculinist fantasy about women living in a harem: "Although the lives of these women were pampered, they were more than mere playthings for the most powerful man in al-Andalus. These women read widely, spoke of politics and history and culture, listened to and made music, created works of art through their weaving and needlework, and even greater works of art through attention to their bodies" (38). Penny's emphasis on the cultural accomplishments of the Sultan's wives does not distract from the objectification of the female form as a "work of art," nor from the unspoken suggestion that life, from this male author's perspective, in a harem does not appear all that bad for medieval women.

All medieval crime fiction authors necessarily portray premodern medical practices and these can range from domestic herbal remedies, to more sophisticated plant-based medicines used in monasteries, to surgical procedures that can challenge a modern reader's sensibilities and, at times, credulity. Thomas Berrington's adept Caesarian section and successful castration procedures have just been noted above. Ariana Franklin's female detective, Adelia Aguilar, performs an unlikely appendectomy on one of Henry II's daughters, discussed in more detail in Chapter Four, while Hugh de Singleton's Oxfordshire practice is comprised mainly of his performance of minor and major operations, rather than the dispensing of medicines. However, one medical activity that offers a conundrum for these authors is the contested practice of autopsy. While not exactly heretical, autopsy was nevertheless frowned upon during the Middle Ages, especially in northern European countries. Autopsy is, however, such an entrenched part of the investigative process associated with today's crime fiction narratives (including literature, film and television) that it is difficult for many writers not to show this procedure. Moreover, when autopsies were performed in the Middle Ages, they were invariably done in medical schools in order to study anatomy (Park 114), and certainly not undertaken for the purposes of collecting evidence concerning a crime.[10] In Starr's *Ashes to Ashes* (2015), Hugh performs an autopsy on his kitchen table, while authors C.J. Stevermer and Keith Souter offer two of medieval crime fiction's more memorable autopsies. The practice of autopsy offers an ideal opportunity to confront the challenge of incorporating a strikingly modern medical procedure into the medieval landscape without incurring a catastrophic collapse of historical authenticity.

C.J. Stevermer published two early medieval crime fiction novels featuring an English alchemist, named (apparently unironically) Nicholas Coffin. At the turn of the sixteenth century, Nicholas has travelled to Rome to seek out the famous alchemist, Nicholas Flamel, now extremely old, amusingly cranky and in the habit of giving Nicholas vague and frustrating advice. In *The Alchemist: Death of a Borgia* (1980), Ercole Borgia—younger brother of Cesare—is murdered and thrown into the river. A cunning and enterprising street thief, Angelo, hauls out the body and brings it to Nicholas, knowing the latter's interest in anatomy and hoping he will pay for the opportunity to use the corpse in his experiments. Nicholas is horrified to discover Angelo has the body on his landing and initially refuses to take it. However, the corpse is tinged with blue and this intrigues Nicholas enough to risk dissecting the body, separating various organs and applying chemicals to them in order to confirm that Ercole was poisoned. Nicholas attempts to dispose of the body, but Cesare Borgia discovers Nicholas's involvement and blackmails him into discovering the identity of the murderer. The general consensus throughout Rome is that Cesare's vaulting ambition is to blame for his younger brother's death and he needs Nicholas's help to circumvent his accusers. Stevermer enjoys depicting Nicholas in situations of dramatic irony, gently mocking her medievalist detective. When Angelo arrives with Ercole's body, he exclaims, "'God's bones, man! This isn't the dark ages! It's 1501! You can't go about carrying bodies through the streets!'" (Stevermer 16). Later, at a dinner given by the novel's *femme fatale*, Nicholas is shocked to be shown the bizarre new instrument for eating, the fork (Stevermer 148). Stevermer also attempts to rehabilitate Cesare Borgia's appalling reputation and recast him as more of a benign dictator; fair but firm: "'I am the law,' Cesare reminded him. 'All the law you will ever know'" (Stevermer 191). Nicholas succeeds in identifying the real murderer, thereby clearing Cesare's name, through an impressive combination of ratiocination and intuition that demonstrates both his scientific and investigative skills.

Keith Souter has written two medieval crime fiction novels that do not form part of a series but share a forensically precise attention to medical detail that reflects Souter's profession as a family doctor. Souter deploys his medievalism in order to showcase his interest in both premodern medicine and the history of his northern England home. In *The Fool's Folly* (2009), Souter's late-fifteenth-century detective is Sir Giles Beeston, Constable of Sandal Castle, which is located outside Wakefield in West Yorkshire. Beeston's superior is John de la Pole, first Earl of Lincoln, President of the Council of the North, presumptive heir to Richard III, and Geoffrey Chaucer's descendant. Souter embraces this literary ancestry: John often composes poetry and displays an acute awareness of the long shadow of his great-great-great grandfather's genius; as the narrator explains, "The blood of the poet ran through his veins and he saw things in his mind's eye that might have evaded those of a less imaginative nature" (Souter 13).

There is a distinct nostalgia in Souter's framing of John's idealization of his poetic heritage that is also present in Souter's participation in the most recent rehabilitation project of Richard III as a person and an effective ruler, as discussed in Chapter One in relation to Jeremy Potter. John desires nothing more than to be worthy of Richard's faith in him both as a leader in the north and as a future king. When Richard appears later in the novel, both characters bemoan the political shenanigans they must engage in and express a desire to return to a more chivalrous past, recalling the nostalgia that suffuses Sir Thomas Malory's *Le Morte Darthur*, written just before the temporal setting of Souter's novel. Despite his idealistic nature, John is a clever politician, managing the difficult lords of the north, especially the Duke of Northumberland, and alert to hints of treason against the king. He is unusually egalitarian, too, insisting that he and the other lords attend the local coroner's court (the Manor Court) to listen to the evidence pertaining to the death of his beloved fool, Ned—much to the other lords' disgust.

Sir Giles conducts the investigation into Ned's death, whose body was discovered in the castle's moat; it is presumed that the jester was drunk and inadvertently drowned. Residing in the castle is Dr. Musgrave, an astronomer, physician and scientist who "had been granted one of the few licences to legitimately practice the art of alchemy" (Souter 16). Sir Giles asks the doctor to examine Ned's body, which leads to an extraordinary autopsy. Dr. Musgrave suggests that opening the jester's body might reveal a quantity of wine still in his stomach that may confirm Ned's inebriation. Sir Giles's young assistant, Will, is horrified at this thought, reflecting the common medieval perception of the sanctity of the body after death: "Will stared at him with open-eyed disbelief. 'But surely we cannot desecrate his body? My lord, you cannot permit this'" (Souter 57). Sir Giles, however, overrules his protest, claiming that "If Dr Musgrave is able to help us detect the cause of Ned Bunce's death, then the law will rule that there is no transgression'" (Souter 57).

The autopsy is performed in the castle's dungeons, a location that is hidden from those who may be outraged by Dr. Musgrave's intention. In an inevitable medievalist cliché, the dungeon is also conveniently home to several rats, to whom the doctor feeds the undigested remnants of Ned's last meal, extracted from the corpse's stomach. The rats die, confirming that Ned had been poisoned and was dead before he fell into the moat. Sir Giles and Dr. Musgrave's innovative evidence gathering is a wonderful example of the ingenuity demonstrated by medieval crime fiction authors in order to ensure their crime narratives are firmly anchored in their premodern landscapes.

These examples of medieval detectives who undertake medical practices in the course of their occupations and their investigations must navigate premodern expectations about the scope of the physician's role and the sacredness of the human body after death. However, for a readership inevitably aware of forensic evidence's indispensability to the solving of crime, it is difficult to ignore the scrutiny and even invasion of the corpse. This presents authors with the challenge of navigating a delicate path between offering a convincing crime narrative—complete with forensic evidence—and irreparably damaging the authenticity of the medieval context within which such practices are performed.

A Scottish Lawyer, a Feminist Peddler and a Romantic Bookseller: Gil Cunningham, Roger the Chapman and Nicholas Elyot

In the early books of Pat McIntosh's series, late-fifteenth-century Glasgow lawyer Gil Cunningham is drawn into helping to investigate murder because he is in the wrong place at the wrong time. In *The Harper's Quine* (2004), the first novel, Gil inadvertently discovers a corpse while walking through the new building work being carried out at Glasgow Cathedral; in *The Nicholas Feast* (2005), he has returned to his alma mater, Glasgow University, for a traditional procession, play and feast, when one of the undergraduates is discovered strangled in the coalhouse. By the sixth novel, however, Gil is firmly ensconced in the service of Robert Blacader, the Archbishop of Glasgow, as an investigator of strange occurrences. Travelling up to Perthshire in *The Stolen Voice* (2009), Gil is tasked with investigating the disappearance of local cathedral singers and the bishop's secretary. He also untangles the uncanny circumstances surrounding the return of a boy who disappeared thirty years ago and has now returned, looking no more than five or six years older, and insisting that he be allowed to resume his place as a singer in the cathedral at Dunblane.

Accompanying Gil is his wife, Alys, whom he met during his first murder investigation. Alys is the daughter of the French master mason, Maistre Pierre. Meeting the young woman confirms Gil's instinct to forego the priesthood; the two eventually marry in the fourth book of the series, *St. Mungo's Robin* (2007). Gil is amazed at Alys's intelligence and learning, startled to discover that she reads Latin, although she admits that theological texts such as

Thomas a Kempis's *De Imitatione Christi* (*The Imitation of Christ*) are not all she reads: "'I have to confess—' The apologetic smile flickered. 'I take refuge in Chaucer when it becomes too serious for me'" (McIntosh, *Harper's Quine* loc. 1163). Gil questions her interest in the "story-tellers on pilgrimage" and, discovering that she is reading the "Clerk's Tale," declares that "I never had any patience with Patient Grissel or her marquis…. Any man that treated one of my sisters so would have got his head in his hands to play with as soon as we heard of it" (McIntosh, *Harper's Quine* loc. 1163). Alys agrees; her interpretation of the power imbalance between the two Chaucerian characters surprises Gil and he thinks to himself, "This girl … was exceptional" (McIntosh, *Harper's Quine* loc. 1163). At the end of the novel, Gil contemplates the success of his quest for justice, while also musing that at the beginning "he had still thought he was bound for the priesthood," whereas "now I have a girl, … who wrestles with her mind" (McIntosh, *Harper's Quine* loc. 5783).

Alys's French family contributes a certain exotic quality to everyday Scottish life, and McIntosh creditably demonstrates the close connection between the Scots people and their Breton cousins through a shared Celtic heritage. In *The Stolen Voice*, Alys impresses and surprises her highland hosts by speaking Gaelic. But, as Alys later confesses to Gil, "'I have only a few words that I have learned from Ealasaidh McIan, and at times I confuse those with Breton'" (McIntosh, *Stolen Voice* 14). Alys spent her childhood in Nantes, Brittany, and she learned Breton from her family's local servants. Probably not realizing the shared Celtic heritage, Alys comments on the similarity of the two languages: "Many of the words are the same, which I find astonishing. *Ty* is a house, for instance" (McIntosh, *Stolen Voice* 14). As McIntosh explains in her "Author's note," "Ever since it became a kingdom, Scotland has had two native languages, Gaelic (which in the fifteenth century was called Ersche) and Scots, …" (*Stolen Voice* 297). McIntosh's Gil Cunningham is an appealing detective and one of the few lawyers and Scots represented in medieval crime fiction. He, like Robb's Owen Archer, relies upon a network of characters to support his inquiries (within which Alys is the most important and often given her own investigative tasks), rendering his methodological approach more aligned with police procedural conventions than hardboiled detective fiction.

Between 1991 and 2013, Kate Sedley published twenty-two novels featuring her peddler-detective, Roger the Chapman. Roger is an appealing mixture of pragmatism and esoteric musings about life, believing that his talent for solving crime is God-given and he therefore has no choice in his investigative occupation. A restlessness consistently comes upon Roger before each mystery that he interprets as a divine signal to walk the roads again searching for someone in need, although he clearly has a naturally itinerant nature. Roger is unusually tall, young and good-looking, which he informs the reader from "the safety of old age" (Sedley, *Saint John's Fern* 1)—each novel in Sedley's series takes the form of a tale recalled from Roger's youth that he is recording for his children and grand-children. Roger's physical attributes and his occupation as a peddler allow him access to most households without suspicion where he can interview witnesses under the guise of selling his wares. The upheavals of the Wars of the Roses intrude into the series because Roger occasionally undertakes clandestine missions for Richard, firstly as Duke of Gloucester and then as King Richard III. While this broader historical context is deftly handled by Sedley, the majority of her novels conform to golden-age conventions and concern southwest England's manor houses, villages and the town of Bristol.

One characteristic of Roger's investigative process is his reliance upon dreams to help him penetrate to the heart of a mystery. Sedley ameliorates the potential ludicrousness of this habit by framing Roger's dreams as his subconscious processing the case's evidence, while appearing to Roger himself as insights placed into his sleeping mind by God. In *The Saint John's Fern* (1999), Roger anticipates visualizing the solution to this case as he falls asleep one night: "Even as I closed my eyes, I knew I was going to dream. Since our meal, I had been suffering from one of the oppressive headaches that sometimes afflict me and are harbingers of those strange visions that crowd my unconscious mind" (221).

Roger's faith in his divine purpose does not preclude his thoughts from straying to proto-Reformation musings, a habit he has in common with many of his medieval crime fiction colleagues. In *The Three Kings of Cologne* (2007), Roger expresses what is an extreme view, especially given his belief that his investigative gifts are God-given: "I couldn't deny it. There were moments when I even doubted the existence of God; moments when the sheer brutality of what was perpetrated in His name appalled me, or when His seeming indifference to the sufferings of His children denied the claim that He was a God of love" (Sedley, *Three Kings of Cologne* 91). But Roger is also grateful that these thoughts may be hidden from others, as he is unwilling to depart from orthodoxy, despite his association with the Lollards of Bristol: he "wasn't even a secret Lollard, like Margaret Walker [his former mother-in-law] and so many of Redcliffe's weaving community" (Sedley, *Three Kings of Cologne* 91). As is expected for a medieval detective, Roger is tolerant of the heterodoxy of others, but nevertheless relieved that "God made our thoughts secret, kept them hidden from view, for I wouldn't like others to see too often inside my head" (Sedley *Saint John's Fern* 133). As well as being proto-Reformist, Roger is also proto-feminist in the manner of many medieval crime fiction detectives, but particularly for the three characters in this section. He frequently considers the unfair position of women in general terms, expressing such sentiments as, "Women, I reflected, not for the first time, were the losers in the game of life; the thankless drudges who smoothed the paths of their men" (Sedley, *Three Kings of Cologne* 226). Roger applies this attitude to his investigations, though at times it seems an unconscious impulse.

However, Sedley takes care to temper the potentially disruptive effects of Roger's modernity. In contrast to the contemporary sensibilities of most of Paul C. Doherty's medieval detectives, for example, Sedley balances her descriptions of the unpleasantness of certain aspects of medieval life with Roger's realistic reactions: "And the stench from the Shambles, where butchers were carving up the freshly killed carcasses of sheep, cows and pigs was over-powering enough this morning to make me retch. Normally, I didn't notice it. I must be sickening for something" (*Three Kings of Cologne* 14). Sedley similarly counteracts Roger's feminist musings with some amusing, if appallingly sexist, behavior. While Roger is sympathetic to his wife, Adela, and the demands upon her, this does not prevent him lamenting the fact that leaving her "cooped up all day with the children" results in her transformation into "a nagging scold, exhausted as much in mind as in body, and ready to fly out at me over every little thing" (Sedley, *Three Kings of Cologne* 2). Roger is also extremely jealous of Adela's close friendship and past dalliance with Richard Manifold, a sergeant working for the Sheriff of Bristol, in an inventive way of manufacturing the conventional opposition between a sheriff and a medieval detective. Roger's attitude is unsurprisingly hypocritical, blaming Adela for encouraging Richard while reserving the right "to ogle and flirt with any female who caught [his] fancy.... But then, as anyone with any sense knows, it's different for a man" (Sedley, *Three Kings of Cologne* 5). Sedley maintains an admirable balance between describing premodern attitudes to women and retaining the modernity of her detective in a largely successful negotiation of the tension arising from comingling an authentic depiction of the Middle Ages with the demands of contemporary crime fiction conventions.

McIntosh and Sedley are authors of series that are ostensibly different, but upon closer inspection, share some unexpected similarities. Both series are set in the later part of the fifteenth century, although in different countries; both Gil and Roger were trained as priests but left their vocations in order to pursue their secular occupations. The two men also marry intelligent, resourceful, practical women who provide invaluable advice, support and not a small amount of pointed criticism. One interesting difference between the two is that Gil is a reluctant investigator, while Roger fervently believes that his talent for solving mysteries is a divine gift.

Ann Swinfen has published, in close succession, several novels in a medieval mystery series set in Oxford in the early 1350s, a town still deeply traumatized by the ravages of the recent Black Death. Nicholas Elyot is a bookseller—a rare occupation in medieval crime fiction—who employs two scribes to copy manuscripts, such as books of hours, that may appeal to wealthy clientele or the university's colleges. Swinfen provides other interesting details about the day-to-day practices of Nicholas's profession as a bookseller, including offering quills that come "pre-trimmed," although Nicholas cannot understand why anyone would not prefer to cut his or her own quill to size (Swinfen, *Bookseller's Tale* 41), and the thriving business of renting *peciae* (copied excerpts of books) to university students so that they may study their texts without purchasing a prohibitively expensive manuscript. Students are charged if they return the *peciae* damaged or marked by spilled ink.

Swinfen offers a sympathetic portrayal of the grief that continues to affect the people of Oxford and informs many of the characters' comments and actions. She also includes poignant details of some rarely mentioned consequences of the plague, such as the slaughter of the city's dogs and cats in the belief that they were harbingers of the disease. Early in the first novel, Nicholas expresses a form of survivor's guilt that he and his community are struggling to overcome: "For those of us who survived, there remained a lingering fear of ever allowing ourselves to love anyone again, so fragile is life, so terrifying the sudden loss" (Swinfen, *Bookseller's Tale* 4). This is a persistent sentiment in Swinfen's novels and, occasionally, its expression verges on an anachronistic questioning of the existence of God in an unmistakable echo of Roger the Chapman's doubts: "Why had God inflicted such punishment upon his children? Was there indeed a God? Why should a man try to live a godly Christian life, when all were struck down alike, sinful and innocent?" (Swinfen, *Bookseller's Tale* 31).

This rhetorical lament is unlikely to reflect contemporary beliefs, but instead reveals Nicholas's innate modernity, as does his proto-feminism. In Swinfen's second novel, *The Novice's Tale* (2016), Nicholas reframes some of the laws constraining medieval women in terms of Wycliffe's reformist agenda. Learning that the law, in some cases, considers women to be of the same status as a child and therefore under the complete authority of a male guardian, Nicholas ponders the capable women in his family and muses, "'It seems unjust, ... I wonder whether that is another ill practice that John Wycliffe opposes'" (Swinfen, *Novice's Tale* 119).

Like McIntosh's Gil Cunningham, Nicholas is a reluctant investigator of crime. His new "profession" begins when, walking home one evening, he spies the body of a young student floating in the river. With no other passersby evident, Nicholas hauls the corpse onto the riverbank with difficulty, eventually and reluctantly assisted by two lay brothers from the nearby abbey. While Nicholas's conscience prompts him to become involved in the ensuing investigation, at that moment on the side of river, he is berating himself: "silently cursing that I had chosen this evening to walk to Yardley's farm. Had I not been crossing the bridge when the body was washed toward it, I should have known nothing about it and would be at home now eating my supper..." (Swinfen, *Bookseller's Tale* 23).

Despite this initial reluctance, Nicholas uncovers the plot behind the student's murder, demonstrating typical detective traits: he notices forensic evidence such as the quality of parchment samples; he recognizes a suspect's hand-writing; and he experiences antagonistic entanglements with local law enforcement. For example, when Nicholas approaches one of the parish constables, the man is typically condescending towards the amateur sleuth: "'I think you take too much upon yourself, Nicholas. Leave these matters to those in authority. We will see to all that concerns the fellow's death. You, on the other hand, have no authority at all'" (*Bookseller's Tale* 214).

While Swinfen demonstrates a knowledgeable and sympathetic portrayal of mid-fourteenth-century Oxford, her detective narrative is not strong. An intriguing mystery too quickly becomes transparent and the loose ends of the investigation are resolved in a series of unlikely coincidences and convenient events. The most disorientating of these is the abrupt suicide of the main perpetrator. *The Bookseller's Tale* (2016) is an example of medieval crime fiction novels that only nominally deploy a detective, mystery or crime plot in order to construct a narrative frame on which to attach their deeper concern with an authentic recreation of the medieval landscape.

Swinfen's second novel reinforces this deliberate privileging of the premodern world over a substantive engagement with crime fiction more broadly. *The Novice's Tale* is set very soon after the events in *The Bookseller's Tale* and continues the main plotlines. The murdered student's young cousin, Emma, is a novice in a nearby priory, forced to take the veil by her evil stepfather who has designs on her inheritance. This sounds very much like the beginning of a gothic novel and Swinfen certainly owes more to this tradition, as well as to the historical romance genre, than to crime fiction conventions. Indeed, there is very little mystery in this second "Oxford Medieval Mystery" for Nicholas to solve, although there is the aforementioned "crime" of confining young Emma in Godstow Abbey, north of Oxford.

Swinfen's overarching concern with depicting the Middle Ages once again overshadows the nominal crime narrative, most pointedly in an extraneous episode in which Emma learns, in great detail, the craft of candle-making. Medieval chandlery appears to be of particular interest to Swinfen, evinced by the scene's long elaboration in her historical notes. In the end, Swinfen transforms her medieval crime fiction novel into a medieval romance: she recasts Nicholas as a knight on a quest to rescue his lady in distress, which he achieves with remarkable ease. On his horse, Nicholas manages to outpace his pursuers who are—in another implausible circumstance—hampered by the antics of their hunting dogs who had, until Nicholas's timely intervention, been seeking Emma as their quarry.

Nicholas is himself seduced by the courtly love conventions that inform his present situation: "Despite the hunt [that is, the pursuers hunting Nicholas and Emma], I was suddenly, gloriously happy. Emma's body was pressed up against mine. I could feel the warmth of it, and her weight against my chest. I would probably never again hold her like this, but I would savour every moment while I could" (Swinfen, *Novice's Tale* 234). Emma responds to the courtly love scenario, squeezing Nicholas's hand and pointing out there is no rush to arrive at the house of her aunt. But, as the couple join the anxious families and Emma exchanges her peasant garb for a deep blue gown that reflects her eyes, her transformation to the lady of courtly love tradition is complete: "She was remote, beautiful, and untouchable" (Swinfen, *Novice's Tale* 250). There are more novels planned in Swinfen's series and it remains to be seen whether she will persist with her overarching "Oxford Medieval Mystery" premise or allow her dalliance with crime fiction to be increasingly subsumed by her historical romance preferences.

The three medieval detectives discussed in this section share a concern with depicting female characters on resolutely equal footing with the medieval detectives they support throughout their investigations. This is not uncommon in medieval crime fiction, as noted throughout this book, but Gil, Roger and Nicholas in particular demonstrate notably proto-feminist leanings. These characters are also of a different class to the noble warriors who dominate this chapter and consequently appear able to circumvent the feudal restrictions more easily than their aristocratic counterparts. The productive tension between medieval and medievalism is at its creative best here in the meticulous recreation of the Middle Ages into which is inserted not only the modern figure of the detective, but also a strong, clever, woman with a recognizably modern independence.

There are several other non-knightly detectives for whom space does not allow detailed examination, but who are nevertheless worth noting. These characters similarly navigate their feudal context with a circumspect freedom that enables the successful performance of their investigative quest, as well as deployment of their proto-modern attitudes. Italian author Alfredo Colitto's trilogy is set in the early fourteenth century and features Mondino de 'Liuzzi, a university anatomist in Bologna, who contends with the superstitious beliefs of both the Inquisition and the remaining tendrils of pagan sects worshipping Mithra. Also in Italy, mercenary sleuth Sigismondo and his "more-faithful-than-clever sidekick, Benno," as the blurb for *Dirge for a Doge* (1997) rather uncharitably describes him, move through the various social strata of "Renaissance Italy" in Elizabeth Eyre's six-novel series.

Margaret Frazer's Dame Frevisse series is discussed at length in Chapter Four, but her series featuring Joliffe the Player offers a character who enjoys as much freedom and access as her cloistered nun experiences restrictions. In the mid-fifteenth century, Joliffe takes advantage of his troupe's peripatetic lifestyle and engagements in the great houses of England in order to solve murders in a wide-ranging suite of locations. Similarly, Alan Gordon's jester, Theophilos (also known as Feste), has an occupation that disguises his membership of the Fool's Guild, a secret organization that seeks to influence political events throughout Europe in the early thirteenth century.

C.B. Hanley's Edwin Weaver is a bailiff who is a little more embedded within his feudal milieu, as he investigates crime for his lord William de Warenne in thirteenth-century south Yorkshire. Toni Mount's recent series is set in fifteenth-century London and participates in the increasingly common rehabilitation of Richard III by medieval crime fiction authors. Sebastian Foxley is a crippled illustrator whose genius catches the eye of Richard, then Duke of Gloucester. Seb arguably faces another handicap in the form of his brother, Jude, a handsome, womanizing scribe whose arrest for the murder of his lover's husband (and Seb and Jude's employer) launches Seb upon his first investigation. Chris Nickson has also selected an unusual profession for his medieval detective. John the Carpenter inherits his tools and his trade from his father, who has died in the Black Death of the mid-fourteenth century. Traveling to Chesterfield from Leeds, in the north of England, John finds work, but, like Seb and many others, is soon forced into the role of detective when the master carpenter is murdered and John is under suspicion.

Postscript: Hardboiled Partnerships

Worth highlighting briefly at the end of this chapter are the delightful partnerships that populate medieval crime fiction, as also noted throughout this book. Partnerships are an important feature of detective fiction convention, whether they are comprised of amateur assistants to private detectives such as Hercule Poirot or Sherlock Holmes (Captain Hastings and Doctor Watson, respectively), or the complementary pairing of the jaded experienced older cop with an enthusiastic, young and naive new recruit that are a commonplace of police procedurals. Medieval crime fiction has a disproportionate share of partnerships—likely and unlikely—and some of the most interesting involve pairs of detectives who are thrown together through circumstances or dire necessity and must overcome differences such as unequal social status and different racial backgrounds.

Edward Marston's medieval crime series is set in the late eleventh century in England and features Ralph Delchard, a Norman soldier, and Gervase Bret, a Saxon lawyer. These two are tasked by William the Conqueror to travel through the counties of England in order to resolve disputes that arise during the compilation of William's extraordinary *magnus opus*, Domesday Book. The narrative conceit is effective in its ability to explore the immediate aftermath of the Conquest, across different regions of the country, as well as depicting the mundane, administrative challenges that conquest of another country entails—something that is often overlooked in the greater excitement of battles, castles and pageantry. Most successfully, Marston explores the inevitable tensions between the conquered English and the incoming Norman elite.

Other partnerships not mentioned elsewhere in this book include Sarah Hawkswood's crusty Serjeant Catchpoll and undersheriff Lord Hugh Bradecote gradually gaining respect for each other in mid-twelfth-century Worcestershire. Danish author Martin Jensen also has an unlikely pairing in his King Knud series, set in pre–Conquest England. Young Halfdan has fallen through the cracks during the new Danish rule of the Saxon kingdoms, despite his heritage as half Dane, half Saxon. He falls in with wandering illustrator Winston, a former monk, as they combine their complementary attributes to solve both mysteries they encounter on their journeys and those imposed upon them by Cnut himself.

Finally, E.M. Powell's Sir Benedict Palmer is discussed earlier in this chapter, but she has commenced another medieval crime fiction series in 2018 featuring a partnership between Aelred Barling and Hugo Stanton, senior and assistant clerk, respectively, attached to the roaming justices who administer King Henry II's justice throughout England in the second half of the twelfth century. Stanton is a reluctant clerk to the court of the king's justices because he harbors a deep resentment stemming from the murder of his beloved that he blames on the king and is consequently skeptical about Henry's so-called "justice." Barling is fussy and pedantic, making him a good foil to Stanton's cynicism and more intuitive approach to investigations. Powell's first novel in this series, *The King's Justice* (2018), opens with an example of why modern readers often find juridical procedures in the Middle Ages challenging. Three men accused of murder are to be put into a pit of water to determine their guilt or innocence: sink and they are deemed innocent, float and they are "hauled out to the gallows to be strung up to die" (Powell, *King's Justice* 1). Powell describes the scene in excruciating detail and the reader is told several times, in various ways, that "[hell] would freeze over before Stanton shouted for the King and his justice" (Powell, *King's Justice* 9). The first man does not sink and so is condemned to hang later that day. The second man does sink, and so is proclaimed innocent, but when he is hauled up he is found to be drowned, much to the dismay of the crowd: "Stanton's stomach dropped. The man was dead. An innocent man was dead. A chorus of shocked gasps and a buzz of questions joined the clamour of those still shouting and praying" (Powell, *King's Justice* 10). Powell wants the modern reader to feel the premodern crowd's shock, but for a different reason. Medieval justice was harsh, arbitrary and, at times, ostensibly illogical, as is the case here. This scene articulates the rarely acknowledged understanding that contemporary popular culture's insistent recreation of the Middle Ages does not include a desire to return there. The medieval detective masks this critical distance by imposing a modern version of justice onto the premodern landscape, perpetuating the fiction that the modern reader, at least, would never have guilt or innocence determined by a pit full of water.

The hardboiled form of crime fiction emerged and strengthened at a time after the First World War when the United States was increasingly focusing its gaze upon itself, as manifested in political isolationism. After the wild west was literally and metaphorically won, the next frontier to offer opportunities for both danger and heroic endeavor was found in the growing and troubled cities. Hardboiled fiction explores the reality of organized crime and institutional corruption, while simultaneously suggesting the possibility of personally based redemption, reflecting modernism's isolationist concern. For the audience, the hardboiled detective epitomizes the hope that there is an innate sense of honor in people, in spite of the corruption that pervades the modern city. The quest for justice that the private eye undertakes—for a fee—rehabilitates those mean streets and burnishes the belief in humanity that has been tarnished by moral decay.

A parallel role is offered historically by the authors of medieval crime fiction. The knight's physical prowess, martial experience and moral focus offer synergies between the hardboiled detective type and what contemporary culture popularly imagines a medieval knight to be. However, secular medieval detectives are also drawn from a wider pool of occupations such as doctors and lawyers, and some of these also productively contribute to the quasi-hardboiled medieval detective tropes. On the other hand, the hardboiled detective's conventional fight against corruption and the futility that threatens to overwhelm him (or her) is echoed in the frustration that medieval non-knightly secular detectives often experience due to their lower social status, physical or mental frailties.

Contemporary hardboiled detectives fight against the city's institutionalized corruption, as well as the criminal underworld, and these systems also confound medieval secular detectives, notably in the guise of corrupt sheriffs, bribable clerks, and sadistic jailers. By identifying this malfeasance—even if they are not always able to expurgate it completely—these medieval detectives ensure that justice is not always circumvented. As such, they also function as interpreters of the medieval city for a contemporary readership. To take just one urban example, medieval London is a fascinating, daunting, familiar-yet-foreign, alluring place. The modern or postmodern literary device of the detective works as an interface between the modern reader and this irresistible city, functioning as translator, guide, crusader or protector. For Paul C. Doherty's hardboiled detective, Hugh Corbett, London's mean streets appear as distasteful and dangerous as they might to modern sensibilities. For Sharon Penman's Justin de Quincy, London is the place where he will experience his journey from innocent squire to hardened detective. Crispin Guest, Jeri Westerson's disgraced knight, finds London's streets to be at times dangerous and at times comforting, but always familiar. These medieval detectives navigate London, observing, interpreting and explaining the geography, dangers and marvels that they witness there. However, this translation is not without risk: these characters also impose a distinctly modern form of justice upon medieval crime fiction's premodern streets, an ethical imperative that threatens to destabilize the authenticity of the carefully constructed historical cityscape.

Chapter Three

Divine Ratiocination

One of medieval crime fiction's defining features is the tension between the modern investigator and the meticulously recreated Middle Ages. This incongruity is nowhere more evident than in novels portraying medieval detectives who are also members of religious orders. While there is, of course, a long tradition of clerical detectives, beginning with G.K. Chesterton's Father Brown and expanding rapidly since then to encompass priests (male and female), rabbis, monks and nuns,[1] a significant number of these religious investigators are characters from the European Middle Ages.[2] Focusing on male religious detectives, this chapter explores the irony generated by the conflict between an entrenched belief in supernatural intervention into earthly affairs and the rational demands of the literary detective; a conundrum that threatens to disrupt the premodern realism of medieval crime fiction.

There is considerable academic interest in both clerical and lay devotional practices of the medieval period—an interest that has more recently encompassed women, rural parishes and the poor.[3] These studies explore, to take just three of many examples, the manner in which priests disseminated Church doctrine to their predominately illiterate congregations, lay devotional tools such as Books of Hours, and the tensions between religious and royal authority over issues such as taxation and clerical appointments. Of particular interest for this chapter is the existence, identification and prosecution of heretical movements in the Christian Middle Ages, such as Catharism, Lollardy, and Waldesianism. Andrew P. Roach and James R. Simpson recently commented that the scale of academic scrutiny for this topic is "such that one might be given to believe modern scholars live in the age of the heretic" (2).[4] Heresy in the European Middle Ages was largely a matter of disagreement about devotional practices, clerical authority or the belief in dualism— that is, the existence of two opposing forces of good and evil that structure the world. However, despite the vitriolic denunciation and ruthless extermination of protest movements by the medieval Church, it is difficult to find evidence that these so-called "heretics" ever denied the existence of God *per se* (including, of course, Jewish and Islamic adherents). In other words, medieval heretics were very rarely atheists, or even agnostics; they were, for the most part, members of sects that disagreed with certain doctrines of the Church. As such, it seems credible that the vast majority of medieval society firmly believed in the possibility of both divine and diabolical intervention into human affairs. This entrenched belief has clear implications for the literary detective who is not only enmeshed in this context of supernatural possibility, but also constrained by the modern laws of "ratiocination."

Without exception, the *modus operandi* of the modern literary detective is a calm collection of the clues, followed by a logical interpretation of the available evidence that will inevitably reveal the all-too-human perpetrator of the crime. This process has been enshrined in detective fiction since Edgar Allan Poe—via his master logician, Auguste Dupin—developed the concept of "ratiocination." Ratiocination is "the process of exact thinking, reasoning" and imposes upon the detective a rational system that is not easily discarded (Merriam-Webster). Alison Joseph describes this process as "a tale told backwards" (190), while Lee Horsley argues that the same basic structure underpins all "classic detective fiction" and is a "characteristic pattern of death-detection-explanation" (12). But what are the consequences for a detective who operates within a social, cultural and religious context that readily accepts supernatural intervention as a perfectly acceptable—indeed "rational"—solution?

The potential for conflict between faith and facts is a conundrum that all religious detectives must confront, regardless of historical period. Joseph suggests that G.K. Chesterton's first novel featuring clerical sleuth Father Brown, "The Blue Cross" (1911), is a meditation on Poe's ratiocination that "deliberately exploits the tension between reason and faith" (192). Ultimately, however, Chesterton privileges reason and allows Father Brown to penetrate arch-villain Flambeau's priestly disguise because, as Brown informs him, "'You attacked reason' [and that is] 'bad theology'" (qtd. in Joseph 192).

Religion and detection have historically strong associations. Author and priest, Giles Fraser, recently pointed out that the atheist detective, currently flourishing in film, fiction and television, is not a particularly original reinvention of the investigator.[5] Following a similar logic to Charles J. Rzepka's, outlined in Chapter One, Fraser argues that the development of literary detective fiction "took off around the same time that Darwin was publishing *On the Origin of Species* (1859) and Nietzsche was proclaiming the death of God" (Fraser). This turn to secularism leaves an epistemological void that religion had previously filled and Fraser contends that "the detective took over the role of the priest, seeking justice, trying to make sense of the mysterious, struggling to bring order out of chaos, facing evil. They are not just whodunnits, but whydunnits—journeys into the sort of human darkness that, for most of us, only exist in our nightmares" (Fraser). Similarly, Carole M. Cusack argues that the increasingly secularized society of the nineteenth and twentieth centuries replaced the traditional religious confessor with the figure of the detective, "in the process of ascribing meaning to the otherwise random *minutiae* of existence" ("Scarlet and Black" 161). Moreover, John Wren-Lewis held that "The detective emerged as a saviour-image as people began to lose faith in those more traditional saviours, the holy man, the righteous ruler, and the knight in shining armour" (20–21).

While most critics of crime fiction appear to accept that the genre's inherent secularism is crucial to the successful application of Poe's ratiocination, Peter B. Ely (S.J.), on the other hand, searches for the religious in the worldly realm of detective fiction by suggesting that Georges Simenon's detective, Jules Maigret, "manifests a profoundly Christian, even priestly character in his approach to solving crimes" (453). Ely argues that despite Maigret's (and Simenon's) professed atheism, "perhaps a residue of their early piety might be traceable in Maigret's character and methodology" (473). In support of this position, Ely cites Julian Symons's assessment that "'There are no great feats of ratiocination' in the Maigret stories, 'and the problems they present are human as much as they are criminal'" (453). A similar evaluation may be made regarding P.D. James's novels, in which Commander Adam Dalgliesh is also, more often than not, concerned with the physical, mental and existential well-being of those affected by the crimes he investigates. While Dalgliesh cannot be characterized as a clerical detective, his father was an Anglican rector and his status as a published poet provides him with a moral underpinning that functions in a similar way throughout James's series.

However, absent from most critical analyses is a consideration of how deeply religious detectives—whose faith insists upon belief in divine intervention such as miracles—are able to identify and separate their opposing impulses. In other words, religious detectives such as Father Brown, the Reverend Sidney Chambers or even Dalgliesh operate under the competing frameworks of ratiocination and faith; a binary opposition that threatens either to compromise their investigations or to undermine their religious commitment. This paradox is thrown into sharp relief for detectives of the Middle Ages, in whose definitively non-secular context the authorities of both religious confessor and secular detective combine to enhance the status of medieval crime fiction's clerical sleuths.

As illustrated by the example that opened this book, Ellis Peters immediately identified this potentially insoluble contradiction for her medieval detective, Brother Cadfael, and addressed it early in her first novel, *A Morbid Taste for Bones* (1977). Cadfael is a master at deploying the significant advantage that his religious status delivers to his investigative purpose. In *The Virgin in the Ice* (1982), for example, young Yves Hugonin believes he has overheard something that implicates his companion, Brother Elyas, in a murder, but the boy is not willing to condemn the monk by passing on this information to the deputy sheriff, Hugh Beringar. Instead, he confides in Cadfael because, "though Hugh Beringar was fair and approachable, Hugh Beringar was also the law, and bound by his office. But Brother Cadfael was not the law, and would listen with an open mind and a sympathetic ear" (Peters, *Virgin in the Ice* 237). Yves's revelations enable Cadfael to identify the killer of the eponymous virgin and while the monk's approachability is, of course, a consequence of his personality—not all clerics demonstrate Cadfael's empathy—his religious status reassures witnesses that their information will remain confidential. As an originator of the genre, Cadfael rightly stands as the epitome of the medieval religious detectives; moreover, religious detectives also feature in medieval crime fiction's only two novels to have been nominated for the prestigious Booker Prize for Fiction, as discussed in the following section.

Metaphysical Morality: John Fuller's Flying to Nowhere *and Barry Unsworth's* Morality Play

Chapter One considered Umberto Eco's triumph of postmodern historiographic metafiction, to use Linda Hutcheon's phrase (*Poetics* 5), in terms of its importance to what Michael Holquist identified as the "metaphysical detective novel" (150). Chapter One also noted the temporal convergence of Peters' Cadfael novels and *The Name of the Rose*. Indeed, critics such as Bruce Holsinger and Stephanie Trigg have wondered at the coincidence of two such different writers as Peters and Eco selecting a similar narrative conceit in close temporal proximity (177). Also coincidentally, in the same year that Eco's novel was published in English, another medievalist metaphysical detective novel appeared in Britain; one that shares a surprising number of characteristics with *The Name of the Rose* but has received little critical attention.

In 1983, British poet John Fuller's novel, *Flying to Nowhere*, won the Whitbread First Novel Award and was shortlisted for the Booker Prize. The novel is brief, only ninety pages in length, and offers a densely allegorical fable that challenges the reader to confront the inevitability of death and decay. The novel's setting is a remote island off the Welsh coast "during the Middle Ages," as the book's dust-jacket vaguely states, and opens with three novices from the island's monastery striding past women working in the fields towards the rocky shore to meet a boat approaching from the mainland. The boat contains an emissary from the bishop, sent to investigate the disappearance of several pilgrims who set out to visit the island's holy well. The emissary's name is "Vane" and this proves to be an apt homonym for both his personality and the futility of his quest. Vane's antagonist is the monastery's nameless "Abbot," whose vague, dreamlike behavior indicates his preoccupation with discovering the precise location of the soul in the human body. To that end, the Abbot has been undertaking autopsies upon the bodies of the pilgrims, whose corpses are washed down into his cellar by the waters of the island's miraculous spring, dedicated to Saint Lleuddad. While there is no evidence that the Abbot deliberately caused the pilgrims' deaths, his dissections are certainly not compatible with the mores of his society or faith. Nor, indeed, does the Abbot attempt to discover why the pilgrims are dying or endeavor to prevent further deaths.[6]

Edward L. Mendelson, reviewing the novel for *The New York Times*, likens the close temporal proximity of *Flying to Nowhere* and *The Name of the Rose* to "two scientists working independently" and making "the same discovery at the same time" (BR9). Mendelson lists the similarities between the two books: a medieval monastery; suspicious deaths; an outsider sent to investigate; first novels by well-regarded academics.[7] A young apprentice, Geoffrey,[8] also accompanies Vane, although their interaction lacks the pedagogical respect and warmth that characterizes the relationship between William of Baskerville and Adso of Melk. Despite the significant difference in length, Mendelson describes *The Name of the Rose* as "a vastly learned joke about language, a book extravagant and glittering but in [his] view ultimately hollow"; *Flying to Nowhere*, on the other hand, "is as rich and exciting as Eco's book, but deeper and more disturbing" (BR9). David Nokes, writing for *The Times Literary Supplement*, also praised Fuller's novel, describing it as "a brief, enigmatic but powerful work of sustained allegory" (480). Nokes perceptively interprets the complex labyrinths that comprise the monastery's subterranean staircases, tunnels and galleries (through which the pilgrims' bodies flow and where the Abbot performs his dissections) as representing "more than an image of the subconscious mind; they are also a symbol of the chain of being and a map of hell" (480). However, not all contemporary reviews of *Flying to Nowhere* were positive. Thomas M. Disch, for *The Washington Post*, writes that while "This is a book I should have liked," he found that Fuller's poetic aesthetics intruded too much upon the novel, resulting in "a vivid situation but no autonomous characters, and prose that, however finely wrought, is without narrative momentum" (Disch).

As mentioned above, literary scholars largely overlooked Fuller's novel. A recent exception is David Matthews, who also notes the peculiarity of it being an "outline version of the same story told by Eco," although he concludes that "The odd consonance between *The Name of the Rose* and *Flying to Nowhere* is unlikely to have been a result of direct influence, but rather the fact that the authors drew on a common store of basic ideas" (127–28). It troubles Matthews that these two "high-art medievalist novel(s)"—referring also to Barry Unsworth's *Morality Play* (1995), discussed in more detail below—place murder at the center of their narratives in the same manner as Ellis Peters' Brother Cadfael series or gothic novels such as *The Castle of Otranto* (1128). Matthews' overall theory is that medievalist cultural products rarely achieve "high-art literariness," nor enjoy critical success (127). By implication, then, the inclusion of "murder at the heart of their plots" condemns these novels to the ignominy of genre fiction and a subsequent lack of critical acclaim, "whatever their high-art ambitions" (Matthews 127, 128). This assertion, according to Matthews, is ostensibly evinced by the fact that "Fuller's and Unsworth's novels were shortlisted for Britain's prestigious MAN Booker Prize, though neither won" (128). Another way to look at this, however, is to consider the effective way in which postmodernism harnesses medievalism for its project of critiquing the present through a critical reevaluation of the past: as well as being "genre fiction," these novels are classic examples of the late twentieth century's productive engagement with the metaphysical detective narrative, as detailed in Chapter One, made all the more compelling for these medieval settings.

While the serpentine tunnels that meander underneath the island's monastery recall Eco's labyrinth of a library, the learning that occurs in the Abbot's "library" is inscribed upon—and derived from—the corpses he dissects in a macabre allusion to the animal skins used in the production of premodern manuscripts. The Abbot is acutely aware of his own manuscripts' previous "lives," as he strokes the leather that binds one of his books and wonders, "Could leather be cured of its curing? Could the sightless hides be reassembled, clasps turn to bells, the branded spines grow tails again?" (Fuller 76). The Abbot's speculation develops into mad delusion in the last pages of the novel, as he hallucinates that the flooding waters of the sacred well are reviving those long-dead skins in his library:

> He stood with his hand upon the knotted bark of the library door in despair as it thudded against his palm with the weight of the huddled herds inside. The living books seemed to have sensed his presence: the bellowing increased as they jostled on the

other side of the strained wood, and the ring of hooves on the flooded stone blended with a fresh trumpeting of panic and rebellion [Fuller 96–97].

In terms of its detective narrative, *Flying to Nowhere* offers parallel, concurrent investigations whose intersection at the end of the novel is a disaster for the two religious detectives involved. Vane represents the conventional medieval religious detective (although figured within a postmodernist framework), whose task seems straightforward enough for a literary sleuth: conduct an investigation into the mysterious disappearance of the pilgrims to the island. Vane follows the evidence he uncovers and accesses the Abbot's convoluted house from the depths of its foundations, having followed the path of the well's spring. But he does not recognize the danger of his situation and continues to ponder his inquiry—which "had rapidly turned into a particular investigation of the Abbot" (Fuller 83)—and to speculate as to why there are no ordained monks on the island when, distracted, he suddenly stumbles into the cesspool containing the putrefying corpses of the missing pilgrims. Thus, having discovered the solution to one mystery, Vane cannot escape the clinging bodies "and he became a corpse himself. The question of the unordained novices remained open" (Fuller 84). Vane's demise is sudden and shocking, particularly when he appears on the cusp of apprehending the truth of the strange monastery. But within the postmodernist framework that Fuller creates, Vane's quest for knowledge, in the manner of the traditional detective, is doomed to failure and death.

The Abbot, on the other hand, undertakes a more mystically profound inquiry into the connection between body and soul; indeed, Mendelson describes the Abbot as "part Dr. Frankenstein and part René Descartes" (BR9). Mendelson's characterization is entirely appropriate because not only does the Abbot dismember body parts, he also shares with Descartes the belief that "the precise physical seat of the human soul" resides in the pineal gland (Fuller 41). For Descartes, the pineal gland was involved in the body's sensation, imagination, memory and the causation of bodily movements.[9] While the Abbot retains what the novel characterizes as a medieval belief in the miraculous powers of the well's water—having observed a corpse's fingernails continue to grow after death and attributing this to the revivification of the corpse—he also demonstrates an Early Modern Cartesian logic, as he contemplates the circumstances under which the soul may operate:

> The seat of the soul had to obey several conditions. Firstly it must be one; ... as, for example, she [the soul] might not see two novices carrying a bucket of water where there was only one. Secondly, it must be very near the source of the animal spirits, ... And in the third place, it must be moveable; ... Conditions nowhere to be met with but in the little gland called pineal! [Fuller 41–42].

Fuller here reveals a complex intertwining of temporalities as the medieval Abbot meditates upon Early Modern Cartesian philosophy and deploys a feminine pronoun for the soul in a signification that owes more to the feminist movements of Fuller's own late-twentieth-century context than to (almost) exclusively male medieval anatomical practices.

While condemning the Abbot for heresy would have been an extreme response, northern Europeans in the high and late Middle Ages strongly disapproved of dissecting corpses for scientific purposes. According to Katharine Park, this was because the French, Germans and English believed that the separation of body and soul was "an extended and gradual process, corresponding to the slow decomposition of the corpse and its reduction to the skeleton and hard tissues, which was thought to last about a year" (115). In a fascinating contrast, the Italians believed that there was an instantaneous rupture: "Thus, while Italians tended to see the recently dead body as inert or inactive, northerners treated it during this liminal period as active, sensitive, or semianimate, possessed of a gradually fading life" (Park 115). Consequently, medical professionals in Italy made use of dissections for teaching and anatomical investigations much earlier than their contemporaries in northern Europe.[10] At the very least, of course, the Abbot's obsession prevents the pilgrims' families from reclaiming their bodies and administering burial in consecrated ground.

It is characteristic of the metaphysical detective novel that, finally, the "mystery" itself is irrelevant. In *Flying to Nowhere*, the infinitely more profound search for the solution to human ontology supersedes the detective narrative. The wonderfully named Mrs. Ffedderbompau penetrates this conundrum as she lies dying after a fall from an apple tree: "'Why,' she asked [the Abbot], 'am I inside myself and not somewhere else?'" (Fuller 65). The Abbot, seated by her side, preparing to hear Mrs. Ffedderbompau's confession, searches for a comforting truth, "But her question was too close to his own enquiries to be easily pursued" (Fuller 66). Fuller grapples with these age-old questions by embedding his novel in a mystical medieval landscape, where the Abbot's scientific experimentation coexists with the miraculous powers of Saint Lleuddad and the ancient Celtic realm of fairies and pagan ritual. While such a world indeed appears to be one in which these questions may be answered, Fuller instead forecloses its efficacy by allowing his postmodern detectives to destroy it all.

Barry Unsworth's 1995 novel *Morality Play* was also shortlisted for the Booker Prize and was released "at the height of the renewed preoccupation with history" that Mariadele Boccardi ascribes to British fiction from the mid–1980s (205). A well-regarded author of historical novels, Unsworth's work ranges over a variety of centuries and locations,[11] and *Morality Play* is his foray into the English Middle Ages. Set in the late fourteenth century, the novel's narrator is Nicholas Barber, a young, runaway priest who encounters a troupe of travelling players while fleeing from his lover's irate husband. Nicholas joins the group—that has just lost one of its members—and travels with the players to an unnamed village in the north of England in order to bury their comrade. The players are desperately short of money and cannot afford the funeral costs; poor troupes such as theirs can no longer compete with the wealthy guilds that are able to mount Mystery plays with extravagant costumes, props and the freedom to conduct them over the course of a week.

The troupe's leader, Martin, decides to write and perform a new play based upon the events surrounding the recent murder of a boy from the village and the young deaf and mute woman, Jane, who awaits trial for his murder. However, once the players begin to gather the facts of the case in order to develop their script, they find several troubling inconsistencies that propel them towards a deeper investigation into what actually happened to twelve-year-old Thomas Wells. Anticipating *Hamlet*, the players act out the crime in front of the townspeople and, later, before the local magnate, Sir Richard de Guise, who comprehends the truth about Thomas Wells's murder and detains the players. When the unnamed Justice arrives to investigate, he is convinced that the players are correct, allows them to leave, and retains the knowledge of the true perpetrator in order to guarantee Sir Richard's future compliance with the king's will.

The New York Times' reviewer, Janet Burroway, characterizes the players as "investigative journalists" and she notes Unsworth's ability "to enter the sensibility of a period—its attitudes, assumptions and turns of phrase—so convincingly that he is able to suggest subtle yet essential parallels between an earlier era and our own" (Burroway). For Burroway, Nicholas's perspective spotlights contemporary social issues such as the plight of women, the abuse of children and the disabled, and political corruption. George Garrett similarly praises Unsworth's ability to present the reader with "a sense of the times in plague-ridden England," describing Nicholas Barber as "an ideal narrator" (460). Barber may be well-educated and intelligent, but he is also relatively innocent about the world outside his monastery, particularly the world of travelling players: "Through Barber we come to know the complex characters of the other players, and through his own hurried training and experience we get a sense of the dimensions of the player's craft" (Garrett 460). Garrett, however, notes a flaw in *Morality Play* that often applies to historical novels, including medieval crime fiction, in that Unsworth attempts "to present the mindset of medieval people in more or less contemporary terms" (460). As such, Nicholas's "faith and belief seem curiously modern, easy enough to cast aside. It is hard for the contemporary author to take medieval Christianity seriously" (Garrett 460).

Garrett identifies the paradox that inhabits the core of medieval crime fiction, especially those novels featuring detectives who are members of religious orders: can contemporary readers truly comprehend the pervasiveness of religious beliefs and practices in all aspects of life in the late Middle Ages? And does inserting the modern device of the literary detective foreclose the possibility of ever achieving that comprehension? Even a writer such as Unsworth cannot help but secularize Nicholas's belief system, as the young man's decision not to return to the priesthood reveals:

> When I was a subdeacon transcribing Pilato's Homer for a noble patron, I had thought I was serving God but I was only acting at the direction of the Bishop.... I was in the part of a hired scribe but I did not know this, I thought it was my true self. God is not served by self-deceiving. The impulse to run away had not been folly but the wisdom of my heart. I would be a player and I would try to guard my soul... [187].

Nicholas ultimately realizes that he is better able to promote moral behavior among his audience as a player than as a priest. Unsworth here suggests that these two roles are not dissimilar in their promotion of ethical modes of living through performance; a decidedly modern assessment that sits uneasily within the novel's medieval context.

On the other hand, Richard Rankin Russell disagrees with Garrett's claim that Unsworth dismisses the seriousness of medieval Christian faith, arguing that Nicholas's transformation throughout the three different performances of the *Play of Thomas Wells* reflects the structure of a traditional morality play: innocence, fall and redemption; that is, "In the process of becoming a player after his fall as priest, [Nicholas] dies to his old self and is reborn with a new self that was latent in him all along" (222). Russell also notes the importance of community to Nicholas, who exchanges his religious community for this new company of players. He argues that "Unsworth has captured the medieval worldview of self-in-community that has been occluded and even denied by the modern world" (225). However, Nicholas's conflation of the two communities—the clergy and the players—underscores the innate modernity in his comprehension that his priestly role owed more to the art of performance than to the dissemination of faith via a true religious vocation.

More recently, Boccardi attempts to rescue *Morality Play* "from the peripheral position it currently occupies" and situate it instead at "the center of a discussion of contemporary historical fiction" (206). Boccardi argues that it maintains its identity as a conventional historical novel, as mandated by Georg Lukács's influential formulation whereby characters must behave according to the social and psychological mores of the past that is recreated (Lukács 42); but it also engages with the historical novels of the late twentieth century and their developing interest in epistemology and fascination with ontology (206). However, Boccardi's conclusion also implicates Unsworth in the postmodern or metaphysical trend of detective fiction through the novel's ambiguous ending: "There is ... a clear divergence between the narrative and ethical resolutions—the former definite, the latter left problematically open" (212). In other words, the novel "resolves" its detective narrative by revealing the perpetrators and mechanics of the crime(s), while simultaneously resisting a satisfied sense that justice has been served and social order restored. Instead, the "Justice" shifts the crime from the judicial sphere to the political realm so that the king may enforce his authority—through blackmail—over a recalcitrant noble.

Nicholas and the troupe of players gradually transmogrify into detectives through a sequence of events that appears neither entirely planned nor completely coincidental. As noted above, Martin suggests a shocking plan to garner the interest of the townspeople: "'Good people,' he said, 'we must play the murder'" (Unsworth 63). The troupe reacts with astonishment and fear that slowly gives way to acceptance and a cautious excitement about the possibilities of this new dramatic form. The fugitive priest, Nicholas, has the strongest reservations, arguing that, "'Players are like other men, they must use God's meanings, they cannot make meanings of their own, that is heresy, it is the source of our woes, it is the reason our first parents were cast out'" (Unsworth 64). Nevertheless, the performance goes ahead, mobilizing the conventions of the traditional "Morality Play" that preceded the mystery plays that were becoming more frequently staged.

In order to gather material for their new work, the players spread out through the town to learn what they can about the circumstances of Thomas's murder. When they stage the first performance, something unusual occurs: the audience is hushed and enraptured by the scene in which Thomas is tempted to go with the woman accused of his murder. As Springer, playing Thomas, moves forward towards temptation, a woman's voice cries out from the audience, "'It was not thus,' she shouted. 'My boy did not go with her.... My Thomas was a good boy,' ...'" (Unsworth 93). Thomas's mother is appealing to the crowd surrounding her and, in response, the audience becomes angry; the players freeze, sensing the violence directed towards them. Martin, their leader, rushes on to the stage, abandoning his mask and shouts over the noise of the crowd, "'Good people, why did he go with her? ... Thomas Wells was not killed by the roadside'" (Unsworth 93). The play continues, but the theatrical fourth wall has been broken, uniting the cast and audience in a mutual interrogation of the circumstances surrounding Thomas's death. Financially, the play more than serves Martin's purpose, taking more money than any of the players could recall for a single performance. But the effect of the play and the audience's reaction ignites something in the players that has nothing to do with financial reward. The troupe agrees to stage the play again, ostensibly to earn more money, although Nicholas perceives a broader motivation: "Thus once again Martin won us over. But there was more to it than money and I think we knew this already in our hearts" (Unsworth 101).

In Martin and Nicholas, Unsworth offers, respectively, an example of the amateur detective paired with the reluctant investigator whose strong sense of justice will not allow him to abandon the search for truth. This effective combination is complicated by Nicholas's status as a rogue priest, distracted by his own existential crisis that is transforming him from a cleric-scribe into a performer. Nicholas's engagement with the both the investigation and the performance is mutable; he is "now an active participant [in the play], now a mere spectator, simultaneously inside and outside the action" (Martínez Alfaro 82). This intermittent detachment recalls Eco's concern with the critical distance of postmodern irony that assists the literary detective to navigate the Middle Ages through the deployment of modern tropes and techniques. However, Unsworth's medieval landscape manages to contain these potential disruptions because the outcome of the investigation garners a residual sense of circumstantial randomness that contemporary readers readily associate with the Middle Ages. For example, the arrival of the Justice coincides with the first performance of the *Play of Thomas Wells* and, as Nicholas discovers at the end of the novel, this Justice is motivated more by a desire to curb the activities of Sir Richard de Guise than to save an innocent peasant girl from hanging. The Justice, more worldly than Nicholas, imparts his cynicism to the young player, saying "Wickedness is too common in the world for us to think much of why and wherefore. It is more natural to ask about the rarer thing and wonder why people sometimes do good" (Unsworth 184). Nicholas resists this bleak assessment, not believing in "such preponderance of wickedness ... except sometimes when [his] spirits are low" (Unsworth 184). However, in order to allow this optimism to flourish, Nicholas must abandon his religious vocation and instead seek to bring truth to his audience through the proto-social-realist drama represented by the *Play of Thomas Wells*.

Unsworth is one of only three medieval crime fiction authors whose work has been adapted to film or television. In 2004, Paul McGuigan directed *The Reckoning*, starring Willem Dafoe and Paul Bettany (every Chaucerian's favorite actor). The film retains the novel's concern with seeking justice through the innovation of presenting a play that reflects real events but alters the narrative in significant ways. The climax of the film portrays the incensed townspeople attacking Lord Robert de Guise's castle (a slight change in name that conflates the father and son de Guise of the novel), burning it and killing the lord in an apparent allusion to the forthcoming 1381 Uprising (the film is set in 1380). In a stark departure from the book, Nicholas loses his life at the end of the film in an unsubtle act of redemptive sacrifice.

The movie was not a success, receiving lukewarm reviews and modest box office returns. Most critics complained that the transparent narrative does not allow the film's potential complexity to develop. Erika Hernandez blames the inexperience of McGuigan, who "crams both story and theme down the viewer's throat," foreclosing interpretation, "a pursuit that is vital to both the Morality play *and* the narrative film" (Hernandez, emphasis in original). Hernandez recognizes the pivotal moment in the history of theater that *The Reckoning* seeks to highlight, where "art and real life merge again." She notes that the morality play genre warrants some examination on screen because it "was an invaluable step in the evolution of Acting and Theater." A.O. Scott, reviewing the film for *The New York Times*, dismisses it as akin to an hour-long television pilot, while nevertheless enjoying the otherness of the medieval setting. For Scott, *The Reckoning* presents the Middle Ages as a distant, barbaric past that destabilizes his "modern moviegoing expectations." Scott uses expressions that are now commonplace to the practice of refiguring the Middle Ages as "foreign": "[it] seems intended to plunge modern viewers into a scary, alien world"; "strange premodern landscape"; and "the medieval landscape … retains its harsh, authentic look." However, into this bleak "time of authoritarianism and repression," Scott, like Hernandez, detects "the awakening of the spirit of modernity" (Scott).

Cinema critics like Scott and Hernandez characteristically immerse themselves in the otherness of the medieval mise-en-scène while maintaining a hopeful eye for hints of an emerging modernity that reassures them they will not be stranded in the Middle Ages. The irony of reviews such as these lies in their insistence that the Middle Ages remains somehow unknowable—"another country"—while the medieval is, in fact, inextricably intertwined with contemporary culture, including, perhaps most effective for the dissemination of medievalism, the medium of film.

Medieval scholars are also interested in the film's attempt to harness the moment that modern replaces premodern. Nickolas A. Haydock believes that

The Reckoning stages the transition to modernity in a *mise-en-abyme* of dramatic evolution: The traveling troop of actors progresses from mystery to morality play and finally to a proto–Brechtian epic theater in its quest to make drama relevant to the lives of its audience [32].

Haydock includes his discussion of *The Reckoning* within a broader examination of three medievalist films in which the "detective monks" fail "to defeat the conspiracies they uncover" (34).[12] Haydock convincingly argues that *The Reckoning, The Name of the Rose* (1986, directed by Jean-Jacques Annaud) and *The Advocate* (1993, directed by Leslie Magahey) thereby evince "the incapacity of post–Enlightenment rationalism to contain or repress the medieval" (34). Christine Neufeld similarly suggests that the film's "ineffectiveness" indicates the tenuousness of "conventional evolutionary views of the arts that reduce the medieval to modernism's barbaric Other" (1). Neufeld argues that *The Reckoning* is a film about redemption, both for the rogue priest Nicholas and for the dramatic arts as the catalyst for personal and social change (3). She points out that the film establishes a "precarious binary … between the medieval as oppressive blind faith and modernity as the liberating impact of empiricism" (4), and this binary is most clearly evident in the final performance of the *Play of Thomas Wells*, which Neufeld describes as "not theatre per se but a lawyer's closing argument" (6). However, as noted above, Nicholas's sacrifice underscores the film's ideological concern with death necessarily preceding redemption; a construction that implies the barbarism of the Middle Ages may only be overcome by the light of modernity.

Both Fuller and Unsworth offer medieval crime fiction novels that showcase the powerful combination of postmodernism and medievalism. As such, they most closely resemble Eco's *The Name of the Rose* in their engagement with questions of historical authenticity and postmodern irony. In keeping with postmodern or metaphysical detective conventions, both novels offer a "failed" investigative process: in Fuller's novel, the detective, Vane, loses his life at the moment of revelation, while Nicholas must accept that the information he has uncovered is too valuable to serve justice alone and is instead more usefully applied to a broader political purpose. While these impressive feats of postmodern medievalist metafiction may contrast markedly with other examples of medieval crime fiction, they nevertheless evince the extraordinary variety of narratives that comprise this genre.

Crusade and War, Faith and Rehabilitation: Bascot de Marins and Brother Athelstan

Medieval crime fiction authors often attempt to challenge the idealized depiction of the various medieval Crusades to the Middle East. Many of the detectives in Chapter Two are weary ex-crusaders, returning to England disillusioned by the cruelty and futility of the crusader cause. Their experiences frequently motivate their desire to seek justice in roles that investigate crime or uphold the law. Maureen Ash's Bascot de Marins not only epitomizes this effort to problematize the "glorious" quest to impose Christianity upon the Middle East by force, he also emerges as a paragon of medieval religious rehabilitation. Bascot is a member of the Knights Templar who returns to England after escaping from an eight-year captivity in the Holy Land. The Templar is severely scarred physically (among other injuries he has lost his right eye), emotionally and spiritually by his experiences: he suffers an existential crisis exacerbated by the discovery that his family (his mother, father and brother) had died during his years as a Saracen slave. Hoping to rekindle Bascot's faith, the master of the English Templars, Amery St. Maur, suggests a sojourn at Lincoln Castle in order to help the knight recover in body and spirit. Thus, in the year 1200, Bascot finds himself in the service of Nicolaa de la Haye, castellan of Lincoln castle, a position she inherited upon her father's death. Nicolaa is married to Gerard Camville, Lincoln's sheriff—both historical figures. In Ash's reimagining, Nicolaa and Gerard's marriage is not a happy one, having been arranged by Nicolaa's father; nevertheless, the couple manage their personality differences in order to ensure that Lincoln functions effectively both as an important commercial center and as a loyal stronghold for King John.

Nicolaa was a formidable leader and resolute supporter of John, resisting several assaults on the castle while her husband was away fighting for John's rebellion against Richard I, and then refusing to yield to rebels supporting the French invasion of 1216. Indeed, one of John's final acts was to appoint her Sheriff of Lincoln (Gerard had died in 1215); this was an unprecedented role for a woman. After John's death and in her sixties, Nicolaa held Lincoln Castle against the French commander, Comte du Perche, who captured the city of Lincoln in early 1217. Despite a personal plea for her surrender from Prince Louis, the future Louis VIII (who had been declared king of England), Nicolaa survived a three-month siege until William Marshal arrived to rout the French and rebel English forces. This so-called "Battle of Lincoln" proved a decisive turning point and began the process of the French retreat from England.[13]

Bascot de Marins understands that the Templar Order hopes he will return: "Sending him to Nicolaa de la Haye had been a way of releasing him, but not quite letting him go" (Ash, *Alehouse Murders* 34). Nicolaa initially uses Bascot's literacy skills to assist with the running of her extensive landholdings. However, when four bodies are discovered in a local alehouse, Nicolaa asks Bascot to investigate. Moreover, both Nicolaa and St. Maur are staunch supporters of King John and they engage in a tacit collusion to harness Bascot's abilities and deploy them in the king's interests. This political agenda becomes clearer as the series progresses.

On Bascot's long journey back to England after escaping captivity, he had encountered Gianni on the streets of Palermo, Sicily; a young, starving and mute orphan whom Bascot rescues and, to all intents and purposes, adopts. While Gianni never regains his speech, he becomes an invaluable assistant to Bascot during his investigations and, upon the knight's eventual return to the Templar Order, Nicolaa allows Gianni to remain at Lincoln Castle and trains him to be a clerk. As Gianni develops his skills, he repays Nicolaa's faith in him by becoming an effective *secretarius* and temporary stand-in investigator when Bascot is not available. Gianni and Bascot's bond remains strong and they continue to work together throughout the series.

Despite Bascot's dedication to upholding the king's law, he nevertheless harbors a definite dislike for John, illustrating the harsh realities of feudalism when obligation and respect do not coalesce. Renowned English soldier, William Marshal, Earl of Pembroke, perceives this dislike when he first meets Bascot and observes the Templar's interaction with the king: "Although courteous, de Marins was not diffident towards the king.... The earl also sensed, from the slight clenching of the muscles in Bascot's jaw while he conversed with John, that the monk felt some degree of antipathy towards [him]" (Ash, *Canterbury Murders* loc. 1074). This antipathy stems from a previous encounter with John, in which the king attempted to bribe Bascot into staying in Nicolaa's service and renouncing the Templar Order completely in return for the restoration of his father's lands (Ash, *Death of a Squire* 239–40). The bribe John used was the boy Gianni, forcing Bascot "to choose between his love for another human being and his faith" (Ash, *Canterbury Murders* loc. 1056). For Bascot, this illustrates John's inherent maliciousness that forecloses respect from the Templar. Ash draws her characters well and imbues them with enough complexity that readers may understand their virtues and faults—even John's. Moreover, countering Bascot's dislike, Nicolaa and Marshal demonstrate consistent respect and affection for John. Ash effectively complicates any preconceived beliefs her readers may have about a king who has traditionally been viewed by history as deeply problematic.

As a Templar, Bascot is as highly trained in combat as any secular knight and he is able to fight when necessary either to defend himself or to apprehend culprits; this is unusual for medieval religious detectives, who rarely engage in violence. In *The Canterbury Murders* (2013), Bascot attempts to arrest Chacal, a mercenary whose band of soldiers was supplementing King John's guards, but Chacal prefers to resist, declaring, "'I must warn you, Templar, … that I do not intend to be taken'" (loc. 2947). Bascot does not bother to reply and the two engage in an impressively staged duel that results (inevitably) in the Templar's victory. However, this scene not only showcases Bascot's battle prowess, it also reveals a disquieting absence of Christian mercy, as Bascot succeeds in severing the upper part of Chacal's sword arm and the mercenary falls to his knees, imploring, "'Grant me a quick death, Templar, I beg of you.'" Bascot, despite knowing that "drawing, hanging and quartering would be the mercenary's certain end," refuses to deliver the death blow and declares, "'You have forfeited your right to such a courtesy'" (Ash, *Canterbury Murders* loc. 2974). In this case, the knight's concern for honor suppresses the man of God's inclination to clemency, in an illustration of the complex and contradictory identities that reside in members of militant religious orders.

Like other ex-crusaders such as Sir Baldwin Furnshill (see Chapter Two), Bascot de Marins is clearly suffering post-traumatic stress disorder as a consequence of his violent past, his long captivity and his disillusionment upon discovering that humanity's worst traits are also rampant in England. St. Maur, Master Templar, perceives Bascot's anguish:

> The master had not expected to see a man who wore the results of his ordeal so plainly. It was not the black leather patch that covered his missing right eye which made it so, but the weary resolution in the vision of the other. Here was a man who had undergone great suffering at the hands of his heathen captors but had kept his devotion to Christ unsullied throughout. It was only amongst those of his own faith that his inner strength had been tested, and the master could see that his long endurance was beginning to flag [Ash, *Plague of Poison* 284].

Over time, Bascot slowly gains some perspective about his experiences that eventually develops into an understanding of human character that recalls the tolerance demonstrated by Ellis Peters' Brother Cadfael and enhances his performance as a medieval detective.

In *Death of a Squire* (2008), the titular victim is seemingly disliked by everyone: "He had been painted blackly, as a disagreeable young man, a braggart and a lecher" (Ash, *Death of a Squire* 59). Bascot realizes that he is relying too heavily upon the opinions of others in his assessment of the squire's character and he muses that there is a "trace of good" or a "redeeming trait," even in "the most evil of men" (Ash, *Death of a Squire* 59). This train of thought takes Bascot somewhere unexpected and he remembers the "infidel lord" who held him captive and commanded the hot iron that removed his eye. Bascot hated this Saracen passionately and, had the chance arose, would have eagerly killed him not only for his cruel behavior, but also for his contempt for Christianity. Time, however, has tempered Bascot's hatred and anger:

> But on reflection, and with the benefit of hindsight, Bascot had to admit he had seen his captor show kindness to those of his own heathen faith, and had seemed genuinely fond of the many children he had sired on the numerous women of his harem. No doubt he had been viewed as a generous and loving benefactor by those receiving his favour [Ash, *Death of a Squire* 59–60].

This grudging acknowledgment of a common humanity—despite deep religious and cultural differences—is a small indication of Bascot's rehabilitation from the trauma of his past experiences. It also provides the broader perspective, tolerance and understanding of the world that is crucial to the make-up of a medieval detective. Another sign of Bascot's gradual recovery is the pull he begins to feel to return to the Templars and resume his fight for Christ. This he eventually does, once he satisfactorily settles the issue of Gianni's future security.

As Bascot slowly regains his faith, he becomes increasingly disenchanted with the role of detective that Nicolaa, and occasionally King John, constantly thrust upon him. For example, having discovered the killer of the aforementioned squire, Bascot is sorely troubled by the murders of a charcoal burner and his two sons that the culprits claim occurred only because the Templar had questioned them in the course of his investigation; consequently, "His satisfaction at discovering the perpetrator of the crime was tainted by the burden of responsibility that had accompanied it" (*Death of a Squire* 235). Ash, however, deftly manages Bascot's disillusionment by allowing Gianni a more prominent investigative role. And, while Bascot de Marins seems the epitome of knightly piety, his traumatic past and the ongoing struggle to overcome its repercussions lend him a vulnerability that engenders nothing but sympathy in readers and a willingness to follow his journey wherever it leads.

As mentioned in Chapter Two, Paul C. Doherty is the author of an extraordinary number of medieval crime fiction novels, comprising several series that span different centuries and showcase various medieval professions. His religious detective is Brother Athelstan, a Dominican friar whose parish is in the unpalatable precincts of Southwark. Doherty reveals in the opening few pages of the series' first novel, *The Nightingale Gallery* (1991), that Athelstan deserted his novitiate to chase glory fighting for the Black Prince in the Hundred Years' War, convincing his younger brother to join him. Athelstan's brother was killed and their parents never recovered from the grief and shock. Like Bascot de Marins, Athelstan is scarred psychologically by his experiences and he returns to his religious order to continue his training. As penance, the Father Prior assigns him the poor parish of St.

Erconwald's, where readers find him in 1377. However, Athelstan's real punishment is to be appointed clerk to London's coroner, Sir John Cranston, whose drunken buffoonery perpetually frustrates the friar, but also conceals sharp eyes and a shrewd intelligence. Together, they have been investigating suspicious deaths in medieval London over the course of eighteen books (so far) in the Sorrowful Mysteries of Brother Athelstan series.

Doherty is a devotee of the clue-puzzle structure of golden-age crime fiction. *The House of the Red Slayer* (1992), for example, features a classic locked-room conundrum in which the Constable of the Tower of London, Sir Ralph Whitton, is discovered with his throat slashed despite the safety precautions he had put in place: "The stairway to his chamber was guarded by two trusted retainers. The door between the steps and the passageway was locked. Sir Ralph kept a key and so did the guards. The same is true of Sir Ralph's chamber. He locked it from the inside, whilst the two guards had another key" (*House of the Red Slayer* 35). *The Devil's Domain* (1998) not only features a locked-room mystery, but also a remote setting that limits the list of suspects. *The Straw Men* (2012) deploys the device of murder in plain sight when two severed heads are left on the stage of a mystery play that Athelstan, Sir John and King Richard's uncle, John of Gaunt, are watching.

John of Gaunt, the Duke of Lancaster, looms large over the series, often demanding that Athelstan and Sir John solve a crime committed against one of his retinue. Doherty embraces the dislike and suspicion that most of England's fourteenth-century population felt towards Gaunt during his years as regent for his nephew, who came to the throne at the age of ten. Neither the members of parliament nor the powerful magnates could ever believe that Gaunt did not secretly wish to seize the throne. Doherty sets up the tension between Richard and his eldest uncle early on, as the Duke contemplates his situation with frustration:

> His father was dead and he was regent but not king. John groaned to himself, clenching a bejewelled fist. He should be king, a man born to the crown with claims to the thrones of Castille, France, Scotland and England. And the only obstacle in his path? A golden-haired ten-year-old boy, his nephew, Richard of Bordeaux, son of Gaunt's elder brother, the feared and fearsome Black Prince [*Nightingale Gallery* 5].

In a recent interview, Doherty draws a parallel between his condemnation of Gaunt—whom he describes as "sinister," "enigmatic," and overshadowing Richard—with the contemporary political climate in Britain: "London is still a very wealthy city with its powerful burgesses and richly brocaded mansions. However, there's a storm coming. The dispossessed are beginning to protest against poor government, high taxes, and the excesses of the rich" (qtd. in Picker 52).

Unsurprisingly, then, there is a distinctly political overtone to Doherty's writing in this series. The novels all anticipate the approaching 1381 Uprising in which bands of disgruntled serfs, farmers, blacksmiths, weavers and other workers ransacked London in protest at exorbitant taxes, the continual war with France, and the excesses of young King Richard's court. Just a few pages into Athelstan's first investigation, he studies the nobles passing him on London's streets, noting the lords' swaggering arrogance and ruthless pride. Athelstan thinks that "Their women were no better, with their plucked eyebrows and white pasty faces" and he reflects upon the contrast between this ostentatious display of wealth and the abject poverty of the streets through which they ride: "God should send fire, he thought, or a leader to raise up the poor" (Doherty, *Nightingale Gallery* 26).

In the series' second novel, Athelstan speculates that the death of the Tower's Constable may be a reflection of the rumors he was hearing about peasants in Kent, Middlesex and Essex forming a secret society called the "Great Community." Furthermore, "Athelstan even vaguely knew one of these leaders—John Ball, a wandering priest; the man was so eloquent he could turn the most placid of peasants into an outright rebel…" (Doherty, *House of the Red Slayer* 37). Athelstan worries whether any of his parishioners are implicated in the rebels' cause and wonders, if the anticipated Uprising does come, which side he should support, revealing a certain sympathy for the rebels: "God knew, [they] had legitimate grievances. Harsh taxes and savage laws were cruel enough to provoke a saint to rebellion" (Doherty, *House of the Red Slayer* 37). In *The Herald of Hell* (2015), it is May 1381, on the eve of the Uprising, and Athelstan's investigation into a chancery clerk's death leads him to the so-called "Herald of Hell," supposedly the harbinger of the rebels, sent to foster fear among the London populace. In the series' sixteenth book, *The Great Revolt* (2016), the Uprising finally arrives.

Historically, the 1381 Uprising originated in the acute labor shortages engendered by the ravages of the Black Death earlier in the century. A repressive governmental response to the increasing mobility of workers in search of higher wages, as well as the latest in a punitive poll tax, culminated in relatively well-organized and large groups of men converging on London from Essex and Kent. The rebels destroyed John of Gaunt's Savoy Palace, executed the Archbishop of Canterbury and the Chancellor of England, and local sympathizers went on a seemingly unconnected rampage against the city's Flemish residents. Famously, the fourteen-year-old king, Richard II, rode out to Smithfield in order to confront the leader of the Kent movement, Wat Tyler, and disperse the armed crowds through undertakings of reform and clemency. While Richard's actions are regarded unequivocally by historians as exceptionally brave and mature, once the crisis was over, the young king (or, more probably, his advisors) reneged on his promise for clemency and a spate of executions followed throughout the offending counties; Richard allegedly dismissed the rebels' concerns by declaring, "Rustics you were and rustics you are still" (qtd. in Ganim 77).

In Doherty's treatment of the Uprising, he suggests that while "the peasant army" had legitimate grievances against their treatment, the rebellion was actually orchestrated by a shadowy and sinister group of criminals known as the "Upright Men" (foreshadowed in several previous novels) and exploited by ambitious noblemen for political gain. However, Athelstan, amid the chaos and political wrangling, finds himself solving two locked-door murders—a standard device for Doherty—one of which has links back to the murder of Edward II, Richard's great-grandfather. It is puzzling that Doherty chooses to distract his readers from this famous historical event by recalling the mayhem of Edward's deposition fifty years earlier, especially since the previous fifteen novels have all, to a greater or lesser extent, progressed in anticipation of this Uprising. However, Edward and his rebellious queen, Isabella, form Doherty's primary academic interest and he perhaps prefers to consider all tumultuous events through the lens of those disruptive years.

In addition to his innate egalitarianism, Athelstan also expresses some unusual theological doubts for a Dominican friar. While praying in his church, Athelstan wonders whether God has forsaken him and whether there was anyone listening to his prayers: "What if there was not? What if Christ had not risen from the dead, and religion was mere hocus-pocus?" (Doherty, *House of the Red Slayer* 96).[14] Furthermore, Doherty appears unable to break the habit of allowing his characters to express seemingly modern reactions to their surroundings, as noted in Chapter Two with regard to Doherty's hardboiled detective, Hugh Corbett. As Athelstan is walking through the streets with Cranston, the coroner asks him a question, "and Athelstan was about to reply when the stench from the poultry stalls suddenly made him gag: ... Athelstan let Cranston chatter on as he held his breath, head down as he passed Scalding Alley" (Doherty, *Nightingale Gallery* 29). No other characters are affected by the squalid surroundings that Doherty delights in describing. All of his medieval landscapes feature filth, poverty and cruelty, emphasizing the dreadful bleakness of life in the Middle Ages. Athelstan's modern sensibilities underscore both the danger and the decay of fourteenth-century London. But his reaction also reassures the reader that he recognizes the injustice that pervades medieval life and that he, in his role as priest and detective, will demystify the otherness of the Middle Ages as he prosecutes his campaign for a distinctly modern form of justice.

Doherty's novels (in this series and his others) are uniformly concerned with recreating the historical period, often to the detriment of the detective narrative. As noted in regard to Hugh Corbett, Doherty's characterization is simplistic, while his depiction of the fourteenth century is impressive if veering occasionally towards the anachronistic. Reviews of his novels discern this imbalance and sometimes struggle to reconcile Doherty's laudable portrayal of the English Middle Ages and his detective narrative. For example, Mary F. Burns notes, referring to *The Great Revolt*, "Doherty writes with conscious assurance about the times and the details, although I found the dialogue somewhat stilted and lacking in depth.... It's a solid mystery, but I thought the characters seemed wooden and two-dimensional; it was hard to care about their fates" (Burns). This review characterizes many of Doherty's forays into medieval crime fiction, across his several series. Doherty has a deep love and understanding for the English Middle Ages, particularly the fourteenth century, and in a reversal of Eco's invocation of the medieval as pretext—that is, invoked as a backdrop upon which to lay another, often modern, tale—Doherty enacts the reverse by using the detective narrative as pretext: an incidental narrative skeleton upon which he builds a medieval body.

Both Bascot de Marins and Brother Athelstan are reluctant detectives, forced into activating their undoubted investigative skills by characters that act as authority figures and mentors. Despite this reluctance, Bascot and Athelstan nevertheless find a measure of comfort in the quests for justice they undertake that goes some way to heal the ongoing trauma they both experience as a consequence of war.

The Good, the Bad, the Conspiracies

As with all genre fiction, there are wide-ranging standards across the field, from the so-called "literary" examples of Fuller and Unsworth, to the consistent and long-running series of Ash and Doherty, to the handful of novels that blatantly undermine the integrity of medieval crime fiction conventions. This section considers a range of novels that do not form part of longer series and represent a cross-section of quality.

Catherine Jinks studied medieval history at the University of Sydney and many of her novels reflect her familiarity with this period. Best known for her children's and young adult fiction, Jinks has also written three novels that may be categorized as medieval crime fiction: *The Inquisitor* (1999), *The Notary* (2000) and *The Secret Familiar* (2006). While these books are not part of a series, nor feature the same characters, they share a fourteenth-century French setting and a concern with the Church's Inquisition into heretical practices. As discussed at the beginning of this chapter, the way in which heresy is defined, identified and subsequently prosecuted is a significant area of interest for authors of medieval crime fiction.

The Inquisitor recounts the events of 1318 in the town of Lazet, in the Narbonne region of southern France. Dominican friar, Bernard Peyre, writes a letter to the Master General of his order, asking for help and protection in the wake of the brutal and shocking murder of his most recent superior, Father Augustin, along with his group of mercenary bodyguards. Bernard's role is to assist the lead Inquisitor in his investigations into local cases of heretical practice and the main suspects for the crime are a group of women, living on an isolated farm, whom Father Augustin suspected of being Cathars. Bernard doubts the women are involved and, through the course of discovering the truth, as well as uncovering the reasons behind other deaths, falls in love with Joanna, the leader of the women. Jinks's second medieval crime novel is set in the same time, the early fourteenth century, in Avignon, and features a young notary, Raymond Maillot, who assists another Dominican friar, Father Amiel, in his investigation of acts of murder and sorcery. The Inquisition still looms large and Maillot is an extremely appealing character. The Inquisitorial theme continues with *The Secret Familiar*, published in 2006 and the last of Jinks's medieval thrillers. This time, the detective is Helie Bernier, who recounts his activities as a spy for the Dominican inquisitor, Bernard Gui, familiar to readers of medieval crime fiction as the antagonist in *The Name of the Rose*.

Jinks's attention to the detail of her medieval world is impressive and her description of the religious, social and historical context surrounding the events in her narrative is detailed and convincing. Her concern with historical accuracy reflects her training as a historian, prompting one reviewer (referring to *The Inquisitor*) to observe, "The dense, conspiratorial result is bracing, though it may prompt simpler souls to wish for good old-fashioned anachronism" ("*The Inquisitor*"). The contrast between the above-mentioned review of Doherty and this one referring to Jinks illustrates the challenging balance these authors must achieve: too much historical detail describing, for example, authentic medieval theology threatens to obscure the narrative or distract the readers just as surely as anachronistic reactions to the squalor of medieval streets do so. In her three medieval crime fiction novels, Jinks demonstrates how the Inquisitorial process fails in its project to eliminate heresy and instead fractures societal trust in both the Church and each other.

In an intriguing coincidence, another murder mystery set in the confines of a fourteenth-century monastery was published in 1983 (the year *The Name*

of the Rose was released in English and Fuller's *Flying to Nowhere* was published) by a couple writing together under the pseudonym, E.M.A. Allison
(Eric W. and Mary Ann Allison). In a nuanced engagement with its medieval
setting, *Through the Valley of Death* recounts the investigative activities of
Brother Barnabas, the cellarer of a Cistercian monastery in Yorkshire. One
of the monks, Brother Anselm, is found strangled and the prior assigns Barnabas the responsibility of discovering the murderer. Barnabas is extremely
reluctant to do so and frequently finds other tasks to occupy himself in order
to avoid the investigation. As a detective, Barnabas has an irritating habit of
procrastination and prevarication, more inclined to contemplate the courtyard garden or the vista from the abbey's walls than to conduct the series of
interviews that the investigation requires. This is partly because Barnabas is
at a loss as how to proceed (he eventually deploys his knowledge of Aristotle
and seeks the "essence" of the crime) and partly because he is entirely inexperienced in the ways of the corrupt world.

Barnabas's father sent him to the abbey at the age of eight and forty years
or so later, he retains a marked innocence that blinds him to the faults of others. As Barnabas probes into Anselm's belongings, he discovers that the dead
monk and several others had been engaged in blackmail and stealing from
the abbey; as the abbey's cellarer, Barnabas oversaw the duties of these monks
and he is therefore ultimately responsible for their crimes. Prior Geoffrey—
an ex-soldier who is as worldly as Barnabas is ingenuous—struggles to accept
that Barnabas was not involved in the conspiracy before conceding: "Barnabas,
I must beg your pardon. I know you to be a good man, and I should not have
doubted you. It is rare that one meets an innocent, but I believe you to be
such" (Allison 98). That assessment is damning for one whose task is to delve
into the bleaker aspects of human behavior, although it is a notable and refresh-
ing contrast to some religious detectives who can appear worldly without any
requisite experience. Allison, perhaps unconsciously, subverts the conventions
of medieval crime fiction's religious detectives by demonstrating the likely
unpreparedness that a monk, cloistered since childhood, brings to the investigative process.

Allison underscores the incompatibility of a cloistered life with the
demands of being a detective by concluding the novel with Barnabas's decision to leave his abbey because he believes "he should go out into the world
… [to] see what good he could do in the world" (184). Given his inept performance as a detective, it seems he also departs to seek those skills and experience that his sheltered life has precluded. Unfortunately, since Allison did
not publish any more novels featuring Brother Barnabas, whether or not he
succeeded remains unknowable.

Stephen Gaspar's *To Know Evil* (2009) recounts the story of Brother Thomas of Worms, a monk in a northern Italian Benedictine abbey, set at the turn of the first millennium. When one of his fellow monks dies in suspicious circumstances, Thomas attempts to investigate the murder but is forestalled by his abbot, who instead assigns him the task of scribal copying in the monastery's library. While there, Thomas discovers a forbidden codex embedded in a book of Gnosticism that leads him to question his commitment to both the monastery and the religion it supports. Gaspar's novel blatantly echoes Eco's medievalist murder masterpiece, from its setting, to its suspicion of knowledge, to its discovery of a lost book that conservative religious thinkers believe will undermine faith itself, to its labyrinth of secret rooms beneath the monastery.

Gaspar appears unconcerned that his detective, Thomas, is decidedly unmedieval in his attitude and actions. Thomas is also supremely arrogant, believing that he possesses a vastly superior intellect to those surrounding him. This exasperates his abbot and Thomas often feels compelled to show off his ratiocination skills, even when they are not wanted: "Something inside Thomas had compelled him to reveal his true belief in the affair.... The situation was not wholly devoid of appeal for him. Though he would never admit it—even to himself—Thomas needed to display his intellect and manner of reasoning" (Gaspar 116). When Thomas's eager and naive assistant, Brother Nicholas, discovers the whereabouts of the secret passage beneath the scriptorium, Thomas reacts to the news not with the excitement that Nicholas expects, but instead is "resentful towards the younger monk for discovering something that should have been obvious" (Gaspar 88). Rather heavy-handedly, Gaspar mocks Thomas's confidence in his own knowledge by having the monk frequently refer to such incontrovertible "facts" that this earth is flat, and the sun revolves around it (123, 176, 177)—the author here winks at his readers in order to assert modernity's superiority over these ostensibly misguided premodern beliefs.[15] Gaspar's engagement with the Middle Ages is unconvincing and the novel suffers from an inauthentic medieval world that is paired with an extremely flawed detective narrative.

David Bland joins the clutch of authors who have written single books featuring clerical detectives in the Middle Ages. In what appears to be his only novel, Bland portrays London in the mid-twelfth century, during the reign of Henry II. His detective is Father Martin, preceptor of the Benedictine monastery situated at Bellins Gate (Billingsgate). Father Martin possesses preternatural observation and analytical skills that he himself does not fully understand. As Bland laboriously explains:

> Martin's talent to unravel mysteries was significantly dependent on his facility for non-consciously collating his visual perception of another person with the tone of voice and mannerisms, set in the location.... Somehow, somewhere, outside his understanding, Martin's perception of human situations went far beyond the evidence that can be gathered directly by any ordinary mortal of another [13].

As may be deduced by this example, Bland's prose is tortuously overblown and his purpose in writing this novel has nothing to do with providing an entertaining historical mystery, but is instead concerned with lecturing the reader on everything from the mechanics of bridge repair according to the tidal fluctuations of the Thames, to the history and politics of English colonization of Ireland and the linguistic relationship between Welsh, East Saxon, West Saxon, Middle Saxon, French, Irish and Norse. *Father Martin and the Hermitage Mystery* (2005) is an ideal, if tedious, inversion of Eco's Middle Ages as pretext: the crime or investigative process is the pretext and matters little to Bland, whose primary purpose is to educate his readers about the aspects of medieval life that interest him.

The Establishment of Genre: Collaboration and Parody

A literary genre achieves some success when variations of that form emerge, such as co-authored books and parodies. This section considers two examples of variations to the medieval crime fiction formula.[16] The first is a successful collaboration among British authors of crime fiction set in the Middle Ages who call themselves "The Medieval Murderers." This group published a remarkable ten novels between 2005 and 2014, in addition to writing their own separate and well-established series. According to one of the founding members, Michael Jecks, "The Medieval Murderers" began as a group of like-minded authors who travelled to literary events together, speaking about writing, publishing and murder in the Middle Ages ("Who Are the Medieval Murderers?").

Eventually, the group's members decided to see whether they could write together and came up with a format that has since remained unchanged: each author writes a novella featuring his or her medieval detective as well as the anchoring device that runs through the book, linking the different stories. The original members are Philip Gooden, Susanna Gregory, Michael Jecks, Bernard Knight and Ian Morson, and these authors continue to form the core writing group, although they have been joined by C.J. Sansom and, most recently, Karen Maitland. The historical period they cover ranges from 1100 to the early 1600s. Strictly speaking, Gooden's Nick Revill series is not medieval, since it is set in Elizabethan England and frequently features William Shakespeare as a character, while Sansom sets his very successful series during the reign of Henry VIII. However, the group does not appear overly concerned with limiting its stories to the Middle Ages: Susanna Gregory at times includes her early modern detective, Thomas Chaloner (mid-seventeenth century), and there are occasional forays into the nineteenth century. The books all conclude with an epilogue by one of the authors that brings the story up to the present.

In the first novel, *The Tainted Relic* (2005), the object that connects the stories is a sliver of the True Cross that has been cursed by Barzak, its Arab keeper, whose family has guarded the relic for centuries. In 1100, the crusaders have taken Jerusalem and slaughtered most of its inhabitants. Before his death, Barzak condemns to death anyone who handles the piece of wood, a fate that occurs as soon as he or she parts from it. The relic travels from Jerusalem to Rome and eventually to England, where its appearance in the various periods and locations of each medieval detective causes a spate of unexplained deaths. For example, a chapman found beaten to death by outlaws outside Exeter in 1194, in Sir John de Wolfe's bailiwick, manages to gasp "Barzak" before he dies, referring to the curse that has claimed his life soon after the relic was stolen from him (Medieval Murderers, *Tainted Relic* 51). Crowner John discovers who has killed the peddler, and then the outlaw who took the relic, correctly attributing the deaths to the greed of the thieves and not to the cursed sliver of wood. Nevertheless, while "still sceptical about Barzak's curse, [John] thought it well to humour Thomas's concerns and leave the tube unopened" (Medieval Murderers, *Tainted Relic* 107)—thereby avoiding the curse himself—and he arranges for it to be sent to Tewkesbury Abbey.

"The Medieval Murderers" do not rely solely upon objects as their overarching device, however. In *House of Shadows* (2007), the focus is Bermondsey Priory, located on the south bank of the Thames, across from the Tower of London. Founded in 1089, the establishment survived until the dissolution of the monasteries in the sixteenth century. All of the medieval detectives visit the Priory for one reason or another and confront the illicit deaths that occur within its precincts.

The books are a successful collaborative effort and the authors' writing styles work well together to produce more or less seamless narratives. It is not clear, however, whether this cohesiveness is due to a concerted effort towards synergistic writing, or whether it instead highlights the formulaic nature of medieval crime fiction more generally. Inevitably, there are occasional lapses in continuity such as the scene in which Bernard Knight's John de Wolfe rides alongside the Thames towards Southwark "to look again at London Bridge, which they had crossed less than a couple of months ago" (Medieval Murderers, *House of Shadows* 41). In the next "Act" (as the novels are structured), Ian Morson's William Falconer also mentions that London Bridge in 1270 was "built only twenty years earlier" (Medieval Murderers, *House of Shadows* 89). A perceptive reader will note the inconsistent dating, since de Wolfe observed the bridge in 1196. It is not clear that either author is correct in this instance, since a local enterprising priest, Peter de Colechurch, initiated construction of the stone London Bridge in 1176 to replace the rickety old wooden bridge and it took thirty-three years to complete, opening in 1209. So, it seems doubtful that de Wolfe would have been able to cross the unfinished bridge in 1196, while Falconer was looking at a structure completed at least sixty years' previously. This is, of course, a rather petty quibble; these criticisms are easy to level at all types of historical fiction. They seem more striking here, perhaps, because these authors' individual series generally offer much more exacting standards of accuracy. The success of the collaboration does seem to come at a certain cost to the authenticity of the medieval landscape that the "The Medieval Murderers" construct.

In addition to collaboration, the emergence of parody is another sign that a genre has embedded itself into contemporary popular culture. Parodies have existed since the mock-epic poetry of Ancient Greece; indeed, Robert Chambers suggests tongue-in-cheek that "the mock epic came first and that the epic is its noble, stately child shorn of its original parodic components" (13). Parody is often a complex and sophisticated reimagining of artistic forms that may encompass satire and irony. As discussed briefly in Chapter One, Linda Hutcheon ascribes significant postmodernist power to parody and its ability to critique the past through ironic revisitation (*Politics* 93; *Power* 39). Parody can also, more benignly, simply and gently mock serious literature or other cultural products for humorous effect. Either way, parody will not work if its target's conventions are not understood. In its simplest form, parody identifies the oddities within the style or subject matter of a preexisting conventional model, magnifies those quirks and combines them with its own "bizarre or inappropriate material" to create a "new context while maintaining an identifiable connection with the model" (Chambers 20).

The parodist "Howard of Warwick," pseudonym of author Howard Matthews, stumbled across some old parchment fragments that recount the experiences of Brother Hermitage, "a monk more medieval than detective, who nonetheless solves mysteries—somehow" (*Howard*). According to Howard, after years of research, "the tales of Brother Hermitage have become the world's bestselling comedy historical who-done-its," although the author concedes, "it's not a very crowded field" (*Howard*). So far, there are ten novels in The Chronicles of Brother Hermitage series, with an additional volume of short stories and three spin-off novels concerning Domesday Book and Magna Carta (the latter produced to tie-in with the Great Charter's 800th anniversary in June 2016). The novels are self-consciously satirical in their treatment of both Brother Hermitage and the medieval world. In order for this humor to work, however, there is an underlying assumption that readers can recognize the conventions of medieval crime fiction that Howard is parodying.

While Eco's *The Name of the Rose* uses complex parody to play with the conventions of literary analysis, detective fiction and postmodernist literature, Howard of Warwick deploys simple parody to try to make his audience laugh. Brother Hermitage is a woefully incompetent detective, who only survives because his companion, Wat—weaver of pornographic tapestries—frequently intervenes. While staging a reconstruction of the first murder the pair tries to solve, Hermitage suggests retrieving the body of the old monk who had died in order to lend the scene "some authenticity" and Wat must point out that "a days-old rotting corpse would be neither authentic nor pleasant" (Howard, *Heretics of De'Ath* ch. 18, loc. 3839). When the opportunity arises to present the solution to the crime in front of an audience that includes King Harold, the Earl of Northumbria, and his own abbot (in true golden-age crime fiction fashion), Hermitage freezes, looks behind him for another monk whom the king may be addressing and begins with an unpropitious "Erm" (Howard, *Heretics of De'Ath* ch. 18, loc. 3992).

The series is peppered with anachronistic language, absurdist situations and a mocking tone in which wry observations about medieval life are frequently made:

> The King's own person was not of course the person of the King. The King's person consisted of about fifty people all of whom had very particular jobs. Most of these involved stopping anyone else getting anywhere near the actual King himself [Howard, *Heretics of De'Ath* loc. 3701].

As is becoming a more common practice, Matthews self-published his first novel and uploaded it to Amazon, where it and subsequent iterations slowly gained traction. Matthews' premise is amusing, and he pokes gentle fun at both detective fiction and those historical novels that tend to take their periods very seriously: as the author-supplied synopsis to *The Garderobe of Death*

(2012) warns, "If you are looking for a poignant evocation of the medieval world, an insightful exploration of the characters of the time, buy a different book. Ellis Peters is quite good" (*Howard*). Wat the weaver takes on an apprentice, Cwen, in the third book of the series, who forms an integral part of the investigative team. Although the humorous writing is sometimes forced, and the similarity of plotlines, standard characters, and insistence on exploring the messy Middle Ages does wear rather thin after ten or more books, Matthews' parodic endeavor is creditable and especially welcome for what its existence reveals about the state of medieval crime fiction as an entrenched, stable genre.

In a discussion about medievalist cinema, Nickolas Haydock notes the number of films that effectively deploy "the precocious modernity of detective clerics" (32). He describes these characters in terms that encapsulate the role that religious detectives perform in medieval crime fiction:

> These figures embody the contradictions inherent in the modern wish to know the medieval past directly from a perspective that is at once within and yet impervious to its radical alterity [32].

In addition to the secular constraints generated by the political and social realities of the Middle Ages, these detectives are members of religious orders where entrenched beliefs insist upon the possibility of divine or diabolical intervention. Consequently, medieval religious detectives must carefully navigate these systems in order not to disrupt the medieval world created by their authors.

Many of the novels featuring religious medieval detectives conform to the conventions of golden-age or clue-puzzle fiction that flourished between the two world wars. Restricting criminal activity to the confines of an abbey, castle, ship or a town acknowledges the relatively limited freedom of movement most medieval *religieux* have, as well as ensuring that the list of suspects remains small and that the trail of evidence is easily followed by both detective and reader.

However, the success of the detective relies upon a certain amount of critical distance from the crime that he or she is investigating, as well as the ability to apply other skills to interpreting the evidence, such as medical knowledge or experience with human psychology. In order to achieve this perspective, many medieval religious detectives have unusual backgrounds and have often come to their monastery or parish later in life. Moreover, they frequently endure significant crises of faith either before or during their time as detective, brought about by experiencing the horrors of war or witnessing the cruelty that individuals are capable of inflicting on one another. Both Bascot de Marins and Brother Athelstan have past experiences that profoundly shake their faith, while at the same time equipping them for their roles as investigators into secular crimes. Rogue priest Nicholas Barber escapes the dullness of the scribal tasks that institutionalized religion has imposed upon him, instead discovering that he can do God's work more effectively by performing onstage than by preaching from a pulpit.

While these detectives almost always successfully combine seeking a secular solution to mysterious and criminal occurrences with maintaining the tenets of the religious systems that surround them, the faith-oriented medieval world is not able to withstand too much intervention from this modern interloper. In Fuller's postmodern novel, all of the characters are trapped within their own webs of superstition, paranoia, fantasy, and, in the case of the Abbot, a heretical obsession with the soul. When an outsider arrives to investigate suspicious occurrences, the interrogative pressure causes the fragile medieval landscape to collapse, destroying the detective in the process and leaving the remaining characters stranded on an island shrouded in confusion and despair.

Nevertheless, despite these nagging incursions of modernity that are arguably unavoidable, these authors strive to maintain the authenticity of their depiction of the Middle Ages. Consequently, their religious detectives often twist themselves through convoluted evidentiary pathways in order to ensure that their solutions to crimes do not threaten their tightly held beliefs. And observing this process is one of the great joys for readers of medieval crime fiction.

Chapter Four

An Unsuitable Job
for a Medieval Woman

While the preceding two chapters have focused on male medieval detectives, this chapter considers the enterprising female sleuths who feature in medieval crime fiction. From the relative independence of Chapter Two's secular investigators—particularly those of noble rank—to the more constrained *religieux* of Chapter Three, these detectives have negotiated constraints ranging from the demands of feudal overlords to the obligatory performance of the daily canonical offices. However, none of these detectives has faced obstacles such as those arising from simply being a woman in the Middle Ages.

Over the past decades, feminist scholarship has successfully challenged the ostensibly patriarchal conservatism of both medieval studies and crime fiction. In the case of medieval studies, scholars have searched for, located and recuperated the previously "absent" voices of the historically marginalized, including women, the poor, the young and the multiracial. In crime fiction, feminist criticism has identified the important contribution women writers have made to the development of the genre from its inception, as well as explored the more subversive appropriation of its conventions by authors such as Patricia Highsmith, Sara Paretsky and Denise Mina.

However, medieval crime fiction offers its own challenges to critics attempting to reframe both the genre and the period along more feminist lines. Medieval women detectives are often presented as unusually knowing and well-informed about the structures and ideologies that constrain women's behavior, and the popularity of women characters who seem to break through the constrictions of medieval patriarchy mirrors a similar trend in medieval historical fiction more generally. At the same time, almost without exception, medieval female detectives rely heavily upon a male protector, partner or mentor without whom they would inevitably fail in their investigations. This reliance suggests that while medieval crime fiction authors might wish to assign their female protagonists autonomy, the Middle Ages that they carefully recreate instead forecloses the possibility of unfettered feminine agency. Similarly, an overly resourceful and independent female detective potentially magnifies the literary device's inherent modernity and threatens to sabotage the genuineness of her medieval landscape. Medieval crime fiction authors and readers, as evinced throughout this book, privilege authenticity above other narratological investments. As Rosemary Erickson Johnsen states, "Accuracy must not be sacrificed, or the feminist motivation will not be well served, but the medieval world's circumscribed roles for women can make it difficult to generate any feminist material at all" (22). A central concern of this chapter is to consider whether *any* medieval crime fiction novel successfully engages with this feminist project. Conversely, it also considers the contribution that the representation of women in medieval crime fiction delivers to both medieval feminist scholarship and feminist crime fiction. What follows is a brief overview of the feminist scholarship within both crime fiction and medieval studies, ahead of a detailed examination of the wonderful women who solve crime in the Middle Ages.

Feminist Crime Fiction

Most critics now acknowledge that women have played an important role in crime fiction from its inception.[1] As Lee Horsley notes, "the role of women in the crime and detective fiction of earlier decades is often more central and complex than is assumed" (243). Merja Makinen goes further and claims that the conventional assumption that detective fiction is a male-based genre

> ignores the fact that women have consistently written detective fiction, and in large numbers, and that the character of the woman detective, or the "lady detective" as she was described in the titles, was a mainstay of detective fiction for writers of both sexes from the 1860s through to the Golden Age [92].

Makinen reminds her readers that "between [Gaboriau's] Lecoq and [Conan Doyle's] Holmes, came Anna Katherine [*sic*] Green" (95). Green was born in Brooklyn in 1846 and she published her enormously successful first novel, *The Leavenworth Case*, in 1878. Between 1897 and 1900, Green wrote her Amelia Butterworth novels, featuring the fiftyish, upper-middle class, redoubtable Miss Butterworth, who disingenuously states in the first line of the first novel (*That Affair Next Door*), "I am not an inquisitive woman, but…" (15). Miss Butterworth certainly is inquisitive and effectively mobilizes this trait in order to solve the murder of a young woman that occurred next door.

In doing so, Miss Butterworth also outshines the patronizing and condescending Inspector Gryce—the protagonist in several of Green's other detective novels, introduced in *The Leavenworth Case*. Anticipating Agatha
Christie's Miss Marple, Miss Butterworth and other spinster sleuths avoided
the fate that young women detectives faced at the hands of their male authors:
"by the end of the novels, these women not only find detective work unsuitable for a woman but also are married off by their creators" (Ross 78).[2] Nevertheless, as Makinen notes, casting elderly spinsters such as Miss Butterworth,
Miss Marple, or Patricia Wentworth's retired governess, Miss Silver, as detectives ensures that their "age prevents their sexuality creating a conflict of representation with their effective ratiocination" (101).

It was not until 1972 that P.D. James created the first professional female
private detective: Cordelia Gray in *An Unsuitable Job for a Woman*. Despite
its titular promise to challenge the patriarchal normativity of detective fiction,
Stephen Knight characterizes this novel as "at best a tentative foray into feminism" and notes that "James herself seems to have been less than committed"
(*Crime Fiction* 164): the sequel to Cordelia's first adventure came after ten
years and much gentle badgering by fans.[3]

However, "regendering the gender" is not simply about substituting a
female for a male detective, as Horsley cautions:

> The recovery of female subjectivity is more complex than this: there are other key roles
> that female characters occupy. The revisionings of the female transgressor—and indeed
> victim—are as significant as the better-known series which recast the investigative role
> [243–44].

Moreover, Horsley admits that "it is unquestionably hard-boiled fiction that
has proven to be the most compelling model and, for the purposes of self-
definition, the key point of reference for post–1970s women crime writers"
(248). Sara Paretsky pioneered this appropriation with her formidable private
investigator, V.I. Warshawski, who admirably replicates the toughness of the
hardboiled type (Knight, *Crime Fiction* 168). More recently, the success in
both print and television iterations of Patricia Cornwell's Kay Scarpetta and
Kathy Reichs's Temperance Brennan suggests a comparable feminist intervention into the laboratories of traditionally male forensic investigators.

Feminist authors have also challenged the heteronormativity of traditional crime fiction through the introduction of investigators such as Katherine V. Forrest's Kate Delafield, generally acknowledged as the first lesbian
detective, appearing in 1984. Other authors soon followed, including Barbara
Wilson, Val McDermid, Claire McNab and Nikki Baker, all of whom "were
published in the 1980s by small lesbian presses such as Naiad and Seal"
(Lake).[4]

There was a similar challenge to crime fiction's historical whiteness with the emergence of ethnically diverse authors and detectives, particularly in the 1990s. As Maureen T. Reddy states, "While the white feminist writers critique the intense masculinity of the hardboiled tradition, for instance, the women writers of colour critique both that masculinity and the normative whiteness of the genre" ("Women Detectives" 202). Black female detectives are, by and large, amateurs—one exception is Valerie Wilson Wesley's ex-police officer, turned private investigator Tamara Hayle—and often confront issues of class in addition to struggling against racism and sexism. BarbaraNeely's [sic] overtly political series features the ironically and pointedly named Blanche White who is middle-aged, overweight and works as a maid for a wealthy white family. While Blanche's lowly position and dismissive treatment by the household deliberately recalls America's ongoing racial and class conflict, "her invisibility in the eyes of her employers affords her the space and opportunity to turn her ratiocinative powers towards uncovering the web of murder and blackmail in which she, inevitably, finds herself implicated" (Pepper 222). Neely's character fulfills the conventions of "detective-by-default," thrust into the role in order to defend herself from erroneous accusations and to escape becoming a convenient scapegoat upon whom to pin the crime. This scenario is common in medieval crime fiction, particularly for women detectives, who often set out to solve a crime in a last, desperate attempt to save themselves or someone close to them who has been falsely accused.

Katrin Sieg's analysis of German author Doris Gercke's detective series illustrates feminist crime fiction's ability to critique contemporary ideological concerns and challenge antifeminist structures. Sieg argues that by linking fascism with globalization, "Gercke shows the resurgence of a neofascist politics and a patriarchal order resting on women's sexual subordination and economic exploitation" (142). In *Genghis Khan's Daughter* (1996), for example, Gercke compares the state-organized violence of the Nazi occupation of Odessa and massacre of its Jewish population "to the privatized violence unleashed by the criminally run fashion industry and the economic restructuring of Ukrainian agriculture in the present" (Sieg 145). Sieg describes this formulation as "the antifascist performative" and claims that it "reiterates history in order to incite both grief and vigilance" (147). *Genghis Khan's Daughter* features Bella Block, Gercke's detective, but also introduces a new character type to crime fiction: Tolgonai, "the feminist vigilante" (146). Tolgonai refuses to accept the two alternatives upon which her family insists— resign herself to her rapist-husband or commit suicide—and instead converts her experiences into a militancy that transforms her into a terrorist. However, as Sieg perceptively observes, Tolgonai "is less a heroic embodiment of resistance than a symptom of the lack of political alternatives" (151).

Sieg's account of the important political work that contemporary feminist crime fiction can achieve is suggestive for medieval female detectives. Most women in the Middle Ages faced choices as stark Tolgonai, with few opportunities for exercising social or political agency. Unlike Tolgonai, however, the women in medieval crime fiction are rarely given the option of militant vigilantism. Indeed, very few female detectives in any period of the Middle Ages can conform to hardboiled crime fiction conventions. These women must navigate their medieval landscape with more subtlety than their masculine counterparts—who already face significant restraints—in order to avoid the anachronism that could potentially dismantle their authors' credible recreation of the Middle Ages. This quest for authenticity precludes the kind of feminine agency exemplified by Gercke's Tolgonai. Instead, female medieval detectives must operate within an innately antifeminist patriarchal feudalism while retaining their own feminist identity; a challenging balancing act necessary in order to appeal to modern readers.

Horsley points out that while "the chick dicks" of recent feminist crime fiction appropriate instrumental qualities from their male counterparts such as physical prowess, tenacity and self-reliance, "What changes most markedly are the social and moral contexts within which these qualities are brought into play" (249). In other words, while the detective's "masculine" agency is important, equally crucial is the "female" community that "is not just a sustaining presence for the protagonist but the linchpin both of plot and of the protagonist's own sense of self-definition" (250). While feminist authors successfully appropriate hardboiled crime fiction, they nevertheless eschew the conventional loner status of the private eye, working outside institutional and familial structures. Rather, they depict detectives who are fiercely and insistently independent, but remain connected to their communities in a way that many male private eyes do not. Medieval female detectives similarly emphasize the importance of community as both a motivating factor and a supportive space. However, while this shared sense of community suggests a generic relationship, a niggling question remains: are medieval women detectives ever feminist without being catastrophically anachronistic? And what does the answer (or answers) to this question mean for the success or otherwise of these medieval crime fiction novels? As this chapter will show, medieval female detectives rely more frequently than their male counterparts upon supernatural intervention—or the appearance thereof—in order to finesse their ostensible lack of historical agency.

Feminist Medieval Studies

In 1997, Joan Ferrante wrote that women have had roles in political, religious and cultural developments from the earliest centuries of the Christian era, "not continuously or ubiquitously but frequently and consistently enough to make it clear that medieval history in any form from the Middle Ages to the present which does not include the role of women is not a true history" (3). Ferrante's assertion reflects the crucial work undertaken in the 1980s and 1990s by feminist scholars who began "to find terms with which to suture the 'pastness' of the Middle Ages with current [feminist] theory" (Stanbury 364). This work has led to seminal studies of medieval female authors such as Christine de Pizan and Margery Kempe, as well as reconsiderations of the depiction of women by male writers and deft analyses of medieval constructions of gender.[5] More recently, Geraldine Heng reiterated the challenge that faces medieval scholars whose material was written centuries ago, "in historical contexts and social conditions almost unimaginable today" (53). In Heng's elegant analogy, "a feminist aesthetics of reading" is "the dance of negotiating a delicate balance between resisting and acquiescing to what we read" (53). This dance is necessary because

> Committed to feminist principles and ideals, feminist medievalists invariably require a critical performance that respects the integrity of the text, and its place in history, by acknowledging the delicate choreography of meaning-making in which the feminist reader and the medieval text both participate, each possessing specific kinds of authority and knowledge, in the moment of reading [54].

Scholars such as M.C. Bodden have reasserted Ferrante and Heng's stance by demonstrating that "women were actively engaged in cultural practices and speech strategies that ... appear to be subversive in undermining [patriarchal] ideology," despite "extensive evidence indicating a wholesale suppression of early women's speech" (2). Bodden's wide-ranging analysis of court depositions, clerical writing, Geoffrey Chaucer, Margery Kempe and the anonymous female author of *The Assembly of Ladies* positions women's voices "as a site of revolt" and she acknowledges her debt "to a generation of scholars engaged in publishing accurate representation of medieval and early modern English women" (143).

Tracy Adams notes medieval literary studies' conventional divide between the "courtly" lady and the "fabliau" lady, observing that "the modern reader of medieval literature is trained by literary criticism to perceive 'courtly' and 'fabliau' ladies as type and anti-type" (81). Adams proposes that one feminine model in medieval narrative that has been overlooked is that of the "clever woman" and she examines two French fabliaux that resist categorization within a "courtly" / "anti-courtly" framework by inviting its readers to focus upon the cleverness of its characters (82). "Cleverness," in Adams's construction, not only "evens out relationships between unequal partners" (82), it also transcends genre (83), enacting a challenge to traditional power structures in obscene, religious and lay works (91). These scholars embraced, and continue to embrace, the task of recovering the voices of medieval women from the margins of masculinist historiography and the entrenched trope of the idealized, unobtainable, and silent lady of courtly love convention.

Adams's identification of the "clever" lady in medieval literature is clearly a productive one for medieval crime fiction. All literary detectives share a particular form of intelligence that assists them in the logical processing of evidence. But, in addition, female medieval detectives make use of a "cleverness" that affords them skills to navigate the predominately male power structures designed to suppress their agency. In this way, medieval crime fiction authors contribute to the ongoing recovery of a variety of female voices from the Middle Ages by medieval feminist scholarship.

Rosemary Erickson Johnsen is one of very few critics to consider the intersection between feminism, the historical novel and crime fiction. Her study, *Contemporary Feminist Historical Crime Fiction*, contains a chapter on medieval crime fiction in which she considers the novels of Candace Robb, Margaret Frazer and, in considerably more depth, Sharan Newman. In the case of Robb and Frazer, Johnsen includes their novels as examples of feminist historical crime novels, but then rather confusingly critiques their feminist credentials. For example, in Robb's series "The feminist content provided tends to be incidental, rather than central, to the plots and the narrative's [sic] focalization" (24). Similarly, "The Frazer series features a female sleuth, Frevisse, but both plots and characterization are weak in feminist terms" (26). Referring to Frazer's *The Squire's Tale*, Johnsen asserts "the particulars of Frazer's development can seem actively misogynistic" (26). These two examples illustrate Johnsen's tendency to restrict her analysis to novels by female authors, which then fail to deliver her anticipated feminist agenda. This restriction leads to some glaring omissions, the most obvious of which is the absence of Peter Tremayne's unquestionably proto-feminist detective, Sister Fidelma.

Peter Tremayne's Sister Fidelma and the Politics of Historiography

One of medieval crime fiction's most popular female detectives is Peter Tremayne's Sister Fidelma.[6] Tremayne, in the comprehensive "Author's Notes" that accompany each of his novels, regularly insists that Fidelma is a realistic portrayal of what was possible for a woman to achieve in seventh-century Ireland. Sister Fidelma, in addition to being a nun, is a *dálaigh* (advocate) of the Irish law courts, committed to investigating legal disputes and discovering "truth," a highly prized concept in Celtic Ireland. She is also sister to Colgú of Cashel, the King of Muman, one of Ireland's five kingdoms. Fidelma's royal blood, her position as *dálaigh*, and her religious status afford her authority in almost every situation she encounters. Fidelma is a product of the enlightened environment that Tremayne carefully constructs; she deploys her considerable talents to solve complicated and obscure mysteries, for which she is famous throughout Ireland. Sister Fidelma's desire to restore order is reminiscent of the conservative detectives of the golden age and Tremayne's novels generally conform to these familiar conventions: the narrative is often contained within a castle, an abbey, on board a ship, a town or village; the list of suspects remains limited; the reader and Fidelma discover clues simultaneously; and Fidelma usually presents her solution to a gathering of the suspects in a stage-managed setting reminiscent of Hercule Poirot.

Fidelma is observant, intelligent, rational, brave and determined. Her disavowal of divine or diabolical intervention into her cases is characteristic of medieval detectives: one of her favorite tenets is "What is the supernatural but nature that has not yet been explained?" which is in keeping with Tremayne's idealized Celtic enlightenment (*Haunted Abbot* 131). However, Fidelma is also arrogant, aloof and waspish when frustrated with the progress of her investigation or the stupidity of others. The main target for Fidelma's shortness of temper is Brother Eadulf, a Saxon monk she meets while attending the Synod of Whitby (664 CE) as a member of the delegation representing the interests of the Irish Church.

The first novel, *Absolution by Murder* (1994), chronicles the events at Whitby, in which Tremayne establishes important tensions that characterize the series. These include the conflict between the Roman and Irish Churches over issues such as the date of Easter and clerical celibacy, the animosity between the "barbarian" Saxons and the "enlightened" Irish, and the perennial opposition between men and women. Eadulf is a member of the Roman Church and a Saxon, two patriarchal systems despised by Fidelma. Despite this apparent incompatibility, over the course of the series Fidelma and Eadulf are betrothed, have a son, and eventually marry. However, Fidelma gradually comes to believe that even the comparatively tolerant Celtic church is incompatible with her independence of mind and she decides to relinquish her position within the church, renounce her vows and focus on her career as a lawyer for her brother, King Colgú.

"Peter Tremayne" is the pseudonym for London-based Celtic historian and journalist, Peter Berresford Ellis, who deploys his knowledge of the period to great effect in his novels. While much of the rest of Europe was struggling out of the so-called "Dark Ages," the seventh century "was a period of brilliance for Celtic culture, especially that of Ireland" (Luehrs and Luehrs 46). The renowned monastic libraries and medical schools attracted students from across the continent, and Irish missionaries were converting much of northern Europe to Christianity. Tremayne's overarching concern is to promote the Celtic Middle Ages as a proto-Enlightenment period and he therefore portrays Fidelma's world as a place of justice and learning, tolerance and freedom, secularism and rationalism. Ellis's popular history monographs promote the same Celtic ideal that suffuses the Sister Fidelma series. He argues that the enlightened, liberal civilization of the Celts across Europe was bludgeoned to death by a combination of barbarian invasion by Germanic tribes and the encroaching influence of patriarchal Roman Christianity. He is particularly concerned with revising the received history of Celtic women, insisting that theirs was a significantly more valued and easier existence than that of their Saxon counterparts, demonstrating his awareness of, but perhaps overstating, the continuing influence of early Irish matriarchal traditions. In *Celtic Women* (1995), Ellis cites examples of women who were able to own property, receive the same inheritance as men, and participate in higher education. Indeed, Ellis states, "There seemed few professions that women could not join, nor was there any barrier to their rising to prominence in such professions as they chose" (*Celtic Women* 116). He describes women as war leaders, physicians, artisans, poets and judges.

Critics have attributed this nostalgia for an ancient Celtic utopia to Tremayne's desire to use his fiction to intervene into contemporary historiographic debates about Irish nationalism. The nationalist school, of which Tremayne is a proponent, assumes the existence of a continuous Irish identity, struggling through centuries of oppression towards nationhood. The revisionists, on the other hand, "call for an Irish history that is more value-free and demythologized, a scholarship less concerned with grand heroes and great villains" (Luehrs and Luehrs 56). Other critics have pointed out Tremayne's selective use of historical sources: Carole M. Cusack, in particular, is scathing in her assessment of Tremayne's depiction of marriage between monks and nuns, mixed religious houses, the medieval Irish legal system, and the interaction between Christianity and paganism in the early Middle Ages. Cusack disputes Tremayne's claim to be "a qualified scholarly authority," dismissing his honorary doctorate and pointing out his failure to cite sources and/or his distortion of those sources he does use ("Fiction" 337). Of course, Tremayne is writing fiction and so Cusack's attack on his research may appear a little harsh in denying him any artistic license. However, Cusack's point is that scholars *should* be calling historical novelists to account: "It is unfortunate that academics do not generally believe that it is a valuable exercise to write critical appraisals of popular writers and pseudo-scholars" ("Fiction" 339). Furthermore, while Cusack acknowledges that "The Sister Fidelma novels are just that, novels," she challenges Tremayne's own claims—in historical notes and through the International Fidelma Society—"that his portrayal of early medieval Ireland is the genuine article" ("Fiction" 340).

With regard to Ellis's nonfiction work, academic historians consistently challenge his historiography, expressing similar concerns to Cusack's. Lisa M. Bitel, for example, opens her review of *Celtic Women* impatiently: "Peter Berresford Ellis has written a rather silly book about women in Celtic societies" (427). Bitel describes the book as "pseudo-scholarly," "historiographically unsound," and she particularly lambasts his deployment of sources as inconsistent and misinterpreted (428). In a milder critique, Katharine W. Swett acknowledges Ellis's engagement with "the tradition of gradual decline from a freer, more egalitarian past for Celtic women," but she is critical of Ellis's lack of scholarly discipline, calling the book "at once too general and too detailed," with no well-organized evaluations of the sources he employs (224). James Allan Evans reviews Ellis's book *Celt and Roman: The Celts in Italy* (1998) and similarly notes a lack of footnotes and "curious errors," concluding that "Ellis's book is good but it could have been better" (522). Finally, Charles D. Hamilton describes the same work as "avowedly sympathetic to the Celts" and points out that "Ellis takes pains to convince the reader that in some respects, Celtic civilization was superior to that of the Romans" (135). Like all academic reviewers, Hamilton also comments on Ellis's cavalier approach to references. While these reviews refer to Ellis's nonfiction books, they illustrate the broader context of the Celtic-centric, uncritical bias that informs Tremayne's medieval crime fiction novels.

A significant theme of both Tremayne's fiction and Ellis's historiography is the tension between Celts and Saxons. In the Sister Fidelma series, this tension manifests on those occasions when Fidelma travels to England, at the time a conglomerate of Saxon kingdoms. In the following exchange with Eadulf in the kingdom of the South Folk, Fidelma displays her unshakeable belief in the superiority of Celtic culture:

> "It is no good my pretending that I like this country with its customs, Eadulf. I find it a place of violent and intemperate nature. A place of extremes, aggressive, presumptuous and inconsiderate of others."
>
> ...

Eadulf flushed in annoyance.

"I do not find this worthy of you, Fidelma," he said sulkily. "There is war, murder, hate and jealousy in your own land, yet you do not condemn it as barbaric."

"Because we have evolved a law system, a social system, in which such things are not the normal way of life. I fear that in your land, Eadulf, even the law seems entrenched in the brutality of life" [Tremayne, *Haunted Abbot* 281–82].

Tremayne's political objective here needs little elaboration. However, what is striking about this passage, and others like it that regularly appear throughout the series, is the similarity of language and theme with the non-fiction, historical writing of Peter Berresford Ellis. In *Celt and Saxon* (1993), Ellis provides the "authority" for Fidelma's views regarding Saxon culture:

Whether fighting the Celts or fighting with each other, the Saxons were constantly at war. A state of perpetual disorder seemed to exist. Blood feuds were common and the mortality rate was high [52].

He goes on to contrast the place of women in Celtic and Saxon culture:

In such a [Saxon] society, women do not appear to have been allowed any prominent role. They are shown as passive, suffering hardship and discrimination but doing little about it…. The Saxon queen appears mostly as a ceremonial object in a male-dominated world.

    …

The woman's place in Saxon society was in total contrast with the happier position of her Celtic sisters…A Celtic woman] could be elected as chief, lead her clan into battle in defence of the territory and, in law, she remained mistress of all she had brought into a marital partnership. She could divorce or hold any office a man could hold [53–54].

The binaries evident in his formulation of early Irish history are not only present in his fiction, they are overly exaggerated: the civilized Celts oppose the barbaric Saxons; the tolerant Irish Church opposes the restrictive Roman Church; the proto-feminist Celtic culture opposes the misogyny of the Saxon kingdoms; and so on. In other words, the Sister Fidelma series is a calculated interpellation of Peter Berresford Ellis's historiographic ideology into the influential platform of his enormously popular fiction series.

Fidelma's decision to forsake her position as a nun emerges from the conflict between her religious calling and her lawyerly profession, a conflict that has always troubled her. Her friend, Abbess Lioch, understands this, telling Fidelma, "'I was not surprised to hear that you had formally left the religious … you were always better suited to law than the religious life'" (Tremayne, *Devil's Seal* 75). Eadulf remains ordained within the Roman church and is not used to seeing his wife dressed as an Eoghanacht princess: "Although Fidelma had quit the religious, Eadulf had not and so still kept to his Roman tonsure and robes, though at times he felt a little drab at his wife's side" (Tremayne, *Devil's Seal* 29). Despite Eadulf's adherence to the church and loyalty to his Saxon people, he gradually becomes more Celtic—more "civilized"—over the course of the series and his behavior and attitude contrast more and more starkly with other Saxons who occasionally visit the kingdom of Muman, including, on one notable occasion, his younger brother.

Tremayne's Sister Fidelma novels are certainly among the most successful of medieval crime fiction. The series enjoys a dedicated following and boasts passionate fans who participate in The International Sister Fidelma Society, founded in 2001, an impressive organization with its own journal, *The Brehon*, and regular pseudo-scholarly conferences that take place in Fidelma's home town of Cashel.[7] Moreover, atypically for medieval crime fiction, Edward J. Rielly and David Robert Wooten edited a 2012 collection of essays examining the Sister Fidelma series, its early Irish context and its place in crime fiction genre more broadly. Although the book's primary purpose is to function as a paean to Tremayne—the editors' preface is particularly sycophantic—it nevertheless contains some perceptive essays that grapple with the situation of women in Celtic Ireland, as well as surveys of Fidelma's contribution to the early-twenty-first century flourishing of Irish crime writing and how she compares to other female detectives (Rielly and Wooten).

The Fidelma Effect: Cora Harrison's Mara and Philip Freeman's Sister Deirdre

As Rielly and Wooten point out, "one obvious literary descendant of Sister Fidelma is a female Brehon named Mara" (4). Set in the first decade of the sixteenth century, Cora Harrison's Burren Mysteries series breaches the temporal parameters set out in the introduction to this book. However, this appearance of another female Irish detective upholding the same ancient Brehon laws that Fidelma revered almost one thousand years earlier warrants a brief mention here. And, indeed, the novels all feature the tagline, "A Mystery of Medieval Ireland," indicating again the arbitrariness of imposing temporal limits upon history. Fidelma's kingdom is Muman, an area which is now in County Tipperary, but Harrison's series is set on the western coast of Ireland in County Clare and encompasses a limestone expanse called the "Burren," a name retained today. Like Fidelma, Harrison's detective is a Brehon, or lawyer, responsible for administering the law in the Burren, as well as supervising the law school of Cahermachaghten. As she explains in an epigraph to her first chapter, Harrison has found the name of her detective, Mara, in one of the British Library's manuscripts, Egerton 88, in which there is a document dating from the beginning of the sixteenth century that contains case notes and judgments signed "by Mara, a female judge, or Brehon, from this era" (*My Lady Judge* 3). MS Egerton 88 also names the ruler of the Burren at this time as King Turlough Donn O'Brien.

The Burren is an expanse of exposed limestone and labyrinths of caves, an evocative landscape well-suited for locating a crime narrative. Harrison beautifully illustrates the connection between past and present in the first line of her first novel's prologue: "It was then, as it is now, a land of grey stone" (*My Lady Judge* 1). This is a clever opening because it is not immediately clear to which "then" and which "now" Harrison is referring. She is introducing the action of her novel (indeed, her series) by performing a doubled temporal move: yes, the landscape has not changed in millennia, but what seems ancient today was just as ancient to the people who lived in the Burren in 1509. Harrison reminds her modern readers that the historical period they travel to in the course of these novels has its own history.

While Mara is Fidelma's Brehon counterpart in the distant future, Philip Freeman sets his series a century earlier than Tremayne's, and he recalls Fidelma's complicated religious vocation for his young nun, Sister Deirdre. Fidelma's dilemma is how to navigate the conflict between her dedication to a secular, rational "truth" and the demands of her Christian faith, while Deirdre finds herself torn between the influence of her Druidic upbringing and her life as a novice in St. Brigid's Monastery in Kildare (probably not coincidentally, this is the same religious house in which Fidelma was a novice). Freeman is a Professor of Classics who has taught at a number of universities across the United States and so brings a similarly credible claim to expertise as Tremayne. He has also written an impressive array of popular history books, ranging from biographies of Alexander the Great and Julius Caesar, to clever reformulations of the works of Cicero, to accounts of Celtic mythology and saints. The two authors do differ in one notable way: Freeman's "Afterwords" are markedly short, just one page, indicating that he does not feel the same impulse to provide detailed historical sources in the manner of Tremayne's essay-like epilogues. Freeman is an example of the intriguing cases in which "professional" historical scholars choose to fictionalize their expertise and embrace the opportunities of popular fiction; the possible motivations and consequences for which are explored more fully in Chapter Six with regard to Bruce Holsinger.

Both series do share an idealization of this early Irish world, as well as the independent minds and spirits of their medieval detectives. Sister Deirdre, like all the nuns of medieval crime fiction, is a challenging character for her abbess, Sister Anna, to manage, as she informs the young nun at the end of the first book in the series (*Saint Brigid's Bones* [2014]):

> Sister Deirdre, you have been a thorn in my side since you put on the veil. You resist authority, you lack discipline, and you seem to think the rules are something you need follow only at your convenience. When I put you in charge of finding these bones, I did so only because of your unique status outside these walls. You were willful and difficult then—qualities you still possess in abundance…. I'm not yet sure that you were meant to be a nun, but I will tolerate your disobedience on this particular occasion [Freeman, *Saint Brigid's Bones* 213].

This complaint about Deirdre's suitability for her vocation and her struggle to conform to the absolute obedience required by the monastery's strict rule is ubiquitous across medieval crime fiction and applies to both male and female *religieux*.

Deirdre's task in this first novel is to recover the monastery's precious collection of bones from one of Ireland's most beloved saints. The loss of the relics has put the monastery's survival into doubt and so Abbess Anna grudgingly assigns Deirdre the task of finding them because the young novice's noble, yet pagan, family background and her training as a bard allows her access to information and society from which others are excluded. Having discovered who stole the bones, Deirdre also demonstrates the golden-age characteristic of a deeply ingrained sense of natural justice that she chooses to heed: she decides there is nothing to be gained, and potential harm to be done, by revealing the perpetrator to the understandably frustrated abbess.

Freeman also offers an appealing image of Christian and Druid cooperation that recalls the religious tolerance of the Celtic church promoted by Tremayne. When the saint's relics are recovered, "Everyone from miles around came to celebrate, Christian or not" (Freeman, *Saint Brigid's Bones* 215). Deirdre's Druid grandmother is there, "sitting at another table with a few of the local druids and a couple of the older nuns she had known for years" (Freeman, *Saint Brigid's Bones* 216). In a similarly convivial scene, the second book in the series, *Sacrifice* (2015), opens with Deirdre visiting her grandmother to celebrate a May Day dinner with her guests: a priest, two other Druids (besides Deirdre's grandmother), and a nun. After an expository dialogue informing the reader about the different specialties that each of the Druid women practice (seer, astromancer, interpreter of dreams, bard), Father Ailbe, the Christian priest, is asked to bless the meal (Freeman, *Sacrifice* 6). The tolerance displayed by both religious adherents is undoubtedly idealized, although Freeman is recreating a time when Christian and Druid communities did interact. By Fidelma's time, just a hundred or so years later, the Druidic presence in Ireland is much less visible.

Feminism and Racial Tolerance: Adelia Aguilar and Catherine LeVendeur

Ariana Franklin's acclaimed series featuring Adelia Aguilar comprises four novels, the first of which introduces the young woman on the road from Salerno to Cambridge at King Henry II's request to investigate the deaths of several children. The final book in the Mistress of the Art of Death series is *The Assassin's Prayer*, published in 2010 before Franklin's death in 2011. In this novel, Adelia is tasked by Henry with accompanying his ten-year-old daughter, Joanna, from England to Palermo in Sicily in order to marry its king, William II. Adelia is returning to her roots through this journey, as she was trained as a doctor in Sicily's Salerno School of Medicine, "probably the only foundation in Christendom to take women as students" (Franklin, *Assassin's Prayer* 13).

Adelia has spent the last three books fighting to have her medical expertise accepted by the recalcitrant English and the intolerant Church, both of which prefer to believe the fiction that her attendant, Mansur, is the doctor and Adelia his assistant and translator. Mansur and Adelia were both born in Sicily, "that melting pot of races" (Franklin, *Assassin's Prayer* 13): she an abandoned baby of Greek heritage, adopted by a Jewish doctor and his Christian wife; he "once a lost boy with a beautiful voice whom the Latin Church had castrated so that he might retain it" (Franklin, *Assassin's Prayer* 13). Adelia's frustration is compellingly expressed by Franklin, even if a trace of anachronism attaches to Adelia's annoyance at the backwardness of her medieval context. Accused of remotely orchestrating through witchcraft the death of a laundress accompanying them on their journey, Adelia despairs of the lack of commonsense that surrounds her:

> *Witchcraft.* Always, *always*, since she'd left Salerno where they knew what she was and what she did and appreciated her for it, superstition had attached itself to her heels so that the skill she'd been granted to benefit mankind must be hidden by stratagems so wearying that she was sick of them…. She felt a terrible grief, for Brune [the murdered laundress], and for the science of reason that always lost to unreason [Franklin, *Assassin's Prayer* 170–71].

Adelia is subtly blackmailed by Henry into undertaking the journey to Palermo when he assures her that he will keep a close eye on her daughter, Almeisan (Allie), who has been placed with Queen Eleanor by Rowley Picot, Bishop of St. Albans, the girl's father and Adelia's lover. This arrangement has been made over Adelia's strong objections, which are also anchored in her innately modern outlook: "'Education? And what sort of education would she get with Eleanor? Needlework? Strumming a lyre? Gossiping? Courtly blasted love?"' (Franklin, *Assassin's Prayer* 29). Rowley and Adelia meet in the first novel of the series, *Mistress of the Art of Death* (2008), when he was Sir Rowley Picot and not yet a bishop. A former crusader and a dedicated follower of Henry II, Rowley works with Adelia to solve the conundrums Henry assigns them and they fall deeply in love. But the bonds of feudalism prove too difficult to break, and Rowley relinquishes Adelia to accept the powerful position of Bishop in order to serve Henry more ably. Adelia is in equal parts heartbroken, resentful and accepting of the politics that forced Rowley's decision. Notwithstanding the unusual circumstances and underlying tension, Rowley and Adelia—at Henry's insistence—work together over the next three books and their relationship remains strong, if unorthodox. Franklin is matter-of-fact about the fiction that was clerical celibacy during the Middle Ages, as noted by Adelia when referring to her "eccentric domesticity": "Scandalous, of course, but nobody in this remote part of England seemed to mind it; certainly Father Ignatius and Father John, both of them living with the mothers of their children, had not seen fit to report it to Adelia's great enemy, the Church" (Franklin, *Assassin's Prayer* 21).

Like the other physicians discussed in Chapter Two, Adelia performs impressive medical feats. She also constantly confronts objections to her methods that are a product of her premodern context. Examining the murdered laundress, found in her own tub, Adelia tackles the ever-thorny issue of autopsy: "Slowly, she sat back on her heels. 'I'm fairly sure she didn't drown, Rowley. I'd like to dissect the lungs, of course...'" Rowley reacts with frustration, "'Oh yes, necropsy would go down *very* well,' the bishop said between his teeth" (Franklin, *Assassin's Prayer* 165). Later in the novel, Franklin subtly parodies medieval crime fiction by having Adelia undertake an autopsy on a beloved pet goat in order to settle a village dispute, much to the physician's disgust: "But I don't *know* about goats" (*The Assassin's Prayer* 289, emphasis in original). Franklin's affectionate portrayal of this minor incident that nevertheless warrants the full detective treatment by Adelia is gently mocking of the investigative process, as articulated by one of Adelia's traveling companions: the young man, Ulf, "grinned. 'Goats, eh? How the mighty are fallen'" (*The Assassin's Prayer* 292).

Towards the end of the novel, Adelia performs an unlikely, though impressive, appendectomy on the young princess, Joanna. Adelia's adoptive father, also a doctor, had once shown her the appendix, attached to the large intestine, on a child's corpse and neither he nor her tutor at the Salerno School of Medicine had been able to explain to her what function it performed. Indeed, her father, Gershom, with impressive prescience, described it as "'an appendix to the caecum of no damned use whatever except to become diseased'" (Franklin, *Assassin's Prayer* 322). Adelia knows that Joanna will die unless it is removed, but she is understandably crushed by the responsibility of doing so, praying to both God and her absent father: "'Father, help me. The only time I've used a knife these last months was on a goat—and that was dead'" (Franklin, *Assassin's Prayer* 323). However, Adelia faces an unexpected obstacle to the procedure in the form of Joanna's lady-in-waiting, Blanche, who had orchestrated the consultation with Adelia regarding the young princess's condition in the first place. Having risked an enormous amount to get Joanna to Adelia, the latter is bewildered that Blanche is now raising objections.

But Blanche is rightly concerned with something that escapes Adelia at first. If, by some extraordinary luck, Joanna survives the surgery, she will nevertheless forever be imperfect, "scarred by an unholy operation" (Franklin, *Assassin's Prayer* 325). The very real fear is that this could jeopardize the alliance with the King of Sicily that is represented by Joanna's marriage. Adelia finally understands and the consequences of her actions take on a political meaning:

> This wasn't just a sick patient they were discussing, it was a bargain between kings and countries. The girl lying on the table in the keep was of international importance. If she died from the operation, and most likely she would, Adelia herself would be accused of killing her. If Joanna survived—as two of Dr Gershom's [Adelia's father] patients *had* survived—her surgeon would be equally culpable of ... what was it this man had said? ... damaging the goods, *royal* goods. Either way, the political ramifications would engulf not only all of them, but a continent [Franklin, *Assassin's Prayer* 325].

This does seem to be a valid consideration that buttresses the unlikeliness of the situation that Franklin has concocted for Adelia. It certainly has the effect of increasing the stakes surrounding the medical procedure: while it is entirely predictable that Joanna survives, the tension remains as to whether or not there are further consequences for Joanna and Adelia once they arrive in Palermo.

When summoned before the king's private secretary to account for her actions, Adelia bravely overcomes her nerves and explains the operation and the reason for it, concluding, "'I am certain that, as a man of sense [the King] would prefer a scarred bride to a dead one'" (Franklin, *Assassin's Prayer* 359). But, once again, the real reason for the secretary's interview is a surprise. The scar is not a concern; rather, they wish to ensure that Joanna's primary future obligation—providing heirs for the kingdom of Sicily—has not been threatened. "Adelia blew an 'oh' of relief. Was that it? Of *course* that was it. She and Blanche had been worrying over the wrong cause. Scarred or not, Joanna's function was to give William sons" (Franklin, *Assassin's Prayer* 359).

Franklin's deft handling of the practicalities of an unimaginably dangerous operation for its time, combined with the political realities that attach to the body of the princess, is an illustration of what makes her four novels compelling. While her narratives are, like most medieval crime fiction, unfeasible and often contain one too many digressions from the central plot, Franklin's female medieval detective is nevertheless one of the most popular of her type.

Franklin beautifully describes Palermo as a polyglot society accepting of all races and religions: "But, marvel though they did, it was the sheer heterogeneity of the city that soothed the souls of the four former prisoners of Aveyron, who'd seen what intolerance could do" (Franklin, *Assassin's Prayer* 347). But this relief is short-lived for Adelia, whose joy at being reunited with her mother and father is tempered by the news they bring her from Salerno, the city in which Adelia trained to be a doctor. Adelia had noticed the encroaching dominance of the Christian Church as she walked through the streets of Palermo and she realizes that the tolerant world she grew up in is disappearing when her father tells her some awful news: "They had stoned her mother, stoned her, in *Salerno*, which had been a boiling pot producing the greatest social, political and scientific advances the world had ever seen" (Franklin, *Assassin's Prayer* 376). Adelia's mother is a Christian, married to Adelia's Jewish father and, as Gershom explains to his daughter, the days have passed when the Christian Church overlooked mixed marriages. Moreover, Gershom tells Adelia that the Salerno medical school no longer accepted women as students, nor permitted the teaching or practice of autopsy. Franklin here offers a pointed metaphor of the sun setting on an enlightened age of learning, as Adelia and her father stand together, "watching the great semi-circle turn to gold and diminish into a final, lustrous arc before it disappeared entirely and left them in the dark" (Franklin, *Assassin's Prayer* 377).

Disappointingly and unusually for Franklin, this book is let down by its ending. Adelia is shamed into leaving the cathedral in which Joanna is participating in her betrothal ceremony to Sicily's King William because she has brought her dog, Ward, into the congregation with her. Ward, as readers familiar with the series will know, has an unbearably offensive smell. However, by leaving, Adelia exposes herself to the murderer who has dogged her journey, causing Rowley to be stabbed in the back trying to protect her, after a protracted chase through the streets. Indeed, throughout the novel, Adelia has been bewilderingly stubborn about accepting the evidence that someone means her harm, despite numerous attempts on her life that she attributes to accidents or to malice directed at someone else. So, the dog that is meant to protect her (and has done so in the past), indirectly causes her danger and this final novel ends with uncertainty as to whether or not Rowley survives

the stab wounds to his chest.[8] Despite this anticlimactic—though understandable—conclusion to the series, Franklin's Adelia Aguilar is a deeply
appealing character who, counterintuitively, sits easily alongside other contemporary feminist detectives, evincing medievalism's productive intervention into, and appropriation of, crime fiction conventions.

Historical novelist Sharan Newman's medieval crime fiction series features Catherine LeVendeur, who is introduced in *Death Comes as Epiphany*
(1993) as a twelfth-century novice in the Paraclete, the French convent established by Peter Abelard for his former lover, Heloise. Johnsen effuses that
Newman's inclusion of Heloise as a significant character in the series is "a
brilliant choice": Heloise not only provides an historical exemplar of the deep
love that Catherine and her future husband Edgar feel for each other—and
which other characters note is unusual—she also illustrates the possibilities
open to women in twelfth-century France in terms of education and the
opportunity to be a female public intellectual (40).

Catherine spends very little time in the convent, however, as Abbess
Heloise soon sends her back to her family ostensibly "in disgrace" for refusing
to curb her prideful nature. In fact, Heloise secretly orders Catherine—"the
most brilliant scholar here" (Newman, *Death Comes as Epiphany* 17)—to investigate the report that a prayer book belonging to the Abbey of Saint-Denis,
originally produced by the convent and overseen by Catherine, has had its
meaning altered in a way that suggests heretical teachings. Heloise fears that
the book's defacement is part of a plot to subject Abelard to more charges of
non-compliance with church doctrines. Catherine's homecoming causes enormous consternation within her family: her mother refuses to acknowledge her
existence and retreats further into the practice of her obsessive piety; her father
despairs that Catherine's cleverness will constantly cause her trouble and wishes
she was a boy who could assist him in his merchant business.[9]

As it transpires, Catherine returns only briefly to the Paraclete and never
takes her religious vows because Abelard, also suspecting something awry in
the Abbey's recent renovations and acquisition of a charismatic hermit, has
sent his own spy to investigate. Edgar, the fifth son of a Saxon lord from Wed-
derlie in Scotland, has travelled to Paris to study with Abelard. Disguised as
an apprentice stonemason, (recalling Malory's tale of Sir Gareth's unpropitious
beginnings in the kitchens of Camelot), Edgar's investigation inevitably intersects with Catherine's and the two fall in love. Over the rest of the series,
Catherine and Edgar's relationship survives long periods of separation, the
loss of several children, a dangerous pilgrimage to Santiago di Compostela,

defending Catherine's sister from an accusation of murder in Germany, a disastrous visit to Edgar's family in Scotland, and an ancient curse placed upon Catherine's mother's family in the time of Charlemagne.

Catherine displays many of Sister Fidelma's characteristics, while blessedly free of the latter's more irritating faults: she is curious, intelligent, brave, resourceful and struggles to conform to the strictures of her medieval life. As Heloise observes, Catherine loves her books more than her Maker, which is why she avoids undertaking her final vows. Indeed, like many a religious medieval detective, Catherine's "adjustment to the discipline of the order had been hard" (Newman, *Death Comes as Epiphany* 17). Here Newman illustrates one of the tensions inherent in medieval female detectives: to succeed in their investigative task, they require the education that is often only available to them through the Church. But their innate interest in human nature and the compulsion to solve problems means they are almost always unsuited to monastic life. Those women who do desire to remain cloistered, like Dame Frevisse (discussed below), nevertheless act upon their impulse to seek justice, often in spite of themselves.

Catherine is determinedly skeptical of the mysticism that permeates her world, assuming the role of modern detective and, in doing so, becoming a cipher for the reader's incredulity. Catherine is unusual for her time—this is the great irony of the medieval woman detective—but, as Newman explains in one "Afterword," her attitudes are not "impossible" for her medieval context. Johnsen applauds Newman's ability to balance Catherine between twenty-first-century expectations and the reality of her twelfth-century world and describes Catherine as a necessary "mediator" between the Middle Ages and the present, suggesting that "On many subjects, typical medieval attitudes unrelieved by a contemporary perspective would be unpalatable..." (37). While Johnsen is not a medievalist, her observation reveals an underlying explanation for medieval crime fiction's appeal: if the reality of daily life in the Middle Ages does indeed require a translator for a modern readership, then this role is efficiently and effectively undertaken by the literary device of the detective whose job it is to make sense of the world around her.

Newman ensures that Catherine treads delicately through her medieval landscape, mindful of disruptions that may threaten its authenticity. For example, Catherine and Edgar briefly consider whether the murdered mason Garnulf was struck down by demons, before dismissing this notion not because of their refusal to countenance diabolical intervention, but because he "was a good man. He'd have no traffic with demons" (Newman, *Death Comes as Epiphany* 82). However, Newman also insists that Catherine's medieval world resonates with modernity, a stance that many medieval crime fiction authors leave unstated yet implicit in their novels. In her "Afterword" to *Heresy* (2002), for example, Newman explains that her description of a riot by townspeople panicked by rumors of an invading army of heretics and demons "is total fiction" and not based on a medieval source. Instead, Newman "drew ... on the recent irrational stories involving the year 2000, along with various panics resulting from rumors spread over the Internet. Our credulity hasn't changed over the past thousand years, only the focus of our fears" (*Heresy* 349). There is no historical basis for her narrative, then, but Newman still participates in the long tradition, identified by Eco, of insisting upon the ongoing relevance of the Middle Ages to contemporary society, and, importantly, vice versa. In this way, Newman takes modern anxieties and reinserts them back into the Middle Ages where they are rendered more comprehensible, illustrating the powerful cultural work that medievalism continues to perform.

However, uncanny events do occasionally challenge Catherine's innate rationalism and modern perspective, allowing her to participate in medievalism's penchant for a fantastical Middle Ages in which the magical realm of faerie intersects with the mundane. Catherine's reaction to her brother's recitation of their family's legendary origins is typically incredulous, despite sensing a certain strangeness in her surroundings: "'I thought the story Guillaume told was preposterous,' Catherine said. 'Magic springs and hidden treasure. But this place does make me feel as if we had stepped into some ancient tale'" (Newman, *Witch in the Well* 131). Catherine dismisses the notion of an otherworldly ancestress who supposedly protects the underground spring from where the family draws its strength and longevity. Newman does not offer a "rational" (that is, "modern") explanation for several characters' unaccountably long lives: Catherine's grandfather, Gargenaud, is more than eighty years old and yet when Catherine first sees him after a long separation, she is shocked: "After twenty years, her grandfather had not changed at all" (*Witch in the Well* 133). While Catherine eventually uncovers the motives and human perpetrators behind a series of murders and mysterious occurrences at her family's castle, she also becomes more accepting of supernatural intervention. When her mother—who had spent the last decade in a state of severe dementia—has her faculties miraculously restored to her, Catherine finally capitulates: "'I take back every doubt I had,' Catherine said through tears. 'There was magic after all'" (Newman, *Witch in the Well* 349).

The Witch in the Well (2004) is the final book in Newman's series and it seems doubtful that more novels featuring Catherine will be forthcoming. Newman presents her readers with something of a conundrum: will Catherine maintain her newly awakened belief in the existence of magic? Or will she revert to her long-held practice of searching for a rational explanation, as befits her detective status? Newman, it seems, seeks to remove her medieval female sleuth from the restraint of crime fiction conventions and instead situate her more firmly in an imaginative Middle Ages that owes more to historical romance.

Crime, Medievalism and Romance

A frequent characteristic of medieval crime fiction novels that feature a female detective is the melding of the detective narrative into what is, to all intents and purposes, a historical romance. This tendency is not restricted to female detectives, of course, as Ann Swinfen's series featuring the bookseller, Nicholas Elyot, demonstrates (see Chapter Two). Consequently, there are times when the crime or mystery narrative appears to exist simply to provide dangerous scenarios from which the female detective may be rescued by her male companion. There also seems to be a greater occurrence of mystical and magical elements, reinforcing the entrenched association between medieval women, mystics, witches, paganism and alternative healers. As the detectives discussed in this section demonstrate, the medieval landscape would seem to foreclose the possibility of the hardboiled type for its women. Doris Gercke's militant vigilante, Tolgonai, is not likely to be found in these pages.

Alys Clare writes a series featuring Abbess Helewise who rules the famous Hawkenlye Abbey, a community of nuns and monks located in Kent, in the late-twelfth century. Mixed religious houses were common, especially in the early Middle Ages, however, in medieval crime fiction they appear rarely. Tyndal Priory, discussed below, seems to be the only other example, and it too is governed by a woman, Prioress Eleanor. Helewise joins the abbey after she loses her husband, Ivo, and subsequently surrenders her two sons to the care of other households. Helewise's companion is Sir Josse d'Acquin, one of King Richard's knights, who arrives to investigate the murder of a young nun in the first novel of the series. Josse and Helewise form an effective investigative partnership and their relationship initially remains chaste despite the tangible desire each holds for the other.

Clare's impulse towards romance is developed in *Girl in a Red Tunic* (2005), in which Helewise's elder son, Leofgar, arrives at Hawkenlye with his young wife and son, seeking sanctuary from a traumatic experience at their home. Leofgar's wife, Rohaise, is clearly suffering from postpartum depression, as well as post-traumatic shock—the latter condition also causing her little boy to remain disturbingly silent. Leofgar's arrival forces Helewise to recall the measures she undertook to ensure her sons' safe upbringing while she retreated into the religious life. Through her description of the "provision" she made for them, the heartbreak that attends such arrangements emerges and Helewise accepts that she no longer knows her own son: "'You ask me what I think of my son's strange behaviour and I have to say that I have no answer. I no longer know what or who he is…'" (Clare, *Girl in a Red Tunic* 95).

At the heart of the novel, however, is Helewise's detailed reminiscence about her first meeting with her future father-in-law, Benedict Warin, and then his son, Ivo. Clare describes Ivo and Helewise's courtship in detail, including their first sexual encounter that results in Helewise's pregnancy and the subsequent need to bring forward the date of their wedding. Helewise's happy life with Ivo and their two sons uncovers the abbess's passionate nature that she has sought to suppress during her years at Hawkenlye. But the unexpected appearance of her son—firstly in her dreams, then in person at the abbey—stirs up these hidden feelings. Helewise also recalls her father-in-law's strong magnetism and the rumors of his frequent infidelities. The consequences of Benedict's past seduction of a household maid, Sirida, have emerged to disrupt the lives of Helewise and her son because Sirida—now an aged recluse living in the depths of the forest—is seeking to claim Leofgar's birthright. The discovery that Benedict is not the father of her child compounds Sirida's bitterness, as does her deathbed realization that she could have loved and been happy with her actual seducer, Benedict's manservant, Martin. Helewise's detective role, then, becomes one of disentangling past romantic encounters in order to ensure the future security of her son's claim to his inheritance.

It is sometimes difficult to maintain a sustained character-development trajectory over the course of long series and like Peter Tremayne, Clare allows her medieval religious detective to leave her abbey and return to a secular life. The difference between the pair is that Fidelma relinquishes her vocation because it no longer conforms to her main desire to seek human, secular solutions to her investigations and she is able to maintain her relationship with Eadulf whether or not she remains a nun. Helewise, on the other hand, leaves the beautiful abbey of Hawkenlye—where she had sought refuge as a widow—because of her love for Sir Josse. Helewise and Josse do, however, maintain their connection with Hawkenlye throughout the remainder of the series. While there is a clear attraction between Josse and Helewise from the opening novel, the relationship takes a long and circuitous route that incorporates Clare's desire for a mystical reimagining of the past. For many years—indeed, from the second novel in the series, *The Tavern in the Morning* (2000)—Josse is in love with Joanna, a woman with strange, unearthly powers, who appears sporadically throughout the series.

Incorporating paganism becomes increasingly important to Clare and by the time of the eleventh novel, *The Joys of My Life* (2008), this narrative reaches a critical point. Joanna, by now a committed pagan leader, travels to France and merges with a spirit called the "Bear Man," sacrificing herself in order to imbue Chartres with the power of the Forest People, ensuring that the site will remain sacred even as the new cathedral is constructed over it. Josse is left deeply bereaved and responsible for looking after his own daughter, his son with Joanna, and her son, whose father is reputedly Henry II. Moreover, in a disrupted, disjointed and disconcerting final chapter, ten years pass and Helewise has left the religious life altogether and is living with Josse in his "House in the Woods."

Clare is clearly fascinated with the implications of the pagan, mystical past and her more recent series, Aelf Fen, allows her to pursue this more directly.[10] While the Hawkenlye series retains the crime fiction formula more securely, Clare nevertheless continues to explore mystical themes. For example, in *A Shadowed Evil* (2015), Josse and Helewise travel to Southfire Hall, the home of Josse's family, because his uncle is dying. The house appears to have some kind of sentience that protects itself and its inhabitants from evil. It was built on the site of an ancient Roman villa and its location was chosen "'because the people from the south [that is, Romans] knew this was a good place, and that any dwelling constructed here would have a nourishing, protective spirit'" (Clare, *Shadowed Evil* 53). Josse feels a deep affinity with the house and his daughter, Meggie, also perceives its spirit: "'To me, it [the house] simply shouts out, and it's not only powerful but undoubtedly benign. Protective of its own,' she added thoughtfully. She shot him a questioning look" (Clare, *Shadowed Evil* 208).

The evil in the house turns out to be Cyrille de Picus, a widow recently remarried to the heir, Herbert, and the house finally takes matters into its own hands and disposes of her, witnessed by her six-year-old stepson, Olivar, whom she had been abusing:

> He looked straight up at her [Helewise]. "The house didn't like her," he said. "I know it can't have done, because I saw what it did." He drew a shaky breath. "She was leaning out of the window, trying to see who was calling, and I crept out to watch. I was standing right behind her." Briefly he shut his eyes, screwing them up tight. Then, opening them wide and staring straight into hers, he said, "The house didn't want her here any more. It gave a sort of a shake, as if to rid itself of her, and she fell" [Clare, *Shadowed Evil* 224].

Clare resists the suggestion that perhaps Olivar had more to do with Cyrille's fall than the house by describing other inexplicable occurrences, as well as restating Josse's ongoing connection with his former lover, Joanna, who died several years ago, but still appears to Josse in visions: "He seemed to hear a voice—his own voice—say, *There is no magic in my family.* Another voice—a beloved voice, that of Joanna, his lost love—replied gently, *There is, Josse*" (*Shadowed Evil* 55, italics in original).

Helewise also experiences prophetic dreams while sleeping in the house, and a local lay brother is overcome with a "brief fugue" in order to become a conduit for an otherworldly warning (Clare, *Shadowed Evil* 110). Finally, one of Josse's cousins, Aeleis, is slowly dying due to fluid in her lungs and she believes that she has been cursed by a "moppet"; a wax doll shaped in her image, found face down in a water trough. Aeleis counters Josse's dismissal of supernatural intervention with her undeniably logical perspective: "'You may say firmly that it's all nonsense, and nobody can harm someone else by such methods, but it does feel a little different when it's done to you, and you realize you're the focus of such extreme malice'" (*Shadowed Evil* 179). Revenge is enacted when Cyrille, the maker of the moppet, is herself drowned.

Cassandra Clark's medieval detective, Hildegard, faces similar circumstances to Helewise, albeit more than one hundred and fifty years later. Upon the presumption of the death of her husband fighting the French in the Hundred Years' War, Hildegard joins the Church as an anchoress, leaving two grown children. After seven years as an anchoress, Hildegard receives confirmation that her husband had, in fact, been killed in the war and decides to emerge from seclusion in order to found her own religious house with the fortune she has inherited. Her prioress is an enthusiastic supporter of the plan because a second daughter house will assist in curbing the interference of the newly installed, and somewhat resented, abbot of the great abbey at Meaux, Hubert de Courcy. At the conclusion of her first book, *Hangman Blind* (2008), Clark claims that the inspiration for Hildegard is a fourteenth-century prioress at Swyne (Swine, East Riding, Yorkshire), who "was caught up in an incessant round of litigation with the monks at Meaux but fought back splendidly, being excommunicated by the pope no less than three times for her temerity in standing up for herself and her nuns—an early example of the feminist spirit coupled with Anglo-Saxon bloody-mindedness" (*Hangman Blind* 309). It is not difficult to understand why this historical figure appealed to Clark, who demonstrates the preference of contemporary authors to gravitate towards what they perceive to be a premodern form of feminism. This is a common project for authors of medieval crime fiction, and medieval historical fiction more generally, who often seek glimpses of tolerance towards other genders, races and religions within the historical figures they portray.

In *A Parliament of Spies* (2012), Hildegard has accompanied the abbot, Hubert de Courcy, to London at a time that coincides with the Wonderful

Parliament of 1386. This was the parliament in which Geoffrey Chaucer sat as a representative for Kent and the poet makes a brief appearance, passing Hildegard and Hubert in the street and stopping for a quick word (Clark, *Parliament of Spies* 392). Clark's description of London during this tumultuous time reminds her modern readers how little information was disseminated to the crowds: no one completely comprehends what is happening during the parliamentary proceedings and rumors abound. Clark sympathizes with the young King Richard and she casts the Duke of Lancaster, John of Gaunt, unequivocally as the villain. Gaunt's mistress (later wife) and Chaucer's sister-in-law, Katharine Swynford, is similarly odious and her son, Thomas, is spoilt, reckless, ruthless and violent. It is Thomas who incites a riot in the streets in which Hildegard is accused of being a witch and threatened with execution. Clark's research is impressively detailed: when the Spanish friar Rivera and Hildegard glimpse Richard in the Tower of London, they note his "regality," which was a common characteristic associated with the young king in contemporary accounts. She also paraphrases Richard's famous response to parliament's insistence upon the removal of one of his favorites, Michael de la Pole: "'I shall not allow the lowest scullion in my household to be dismissed at the behest of the council'"; and she captures the fear of an imminent invasion from France that suffused London and the south of England during the late summer, autumn and winter of 1386 (*Parliament of Spies* 319, 341, 148).

Hildegard demonstrates the now-familiar traits of medieval female detectives, including the one fault that is common to them all: "'My prioress is always warning me to be less impatient. The patience required to wait for their verdict is sent as a lesson to me'" (Clark, *Parliament of Spies* 347). She is frustrated at her treatment by dismissive men, but she is also able to mobilize this masculine contempt in order to aid her investigation: "He addressed the two men as if Hildegard were invisible. She didn't mind, of course, it was a lesson in humility and gave her a chance to observe the cook more closely than she would otherwise have been able" (Clark, *Parliament of Spies* 54). Although Hildegard does seem to be more than usually alone, she still has a contingent of male protectors, including the abbot, Hubert (with whom she is clearly in love, and vice versa), Thomas, the ingenuous monk who is her confessor, and Ulf, a Saxon archer also in love with Hildegard.

But, more than most, Clark's modernity intervenes into her series in distracting ways. There is some truly egregious anachronistic language, including "Dark Ages" and "She had decided to visit St Hugh's shrine before other pilgrims turned up and turned it into a bunfight" (Clark, *Parliament of Spies* 54, 76). Hildegard is, even by medieval crime fiction standards, a very secular nun, who rarely prays, is trying to establish her own priory in order to provide a refuge for women now rather than for contemplation of the next life, and directs an almost heretical skepticism towards the Church's teaching: "Hildegard had never been able to make up her mind about the existence of other worlds, heaven, hell, because where was the evidence?" (Clark, *Parliament of Spies* 280). She also demonstrates a rather condescending attitude towards the unruly mob, reminding herself that "forced to live like brutes, they behave like brutes" (Clark, *Parliament of Spies* 351); a sympathetic stance indeed, considering that these "brutes" are attempting to burn her as a witch.

Helewise and Hildegard also share a surprising (and highly unlikely) autonomy in the freedom of their movement outside their respective religious houses. Helewise frequently journeys through the Kent countryside alone or accompanied by Sir Josse, but without the presence of another nun as chaperone, as was the usual practice when circumstances forced religious women to leave their houses. Such a habit exposes Helewise to dangerous situations, such as the time when she inadvisably accompanies a strange man who arrives at the abbey claiming to bring a message from Sir Josse and the local sheriff. Hildegard, in *Hangman Blind*, embarks upon a mission across the Yorkshire moors on behalf of her prioress, "armed with a stave and two trained hounds" (6). Hildegard is confident and capable, navigating the countryside with ease, skinning and cooking rabbits captured by her dogs, and repelling potential rapists with her knife. However, like Helewise, Hildegard unwisely accompanies strangers with false messages, necessitating her frequent rescue. In *A Parliament of Spies*, Hildegard requires rescuing by the dashing friar, Rivera, on three occasions when her life is seriously threatened.

Devastatingly, the last time Rivera intervenes, he sacrifices his own life to save her from the aforementioned bloodthirsty London mob. Episodes such as this are difficult to assess in terms of both the crime narrative and the authors' medievalist project. On the one hand, navigating dangerous situations in the course of an investigation is a conventional element of crime fiction. These situations, however, often feel gratuitous and serve to progress the plot at the expense of an authentic recreation of the Middle Ages. In other words, these scenarios appear even more contrived given the flagrant anachronism that often accompanies them, particularly concerning medieval religious women's freedom of movement. Here, medievalism functions as a pretext for a Middle Ages fairy tale.

Priscilla Royal's medieval crime fiction series is based at Tyndal Priory, situated on the remote East Anglian coast during the reign of King Henry

III, in the 1270s. Appointed as a favor to her father, a favorite baron of the king's, new prioress Eleanor comes to Tyndal as a twenty-year-old from her aunt's priory in Amesbury, where she has lived since the age of six. Eleanor's appointment causes much consternation to the priory's occupants who had already elected one of their own to the position of prioress soon after the death of Felicia, the beloved previous incumbent. Eleanor therefore begins her career at a distinct disadvantage, forced to combat the resentful hostility of her nuns and monks. Royal establishes the theme of unrequited love in the first novel of the series, *Wine of Violence* (2003), which remains prominent throughout the remaining books. When Eleanor meets Brother Thomas, himself newly arrived at the priory, she is struck by an immediate physical attraction to him that she instantly attempts to suppress. The two form a close attachment and become an effective investigative team, but Thomas, even if his vows permitted, cannot reciprocate Eleanor's desire.

Unlike Eleanor, Thomas has no vocational calling, having taken minor orders at the insistence of his father, an earl who is unable to make further provision for his illegitimate offspring. The son of one his father's barons, Giles, joins him at the cathedral school, continuing their lifelong friendship. The morning after one night of "wining and wenching" together, Thomas initiates a sexual encounter with Giles that is ardently pursued until the couple is discovered. Giles subsequently denies all compliance in the encounter, abandoning Thomas to the emotional despair of rejection and to the dungeon to await execution. Fortunately, a mysterious visitor releases Thomas from prison upon the condition that he becomes "a priest with unquestioning obedience to a master whom you will never meet" (Royal, *Wine of Violence* 25). In a sadistic twist, Giles accompanies Thomas to Tyndal, where he spits out his contempt and leaves Thomas at the door of the priory, wiping away tears "as the ache of grief burst into his hollowed-out heart" (Royal, *Wine of Violence* 26).

Investigating suspicious deaths with Eleanor becomes an escape for Thomas and offers a tenuous reflection of the life he may have hoped to enjoy in the secular world. Thomas is also blackmailed into undertaking dangerous expeditions on behalf of a disguised figure described as the "raven-clad spymaster" (Royal, *Sorrow Without End* 41), who knows about his past and threatens to prosecute him. At one stage, it all becomes too much for Thomas and he lives for a time as a hermit, near Tyndal Priory. However, in *Covenant with Hell* (2013), Thomas meets a Norwich merchant, Durant, and their brief encounter "had changed something within him"; in amazement, Thomas "realised that he no longer grieved for Giles" (Royal, *Covenant with Hell* 213). Thomas's sexuality contributes to medieval crime fiction's ongoing participation in the project of troubling the heteronormativity of crime fiction more broadly. It also usefully circumvents the predictable attraction between the two main protagonists that structures many other examples of medieval crime fiction that have dabbled a little too deeply into historical romance.

Robin Maxwell has reframed the story of the little princes in the tower as a historical romance with a fast-moving, investigative plotline that rescues it from the sentimentality that threatens to subsume the novel. Maxwell participates in the rehabilitation project undertaken around the world by numerous Richard III societies, as well as historians and historical novelists, including several of the medieval crime fiction authors discussed throughout this book. Richard's most serious charge, of course, is the alleged murder of his young nephews in the Tower of London in 1483. In order to absolve him of this crime—first brought by Thomas More and cemented into truth by Shakespeare—most authors prefer to offer another suspect. Maxwell's villain is Margaret Beaufort, great-granddaughter of John of Gaunt and Katherine Swynford and mother of Henry Tudor, the future Henry VII. Maxwell's detective is Nell Caxton, beloved daughter of William, England's first printer, and best friend to "Bessie" of York, eventual wife of Henry and Queen of England. Nell is presented as a spymaster extraordinaire, able to perceive "an entire *world* of intelligence lurking beneath the one we see. A network of sorts … a second web. *Invisible* to the eye. But just as real" (Maxwell 38, emphasis in original). Nell consults her "invisible web" to great effect throughout the novel, although much of her detective work involves being in the right place at the right time to overhear a crucial piece of information.

Maxwell also explores the ideas of courtly love through the parallel female gazes of Nell and Bessie towards Anthony Woodville, Lord Rivers, and Richard III, respectively. Both girls have crushes on these middle-aged, powerful men and this allows Maxwell to situate them in a light suffused with the rosy glow of teenage love. At one stage, Rivers and Richard face each other in a joust and request tokens from Nell and Bessie in a classic tournament set piece. Nell has more opportunity to realize her desire, spending several weeks in close proximity to Lord Rivers as she tutors young Prince Edward in Latin at Ludlow Castle in Wales, where Rivers is responsible for raising the heir to the English throne: "But to this date their romance had not proceeded beyond an intense incarnation of chivalric love. Courtly love. They might sit side by side for hours, poring over a Latin translation. When they spoke together, debated, laughed, punned, their eyes were locked together, as if searching for a way into the other's soul" (Maxwell 89).

Rivers and Nell "heroically refrained" from consummating their desire because of strictures imposed by the prince's father, Edward IV, to ensure that a "sin-free" and "pure" environment surrounds young Edward (Maxwell 90). This does not prevent Nell from wanting to lose her virginity, "for she had long wished to lose it like other girls of her station, and to delight in the carnal pleasures Master Chaucer had written of in his *Canterbury Tales*" (Maxwell 90). The ideal of courtly love that Maxwell embraces is also suggested by Prince Edward's comparison, upon reading Malory's *Le Morte Darthur*, of Ludlow with Camelot, casting himself as Arthur, Rivers as Lancelot and Nell as Guinevere. Lord Rivers proves woefully naive—in keeping with his status as ideal chivalric knight—and, upon hearing the news that Edward IV has died and his young charge is now king, promises the boy that he would always be there for him, the people will love him, and peace will continue (Maxwell 95). He then leads the boy into a trap sprung by Richard III and the Duke of Buckingham.

Despite the rather ludicrous yet entertaining plot, the strength of Maxwell's novel lies in its portrayal of the power that fifteenth-century women wielded in terms of patronage, politics and espionage. Nell is offered a job as secretary for Margaret Beaufort, allowing her not only to comprehend the vastness of Margaret's wealth and influence, but also to be perfectly placed for spying. Maxwell also offers an excellent, feminist portrayal of Margaret Beaufort's work ethic, religious devotion and administrative skill, although Nell allows herself a small critique of Margaret's parenting style: "Mother [Margaret] and son [Henry Tudor] wrote to each other every single day, which seemed to Nell—herself a loving and diligent daughter—somewhat excessive" (Maxwell 201).

Helewise, Hildegard, Eleanor and Nell are capable, clever and brave examples of medieval crime fiction's female detectives. They confront similar obstacles and restrictions—not least of which is breathtaking misogyny, often excused by the medieval setting—and seek creative solutions to their investigations, mobilizing their innate detective traits and manipulating those around them. But these novelists (Clare, Clark, Royal and Maxwell) intertwine their crime narratives with prominent romance themes that generate tension and, occasionally, distraction. While this strategy generates religious characters with rather unconvincing vocations (excepting Nell), it also demonstrates the irresistible lure of the romantic Middle Ages.

Manipulating Patriarchal Feudalism

As noted above, there is a tendency for authors of medieval crime fiction to overemphasize the misogyny of the Middle Ages. Of course, patriarchal feudalism is not exactly a social system that promotes the rights of women, but the heavy-handedness of some of the masculine portrayals is so melodramatic that even the other characters in the novels recognize the ludicrousness of their attitudes. For example, in Royal's *Satan's Lullaby* (2015), Father Devoir, sent to investigate accusations that Eleanor and Thomas are engaged in "carnal relations," is so deeply misogynistic that it is impossible for anyone, readers and characters alike, to take him seriously (51). Nevertheless, an important skill for medieval female detectives is to recognize, accept and manipulate the antifeminist context in which they are placed, and adjust their investigative techniques accordingly.

Roberta Gellis has an intriguing setting for her medieval detective. Magdalene la Bâtarde is a widow and former prostitute who leases St. Mary Overy Church's Old Priory Guesthouse from the Bishop of Winchester.[11] In the 1140s, this Bishop is Henry, brother and powerful rival to King Stephen. Magdalene uses her Southwark premises as a discreet brothel—officially recorded as "a house of needle workers" in order to discourage unwanted clientele walking in off the street (Gellis, *Mortal Bane* loc. 122)—that maintains an unusual level of cleanliness and care for her small number of practitioners. Also unusual are the characteristics of each prostitute: Sabina is spectacularly beautiful and blind; Ella has a childlike mind but is completely uninhibited in her enthusiasm for her occupation; Letice is darkly exotic and mute. Magdalene herself is described as having "A face like an angel's, a mind like a trap" (Gellis, *Mortal Bane* loc. 1406), perhaps not unlike her biblical namesake. Also included in the household is Magdalene's deaf cook, Dulcie.

Certain members of the adjoining church remain incensed at this arrangement and the sacristan, Brother Paulinus, is particularly determined to rid St. Mary's from the scourge of fallen women. In the first novel of the series, *A Mortal Bane* (1999), Paulinus accuses Magdalene and her women of murdering a stranger who turns out to be a papal messenger, Baldassarre, and who had recently visited the Old Priory. In the manner of those characters who reluctantly assume a detective role in self-defense (as noted earlier with Neely's Blanche White), Magdalene realizes that she "'must do something to save ourselves'" because, as she concedes, "'We can swear and swear that Messer Baldassarre was never here, but we are whores. Who will believe us?'" (Gellis, *Mortal Bane* loc. 827). Bishop Henry is sympathetic to Magdalene's reasons for wanting to help find the murderer, but also understands that "a woman is too confined by custom to move about and freely question" (Gellis, *Mortal Bane* loc. 1020). He therefore assigns one of his trusted knights, Sir Bellamy of Itchen, to assist Magdelene's investigation. Predictably, "Bell" and Magdalene form an intense bond that develops into an effective detective partnership. Bell, however, wants more and at the end of this first novel, Magdalene must remind him of her true occupation: Bell says to her, "'You said you were retired.' 'So I am, but that does not change what I am,'" Magdalene replies (Gellis, *Mortal Bane* loc. 4441).

Magdalene is adept at manipulating the patriarchal constraints that structure her medieval world. She maintains a working relationship with the Bishop not only because "she pays her rent on time and in full; ... [and] no one has made any complaint against her" (Gellis, *Mortal Bane* loc. 1094), but also because her resourcefulness, intelligence and discretion make her extremely useful for undertaking secretive tasks. Henry has a pragmatic view of Magdalene's business, considering such establishments to be a necessary evil: "'Lechery is foul in itself, but when contained in one place, it does not contaminate the whole body of society'" (Gellis, *Mortal Bane* loc. 965). In support of this approach, Henry quotes Horace's *First Satire* and posits that if "powerful and godless men" have no outlet for their lusts, then "innocent sisters, wives, and daughters" are at risk (Gellis, *Mortal Bane* loc. 965). However, Magdalene cannot help but point out to the Bishop her proto-feminist view that "'whores do not lust, my lord, ... To a whore, coupling is a piece of work for which she is paid as a weaver is paid for a piece of cloth'" (Gellis, *Mortal Bane* loc. 965). Henry is predictably skeptical and though Magdalene continues her argument, she is wise enough to understand that "It was not worthwhile to continue to press her point and perhaps strain the bishop's friendship" (Gellis, *Mortal Bane* loc. 974).

While Magdalene is useful to Henry, her main protector is William of Ypres, who had initially convinced the Bishop to lease Magdalene the Old Priory. William's loyalty to King Stephen means he is at times working towards a political outcome contrary to Bishop Henry, but they nevertheless maintain a wary allegiance. Bell, however, is not at all pleased to learn of William's importance in Magdalene's life and she must explain it to him in the chivalric terms he comprehends:

> "William has a right to my loyalty. He has been my patron, my protector—my lord, since you will understand that term best—for over ten years. I am no man's woman, not even William's, but I do put his interests above those of others. If you cannot understand and accept that, I am most truly sorry" [Gellis, *Mortal Bane* loc. 4431].

Magdalene demonstrates not only her deep awareness of the patriarchal systems that dictate her tenuous position, but also her ability to manipulate those systems to protect herself and her women.

Through her series, Gellis brings to life those marginalized voices from the Middle Ages that medieval scholarship (particularly with a feminist, cultural and political focus) has endeavored to recuperate in recent decades, an enterprise that has not gone unnoticed by reviewers. *Publishers Weekly* notes that Gellis's second Magdalene la Bâtarde novel, *A Personal Devil* (2001), offers "poignant glimpses into the humanity of her characters, particularly the women of the guesthouse," her depiction of relationships "certainly speak[s] to the position of women in medieval society," and her "focus on the 'little people' of the period is most welcome" (*"Personal Devil"*). However, Gellis sometimes falls into the extremely common practice of allowing the details of her medieval world to overwhelm her narratives and detract from her interesting and popular detective, Magdalene. *Kirkus Reviews* had a rather scathing assessment of Gellis's first novel, complaining that *A Mortal Bane* was "burdened with endless details of church rituals and politics," rendering it "heavy-going despite its intriguing heroine" (*"Mortal Bane"*). But, by the fourth and final book, *Chains of Folly* (2006), the same publication is more tolerant: "The extensive roll call of historical and fictional characters is occasionally bewildering, but marvelous Magdalene and stout-hearted Bell make the effort to keep them straight well worthwhile" (*"Chains of Folly"*). Even the more positive *Publishers Weekly* reviewer struggles a little with Gellis's attention to detailed historical context, noting that "the large number of characters means the action plods at times" and that reference is needed to the Author's Note at the end of *Bone of Contention* (2002) in order to "clarify the many historical personages involved" (*"Bone of Contention"*).

Gellis offers a compelling medieval female voice that, while fictional, nevertheless participates in the shared concern demonstrated by both medieval and medievalism studies to represent medieval women. But Gellis also illustrates the difficulty faced by many authors of medieval crime fiction in finding the balance between creating an authentic medievalist space in which those women can credibly function and not subsuming their narrative under the weight of extraneous detail.

Another female medieval detective adept at concealing her thoughts and emotions from the men who attempt to control her is Agnès de Souarcy. Andrea H. Japp is the pseudonym for French crime writer Lionelle Nugon-Baudon. Trained as a toxicologist, Japp has translated into French the novels of Patricia Cornwell, featuring forensic scientist Kay Scarpetta, in addition to writing over twenty novels. Her medieval mystery series comprises four books featuring embattled widow Agnès, the first three of which have been translated into English.

Agnès occupies a significantly more precarious position than her English (or Welsh, or Scottish, or Irish) counterparts. The first novel in Japp's series, *The Season of the Beast* (2006, translated 2008) opens with her attempted suicide in the middle of the brutal winter of 1294 in northern France. Recently widowed at only sixteen, Agnès already has a young daughter and struggles to maintain the livelihoods of the peasants, serfs and craftspeople who are now her responsibility. Rescued by her practical, middle-aged serving woman, Agnès is convinced to carry on with the added burden of caring for the baby of a young, runaway girl who is too weak from starvation to survive the birth of her child. This melodramatic beginning anticipates the tone and themes for Japp's series that owe more to Dan Brown's *The Da Vinci Code* than to conventional detective fiction, with a focus on mysticism and an obsession with bloodlines.

There are several murders, however, as well as one overarching mystery to solve. The clues to this mystery are contained in "one of the most prestigious and the most dangerous [libraries] in all Christendom," housed in Clairets Abbey, where many of the murders eventually occur (Japp, *Season of the Beast* 67). The library is the repository of works collected from all corners of the world by scholars, counts and bishops of Chartres, princes and kings. The Abbess, Éleusie de Beaufort, a woman of great learning and Agnès's aunt, is "the secret guardian of this science, of these books" (Japp, *Season of the Beast* 67); the library is both secret and dangerous because of the blasphemous nature of the works it harbors.

Agnès, as is explained a little more fully (but not completely) in the second novel, *The Breath of the Rose* (2006, translated 2009), is the focus of a search by the Templar and Hospitaller knights, as well as the Inquisition, to whom she is betrayed through the machinations of her evil half-brother, Eudes de Larnay, who has designs on her land. Agnès survives torture at the hands of the sadistic Grand Inquisitor, thanks to her "divine blood," and returns home to learn that her daughter, Mathilde, was also responsible for her betrayal. Japp depicts her heroine's daughter as a deeply unpleasant, self-obsessed adolescent in a departure from the usually affectionate and appealing children that populate medieval crime fiction. Eudes, Agnès's odious half-brother, seduces Mathilde by deploying the conventions of courtly love, encouraging her to believe that she has become an "inaccessible goddess before whom men prostrated themselves. What a delightful idea" (Japp, *Divine Blood* 63). Despite Mathilde's reprehensible behavior, Agnès never gives up fighting for her daughter's return.

There are some aspects to Japp's novels that suggest a slightly different form of medievalist recreation from that which characterizes Anglo-American medieval crime fiction. For example, the latter's tendency is to focus on the scarce, unappetizing nature of the food available to their characters: as noted with regard to Paul C. Doherty (and others), a disgusted reaction to the stale and rotting food is one way in which a medieval detective reveals his or her innate modernity. Japp, on the other hand, offers the most wonderful description of a proto-Michelin-starred dégustation that suggests restaurants replaced taverns in France much earlier than in England (Japp, *Divine Blood* 251). Japp's series also portrays a more brutal feudalism than is generally present in other medieval crime fiction novels: the precariousness of Agnès's situation is illustrated by the ease with which her half-brother betrays her to the Inquisition (by accusing her of sleeping with her priest). This betrayal is effortlessly enacted despite Agnès's careful manipulations designed to circumvent Eudes's desire to take over the estate she has inherited from her husband—a claim based solely upon Eudes's position as her closest male relative. Furthermore, one of the heroes of the novels—the "good guy" who is in love with Agnès, Comte Artus d'Authon—responds to an innocuous critique from a scribe who has helped Agnès escape imprisonment by having to suppress his feudalist-conditioned response: "The young man's unexpected boldness, not to say impudence, flabbergasted Artus, who breathed: 'Heavens! What candour! Are you aware, young man, that I have run men through for more trifling impertinences than this?'" (Japp, *Divine Blood* 253). The fact that Artus resists the temptation to "run [the young man] through" presumably speaks to his designation as Japp's hero, as well as the desire of medieval crime fiction authors to imbue their heroes with glimpses of modern tolerance.

Another of these nods to modernity is Japp's representation of her female characters: an interesting combination of proto-feminism and a rather clichéd depiction of female hysteria. Agnès is brave and sometimes foolhardy, demonstrating an agency that attempts to counter the precariousness of her widowed status. In *The Divine Blood*, she rescues young Clement (her adopted son) from assassins by running them down on her horse and killing them with a knife. As mentioned earlier, Agnès's aunt, Éleusie de Beaufort, abbess of Clairets, is a woman of high intelligence, education and resourcefulness, although she makes some questionable decisions and assumptions concerning the apprehension of a murderer who is one of her nuns. Éleusie consequently fails in this endeavor and succumbs to the poisoner, a devastating scene in which Japp provides a beautiful description of a person who dies in complete certainty of her faith (*Divine Blood* 133). Assisting and then continuing with

Éleusie's investigation is the abbey's apothecary, Annelette, the most feminist character in the series.

Annelette wished to follow her father and brother into medicine but faced derision from both. Not blessed with even average good looks, as the reader is told, she failed to find a husband and chose to join a convent as an apothecary as the least demeaning path for her life. Éleusie finds comfort in the abbey, informing Annelette that "'these nunneries where we are allowed to live in peace, to work, to act, to make decisions are a blessing to women'" (Japp, *Breath of the Rose* 236). Annelette, however, is still bitter and responds with a comment on women's untenable position in the medieval world:

> Annelette shook her head.
> "Behind this blessing lies a harsh reality: we women enjoy almost no rights in the world. Those who, like yourself, are better off might be fortunate enough to marry a man of honour, respect and love, but what about the others? What choice do they have? Freedom, it is true, can be bought like everything else. I was prepared to pay a high price for mine, but nobody was interested in my opinion, certainly not my father, who never even asked for it. As an unattractive spinster with no inheritance I could either look after my brother's children—my brother who was a mediocre doctor but a man—or join a nunnery. I chose the least demeaning of the two alternatives" [Japp, *Breath of the Rose* 236].

Annelette's frustration and disappointment are completely understandable because of her undoubted intelligence. The extraordinary revelation that the Ptolemaic system of the earth fixed at the center of the universe is "totally erroneous" (part of the knowledge secreted in the abbey's library) triggers a flash of comprehension for her: "'Now I understand everything.... What an idiot, what a fool! And I call myself a scientist!'" (Japp, *Divine Blood* 24). However, in an unfortunate counterpoint to Éleusie's and Annelette's intelligence, Japp depicts the other nuns as mean-spirited, spiteful, really quite stupid and prone to melodramatic and hysterical overreaction. This lack of differentiation among the women also impacts upon Japp's crime narrative: when the perpetrator of the murders in the abbey is revealed, it is difficult to remember who she actually was. Annelette does experience some appreciation for her intelligence and initiative when the Knight Hospitaller, Francesco de Leone, includes her in his investigation and confides in her about his investigation into the "divine blood" shared by his mother and his aunts, two of who are Éleusie and Agnès's mother. But the inconsistency of Japp's treatment of women throughout her series indicates the challenges of navigating the medieval past through a "modern" female detective, despite the best feminist intentions.

Paganism, Witchcraft and Herblore: Evidence of Agency

The "wise woman" or "healer" is a popular character in medieval crime fiction. These women are frequently viewed with suspicion, living on the margins of society, in the forest or close by a river. They are often in danger of being accused of witchcraft and may become the scapegoat for adverse occurrences in their local vicinity. In Candace Robb's Owen Archer series, Magda, "the river woman," frequently assists Owen's wife, Lucie, with her dispensation of herbs and she also provides advice concerning pregnancy, abortion and childbirth to local women. Magda willingly offers her knowledge to everyone including—improbably but wonderfully—the Archbishop of York, John Thoresby, as he lies dying in Robb's *A Vigil of Spies* (2008). Thoresby recognizes the irony in "the unlikely friendship" between "a pagan healer and an archbishop," but also acknowledges that while Magda was "always quick to reject his prayers for her, … she gave of herself in a most Christian way" (Robb, *Vigil of Spies* 3). He had come to the rather enlightened conclusion that Magda's "good works far outweighed those he must disapprove of as a leader of the Church" (Robb, *Vigil of Spies* 4).

In Alys Clare's *Girl in a Red Tunic*, embittered former housemaid Sirida resorts to "a few little ruses" of her own in order to stay alive once the father of her child rejects her. In one example, Sirida poisons a local well and informs the sick villagers that they have offended the spirit of the spring and need her charms to save them. When the villagers pay her, Sirida stops putting the potion in the well and the people miraculously recover. Sirida defends her actions, answering the horror on abbess Helewise's face: "don't look like that, Helewise! It wouldn't have killed them, for I know my herbs better than to kill where I don't intend to…" (Clare, *Girl in a Red Tunic* 236).

In Barbara Reichmuth Geisler's Dame Averilla series, a local woman, Galiena, leads the local villagers into paganism, culminating in a battle against the bailiff's men in the forest surrounding Shaftesbury. Galiena is accused of witchcraft and subjected to an ordeal by hot iron, from which she emerges unscathed. At her trial, Galiena, like Sirida, challenges the charges against her, reminding her accusers that "both Margaret of Scotland and Henry the late king were interested in prophesy…. Neither of them was condemned for witchcraft. Geoffrey of Monmouth has recommended baths of water run over the stones on Salisbury Plain" (Geisler, *Other Gods* 210). The son of the bailiff wonders why Galiena was not hanged and his father supposes that "they didn't want to hang her because hanging is considered an honor in the old religion" (Geisler, *Other Gods* 210).

Geisler signals her intention to privilege alternative religious practices in the opening pages of her series: a young nun creeps around her abbey, stealing some pieces of the host (the non-consecrated bread since she is unable to summon her courage to touch the consecrated host, which appears to be protected by an invisible wall), some bones from the abbey's reliquary and a precious book of herbal lore from the infirmary. These items she gives to a messenger for delivery to Galiena.

Other Gods (2002) is set in the Abbey of the Virgin Mary and Edward, King and Martyr, in Shaftesbury in 1139. Unusually for a medieval detective dedicated to rational explanations, Dame Averilla—the central character of Geisler's series—possesses an uncanny ability to discern the thoughts and feelings of those around her. Abbess Emma initially views Averilla's "gift" with irritation, annoyed at "these forays into hysteria, which had rumpled the calm of her abbey" (Geisler, *Other Gods* 214). But even the abbess cannot dismiss Averilla's clairvoyance when the nun faints in a chapter meeting after feeling the searing heat of the hot iron that was, at that moment, being applied to Galiena's inner arm as part of her ordeal. After the prescribed three days, Galiena's bandage is removed to reveal no wound and only slight redness, while Averilla awakens in the abbey's infirmary to find that "An angry red blush, blistered and oozing, marred the inside of her arm" (Geisler, *Other Gods* 214).

Averilla's supernatural tendencies trouble the underlying rationality of medieval crime fiction, while the forceful Galiena promotes a paganism that appears entirely logical and appealing to the local townspeople. Moreover, Averilla's ability to discern the thoughts and feelings of others potentially displaces or even curtails her search for a secular, worldly solution to mysterious circumstances. In Geisler's series, the medieval detective's pragmatic rationalism resides in Emma, the abbess, who accepts what she cannot change, while admitting that initially the disruption that Averilla's "gift" caused "grated on the skin of my flesh like a fingernail on a slate" (Geisler, *Other Gods* 216). However, Emma reflects upon St. Paul's belief that everyone has their own particular gifts and she grudgingly concedes, "'Though I understand them not, I will accept that you have them. I will not try to root them out. But only,' her eyes rested on Averilla's with steely determination, 'insofar as they do not disturb tranquility of the community'" (Geisler, *Other Gods* 216). Consequently, Emma removes Averilla as infirmaress—where arguably her insights are most useful in discerning patients' ailments—and appoints her as sacrist, so she will have more time to contemplate God's purpose in bestowing upon her these unsettling traits.

Dame Frevisse: Ideal Medieval Nun, Ideal Medieval Detective

Margaret Frazer's Dame Frevisse epitomizes the religious female detective. The first six books of the series were co-authored by Gail Frazer and Mary Monica Pulver, after which Frazer continued alone, completing another eleven books, before her death in 2013. The series' opening novel, *The Novice's Tale* (1992), introduces the modest, "not poor, but neither ... rich" (5), priory of St. Frideswide's in Oxfordshire and its small contingent of Benedictine nuns. In 1431, the priory's only novice, Thomasine, is about to take her final vows when the arrival of her great-aunt, Lady Ermentrude, throws the ceremonial arrangements and the priory into chaos with her insistence that her young niece makes a secular marriage instead of becoming a bride of Christ. Dame Frevisse is the priory's hosteller, responsible for providing hospitality for its guests. Her position forces her to deal with Lady Ermentrude's rowdy retinue and to investigate the old woman's subsequent murder, a task made more urgent when suspicion falls upon Thomasine. Frevisse's career as a medieval detective progresses over the next sixteen books, covering approximately twenty years. Eventually, in the series' final book, *The Apostate's Tale* (2008), Frevisse is elected prioress.

In the opening pages of *The Novice's Tale*, the prioress and Frevisse are entertaining Thomas Chaucer (son of Geoffrey), described as "one of the richest and most powerful commoners in England" (5). Indeed, Chaucer's cousin Henry Beaufort, Cardinal and the Bishop of Winchester, "was pleased to ask his advice" (Frazer, *Novice's Tale* 5). The Beauforts were the four children of Philippa Chaucer's sister, Katherine Swynford and John of Gaunt, who, after the couple's marriage, were legitimized through an act of parliament. The unworldly Thomasine is appalled to witness the easy familiarity between Frevisse and the esteemed visitor, prompting Frevisse to explain, "It's all right, Thomasine. Master Chaucer's lady wife is my aunt and I spent eight years of my growing up in her household. We're kin and have known each other for as long as you've been alive" (Frazer, *Novice's Tale* 8). They discuss the marriage of Chaucer's daughter, Alice, to the Earl of Suffolk, as well as Chaucer's recent resignation from the King's Council. Thomas, it transpires, has "bought" his way out of a title, avoiding the additional duties and taxes that such a position entails. Thomas Chaucer plays a significant role in the early novels of the series, encouraging Frevisse's developing skill as a solver of mysteries. After Chaucer's death in 1434, described in *The Bishop's Tale* (1994), Frevisse spends more time with her cousin Alice, now Duchess of Suffolk, and, through this connection, becomes embroiled in the intrigues of court.

Dame Frevisse, unlike many of the other religious female detectives considered in this chapter, entered her priory with a true vocation. She maintains a deep, complex and evolving relationship with her faith, acknowledging the weaknesses and frustrations that are born of her natural inclination towards impatience and disobedience, while always finding solace in the performance of the religious offices and the maintenance of the priory's routine. In *The Servant's Tale* (1993), a group of traveling players arrives at St. Frideswide's seeking accommodation and bringing with them the body of the priory's kitchen maid's husband. During the ensuing investigation Frevisse finds herself drawn to one of the players, Joliffe, and when she examines these feelings with characteristic self-awareness, she recognizes that "She was caring too much about Joliffe, instead of about the truth" (Frazer, *Servant's Tale* 200). In her efforts to ensure that the odious coroner, Master Montfort, does not follow through with his threat to hang Joliffe and his companions for murder, she also realizes that the travelling group arouses in her "a long-dormant love for the endless journeying of her youth. They had brought alive again a part of herself she had loved and never fully left" (Frazer, *Servant's Tale* 200).

Frevisse contemplates the familiarity of her nun's garb and comprehends both its meaning and constriction: what it bestows upon her and what it denies her. Seeking relief, she forces herself to concentrate on the service that surrounds her, "losing herself in the chanted repetition of the psalms, soaking in the words with her mind and soul, listening with a novice's fervour for answers that had to be there" (Frazer, *Servant's Tale* 200). Frevisse obtains those answers, as she always does, and experiences a sense of danger avoided, sure of her vocation and her rightful place once again. The nun's self-reflexivity and ability to find solace in the contemplation of the liturgy is unusual, perhaps unique, among medieval religious detectives and contributes significantly to Frevisse's depth of character.

She is also one of the more diligent in her religious practices; when she is not able to attend a church to hear the daily canonical offices, Frevisse always finds a quiet corner or window embrasure in which to kneel and recite the psalms to herself. Not many share her conscientiousness: on one occasion, when traveling with her prioress, Domina Elisabeth, Frevisse thought it "reasonable to suppose they would say the Office" before going to bed. Elisabeth, however, is tired, saying, "'I think we can forgo prayers tonight. God surely understands our weariness'" (Frazer, *Clerk's Tale* 98). Frevisse says nothing, but later speaks a little sharply to her prioress, "already offended ... at having Compline so lightly dismissed" (Frazer, *Clerk's Tale* 99).

As a consequence of this true vocation, and again unlike other religious detectives, Dame Frevisse resists the need to leave her priory, feeling frustrated when called upon by outsiders to perform services that she frequently questions. By the penultimate book of the series, *The Traitor's Tale* (2007), Frevisse is thoroughly tired of the Duchess's summons to attend to her once again: "For her cousin Alice of Suffolk's sake she had been out of St Frideswide's all too lately, ... And now her cousin needed her again and Frevisse had been given leave to go to her" (Frazer, *Traitor's Tale* 26). In fact, Frevisse has been ordered to go to Alice by Domina Elisabeth not because the prioress is overly concerned about Alice's need for Frevisse, but because of the Duchess's potential as a benefactor to St. Frideswide's. Frevisse prays "not only for strength to do what she did not wish to, but that she be not angry at Alice for demanding her help and even angrier at Domina Elisabeth for sending her away so readily" (Frazer, *Traitor's Tale* 26).

However, this reluctance in no way compromises the effectiveness of Dame Frevisse's performance as a medieval detective. She is highly intelligent, resourceful and preternaturally perceptive. Indeed, the younger nuns view Frevisse with some trepidation, believing that she is able to perceive their thoughts. Novice Thomasine feels Frevisse's scrutiny sharply, uneasy at the older nun's ability to read her mind: "Her eyes were still resolutely down and she did not think she had moved, but Dame Frevisse, with her discomfiting skill at knowing what someone else was thinking, ..." answered her unspoken concern (Frazer, *Novice's Tale* 8). As is the case with every medieval detective, Frevisse also refuses to consider supernatural intervention, briskly dismissing the rumor among the young nuns of the priory that the appearance of demons caused their cook's heart to fail: "Frevisse let her impatience show. 'I doubt it,' she said crisply. 'There was distinctly no smell of brimstone in the room'" (Frazer, *Servant's Tale* 74).

Frevisse shares with Peter Tremayne's Sister Fidelma frequent feelings of frustration with the shortcomings of others; unlike Fidelma, Frevisse endeavors to curb her natural impatience, although her intolerance of foolishness often reveals itself. For example, Cecely, returning to the priory after forsaking her vows and running away several years previously, ruefully ponders, "Among everything Cecely had willingly forgotten about St Frideswide's was Dame Frevisse. Always one of the older nuns, the woman had a way of never showing on her face what she was thinking.... Dame Frevisse had mostly kept to a forbidding silence that always made Cecely certain that, whatever the woman was thinking, it was unkindly" (Frazer, *Apostate's Tale* 10).

Frevisse's rational intelligence enables her to comprehend the solution to a mystery or to identify the murderer before anyone else: "The pieces went together in Frevisse's mind with the silver chink of dropping coins.

They had not finished falling before she was on her feet and running" (Frazer, *Novice's Tale* 218). In keeping with her innate modesty—and in stark contrast with Fidelma's grandstanding—Frevisse never commands a roomful of people in order to explain the solution to her investigations, preferring instead a discreet discussion with her prioress, her cousin, or other close associate.

Frevisse elegantly navigates her medieval landscape, ensuring that her incarnation as a modern literary detective causes minimal disruption. Frazer has embedded Frevisse so deeply and successfully into her premodern religious role that her declaration in *The Traitor's Tale* that she is the lover of the Duke of Suffolk—at Joliffe's insistence and for the sake of their joint investigation—is entirely ludicrous and wrenches the reader out of Frazer's carefully reconstructed fifteenth century. Frevisse (reluctantly) acquiesces to the demands of the patriarchal system that dominates her world, while also manipulating that system to ensure justice is found. In the early novels, Frevisse is confounded by the King's coroner for northern Oxfordshire, Master Morys Montfort, whom Frevisse considers "an arrogant fool" (Frazer, *Servant's Tale* 173). Despite her poor opinion of him and Montfort's breathtakingly bad decisions, Frevisse manages his interference by ostensibly conceding to his misplaced opinion about women, nuns and Frevisse herself: "He glared at Frevisse. 'Someone is interfering in what is not their business. Again';" and later in the same interview with Domina Edith, "'Collecting gossip from a priory nun is hardly likely to prove valuable,' Montfort said, ... Frevisse, not wanting to quarrel, or to lie by seeming to agree with him, bowed her head again and tucked her hands even further up her sleeves" (Frazer, *Servant's Tale* 174–75).

Such demonstrations of ostensible capitulation may be difficult for Frevisse to endure but represent an important part of her success as a detective. In a common scenario, particularly for women detectives, Frevisse is forced to undertake the investigation herself in order to prevent Montfort's prosecution of the wrong suspect. In this way, Montfort occupies the medieval crime fiction trope of hostile sheriff; indeed, it is unusual that a coroner plays the role of the incompetent, corrupt representative of the law. Ironically, Frevisse finds herself investigating Montfort's own murder in *The Clerk's Tale* (2002).

Dame Frevisse, eventually Domina Frevisse, is not only an effective detective, she appears perfectly suited to her medieval life. Frazer is therefore among the more successful in achieving the difficult balance between creating an authentic, well-researched and sympathetically reimagined fifteenth century, and the depiction of an appealingly competent literary detective.

Medieval Women Detectives in Brief

There are more medieval crime fiction detectives than there are available pages to do them justice. This is especially true for the women of medieval crime fiction, too many of whom have been necessarily omitted. While not able to undertake a considered analysis here, there are several authors and characters who are worth mentioning in brief.

As discussed in Chapters Two and Three, Paul C. Doherty is the author of many different series of historical fiction, most of which involve mystery or crime narratives. Doherty has two series featuring medieval women, Kathryn Swinbrooke and Mathilde of Westminster. Swinbrooke is an apothecary and physician living in Canterbury in the latter half of the fifteenth century. As is customary, she has a male companion, Irish soldier Colum Murtagh, who works for the crown and consequently affords Kathryn the requisite authority that is sometimes required for her investigations. Kathryn is wonderfully independent, even after marrying Colum, and maintains her occupation as the pair's "lead detective." With Mathilde of Westminster, Doherty returns to the historical period of his greatest expertise, the early fourteenth century and the reign of Edward II and Queen Isabella (Doherty's doctoral thesis examined the queen and her lover, Roger Mortimer). Mathilde is a physician, well-regarded in London, unusually unencumbered with a masculine assistant, and, with the benefit of hindsight, she recounts her past experiences as a lady-in-waiting for Isabella.

Maureen Ash, in addition to her Bascot de Marins series (see Chapter Three), has written two novels in her Anglo-Norman series featuring Estrid, a widow who is forced into the role of detective in order to save her son from an accusation of murder. Set in 1088, just after William the Conqueror's death, in the town of Rochester, Estrid is reluctantly well-suited for her new occupation because she is the daughter of an English nobleman killed at the Battle of Hastings. In her second novel, Ash continues to explore the tensions between conquerors and conquered through Estrid's (again reluctant) investigation into the death of an English bride during her marriage to a Norman knight.

Another recent series with only two novels so far is the The Chaucy Shire Medieval Mysteries, by New Zealand author Odelia Floris (a beautifully medievalist name). Set in southwest England in 1430, Rowena Walden is forced by a malicious relative to assist as clerk to the local sheriff, Sir Richard. The novels are overlaid with strong romance tropes, as well as an exploration of the pagan implications of the "forest-dwellers" who appear in both.

Not so recent, but also comprising only two novels is Judith Koll Healey's Alais Capet series. Alais is a princess of France, sister to King Philip, and rumored to have had a child with England's Henry II. Set in England and France around 1200, Eleanor of Aquitaine still has influence and directs Alais's actions. Healey achieves an interesting combination of feminist themes, court intrigue, mystery and romance, but tempers a potentially disruptive modernity by overlaying Alais's refreshingly elitist (for medieval crime fiction) worldview: "The independence I so admired earlier now annoyed me no end. After all, I was a *princesse royale*. And who was this peasant to talk of honor? Monks running around commanding armies, peasants thinking they had honor to protect. The entire world was in disarray" (276). There are also references to medieval literature such as *Sir Gawain and the Green Knight* and a wonderful description of Alais's half-sister, Marie of Champagne, insisting that her court pledge allegiance to the code of love developed at her direction by the monk, Andreas Capellanus (Healey 245–46).

Candace Robb's medieval studies credentials are well applied to her Owen Archer series (see Chapters Two and Six), in which Owen's wife, Lucie, could easily be described as a medieval detective. Robb also has two other medieval crime series featuring women. Robb's three novels featuring Margaret Kerr are set in Scotland in the turbulent late thirteenth century and are perhaps better described as a spy or thriller series than conventional detective narratives. Margaret is an excellent character, demonstrating impressive and believable ingenuity in order to navigate the restrictions on female agency that Robb brings to the fore while Margaret searches for her missing husband. Robb's new series features Kate Clifford and comprises two novels so far (written in 2016 and 2017). Robb returns to her favorite town of York at the very end of the fourteenth century, during the period leading up to Richard II's deposition. Kate is another independently minded young woman, determined to manipulate the patriarchal hierarchy of the Middle Ages and, recalling Roberta Gellis's wonderful Magdalene, she sets up a guesthouse that also caters discreetly for the powerful men of York and their mistresses. In the second novel, Kate's unlikeable mother returns from France and the realistic tension between mother and daughter evinces Robb's talent for creating believable medieval female characters.

Authenticity is not, however, a characteristic of Sarah Woodbury's Gareth and Gwen medieval mysteries, set in the twelfth-century Welsh kingdoms. Gwen is an itinerant bard's daughter who meets and eventually marries a young knight, Gareth. The series is dreadfully anachronistic in language and plot, although the ten novels and one novella published since 2011 speak to its appeal to readers.

It is also worth mentioning one novel by Barbara Cherne, *Bella Donna* (2001), with the interesting character of Giuditta, the cook for a wealthy Florentine family, set in 1494. Giuditta may be the only cook who also functions as a detective, male or female, in medieval crime fiction. And Ned Hayes's novel, *Sinful Folk* (2012), features another unusual detective-character in Mear, a former nun living disguised as a mute man in the northeast of England in 1377, who conducts her "investigation" throughout a heartbreaking pilgrimage accompanying villagers who are conveying the bodies of their dead children to the king in order to demand justice.

Finally, Karen Maitland is the author who has caused the most difficulty in the decision whether or not to include her novels in this book. She is a member of the Medieval Murderers, discussed in Chapter Three, but she has also written several medieval thrillers that are almost—but not quite—detective narratives. Her novels are not part of a series and, while they do feature mysteries to unravel and deceptions to penetrate, there is often more than one character who could be designated as the "detective," and, more concerning for the parameters of this book, there is a preponderance of supernatural themes that make for fascinating narratives, but counteract the human solution demanded by crime fiction conventions. This addendum is intended as an acknowledgment of Maitland's female characters who are complex, captivating and compromising (such as the protagonist and antagonist in *Company of Liars* [2008] and the brave women in *The Owl Killers* [2009]), and who certainly earn a mention in a chapter celebrating contemporary crime fiction's depiction of medieval women.

This chapter considers a selection of the wonderful women who populate medieval crime fiction. These women vary in age and occupation, family and vocation, but they all share a deep sense of justice, as well as the requisite bravery and intelligence to overcome the restrictions of their premodern context in order to ensure that justice is served.

Like male religious detectives, many women join monastic orders for reasons other than vocation, as was certainly the case in the Middle Ages. Clark's Hildegard, for example, wants to establish her own priory because "Only by joining forces with other like-minded women in our own houses can we garner the power to change anything" (*Hangman Blind* 13). It also appears that medieval female religious detectives are more likely than their male counterparts to leave their calling in order to pursue love (in the case of Helewise and Catherine LeVendeur) or logic (as does Fidelma). Dame Frevisse and Prioress Eleanor are two exceptions in that they both demonstrate a true vocation and only reluctantly direct their considerable intelligence and powers of observation towards solving crime.

There is no doubt that medievalist ideas about mysticism, paganism, herblore and other "spiritualist" practices emerge more strongly in medieval crime novels featuring female detectives than in other versions of the genre. This may be due to the perception that women of the Middle Ages were fated to heavily restricted lives that precluded the activities necessary for performing the role of detective. And this is, for the most part, true. Medieval women were primarily controlled by the wishes and needs of the men that surrounded them: fathers, husbands, brothers, guardians, kings. But for medieval crime fiction authors to discount female agency to such an extent that they require supernatural intervention in order to succeed in an investigation is to detract from the achievements of medieval women such as powerful queens, determined pilgrims, independent widows and efficient wives.

These medieval female detectives potentially trouble the feminist appropriation of crime fiction because rarely are they able to act with complete autonomy: they are almost always accompanied by a male protector, guide, or partner. In particular, medieval women detectives struggle to take advantage of Horsley's identification of hardboiled fiction as "the most compelling model" for feminist appropriation (248). While all of these medieval women are brave and, to a greater or lesser extent, able to protect themselves physically, none is as capable of trained, systematic violence in the manner of Paretsky's V.I. Warshawski, to take one familiar example. Unlike other women depicted in contemporary medievalism—such as the shield maidens of the History Channel's *Vikings* series or Tolkien's Rohirrim warrior-princess Éowyn—medieval crime fiction's women are not expected to fight, nor are they trained to do so. While they do demonstrate initiative, strength and bravery in situations of extreme peril, their methods for protecting themselves generally involve making haphazard use of whatever comes to hand in an uncomfortable allusion to feminine household practicality.

Across medieval crime fiction, this surprising conforming to type for female characters not only suggests a conservatism that is absent from other forms of crime fiction, it also indicates the authors' own desire to perpetuate the view of the Middle Ages as a period generally lacking in female agency. While this perception can certainly be challenged in relation to other aspects of medieval life for women such as financial autonomy or independence of movement, creating a female detective who behaves in a recognizably hardboiled manner, for example, will certainly undermine the authenticity of her medieval context. However, as Horsley also notes, simply substituting a woman for a male detective is too simplistic to serve the feminist appropriation of crime fiction (243). There are other roles that female characters may occupy (including the perpetrator of crime) to assist in portraying the diversity of medieval women, and medieval crime fiction performs admirably in the creation of the variety of characters who surround and support the female detectives of the Middle Ages. Moreover, by depicting women who complicate the traditional divide between "courtly" and "fabliau" ladies in medieval narratives, these female detectives reinforce the recovery of the "clever" lady by feminist scholars of the Middle Ages (Adams 82).

Chapter Five

"There are no Jews in England"

There is a scene in Margaret Frazer's *The Sempster's Tale* (2006) that encapsulates the way medieval crime fiction typically represents Jewish characters, depicts the so-called blood libel and finesses the reality that there were no Jewish people living in England (legally) in the later Middle Ages. It is summer, 1450, and in the crypt of St. Swithin's Church in London, the body of a fifteen-year-old boy lies in the fashion of a crucified Christ, with stab marks to his feet, hands and through his right side. More disturbingly, his chest and stomach are covered in shallow wounds that appear to form Hebrew letters. The horrified observers surrounding the week-old, decaying corpse include Brother Michael, an English Franciscan friar attached to the French Inquisition currently visiting England to preach against and investigate Lollardy. Brother Michael immediately interprets the signs on the body as evidence that "'This was no plain killing. This was done by Jews. It was one of their ritual murders!'" (Frazer, *Sempster's Tale* 118). The other onlookers in the crypt instantly recall England's two boy-saints, William of Norwich and Little St. Hugh of Lincoln, also believed to have been murdered by Jewish perpetrators. However, those killings occurred in 1144 and 1255, respectively, and this is the year 1450. As St. Swithin's priest, Father Walter, rather desperately claims, "'There've been no Jews in England for a hundred years and more,'" while Frazer's medieval detective, the nun Dame Frevisse, carefully points out that "'Pope after pope has decreed there's no such thing as ritual murder by Jews'" (Frazer, *Sempster's Tale* 117, 119).

In November 1290, Edward I asked the English parliament to issue a series of expulsion orders aimed at forcing the country's Jewish population to leave. Jewish people had arrived with the Norman Conquest (there is no evidence of Jewish settlement in England prior to this event) and by the time of the expulsion, this population was still very small, numbering between 2,000 and 5,000 (Barkey and Katznelson 476). Jewish people did not return officially to England until three hundred and sixty or so years later, during Cromwell's interregnum in the 1650s. One of the more insidious accusations frequently leveled at Jewish communities throughout medieval Europe was the participation in the ritual murder of children, mainly boys, and several cults arose around the martyrdom of "saints" such as William of Norwich and Hugh of Lincoln. While most of these English cases occurred in towns where there were thriving Jewish populations, before the time of the expulsion orders, there were persistent rumors that some Jewish people remained in England after Edward's edicts, practicing their religion in secret. Compounding these rumors was the belief, consistent throughout the Middle Ages, that the crucifixion of Christ was a distinctly Jewish (as opposed to Roman) crime and large sections of the population suspected that this scene was secretly reenacted during Jewish Passover rituals.

The portrayal of Jewish characters in medieval crime fiction is surprisingly widespread, especially given the fact that many of these novels confront the historical challenge of being located in England during the time of Edward's expulsion orders. More strikingly—and crucially for what it reveals about the motivation of medieval crime fiction authors—these Jewish characters are inevitably described in positive terms and, while they are always suspected of the crimes, they are never the culprits. Consequently, a common *modus operandi* is to have the real murderers adorn their victims with strange symbols or position them in a crucified pose in order to direct suspicion towards local Jewish residents. By adhering to this narrative so consistently, medieval crime fiction authors engage with the challenges of depicting premodern constructions of race in today's post–Holocaust era. Anti-Semitism was an unavoidable and persistent feature of the Middle Ages, resulting in pogroms against Jewish communities, accusations of ritual murder, and the anti–Jewish polemic found in many medieval texts. But not in medieval crime fiction: this chapter demonstrates how contemporary debates about race and recent work on medieval Jewish history have seemingly foreclosed replication of the anti-Semitism that constituted a significant part of medieval life.

While this chapter focuses upon the depiction of Jewish characters in medieval crime fiction, due to their preponderance throughout the genre, there are a few examples of Muslim characters, as well as the occasional reference to African and Asian peoples. In Ariana Franklin's series featuring medically trained Adelia Aguilar, for example, Adelia resentfully hides behind the fiction that her Muslim protector, Mansur, is the doctor and she is his assistant, in order to combat the misogynistic suspicions of thirteenth-century England (see Chapter Four). For Franklin, it seems, the prejudice against women in the Middle Ages is more irksome than racial tensions. Described in more detail below, Caroline Roe's Jewish detective, Isaac, has a Moorish assistant, Yusuf, whose elite Muslim family features in several of her novels. David Penny's English physician-detective Thomas Berrington, discussed in Chapter Two, is embedded in his Muslim world in the last years of Moorish Spain.

It is now common to see examples of popular culture that justify violence on the basis of their "medievalness." The glaringly obvious example is HBO's *Game of Thrones*, but the language of medieval violence also appears in political scenarios such as the so-called "War on Terror" and the "knights" and faux-medieval heraldry of the Ku Klux Klan and other extreme-right groups.[1] Helen Young argues that scholars of medievalism are familiar with the overlap between nationalisms and medievalisms in the modern period (2), but that theories of "race" have been largely ignored because of the assumption that this is a "post-medieval construct" (3). Young points out that "Studies of medievalism skirt around the edges of contact with race, but only rarely do more than dip their toes in those difficult waters" (2). Recently, however, scholars have attempted to do more than "dip their toes" with regard to race both in the Middle Ages and in contemporary, popular reimaginings of the medieval, evinced by the excellent scholarship listed in a collaboratively produced bibliographic resource, curated by Jonathan Hsy and Julie Orlemanski ("Race and Medieval Studies").[2]

As this chapter shows, medieval crime fiction's engagement with race appears overwhelmingly concerned with rejecting the anti-Semitism of the European Middle Ages. In this way, the genre's depiction of Jewish characters reveals the reluctance of modernity to inhabit completely and authentically the world that medievalism constructs. Furthermore, this depiction represents an ideal instance of Umberto Eco's postmodern irony combined with Lacanian *jouissance*: what contemporary popular culture desires most is to keep desiring the medieval, without ever having to return to the historical Middle Ages.

The Blood Libel and Child Martyrs

While medieval anti-Semitism is undeniable, the so-called blood libel was actually more prevalent in later periods. Many still consider accusations of child ritual murder to be a medieval phenomenon, often cited as representing "all that is darkest about the Middle Ages," but E.M. Rose points out that "it spread most widely during the modern period" and that "in fact the twelfth century was a fairly peaceful time for them [Jewish communities]"

(1, 11, 6). Similarly, Karen Barkey and Ira Katznelson state that "Although punctuated by a small number of allegations of anti-Christian ritual killing and extensive popular assaults in 1189–90, the initial twelve decades of Jewish settlement in England were a time of relative prosperity and coexistence" (485). Indeed, the libel surfaced more frequently in the Early Modern period than throughout the entire Middle Ages, while more occurrences emerged in the nineteenth century than the total number of cases in the preceding centuries (Rose 11).[3]

The blood libel accusation is also not restricted to Europe. Disturbingly, as late as 1928, in the upstate New York town of Massena, a local cafe owner started a rumor that his town's Jewish population had abducted a missing four-year-old girl in order to use her blood in a Yom Kippur ritual. The mayor and police took the accusation seriously enough to call in the town's most senior rabbi for questioning. In the meantime, with the tacit approval of the mayor and police, volunteer fire fighters searched the premises of Jewish shop owners. The little girl had fallen asleep under a tree after becoming lost in the surrounding woods and was found safe, but this did not prevent a mob of people taunting Jewish worshippers as they congregated on the eve of Yom Kippur.[4] In another example, during the 2003 Israeli election controversy erupted over the publication of a political cartoon depicting Prime Minister Ariel Sharon devouring a baby's torso, with the caption, "What's wrong ... you never seen a politician kissing babies before?" While the title of the cartoon references Francisco de Goya's eighteenth-century painting, *Saturn Devouring his Children*, it also "makes appalling sense within a vintage antisemitic ontology of Jewish child-murder" (Bale, *Jew in the Medieval Book* 7). More recently, in an opinion column for the *New York Times* in December 2015, Sara Lipton connected language that "killed medieval Jews" with the hate speech that is prevalent in contemporary America, concluding that "harsh words do lead to violent acts" (Lipton). For scholars such as Anthony Bale and Lipton, today's fraught race relations have partial origins in medieval constructions of race that had no historical basis in factual events or beliefs. In addition to the considerable scholarly interest in reassessing and reframing the historical evidence, as briefly touched on below, medieval crime fiction intervenes into this discourse by attempting to rehabilitate the erroneously slandered medieval Jewish communities.

In a compelling analysis of the historiography surrounding the ritual murder accusation, Hannah R. Johnson contends that while this "legend occupies a tiny corner of historiography," it functions as "an overloaded circuit" when mobilized to account for "the difficult course of Jewish-Christian history, the violence of the Holocaust, and even modern Israeli politics" (2). Johnson acknowledges that the historical indeterminacy of the actual events that lay behind accusations of ritual murder contributes to speculation and anxiety, even though historians may be confident "that Jewish communities did not engage in conspiracies to murder Christian children" (3). Similarly, Rose notes that "No charge [of ritual murder] has withstood historical scrutiny" (1).

Nevertheless, the historical indeterminacy that Johnson identifies offers a rich vein of narrative possibilities for authors of medieval crime fiction: because Christians in medieval Europe were generally deeply mistrustful and fearful of Jewish people, the latter served as easy targets for blame when an unexplained murder or suspicious disappearance occurred. Most people were happy to accept the convenient explanation that "Jews" killed "Christians" out of spite or to enact mysterious religious rites. Medieval crime fiction's response to the challenge of depicting premodern racial prejudice in the post-modern era is twofold: firstly, the medieval detective must overcome this embedded, yet casual, anti-Semitism and work to dispel erroneous superstitions; and secondly, the genre ensures that its Jewish characters are sympathetic, intelligent and kind—and certainly not involved in murder, let alone of a child. Johnson, however, warns that the historiographic project of assigning blame for past deeds is ethically fraught: "Blame only has meaning under a certain version of responsibility, and it concerns how answerable we are, as nations, cultures, or religious groups, for past sins committed in our name" (8). In other words, historicism that is concerned with blame may be limited by "a politics of reparations and essential identity" (Johnson 8). Authors of medieval crime fiction contribute to this historiographical complexity—consciously or unconsciously—through their depiction and rejection of medieval anti-Semitism.

The earliest written account of an accusation of child ritual murder by Jewish perpetrators concerns a young, twelve-year-old apprentice, William of Norwich. The boy's battered body was discovered in Thorpe Wood, outside the town, on the day before Easter, 1144.[5] At the time, William's uncle, a priest, publicly accused the town's Jewish population of his murder at a diocesan synod (McCulloh 701); however, no one was condemned for the crime and interest in the case soon petered out. Sometime before 1150, a Benedictine monk named Thomas of Monmouth arrived in Norwich and began to compose a hagiographic treatise about William, titled *The Life and Passion of Saint William of Norwich*, which he completed more than twenty years later. Thomas undertook an investigation into the case, describing his personal visit to the scene of the crime and interviewing witnesses who had not spoken out in 1144. Indeed, "The story, as Brother Thomas was later to recount it, offered an intriguing mystery, one in which he features himself prominently as a crusading detective" (Rose 15).

Thomas's work is divided into seven books: the first two contain a detailed account of William's murder and outlines the case against the "Norwich Jews"; the last five books recount the multiple reburials of William's body and the miracles that had since occurred at his tomb and elsewhere (Thomas). Thomas's most damning piece of evidence comes from Theobald, a convert to Christianity after hearing about the miracles attributed to the boy saint. Theobald stated that Jewish communities yearly sacrificed a Christian "in contempt of Christ" and that in 1144, the rabbis and leaders in Narbonne had decided that the ritual would take place in England. Subsequently, all of the English Jewish communities had agreed upon Norwich as the location (McCulloh 703). Theobald's testimony also allowed for the possibility that ritual murder was a regular occurrence and could therefore account for unexplained or suspicious deaths in the past and in the future.

Rose connects William's death with another murder: a Jewish banker killed by servants of Simon de Novers, a knight recently returned from the Crusades and deeply in debt to the banker. The trial reached the royal court in London, where a bishop, William Turbe, defended de Novers by claiming that, instead of his client facing the accusation of murder, the entire Jewish community, including the banker, should be charged with killing William of Norwich. Rose suggests that this accusation by Turbe heavily influenced Thomas's *vita* (3). Thomas's hagiography also created a common enemy that served to unite the Norwich populace. In a postcolonial analysis, Jeffrey J. Cohen examines the nationalist work that Thomas's *vita* undertakes by providing a cultural and religious other that coheres the Normans and Anglo-Saxons of the town in their shared hatred: "A neglected and impoverished leatherworker in life, dead William is transfigured in Thomas's text into a new patron for a city that had been riven by the conquest" (28).

Johnson, attempting to problematize the historiography of blame surrounding accusations of ritual murder, draws a parallel between Thomas's effort to canonize the life of William and condemn the Norwich Jews, and twentieth-century anti-Semitism historian Gavin I. Langmuir's concern to rebut those claims. Both of these men, Johnson claims, share "a preoccupation with assigning blame and determining guilt": like the twelfth-century monk whose work he condemns, Langmuir's "moralization of history is also an explicit project of judgment" (24). Johnson's observation raises a dilemma for authors of historical fiction generally and those writing about medieval race relations in particular. Do contemporary post–Holocaust racial sensitivities preclude particular narratives that may inadvertently raise the specter of child ritual murder during Jewish religious practices?

Between the mid–twelfth century—when Thomas of Monmouth was composing his *vita* of young William—and the mid–thirteenth century, Langmuir counts four shrines established in England to the alleged victims of Jewish ritual murder ("The Knight's Tale" 463). Notably, in each of these cases, as well as for the victim of the single shrine in France, no French or English king had condemned their Jewish communities for these murders (Langmuir, "The Knight's Tale" 464). Barkey and Katznelson confirm his findings, pointing out that before the mid-thirteenth century, kings did not respond to anti–Jewish demands from their barons or the populace, despite the strong anti-Semitic sentiments expressed in contemporary ballads, chronicles and sermons: "Indeed, over most of the course of Jewish settlement, kings staunchly shielded 'their' Jews from such pressures" (478).

Rather than attribute the appalling treatment of medieval Jewish people solely to unfettered anti–Semitism, Barkey and Katznelson instead argue that the expulsion of the Jewish populations from both England and France was directly affected by the 1214 Battle of Bouvines, after which the countries embarked upon "separate trajectories of state building" (480). The authors explain that:

> Before Bouvines, Jews had been part of dynastic rule, where their presence produced clear economic advantages. After Bouvines, new goals of state building and new extractive bargaining relationships with urban and rural society deeply affected the fate of Jews in both countries [481].

In England, for example, all Jewish people were the "property" of the king, while in France they belonged to any of the numerous and powerful barons, of which the king was just one (Barkey and Katznelson 482). So while Edward I's expulsion edicts applied to Jewish communities throughout England, decisions by Philip IV could only affect those from the royal demesne and not those residing in jurisdictions controlled by other French barons (Barkey and Katznelson 482). Jewish populations were thus subject both to the unpredictable vicissitudes of mob-fueled anti-Semitic violence and to the political imperatives of their monarchs.

The period of non-intervention by English kings into the circumstances surrounding accusations of ritual murder ended abruptly in 1255 with the case of Little St. Hugh of Lincoln. On 31 July, twelve-year-old Hugh disappeared and his body was discovered about a month later, on 29 August, in the well of a local Jewish man named Copin (or Jopin).[6] Suspicions were immediately directed towards Lincoln's Jewish citizens, swelled by the presence of a significant number of visitors who had recently gathered in Lincoln to celebrate a wedding. On 4 October, Henry III arrived in Lincoln and ordered the execution of Copin and the arrest of ninety-one other Jewish men who were then committed to stand trial in London. Eighteen of these were executed for refusing to submit to a verdict handed down by a Christian jury. Having been condemned to death at their Westminster trial on 3 February 1256, the remaining prisoners were subsequently released at the behest of the king's brother, Richard of Cornwall, to whom Henry had temporarily assigned his rights over the Jewish people of England.

Henry's intervention into this case remains unusual. No other king had ever executed a Jewish person for ritual murder and, at the time, "Frederick II and Innocent IV had already officially declared their disbelief in the related blood libel" (Langmuir, "Knight's Tale" 479). Langmuir speculates that a canon of Lincoln Cathedral, John de Lexinton, forced a confession out of Copin and promised him clemency. De Lexinton then presented the king with written evidence of a crime that Henry might have otherwise dismissed. Instead, Henry overturned Copin's immunity and had him immediately executed. Langmuir believes that "Had the fantasy of ritual murder never developed, young Hugh would have remained but one of thousands of unrecorded victims of homicide or accidental death" ("Knight's Tale" 461).

The story of Hugh achieved widespread notoriety because of the sensationalist account by Matthew Paris, the well-known thirteenth-century chronicler. As Langmuir points out, however, Paris is famously unreliable in his narrative and while "His ability to tell a compelling story is indubitable, ... even his basic chronology of the Lincoln affair is wrong" ("Knight's Tale" 464). Paris's version of the Hugh story is probably the one known to Geoffrey Chaucer. As with other examples of the blood libel, the tale of Little St. Hugh has proven to be unsettlingly tenacious. Langmuir suggests that the murder "did not seem distant to Chaucer some 135 years later" and he goes on to outline recurrences of the boy's story down the centuries: in the early eighteenth century, the *Acta Sanctorum* established 27 July as his martyr's day; in the early nineteenth century, Charles Lamb is afraid to enter a synagogue because of the tale of Hugh's death; and in 1911, a Lincoln brochure directed tourists to the well into which Hugh's body had been thrown (Langmuir, "Knight's Tale" 460).

It was not until 1928 that it was discovered that this famous well belonging to "the Jew's house" was in fact built by a worker in order "to augment the antiquarian value of the house" (Langmuir, "Knight's Tale" 461). The cathedral's shrine to Little St. Hugh was destroyed during the Reformation, not as a redemptive act for the falsely accused Lincoln Jews, but instead in the name of the protestant denial of saints. In 1959, the authorities in Lincoln

Cathedral erected a plaque next to the ruins of Little St. Hugh's shrine, acknowledging the "trumped-up" nature of the ritual murder accusations and, with masterful understatement, conceding that "such stories do not redound to the credit of Christendom" (Bale, "Afterword" 297). The plaque goes on to ask God for forgiveness—but not the Jewish people.

Langmuir's characterization of Thomas's *Life and Miracles of William of Norwich* as the point of origin for the "fantasy" of Jewish ritual murder has maintained its critical currency since his groundbreaking 1984 essay, in which he casts Thomas as the earliest example of the English amateur detective. As Langmuir explains in his memorable and apposite opening:

> The detective story in which the investigator is an amateur without official standing is a peculiarly English genre. Perhaps the earliest example, telling of an investigation that was pursued unofficially by an individual who arrived on the scene after the crime, disagreed with the official stand, pursued his own investigation, and reported the results, is "The Life and Passion of Saint William the Martyr of Norwich," which Thomas of Monmouth started in 1149/50 and completed in 1172/73 ["Thomas of Monmouth" 820].

More recently, critics have expanded Langmuir's historicist approach and considered the long-term cultural impact of the entrenched belief in the blood libel throughout the later Middle Ages. Bale acknowledges that the accusation was partly responsible for the execution and expulsion of Jewish people from Bury St. Edmunds in 1190, Lincoln in 1255 and Le Puy in 1320–21. However, he also points out that historians are "well aware that the medieval expulsions of Jewish communities ... which played such a massive role in Jewish lives and Jewish history were not dependent on generalized 'hatred' and 'mob violence' but also required specific, local circumstances, involving politics, finance, internal Christian divisions and other factors" (*Feeling Persecuted* 184). Importantly for Bale, after these expulsions—particularly in England—the tales of boys such as William of Norwich and Hugh of Lincoln provided some meaning to Christians long after it became highly unlikely for Jewish perpetrators to carry out these murders: "The English context of 1290 to c. 1650, in which there was no visible or organized Jewish community, allows us to retreat from an emphasis on actual victimhood and consider instead its cultural resonances" (*Feeling Persecuted* 13).

Chaucer's *The Prioress's Tale* is the best-known example of such a resonance, written about one hundred years after Edward's expulsion edicts. Other examples include the Croxton *Play of the Sacrament*, a late-fourteenth-century drama that features a piece of consecrated host that confounds and then converts its Jewish abductors. Tales of miracles involving the Virgin Mary also proliferated during this period and often featured the saint inter-

vening on behalf of Christian adults and children who suffer Jewish persecution. Medieval Christians understood that Mary was historically a Jewish
woman, but she was also the virgin mother of the Messiah, which is a fundamental point of contention between Christianity and Judaism. Consequently, Christian worshippers considered Mary "a particularly appropriate
intercessor in stories involving Jewish characters or concerned with Christian
self-definition in opposition to Jewishness," which accounts for the greater
amount of anti–Judaism that Marian miracle stories depict when compared
to most other medieval genres (Boyarin 12).

This introduction conveys a sense of post-medieval resonances of the
blood libel in historiographic anti-Semitism debates, as well as the existence
of its disturbingly tenacious tendrils through to the twenty-first century. The
consequences for the authors considered in this chapter are challenging: they
must portray a deeply anti-Semitic world to a post–Holocaust audience and
navigate the emotions that this complex history engenders. The aim of this
chapter is to assess how successful they have been both in this portrayal and
in finding a credible balance between dismantling an egregious accusation
and participating in what could potentially amount to an over-sanitizing of
history.

"There are no Jews in England": Sister Frevisse and Suppressing Anti-Semitism

Returning to the murder scene in Frazer's novel, Master Crane, the constable responsible for enforcing the law in the local ward, questions why the
Franciscan, Brother Michael, is so insistent that Jewish perpetrators performed this act, reiterating, "'There've been no Jews in England—'" (*Sempster's
Tale* 118). Michael repeats his interpretation of the strange markings on the
boy's body and another of St. Swithin's parish priests, Father Tomas, timidly
denies that the symbols are Hebrew. Brother Michael whirls on him sharply
to demand how he would know: "Afraid though Father Tomas openly was,
he lifted his head, bracing for an attack he knew would come, and said,
'Because I saw my grandfather's Jewish books when I was young'" (Frazer,
Sempster's Tale 119). Father Tomas was born and baptized in Antwerp, where
his parents had fled from persecution in Portugal, despite having converted
to Christianity. They had taken Tomas's grandfather with them. Remaining
unconverted, he spent his last years hidden in a back room where he read
his Hebrew texts of poetry and religion to his grandson. Brother Michael
pounces upon this revelation and attempts to interrogate Father Tomas fur-

ther, before being forestalled by Dame Frevisse, who redirects everyone's attention back to the body, understanding that the "friar's claim was too dangerous to leave unchallenged" (Frazer, *Sempster's Tale* 122).

Frevisse uses her forensic observation skills to point out that the boy was not actually crucified because the wounds in his hands and feet were made by a dagger, not nails, and were administered after death. Moreover, none of the wounds could have been used to drain blood for use in other rituals. Finally, another observer in the crypt, Master Weir, a Jewish merchant visiting—incognito—from Bruges, questions the timing of the murder: "'Isn't part of the purpose said to be to get blood for their Passover rites? That's at Eastertide, not midsummer'" (Frazer, *Sempster's Tale* 122). At the end of this scene, Sir Richard, the "under-crowner," arrives to take charge. Sir Richard is similarly skeptical about Brother Michael's assertion regarding Jewish ritual murder and the recovery of the victim's clothes confirms that the lad died from three stab wounds to the back of his chest. These tiny variances in interpreting the evidence may seem inconsequential: after all, whether the wounds were made by a dagger or a nail, the body's position is unmistakably designed to represent the crucifixion of Christ. However, these distinctions are important for medieval detectives because they allow the crime to be dislodged from an erroneous or unfeasible narrative without destabilizing the authenticity of the detective's premodern context.

In this scene, Frazer not only demonstrates the variety of ways Jewish characters feature in medieval crime fiction, she also explores the after-effects of the expulsion of Jewish communities from England both on those who chose to stay and those who risked their lives returning to England to trade. Firstly, the combination of the observations made by Father Tomas, Dame Frevisse and Master Weir effectively debunks Brother Michael's rash assumption of Jewish ritual murder and directs the investigation towards discovering who benefits from implicating Jewish people who may be visiting or hiding in London. Secondly, Father Tomas's brave admission of his Jewish heritage hints at the ongoing trauma that Jewish people endured in England and across Europe. With the advent of the Inquisitions in Portugal, Spain and France, in particular, third or fourth generations of converts to Christianity were viewed with suspicion, despite having only experienced a Christian way of life themselves.

Earlier in the novel, Mistress Anne Blakhall—the eponymous "sempster"—visits the House of Converts to deliver a letter to one of the longstanding residents there. Founded before the expulsion orders of 1290, the House offered sanctuary to Jewish converts to Christianity who had consequently forfeited their property. By the time of Frazer's novel, in the mid-fifteenth century, the number of residents in the House had dwindled to just four. Anne meets a woman, Alis, who has lived in the House for forty years. Anne gives her a letter from long-forgotten European relatives who had disowned her mother, Joanna, when she had been forced to convert to Christianity by the English authorities or suffer execution. After the death of the head of the family, the remaining relatives reach out to Joanna, who had died the year before. Father Tomas, too, relies upon the secret transmission of letters between himself and his sister in Poland.

Anne is in possession of the letter due to her relationship with Daved Weir, the merchant from Bruges, who has been her lover for several years. Daved is Jewish but pretends to be Christian when conducting business in England and elsewhere throughout Europe. Like the physician, Jacob, in Westerson's *The Demon's Parchment* (discussed below), Daved and his uncle, Master Bocking, smuggle in items that cannot enter England any other way. In Jacob's case, he brings with him Hebrew scriptures used by London's secret Jewish community. Daved not only brings letters such as Alis's but also smuggles in gold for England's nobility, as he has done in this case for Frevisse's cousin Alice, the Duchess of Suffolk. The state of the body in St. Swithin's crypt warns Daved that someone else knows there are Jewish merchants who secretly conduct business in London.

Dame Frevisse observes both that Daved is Jewish and that he and Anne are deeply in love. This knowledge and her growing acquaintance with Daved cause Frevisse to question why this love should be forbidden. However, Frevisse's status as a nun prevents her from delving too deeply into this theological dilemma, especially when she compares Anne and Daved's courage and good sense to the "darkness of heart and mind" of the killer she is seeking. Frevisse feels deep pity

> that she [Anne] and Daved Weir should be forbidden to each other and that their love had brought their bodies and souls into danger of death and damnation…S]et against the darkness of heart and mind of [the murderer] …, Anne and Daved's love seemed far less worthy of damnation, no matter that Daved was Jew. Better a man of courage and honest heart than—
> Frevisse stopped that thought short. Those were matters for priests and scholars to determine and debate. Murder was what she must needs have in mind… [Frazer, *Sempster's Tale* 273].

Here, Frazer illustrates the fraught consequences of allowing Jewish characters to enter her carefully constructed fifteenth-century world: Frevisse's feelings for Daved reveal the modernity of her outlook and threaten the authenticity of her medieval context. Instead, Frevisse retreats from a train of thought that leads dangerously close to heresy and, as befits a medieval detective, distracts her mind with the relatively safe subject of murder.

Only One Jewish Detective: Isaac of Girona

Frazer's sensitive account of the complex entanglements that arise when depicting the deep anti-Semitism of medieval accusations of Jewish ritual murder offers an excellent case study for the manner in which medieval crime fiction authors generally handle this material. But only one author has positioned a Jewish character at the center of their series and explored the implications of casting him as a medieval detective.

In medieval Girona, in the northeast of Spain, Caroline Roe has resurrected the name and physical infirmity of a famous French rabbi and mystic, Isaac the Blind, who lived in Provence in the late-twelfth century and was an important influence on the development of Kabbalah. A century or so after Isaac the Blind's death in 1235, Roe's medieval detective appears in her first novel, *Remedy for Treason* (1998), set in mid-fourteenth-century Spain. The novel opens in 1348 with Girona in the horrifying grip of the Black Death and Isaac, a Jewish physician, powerless to prevent its devastation (a remarkably similar situation to Susanna Gregory's Cambridge doctor, Matthew Bartholomew, discussed in Chapter Two). The effects are sobering: of the seven hundred and fifty-odd people living in Girona's Jewish Quarter, a mere one hundred and thirty are left alive after the plague retreats (Roe, *Remedy for Treason* 1). Isaac loses his young apprentice, Benjamin, to the disease and he realizes that his inexorably failing eyesight will hinder his ability to maintain his medical practice without the aid of the young man's vision.

Five years later, Isaac's sight is completely gone and his new apprentice is his second daughter, Raquel, who examines his patients and describes the appearance of their physical ailments to her father. Roe acknowledges the historical antecedents of her Isaac by making her characters aware of the connection: the local rabbi's wife begs Isaac to save her ill child, telling him that his sight was taken because, as everyone knows, he is "the successor, the incarnation of the great Master Isaac of the Kaballah" (Roe, *Remedy for Treason* 39). Isaac is horrified by the woman's words and shudders in alarm that these rumors, which he had heard before, should gain credence in the mind of the rabbi's wife.

Early in this first novel, Isaac meets twelve-year-old orphan Yusuf, who rescues the physician from the middle of a drunken mob and leads him safely back to his house in the Jewish Quarter. Yusuf is a Moor from Valencia and,

despite Spain's racial and religious (semi)integration, Isaac hints at the precariousness of this cultural mélange in his question for Yusuf: "And what is a
Moorish lad named Yusuf doing in the middle of a riot, helping a Jew, on the
eve of a Christian holy day? It is as dangerous for you to be here as it is for me"
(Roe, *Remedy for Treason* 30). Isaac is philosophical about the attack. As broken
tiles and stones pepper the Jewish Quarter, Isaac sits in the covered walkway
that surrounds his courtyard and muses that "The stout roof above him seemed
well designed to cope with such puny weapons of war" (Roe, *Remedy for Treason*
33). But while Isaac may stoically endure the occasional violence meted out by
a Christian mob, he is fully aware that the Jewish people of Girona maintain a
happy and prosperous existence under the "illusion of security that the protection of powerful men offered them" (Roe, *Remedy for Treason* 41).

One of those powerful men is the bishop of Girona, Berenguer de
Cruilles, one of several historical figures featured by Roe throughout her
series. Another is Don Pedro, king of Aragon, to whom the Jewish people
owe much for their protection, as Isaac reminds his daughter Raquel: "He
has saved us many times already from the ignorant rabble" (Roe, *Remedy for
Treason* 59). Bishop Berenguer is a friend and patient of Isaac's and, in Roe's
first novel in the series, he calls upon the physician both to help his extremely
ill niece, Isabel (the illegitimate daughter of the king and a ward of the local
Benedictine nunnery) and to help investigate the murder of one of the nuns
whose body is discovered floating in the city's bathhouse. The recent town
riot, the young woman's murder and the abduction of Berenguer's niece—
along with Raquel, who had remained with Isabel to nurse her—are the events
that lead Isaac and the bishop into a succession of interconnected plots involving treason, murder and religious fanaticism.

Remedy for Treason is narratively complex, as are the other novels in
Roe's series. In *A Poultice for a Healer* (2003), there are two or three young
men who may or may not be impersonating each other and at least two of
them are in Girona under false pretenses. One of the youths is crucial to the
outcome of Isaac's investigation into the deaths of several patients of another
young man, training to be a herbalist, and yet this first character is rarely
glimpsed throughout the novel. These young men all interact with Daniel,
who is engaged to Isaac's daughter, Racquel, and whom Isaac sends to Mal-
lorca to investigate the backgrounds of the young men, resulting in the post-
ponement of the wedding. Generally, it is not difficult to grasp the plotlines
in medieval crime fiction, but the lack of distinguishing characteristics among
numerous and interchangeable lads (which recalls Paul C. Doherty's similar
habit of not differentiating between suspects) does contribute to what is a
"slightly convoluted story" (Gelly).

In the last book in the series (of eight), *Consolation for an Exile* (2004), part of the action takes place in the Muslim region of the medieval Iberian Peninsula. Isaac's young apprentice, Yusuf, returns to his home, the kingdom of Granada, where his distant cousin is the sixteen-year-old emir, Muhammed V. In this novel, Roe has Yusuf dealing with the reunion with his family, palace intrigue and murder in his homeland, while, at home in Girona, Isaac convinces one of his patients, Master Raimon, that his illness is not caused by his strange and disturbing dreams. Later, Raimon unfortunately dies from taking one of Isaac's herbal draughts that has been poisoned by the murderer. In addition to Muslim, Christian and Jewish entanglements, Roe tackles the Cathar heresy: it seems that Raimon's nightmares consisted of witnessing people burning and of being chased through dark mountain passes. Isaac makes the connection between Raimon's dreams and "the last wave of condemnations of the Cathars" (Roe, *Consolation for an Exile* 194), which resulted in refugees coming from France over the mountains into the Spanish kingdoms. Isaac estimates that Raimon would have been four or five at this time and, while he had lived an orthodox Christian life since then, the dreams indicated a residual trauma. The irony of a Jewish doctor discussing the possible heresy of one of his patients with a Christian bishop is not lost on Roe. When Berenguer asks, "'Did Raimon say anything to you about his religious beliefs?'" Isaac replies with understandable asperity:

> "Your Excellency, the last thing I would discuss with any of my Christian patients is their faith; the only thing that Raimon ever said to me on the subject of religion was that he had prayed for relief from his symptoms, and if that made him a heretic, then most of the rest of my patients are heretics too, including at times, I suspect, Your Excellency" [Roe, *Consolation for an Exile* 195].

Isaac, both despite and because of his blindness, is an effective detective and demonstrates the open-minded tolerance and skepticism that medieval investigators characteristically possess. While Isaac is devout, he does not display the stern adherence to the laws of his faith that his wife, Judith, practices. For example, Isaac's eldest daughter, Rebecca, has married a Christian clerk and become a *conversa*. Judith refuses to acknowledge her daughter and little grandson for more than a year and when circumstances do eventually throw them together, she grudgingly concedes that, "'I won't say that I've forgiven you.... But I am very happy to see you'" (Roe, *Cure for a Charlatan* 252). Isaac admits that his wife is "many times more religious and virtuous" than he is, but also that, despite his years of study, he has "never achieved that much certainty concerning what is truth, and what is righteousness" (Roe, *Remedy for Treason* 51).

Isaac must also manage a tendency to depression that haunts him and occasionally envelops him in a paralyzing despair. After his daughter Raquel is abducted, his fear for her safety overcomes his rational mind and "his old enemy darkness, unformed, uncontrolled and uncontrollable, pressed in.... Having already deprived him of sight, darkness snatched away movement and reason" (Roe, *Remedy for Treason* 105–06). He sits alone in his study, spiraling into what appears to be a psychological breakdown, manifesting in his extreme panic and hysterical laughter. Eventually, his mind reasserts itself and he finds peace in his soul, "and with it a profound and irrational conviction that Raquel was still alive" (Roe, *Remedy for Treason* 109).

These plotlines are all interesting and a testament to Roe's meticulous research and deep knowledge of medieval Spain; however, they do occasionally undermine her detective narratives. Lorraine Gelly, reviewing *A Poultice for a Healer* for the Historical Novel Society, offers an accurate description of Roe's particular brand of medieval crime fiction:

> As always, it is a pleasure to read about Isaac, his large and interesting family and his relationship to the Bishop, who is his patron, as well as a most important patient. Much of the day-to-day life of Spain in that era, especially Jewish life, is set out for lovers of historical novels. The research by the author, a medieval scholar, is thorough, and reading these books is surely akin to traveling in time back to medieval Spain. That fact keeps the reader coming back each time, even when the mystery plot is as thin as in this book. But old friends are the best, and loyal readers will continue to read about this engaging protagonist [Gelly].

While it is an exaggeration that Roe's novels enact a time-traveling experience, Gelly's assessment not only applies to numerous authors of medieval crime fiction, but also points to one of the most appealing aspects of crime fiction more broadly: the identification with, and affection for, the detective character and details about his or her life.

Isaac seems to be the only Jewish detective in medieval crime fiction and Roe's series is also unusual in that it occasionally presents Jewish characters as murderers. Roe is the only one of the many medieval crime fiction authors who does this. It appears that having a Jewish detective somehow circumvents the compulsion to rehabilitate medieval anti-Semitism by avoiding criminal Jewish characters altogether.

Crispin Guest's Jewish Encounter

In Jeri Westerson's *The Demon's Parchment* (2010), Crispin Guest, the tarnished knight of the London streets, encounters a character that causes him to question his prejudices about both Jewish people and homosexuality. Finding himself desperately short of money (as usual), Crispin reluctantly agrees to accept a case from a Jewish physician named Jacob, despite his strong misgivings about dealing with a "Jew." The presence of Jacob and his son, Julian, in London is curious because the novel is set in the winter of 1384, a time when the expulsion edicts were still in force throughout England. Jacob is from Provence and is residing at Westminster Palace at King Richard II's request so that he may attempt to overcome the infertility of the queen, Anne of Bohemia. The doctor wishes Crispin to recover some sacred papers that have been stolen from his rooms in the palace. Crispin is extremely wary of Jacob and resists the grudging respect he begins to feel as the physician demonstrates his intelligence, his learning, and his compassion. This respect, however, does not extend to Jacob's son, who bears as much contempt and malice for the *gentiles* as Crispin feels towards him. At the same time, Crispin is pursuing another investigation into a series of gruesome murders of young, poor boys, all found having been beaten, sodomized, their bellies slit, and their entrails removed. Crispin is deeply affected by these murders, recognizing that the boys' distressing deaths could easily have been the fate of his young apprentice, Jack, if the lad was still scratching a living on London's streets.[7]

The two cases appear to be connected and Crispin begins to believe that Jacob's fear that his stolen papers have been used to create and unleash a *golem* is justified.[8] Crispin's old friend, Nicholas, the Abbot of Westminster, lends him a copy of Thomas of Monmouth's *Life and Miracles of Saint William of Norwich* (discussed above) and Crispin reads about the practice of ritual murder with mounting fury: "The more he read, the angrier he got. He had thought little about Jews before, but that they would scheme to kill an innocent boy for their strange rituals was unthinkable. Yet it was all there, inked on this parchment" (Westerson, *Demon's Parchment* 175). Having read the *vita* and piecing together some other circumstantial evidence, Crispin leaps to the conclusion that Jacob's son, Julian, is the killer and goes to Westminster to confront him. Crispin acts upon the common medieval belief in Jewish ritual murder, based largely upon the "authority" of Thomas's account of young William—incontrovertible proof due to its rendering, as Crispin notes, on "parchment." Crispin angrily accuses Julian of the murders, paraphrasing Thomas's charges from two hundred years previously:

> "Is that why you killed those boys? Because you hate Christians so? Or was it to experiment on them in your vile ways? Oh, I know about you Jews and your Passover sacrifices. The lots that are drawn to determine which town will do the slaughter. The drinking of blood. The eating of human flesh" [Westerson, *Demon's Parchment* 194].

Julian, of course, vehemently denies Crispin's wild accusations and forcefully defends himself, quoting passages from the Old Testament forbidding participation in sacrifices or consuming blood. However, in keeping with the ratiocination process to which medieval detectives must adhere, Julian's most convincing argument comes not from scripture, but practical logistics, framed in rhetorical questions that Crispin is unable to ignore:

> "We draw lots, do we? Such fascinating organization. Across seas? Across borders? How do we accomplish this feat, we who are watched wherever we go? It is decided that this year a boy in ... in London is it? ... is to be sacrificed, no? For the Passover? Is your Michaelmas near Passover, our feast held in the spring?" [Westerson, *Demon's Parchment* 195].

Julian continues his argument, also appealing to Crispin's intelligence and honor. Crispin, while not completely convinced, nonetheless experiences enough doubt to jettison his original plan of hauling Julian before the sheriffs at Newgate prison.[9] Crispin allows his burgeoning familiarity with Jacob, Julian (eventually revealed to be Jacob's daughter, Julianne, in disguise) and the hidden Jewish community of London that he has discovered in the course of his investigations gradually to dissipate his innate, but unexamined, anti-Semitism.

This process is successful enough that Crispin returns to Abbot Nicholas in order to challenge the veracity of Thomas of Monmouth's account of William's death. Nicholas defends Thomas's scholarship and is insulted when Crispin refuses to take his word and instead asserts, "this is more important than friendship" (Westerson, *Demon's Parchment* 242). Crispin's defense of Norwich's Jewish population is remarkable for both his dismissal of a treatise by a monk at a time when written accounts of historical events carried significant authority, and his willingness to sacrifice a longstanding relationship with the Christian abbot on behalf of a people he barely knows, let alone understands. Complicating the situation is the presence in London of an inquisitor sent by the Archbishop of Canterbury to investigate the rumors of Jewish communities living in secret throughout the city (rumors Crispin has confirmed), as well as to obtain the missing Hebrew papers. The inquisitor is operating incognito and Crispin initially suspects him of being responsible for the abduction and murder of the boys.

Having overcome his surprise that Julian is female, the relationship that Crispin then tries to pursue is immediately stalled by Julianne's revelation that she has, in fact, produced a *golem*, following the instructions in her father's pages of Creation (Westerson, *Demon's Parchment* 294). Julianne's intention was to wreak vengeance on "Christians" for the suffering she and her father have endured over years of persecution. Crispin recoils from her in horror, imagining that the shadows "chang[ed] her angelic features to those of a darker angel" (Westerson, *Demon's Parchment* 295). Julianne's admission shatters Crispin's conviction that the strange creature he had glimpsed several times in London's streets was a man (the potter, Odo) and significantly troubles his ability to seek a rational explanation for events. While Crispin remains wracked with uncertainty about the supernatural creature's existence, he has no doubts about his rejection of a girl he so ardently desired just a few moments before.

The potential of Crispin and Julianne's affair is an example of the star-crossed lovers' scenario that appears in many of the novels discussed in this chapter. In Sharan Newman's series, Catherine LeVendeur's Jewish cousin, Solomon, and her Saxon sister-in-law, Margaret, fall in love but accept that they can never marry. Margaret Frazer's Dame Frevisse perceives Anne and Daved's passionate and illicit affair. Jewish physician Isaac of Girona's daughter converts to Christianity in order to marry a gentile and sacrifices her relationship with her mother. In all of these examples, the authenticity effect that is an overarching concern for these authors precludes the possibility of these relationships.

Westerson's novel stops short of an unfeasible rehabilitation and reintegration of the Jewish community into medieval English society. Crispin and Julianne's strong attraction to each other hints at this possibility, as does Crispin's grudging acceptance of Jacob. Instead, Crispin leaves Jacob preparing to depart England, full of regrets about raising his daughter as a son and smuggling scriptures into England. Crispin sends an anonymous message to the secret Jewish community, warning them that the Christian Church knows of their existence and of the presence of the inquisitor who is seeking them throughout London. This prompts a minor self-expulsion as, soon after, "there was a sudden selling of many properties near the Domus and several of London's most successful citizens had departed the city for parts unknown" (Westerson, *Demon's Parchment* 297).

Westerson floods *The Demon's Parchment* with a complex range of controversial events and persons drawn from two centuries of medieval history: accusations of child ritual murder by Jewish people; the mythical *golem*; the transvestite Eleanor/John Rykener (discussed in more detail in Chapter Two); the murder of William of Norwich; French serial killer Gilles de Rais; occult practices; and the Inquisition. The result is a complicated plot that (more or less) successfully intertwines these disparate narratives, creating the opportunity for Crispin to untangle them while learning more about himself, and the chance for Westerson to demystify the historical aspects of the Middle Ages that interest her most.

Lord Godwin's Jewish "Problem"

Sara Conway completed only two novels in her promising series featuring Lord Godwin (no other name is provided), bailiff of Hexham, in northern Yorkshire. The first, *Murder on Good Friday* (2001), is set in 1220. Godwin, like many other medieval crime fiction detectives, has returned from crusade weary and disillusioned. In addition to his lingering guilt over his role in the religious wars and the fact that he survived when his beloved cousin did not, he is also deeply saddened by the death of his wife in childbirth soon after his return. He seeks solace in the duties of bailiff—a position that someone of his rank would usually disdain—reconsidering his previous chivalric pursuits and believing that "Rendering justice had seemed a noble course to follow" (Conway 22). Godwin attempts to carry out his duties justly, especially when it comes to collecting outstanding debts or fines on behalf of his "greedy" feudal lord, the Archbishop of York.

In late March, the body of a young boy, Alfred, is discovered in a field just outside Hexham, with the familiar wounds of a child who has been crucified. Moreover, the boy appears to have been murdered on Good Friday, an inconceivably wicked act beyond the comprehension of the horrified townsfolk. They confront Godwin, seeking information, and he recognizes and despairs of the fearful, superstitious dread that starts to circulate through the crowd: "Godwin heard the words *demon* and *Satan* murmured fearfully and struggled to control his impatience with such nonsense" (Conway 38). However, the townspeople soon find a substitute for the elusive demons in the form of the town's small Jewish population. Comprising only three families, they are forcibly rounded up and imprisoned in the local keep, to their bemusement and Godwin's dismay. The young boy's body is taken to Hexham's priory where it is laid out in one of the cathedral's chapels.

As Godwin begins to dismantle the case against the town's Jewish families, the situation becomes much more fraught when one of the canons, the deeply pious Brother Elias, announces to the crowd gathered in the cathedral's courtyard, "Young Alfred, the innocent child slain on Good Friday, has wrought a miracle. He has cured a crippled man of a lifelong affliction" (Conway 75). Even by the high standards of divine grace, the appearance of this miracle is ludicrously fast. Even more unseemly, the priory's monks begin to sell vials of holy water, created by soaking the cloth that Alfred's body had been lying on when the crippled man was cured. Not even a week has passed since Alfred's body was found and yet pilgrims are lining up outside the cathedral for the chance to see the tomb and purchase some hope. Inflaming the supernatural legend beginning to coalesce around Alfred's "martyrdom" is another "miracle": the canons supervising the chapel notice that a man kneeling at Alfred's tomb is surreptitiously stealing the silver coins that have been left there as offerings. The canons chase the man through the cathedral, but he is crushed to death beneath the sudden collapse of an archway over one of the doors. No one else is harmed and the watching priests immediately attribute the collapse to "Alfred's divine vengeance," claiming that the marvel was "a twofold one, for it is a miracle that only the thief was taken and no one else" (Conway 209).

Godwin's investigation into Alfred's death is hampered by the Archbishop of York's political maneuvering behind the scenes, as he attempts to wrest jurisdiction over Hexham's Jewish community from the royal regent, Peter des Roches, Bishop of Winchester.[10] The Archbishop, seeking to take advantage of the murder accusation, wants this jurisdiction because if they are found guilty of Alfred's murder and hang for the crime, then the bonds they hold would revert to the Archbishop. In other words, the local townspeople, the priory and nobility who have borrowed from Jewish moneylenders are not released from their debts if the latter flee the town or are executed; instead, the debts must be paid to the crown or Archbishop. Conway here explores the precarious political position that Jewish people occupied in medieval England before their expulsion in 1290. They were extremely useful to the king as a source of revenue, which is why they were considered part of the royal demesne, as the Archbishop's agent, Fulk de Oilly, explains to Godwin: "the crown protects the Jews and their livelihood of money-lending, and when the king needs cash, he squeezes them. If the Jews can't pay, their bonds are confiscated and the money is demanded instead from the borrowers" (Conway 160). Thus, as Fulk observes, it makes no sense for anyone to murder a Jewish lender in order to avoid repaying the debt, since the king's agents would then be free to pursue repayment, doubtless in a significantly more timely and aggressive manner.

From the king's point of view, the persecution or protection of Jewish communities depended upon financial and political circumstances and had little to do with anti–Semitic antagonism. As noted above, these communities were considered a tool in a ruler's arsenal that could be wielded to promote state-building and to gain political power over opponents, both domestic and overseas. This pragmatic and ruthless manipulation of Jewish businesses for financial and political purposes is a direct contrast to the irrational hysteria that priests and people of towns often demonstrated when accusing their Jewish neighbors of responsibility for an unexplained death. Medieval Jewish people occupied a precarious position between opposing forces of political pragmatism and religious fanaticism, both of which represented a significant danger to their lives and livelihoods. One of the Hexham Jewish characters, Isaac, describes this uncertainty from his perspective: "For Jews, life is unpredictable, serving the whims of powerful men. We are possessions, servants of the crown, to be used as the king desires. Only in our law do we find stability and security" (Conway 242).

However, this retreat into the comfort of ancient Jewish religious and cultural practices only underscores their outsider status and inflames the suspicious intolerance of the community, perpetuating the cycle of periodic anti-Semitic abuse. Conway, in the manner of all medieval crime fiction authors who portray Jewish characters, represents the Hexham families as peaceful, quiet, longstanding citizens of the town, while she characterizes the Christian townspeople who accuse them of Alfred's murder as ignorant, superstitious rabble. Lord Godwin and his cousin's widow, Constance, in addition to discovering Alfred's real murderer, function as a buffer between medieval Christian and Jewish communities.

Alfred's parents, Ada and Gamel, are Hexham's brewers. They are shocked and deeply saddened by the death of their son, but also somewhat bemused at his instant elevation to sainthood. The "dratted canons" from the cathedral keep accosting Ada in her home to collect Alfred's possessions (clothes and toys) to be used as relics and housed beside his tomb. When Lady Constance tentatively asks Ada whether she believes that Alfred has indeed become a saint, her reply is a touching combination of maternal grief, affection and realism:

> "I'm not sure what I think, lady," [Ada] answered slowly. "I'd like to believe that he's behind the miracles, that he's been singled out by God. It would make me feel easier about losing him—like he had a greater purpose to serve than just being my boy.... Yet, I can't help remembering how he hated going to Mass, how he squirmed and chafed to be outside playing. I was lucky if I could get him to say a *paternoster* at bedtime. So to hear everyone talking about my little boy as if he was a saint ... well, it's going to take some getting used to" [Conway 237].

Ada goes on to wonder why there was never any inkling of her son's saintly destiny, as is the case with so many of the saints' lives with which she is familiar. Furthermore, Ada doubts that Isaac's family, her neighbors, could have murdered Alfred in the manner that is claimed.

Conway writes poignantly and sensitively about the emotional reality of losing a child. This reality is all but forgotten in the subsequent chaos of laying the blame upon the Jewish characters for the murder, and the callous appropriation of the boy as a "saint" in order to gain financial benefit and prestige for the local cathedral. Medieval crime fiction—indeed, historical fiction more broadly—performs its most effective cultural work in depicting these scenes, providing a relatable narrative to broader historiographic analyses of medieval anti-Semitism, boy saints and the religious-political context of the Middle Ages. Alongside their determination to counter erroneous accusations directed towards medieval Jews communities, these authors also discern and describe the grief attached to each case.

Catherine LeVendeur's Jewish Relations

As discussed in Chapter Four, Sharan Newman's medieval detective, Catherine LeVendeur, abandons her novitiate at Heloise's Paraclete convent in order to marry the Saxon nobleman, Edgar, in 1139. As Catherine discovers in the opening book of the series, *Death Comes as Epiphany* (1993), Hubert LeVendeur, her father, was born into Judaism. Although Hubert was baptized as child by a Christian family who took him in after his mother and sisters were killed in one of the regular pogroms that erupted across Europe throughout the Middle Ages, he has never relinquished contact with his Jewish family. He conducts business with his brother, Eliazar, and nephew, Solomon (the son of another brother, Jacob), importing and exporting goods to Paris. Eliazar's family lives in Paris's Jewish Quarter and, on several occasions throughout this first novel, Catherine and Edgar seek sanctuary in Eliazar's house and its secret passages under the city.

Catherine's mother, Madeleine, knows of Hubert's Jewish birth and has been able to suppress her misgivings for most of her marriage. But the ongoing guilt she experiences because she married a "Jew" compels her to sink even more deeply into an obsessive piety that gradually develops into a form of dementia. At the end of *Death Comes as Epiphany*, Madeleine has a complete breakdown and spends the next ten years being cared for in a local convent, seeking refuge in an imagined past where her children are all alive and little again. Hubert blames himself for Madeleine's mental anguish and, in *The Difficult Saint* (1999), confronts his own ontological crisis and returns to his Jewish faith. As briefly noted in Chapter Four, at the end of the final novel in the series, *The Witch in the Well* (2004), Madeleine apparently overcomes her dementia and returns to the present, leading to Catherine's tearful admission that perhaps there can be supernatural intervention into the world after all.

Catherine accepts her Jewish relations and develops a close relationship with them over the course of the series. Indeed, her husband Edgar goes in to business with Solomon (taking over from Hubert when he converts back to Judaism) and the two families spend much time together. However,

Hubert's son, Guillaume, does not know about his father's Jewish heritage and bitterly resents Hubert's—and Catherine's—interaction with them. Hubert's younger daughter, Agnes, discovers by accident her father's secret and, unlike Catherine, reacts with horrified anger, refusing to acknowledge Hubert for a long period and blaming him for Madeleine's unstable mental state. As her uncle Eliazar reflects, Catherine is exceptional for her tolerant acceptance of them. Newman works to suppress the potential anachronism of Catherine's (and Edgar's) tolerance by making frequent reference to the deep anti-Semitism that surrounds and affects her Jewish characters. Rosemary Erickson Johnsen believes that this is enough "to make the point that Catherine's perspective is—as Newman puts it—unusual but not impossible" (37). From the beginning of the series, Newman presents Catherine as possessing high intelligence and a practical mind, which, along with the strong influence of Heloise, no doubt contribute to her tolerant outlook. In this way, Catherine reflects other medieval detectives, such as Brother Cadfael, whose innate modernity may be explained by their backgrounds and experience.

The precarious position that Jewish communities occupy in twelfth-century Paris is a recurring focus for Newman throughout her series. Newman's Jewish characters are frequently abused, subjected to rioting students and accused of crimes they did not commit. In *The Wandering Arm* (1995), a relic (the arm of St. Aldhelm) from Salisbury Cathedral in England is transported to Paris, where it is hidden. Within the complex network of Jewish and Christian merchants who traverse Europe, trading their goods, there appears to be a number who are willing to traffic stolen artefacts, such as relics, chalices, candlesticks and other precious items stolen from churches. One of these merchants, Natan, is found murdered and blame is instantly and unjustly directed towards his Jewish colleagues. Newman also extends this concern into Germany, where Catherine's sister, Agnes, is to be married to a German lord. In *The Difficult Saint* (1999), Newman explores in detail anti-Semitic violence, as well as the brutal suppression of the Cathar heresy. *The Outcast Dove* (2003) features Catherine's cousin Solomon as the main protagonist (and stand-in detective) as he travels to the south of France and north of Spain. One of the Jewish traders travelling with Solomon is murdered and, while investigating, Solomon interacts with the southern Jewish communities who are more assimilated than their Parisian counterparts. Newman's insistence on incorporating Catherine's Jewish relations into every narrative even leads to the unlikely scenario in which a group of Jewish merchants, including her cousin, uncle, and a converted Jewish monk, form part of a group going on the Christian pilgrimage to Santiago de Compostela in Spain, recounted in *Strong as Death* (1996).

As well as the broader, public dangers that Jewish people faced with periodic riots and the necessity of boarding up their houses during Christian holidays, Newman also depicts the effects upon individuals. Solomon, Catherine's Jewish cousin and Edgar's business partner, and Margaret, Edgar's Christian younger sister, are deeply in love, but know that theirs is an impossible union. Neither is able to convert due to their own deeply held religious convictions; however, as Solomon also points out, even if he did become a Christian, the couple could not overcome the demands of feudalism: "Your grandfather has other plans for you" (Newman, *Witch in the Well* 345). Newman, more than most medieval crime fiction authors, ensures that her political concern with retelling stories of Jewish persecution during the twelfth century is insistently foregrounded throughout her series.

The Irresistible Case of Rejecting Medieval Anti-Semitism

While the detectives so far discussed in this chapter represent the most sustained engagement with exploring Jewish communities in the European Middle Ages, most authors of medieval crime fiction find it difficult to resist participating, even peripherally, in overturning the anti-Semitism of medieval history. This chapter closes with some brief examples.

In fifteenth-century Bologna Mary Ellen Cooper features the young widow, Avisa Baglatoni, who works as a locksmith. Avisa's skill is invaluable during one traumatic encounter with the mayor's nephew and would-be rapist, Ippolito, whom she maneuvers towards an open trunk, stabs his foot with her file, then pushes him into the trunk, slamming the lid and securing it by "work[ing] the lock closed, putting a metal rod between the hasp and the hinge" (M. Cooper, *Key Deceptions* 157).

A female locksmith is unusual enough, but Cooper complicates Avisa's situation by attaching a young, Jewish apprentice to her business. Bernardo arrives at Avisa's door one night, on the point of starvation, searching for a long-lost relative who, it turns out, had died two years previously. As he has nowhere to turn, Avisa grudgingly accepts Bernardo's services, maintaining the fiction that he is her cousin from southern Italy, while aware of the danger they both face daily:

> Jews were forbidden under pain of death from learning the skill of locksmithing. The prohibition had never meant much to her; she scarcely knew any Jews. But now if she were discovered teaching a Jesus killer the intricate art of making keys, they might both be burned at the stake [M. Cooper, *Key Deceptions* 17].

Despite these justifiable fears, Avisa begins to teach Bernardo her trade and develops a fondness for the young man. However, Cooper's depiction of her Jewish characters is rather cursory and forms a peripheral strand to her crime narrative. In her second novel featuring Avisa, *Key Confrontations* (2002), Bernardo has travelled to Jerusalem on pilgrimage, rendering the intriguing relationship between the Christian locksmith and her Jewish apprentice irrelevant to Avisa's other problems; namely, she is falsely accused of murder and forced to take refuge in a convent.

As discussed in greater detail in Chapter Four, Ariana Franklin's Adelia Aguilar was not only brought up in the markedly tolerant city of Salerno in Italy, she is also the adopted daughter of a Jewish father and Christian mother. As such, she is horrified to discover the deep-seated intolerance towards the Jewish population in twelfth-century Cambridge. In Franklin's first novel, *Mistress of the Art of Death* (2007), there are a spate of child murders in Cambridge and the local populace blames the town's Jewish population. Henry II relies heavily upon the Jewish merchants of Cambridge for revenue and does not want them convicted, leading to his appropriation of Adelia's services to solve the crimes and thus launch Franklin's successful series.

Priscilla Royal's novel, *The Sanctity of Hate* (2012), concerns Jacob, a young Jewish father-to-be, traveling to Norwich with his wife and mother-in-law, wrongfully accused of murder. Prioress Eleanor of Tyndal Priory ensures that Jacob is released and the real murderer discovered, developing an affection for the family that prompts her to echo Dame Frevisse's tolerance:

> Although their faith was not hers, they were of kind heart and gentle manner. If Jacob ben Asser and his family had been Christians, she would praise them for holding to their beliefs despite threatened slaughter. Indeed, most would condemn them for this obstinacy, but she confessed to God that she admired them anyway [Royal, *Sanctity of Hate* 211].

As Eleanor farewells the family and watches them travel down the road, she is struck by the likeness of the mother and baby on the donkey and father walking beside to "The Holy Family," imagining circles of light around their heads in a vision that would be attributed to Eleanor's reputation for holiness. Despite her exoneration of Jacob, Eleanor remains uneasy with the residual hatred towards the Jewish family demonstrated by the local villagers. Royal has set her series in the years leading up to Edward I's 1290 expulsion orders and she continues to explore the consequences of the mounting anti-Semitism in England in subsequent novels.

Tim Shaw's *A Death in Catte Street* (2013) not only features a young Geoffrey Chaucer as detective, it also describes the position of Jewish converts and visitors to fourteenth-century London. Chaucer is shocked to discover that the House of Converts is located within his parents' neighborhood and he had never been aware of its existence; he also recalls the child martyr, Little St. Hugh of Lincoln, in connection with his investigation into the murder of an old Jewish merchant, anticipating the poet's subsequent reference to St. Hugh in his *Prioress's Tale.*

Finally, in Barbara Reichmuth Geisler's mystically infused series, The Averillan Chronicles, book two, *Graven Images* (2004), similarly depicts mob violence against a local Jewish goldsmith, Master Levitas, who is inevitably and falsely accused of the murder of a young girl. And the second book in Joyce Lionarons's recently published Matthew Cordwainer series has the coroner of late-thirteenth-century York wrestle with increasingly hostile Jewish-Christians relations in the pointedly titled *Blood Libel* (2018).

In his consideration of the challenges that critics and teachers face when exploring Chaucer's *Prioress's Tale* in the post–Holocaust era, Michael Calabrese claims that "foregrounding ethics at all is dangerous because criticism does not meet the basic criterion for ethics. Literary criticism does not solve political problems" (70). However, an examination of how the authors of medieval crime fiction depict Jewish people in general, and their Jewish characters in particular, reveals an ethical and political concern with correcting premodern anti-Semitism. These novels invariably present Jewish characters in positive terms: living quiet, productive lives and frequently forming an important part of their local communities. They also navigate a precarious existence as their authors recreate the deep suspicion and resentment that surrounded them and infused each day with an underlying unease. This threat manifests in the false accusations of murder that Jewish characters inevitably face in most examples of medieval crime fiction. Specifically, this charge is frequently connected with accusations of ritual murder whereby a Christian person, usually a young boy, is killed in a manner designed to rehearse the crucifixion of Christ so that the Christian faith may be mocked and blood collected for religious rites, often connected with the Passover holiday. As historians have categorically demonstrated, there is no evidence that this so-called "blood libel" ever occurred, although this insidious accusation has persisted throughout the centuries and represents an erroneous basis for historical tensions between the Jewish and Christian religions.

In depicting Jewish characters, these authors attempt to redress the historical anti-Semitism of the period they choose to recreate. This political project is most effectively achieved through the figure of the medieval detective, whose innate modernity imbues the reimagined Middle Ages with a racial and religious tolerance that eludes most of the historical record. Sometimes, the medieval detective must overcome his or her own ingrained anti-Semitism, as most obviously demonstrated by Westerson's Crispin Guest, and this offers an opportunity to attach an ontological character arc to the crime narrative. Strikingly, medieval crime fiction uniformly portrays Jewish characters in positive terms, as if conforming to an unspoken agreement that the genre participates in the reversal of the prejudice inherited from the Middle Ages. In the one exception where Jewish characters are, occasionally, murderers, Roe ensures that her Jewish detective demonstrates enough religious moderation to render these aberrations irrelevant. Roe's achievement goes further and succeeds in balancing racial and religious differences so effectively that, in the end, the religion of the criminal is moot.

But medieval crime fiction novels cannot rewrite history, as so many time-traveling stories attempt to do. The genre's adherence to historical authenticity precludes a happy ending in which religious tolerance exists throughout medieval Europe (just consider the Crusades). However, the crime narrative offers comfort here where medieval history does not: through the device of the literary detective, medieval Jewish victims and the falsely accused are afforded justice that has nothing to do with their religion and depends entirely on the successful completion of the detective's investigation. Medieval crime fiction not only critiques the many constraints and abuses to which medieval Jewish communities were subjected, it also staunchly exonerates them from the egregious accusation of ritual murder.

Chapter Six

Poet or PI?

As the preceding chapters demonstrate, a crucial feature of all types of medieval crime fiction is the meticulous reconstruction of an authentic Middle Ages. This recreation almost always requires a portrayal of the historical figures who lived and breathed the medieval world that these authors carefully describe and, consequently, they frequently intertwine their narratives with the actions that the historical record claims these figures performed. A relatively recent trend in historical crime fiction shifts these recognizable people from the periphery of the narrative to the central plotline by casting them as detectives. The range of novels that feature "real life" detectives from history is extraordinary: Jane Austen, Arthur Conan Doyle, Charles Dickens, Elizabeth I, Mark Twain, Benjamin Franklin, Oscar Wilde and many others have all been recruited to seek justice and restore the status quo, as the conventions of crime fiction demand. Medieval crime fiction also has its share of historical figures recast as detectives and this chapter explores the manner in which this is achieved, and considers the consequences of creating a revisionist biography of canonical authors such as Geoffrey Chaucer. While Chaucer is by far the most popular medieval figure to be fictionalized in this way, this chapter also examines novels featuring John Gower, Leonardo da Vinci, Dante and Lucrezia Borgia as investigators of crime.

There are both dangers and rewards attendant upon transforming famous figures from the past into detectives. Readers of historical fiction derive pleasure from identifying inconsistencies and anachronisms and so fictionalizing someone whose life and work is well-documented greatly increases the opportunity for readers to be distracted by the admittedly enjoyable game of spot-the-historical-mistake. For this reason, authors look for poorly chronicled periods in the biographies of historical figures to exploit. Stephanie Barron, for example, has taken advantage of the "mystery" of Jane Austen's activities between 1801 and 1804 to create a popular series of novels in which the acute observer of English manners directs her considerable talents towards solving crime: a Georgian precursor to Miss Marple. John Scaggs characterizes Barron's decision to exploit spaces in the historical record as derived "from the narrative impulse to 'fill in the gaps' that motivates both detectives and historians" (128). Indeed, historians are commonly described in terms that cast them as "detectives" in their search for evidence of past lives and events.[1] Anita Vickers argues that Barron's creative endeavor successfully "reinvent[s] Austen's biography," rescuing Jane from the "stilted, lifeless portrait" that her "official" life story depicts (215). However, the success of Barron's series has necessitated an expansion of Jane's activities outside this three-year lacuna and Barron sets her most recent novel, *Jane and the Waterloo Map* (2015), in London just after the Battle of Waterloo in 1815. Moreover, Barron is close to colliding with the immovable wall of historical reality. As one reviewer notes, "Jane Austen died two years after the events of Waterloo; one hopes that Barron conjures a few more adventures for her beloved protagonist before historical fact suspends her fiction" (Mortensen 80). Barron's series is part of the "Jane Austen industry" that rivals the Middle Ages for its sheer volume of creative reimaginings in fiction, film, television, tourism and online gaming.[2]

Authors of medieval crime fiction must decide whether and how to insert their fictionalized versions of historical poets into a narrative that also reanimates those poets' own characters, creating a complicated and potentially confusing metanarrative. Alternatively, reimagined historical authors may remain separate from their characters and instead discuss their writing or encounter inspiration for their well-known works within the frame of the historical novel in which they find themselves. In medieval crime fiction, the most common strategy for authors featuring Chaucer, for example, is to mobilize the characters in his *Canterbury Tales* for the purposes of the crime narrative.

Tales of Two Chaucers

While most of the literary greats of the European Middle Ages appear in some form or other in medieval crime fiction, the most popular poet-turned-private-investigator is Geoffrey Chaucer. Chaucer, the man, is famously elusive. For centuries, medieval scholars have sought to glean snippets about his life from his poetry, which is notable for its lack of direct allusions to contemporary events. Some five hundred archival documents relating to Chaucer form the *Chaucer Life-Records*, published in 1966 and edited by Martin M. Crow and Clair C. Olson, based upon the significant collection compiled by legendary Chaucer scholars, John M. Manly and Edith Rickert. This is an invaluable resource for those interested in details such as property deeds, payment records and other minutiae pertaining to the administration of Chaucer's fourteenth-century daily life.[3] Several important biographies have also contributed to developing a picture of the historical Chaucer, including Derek Brewer's *Chaucer and His World* (1978), Derek Pearsall's *The Life of Geoffrey Chaucer* (1992), Paul Strohm's *Social Chaucer* (1989) and, most recently, Strohm's fascinating description of 1386 as the year that shaped the *Canterbury Tales*, *The Poet's Tale* (2014). An impression emerges of Chaucer's rather successful life as a young squire attached to Prince Lionel's household (Edward III's youngest son), a senior customs agent and public servant, and husband to Philippa, whose sister, Katherine Swynford, was John of Gaunt's third wife.

In his poetry, Chaucer is usually self-deprecating—when he refers to himself at all. An eagle in the dream vision, *The House of Fame*, describes Chaucer as "noyous for to carye!" (troublesome to carry) (II.574),[4] implying that Chaucer is perhaps a little overweight. Harry Bailey, the proprietor of the Tabard Inn and host of the tale-telling competition the pilgrims undertake on the way to Canterbury, wonders why Chaucer always stares at the ground, as if looking for a hare, and goes on to describe Chaucer's physical appearance:

> This were a popet in an arm t'enbrace
> For any womman, smal and fair of face.
> He semeth elvyssh by his contenaunce,
> For unto no wight dooth he daliaunce
> [*Prologue to Sir Thopas*, VII.700–04].

Chaucer gently mocks his poetic ability with the first tale his pilgrim persona recites to the group, *Sir Thopas*. A tale devoid of plot and tedious of rhyme, Harry Bailey finally interrupts Chaucer-the-pilgrim, exploding, "Namoore of this, for Goddes dignitee," and claims that his ears are aching listening to Chaucer's "drasty speche," famously declaring, "Thy drasty rymyng is nat worth a toord!" (*Sir Thopas*, VII.919, 923, 930). Chaucer innocently insists that he is doing the best rhyming that he can, before switching to his second story, *The Tale of Melibee*, a highly moral prose parable. Chaucer also pokes fun at mundane problems in his life such as his scribe, Adam, making mistakes and the poet having to correct them himself ("Chaucer's words unto Adam"). In another short poem, he addresses his empty purse and he begs the new king, Henry IV, to maintain his annuities. As demonstrated in the examples that follow, most authors of medieval crime fiction respond enthusiastically to this Chaucerian playfulness, harnessing the poet's mode of inserting himself into his poetry and participating in the centuries-long project of seeking this, as John Dryden first claimed, "congenial soul" (Trigg, *Congenial Souls* 38).

There are two types of Chaucerian medieval crime fiction: those that feature the historical Chaucer and those that deploy Chaucer as a character in his own works of fiction, interacting with the embodied pilgrims from his *Canterbury Tales*. As Kathleen Forni correctly observes, depictions of Chaucer such as these rehearse the easy affinity with which readers have embraced both the poet and his work through the centuries. The generally affectionate portrayal of Chaucer in medieval crime fiction demonstrates not only the enduring strength of this virtual communion, but also medievalism's powerful ability to conflate centuries of history, allowing contemporary popular culture to recognize and embrace Chaucer himself.

Forni is one of very few scholars who considers the consequences of Chaucer-as-detective, concluding that the poet's association with crime "may be a logical choice, for, as Patricia J. Eberle suggests, 'a very high proportion of the [Canterbury] tales deal ... with the subject of 'crime' ... treason, murder, and rape appear, together with various forms of theft and assault'" (62). Furthermore, Forni identifies the conservatism shared by a large proportion of crime fiction and some of Chaucer's poetry:

> Detective fiction generally defends the existing social system, neutralizing those who try to disturb the established social order, serving as cautionary tales and modeling acceptable social behavior, similar to much of Chaucer's oeuvre from the sociopolitical conservatism of the *Knight's Tale* to the penitential *Parson's Tale* [62].

Chaucer's ability to observe and record the foibles of human nature while maintaining a reasonable social status appeals to writers of crime fiction, who identify in him a combination of the classical type of detective, endeavoring to restore the status quo, and the hardboiled form, "not naïve [and] recognizing the depravity of social elites and the partisan nature of the justice served" (Forni 61).

Tison Pugh, on the other hand, deeply distrusts historical mysteries that refigure famous authors as detectives in an effort, as he claims, to "invigorate the cultural cachet of detective fiction" (412). Pugh argues that mystery authors such as Philippa Morgan (discussed below) rely "on high culture's high fathers and mothers to imbue their works with the imprimatur of canonical literature" (412). For Pugh, the irony of this fiction lies in the fact that, by "stripping [him] of [his] poetic complexity," Chaucer "fail[s] to perform the high-cultural work for which [he is] enlisted" (412). Pugh seems unsettled by a Chaucer denied the prestige commonly attached to him through his poetry. But the difference Pugh perceives arises not because of an intention to draw Chaucer (and his poetry) into an "inferior" popular genre such as mystery fiction. Instead, by casting Chaucer as a detective, Morgan and others make him "modern"; and thus the preeminent English poet of the Middle Ages no longer sits comfortably within the medieval landscape that produced his rich and complex work. Pugh's article reflects the trace of uneasiness with popular cultural expressions of both crime fiction and medievalism that remains in literary scholarship.

Tales Chaucer Might Have Written: Philippa Morgan/ Philip Gooden

British author Philip Gooden wrote three novels under the pseudonym Philippa Morgan that feature Chaucer as a diplomat travelling to France, Italy and the Devon coast. Gooden has lately reissued these novels under his own name and added a short prequel, *Chaucer and the Vintry Ward Death* (2013), set in 1359—unusually early for Chaucerian historical novels. Forni notes the English country house and gothic traditions that characterize Gooden's work: an invocation of golden-age detective fiction that is further reinforced by these novels' recognition of social injustice while nevertheless ending "with a restoration of the existing social order" (70). But what interests Forni most about this series is Gooden's "practice of Chaucerian intertextual pastiche" (71). Gooden punctuates his novels with Chaucerian proverbs and he enjoys rewriting Chaucer's poetry, as may delight or dismay readers who are familiar with the original *Canterbury Tales.*

In *Chaucer and the Vintry Ward Death*, a young Chaucer listens to a storyteller in the Tabard Inn recount what is, in essence, his own *Pardoner's Tale.* The tale unsettles Chaucer, who leaves before it is finished and hopes that the three wastrels of the story do not represent himself and his two young companions, "cocky and foolish," and heading off to war, "convinced that they too could come away unscathed from an encounter with death" (Gooden, *Chaucer and the Vintry Ward Death* 25). The three squires from the Countess of Ulster's household are enjoying the pleasures of Southwark for a night or two before embarking for France and King Edward's war. Chaucer crosses the river to the Vintry Ward to visit his parents, during which time one of his father's associates is found dead in his wine warehouse.

This novella conforms closely to golden-age crime fiction conventions in its presentation of the classic locked-room conundrum and a victim who is so despised by everyone that the authorities are happy to ignore the fact that he was murdered, thereby protecting the perpetrator from repercussions. Chaucer, intrigued by the decision to cover up what is clearly a crime, undertakes to discover the murderer for himself, which entails treading carefully at times to maintain the official verdict of accidental death:

> "Because if Nicholas Lombard had been shot—which he wasn't—the only place from which such a shot could have been fired was on a level with the upper floor of the warehouse. Yet the tide was on the turn and the *St Vincent* would have been lying too low in the water for the attempt to have been made—which it wasn't. This is all hypothetical" [Gooden, *Chaucer and the Vintry Ward Death* 80].

Gooden here recalls a reasonably common convention of golden-age detective fiction in that he allows Chaucer to unravel the solution to the mystery, fulfilling his investigative obligations, but he does not bring the murderer to justice because of an unspoken consensus that the killing was justified.

In Gooden's *Chaucer and the House of Fame* (2004), the poet is travelling by boat from Calais to Bordeaux in the company of two young retainers from John of Gaunt's household in 1370. The name of the vessel is *Arverargus* and it forms part of a small fleet with two others called *Aurelius* and *Dorigen*. The young men request a story from Chaucer to pass the time and the poet obliges, commencing a narrative that readers may recognize as the *Franklin's Tale*. However, Gooden alters Chaucer's original in several significant ways: Dorigen believes that Arveragus drowns after being shipwrecked on the black rocks off the coast of Brittany as she watches from the cliffs above; the impossible *demande d'amor* she imposes on Aurelius is to retrieve Arverargus's bones; Aurelius, while attempting to drown himself in despair, instead rescues Arverargus from a second ill-fated ship dashed against the rocks; and Aurelius finds solace in the love of Agnes (Chaucer's mother's name), a beautiful maiden living by the beach who witnesses his bravery. Additionally, the two young men accompanying Chaucer offer the poet a suggestion for the *Reeve's Tale* by their amorous encounters with the wife and daughter of an innkeeper. The novel also contains references to the great French poets of courtly love, Guillaume de Machaut and Eustache Deschamps, as well as an amusing vignette recalling *Sir Gawain and the Green Knight* in which the lady of the house where Chaucer is staying as a guest visits the poet in his bedchamber while her husband is out hunting wild boar. However, as Forni similarly laments, the "flirtatious Rosamond" is "hunting, alas, only for gossip" (71).

Chaucer and the Legend of Good Women (2005) describes Chaucer's journey to Italy, in 1373, in order to secure funds for Edward III from a Florentine banking house. Gooden intertwines several of Chaucer's tales into this novel. One of the characters, Lorenzo Lipari, is largely blind, married to a much younger, faithless woman whom he catches with her lover up in the branches of a pear tree in Lorenzo's private garden. Lorenzo falls out of the pear tree three times, the final time to his death. Lorenzo's brother Antonio is married to Emilia and they have a daughter named Philomela; a reference to Chaucer's *Legend of Good Women* and its sequence of Ovidian narratives. While Lorenzo's partial blindness, insane jealousy and young wife recalls the *Merchant's Tale*, Gooden undermines his novel's title by having his cast of "good women" behave in ways that certainly do not echo the virtue and faithfulness demonstrated by the classical women Chaucer celebrates. Finally, the novel's Florentine setting necessitates multiple references to Dante Alighieri and his poetry: Chaucer-the-detective comes to a crucial realization thanks to a copy of Dante's *Inferno*.

In *Chaucer and the Doctor of Physic* (2006), set shortly after his return from Florence, John of Gaunt's secretary, Sir Thomas Elyot, sends Chaucer to Dartmouth to investigate the theft of the cargo of a Genoese ship, wrecked on the Devon coast; an incident that threatens to destabilize the treaty negotiated by Chaucer himself on his recent journey to Italy. Early in the novel, Chaucer recounts a story to his two eldest children, Elizabeth and Thomas, inspired by a small farm he passed on the outskirts of Florence. Chaucer must interrupt his tale of the proud rooster, Chantecleer, and his wives in order to undertake his assignment to recover the stolen materials. Once again, Gooden alludes to several Chaucerian narratives and imagines some fictitious relationships. The local mayor is William Bailey, brother to the Tabard Inn's proprietor, Harry. William's wife is Constance (an allusion to the *Man of Law's Tale*), who endures her husband's infidelity with a local prostitute, Juliana, up to a certain point. The physician of the novel's title is Richard Storey, "A gentleman of influence … and well known to us because he has given an opinion more than once on the afflictions of our Prince Edward," as Sir Thomas explains to Chaucer (Gooden, *Chaucer and the Doctor of Physic* 42). During the course of Chaucer's investigation, two murders are committed and the poet finds himself untangling a complicated network of relationships and unfettered ambition in order to reveal the thief and murderer.

For Forni, quoting Stephen Knight, "recognizing the many Chaucerian allusions provides an intellectual pleasure for the reader not unlike the pleasure associated with 'the sheer act of solving … the puzzle of detection'" (72). Forni, however, does not speculate as to why Gooden chooses to rewrite Chaucer's narratives rather than simply rehearse them and, unusually for medieval crime fiction authors, Gooden does not provide explanatory notes that offer insights into his writerly motivations. Perhaps it is due to a desire to participate, however remotely, in the creative production of a beloved canonical poet. It could also be an allusion to the unstableness of textual reception, particularly of medieval texts, implying that the narratives attributed to Chaucer may not be what he actually wrote and reversing the Early

Modern misattributions of texts such as *The Tale of Gamelyn* and *The Floure and the Leafe* to Chaucer. Gooden's fiction embraces the medieval tradition of appropriating other texts and rewriting the narratives as a response to a new cultural context. In doing so, Gooden does not "strip Chaucer of his poetic complexity," as Pugh claims (412), but instead demonstrates the powerful elasticity of Chaucer's poetry that allows it to participate in such genre-crossing reimaginings.

Chaucer the Public Servant: Gertrude and Joseph Clancy

Death is a Pilgrim: A Canterbury Tale (1993) is a novel by husband-and-wife writing team, Gertrude and Joseph Clancy. Gertrude Clancy, who passed away in 2013, wrote short stories, amateur plays and published one volume of poetry. Joseph Clancy, an Honorary Fellow of Aberystwyth University, is primarily known for his translations of Welsh poetry, modern and medieval, including Gwyn Thomas, Saunders Lewis, Alun Llywelyn Williams, medieval Welsh lyrics and Welsh folk poems. Now living in Glasgow, Clancy's most recent publication is *The Poems of Dafydd ap Gwilym* (2016). *Death is a Pilgrim* is the Clancys' only jointly authored novel and the only work featuring Chaucer or crime narratives for either.

The novel is set at Saint Innocent's Priory, near Rochester Castle, where Chaucer and his fellow pilgrims seek shelter during a sudden thunderstorm. The prioress, Madame Eglantine, and her deputy, Dame Cecily, are a little overwhelmed by the number of pilgrims that have arrived on their doorstep—twenty of them—but nevertheless receive them graciously, despite their leaking guesthouse. During the night, one of the pilgrims, the pardoner Nicholas de Bury, is murdered in the priory's chapel. The storm has caused fallen trees to block the road in and out of the priory, conveniently creating the conditions for a clue-puzzle mystery, and so the suspects remain confined within its grounds until help arrives. Thomas Pinchbeck, the sergeant-at-law, takes charge of the investigation and each of the witnesses describes his or her evidentiary tale to Pinchbeck, Chaucer and the Oxford clerk, Thomas Owen. In keeping with golden-age conventions, most of the pilgrims have had past dealings with the pardoner and, when the murderer is unmasked at the end of the novel, the group swears an oath not to reveal the perpetrator's identity because of the extenuating circumstances that motivated the attack on Nicholas.

As Forni observes, "The Clancys' forte ... is their success in animating or vivifying the pilgrims, that is, in providing psychological motivation in place of estates satire" (63). The novel portrays its characters with an emotional and psychological depth that is certainly uncommon in medieval crime fiction. The Clancys enhance this richness of characterization by a subtle use of allusion both to the pilgrims' portraits in Chaucer's *Canterbury Tales*, and to their own tales. For example, the priory holds one of Little St. Hugh's relics and Madame Eglantine, like the *General Prologue* Prioress, speaks French with a London accent, as Chaucer notes in the novel (Clancy and Clancy 33). Alice Webster, a widow from just outside Bath, sets her sights on the young clerk, Thomas, who confides to Chaucer that he could do worse. In an echo of the *Wife of Bath's Prologue*, Chaucer laughingly assigns Thomas a reading list that includes Jerome, Tertullian, and Chrysippus, telling him, "they should be enough to discourage thoughts of marriage!" (Clancy and Clancy 216). The Clancys depict Chaucer himself just as one might imagine an experienced medieval public servant: discreet, unassuming, perceptive and knowing. As for the unfortunate pardoner, Forni argues that the Clancys endow Nicholas with "the most psychological depth" of all the pilgrims; he "is a sympathetic character" and this undermines the neatness of the novel's clue-puzzle structure because there is "a sense of unease rather than satisfaction in the successful detection and punishment of the crime" (63). While Nicholas's circumstances do evoke some pity—he had experienced a genuine vocation but his social status prevented him from joining the priesthood—his past behavior, as gradually revealed by the evidence of the other pilgrims, suggests that such a fate was inevitable.

The Clancys place themselves firmly in the community of scholars and authors who claim a kind of virtual friendship with Chaucer, referring to him in terms that are both familiar and reverential. This imagined affinity is particularly evident at the end of their novel, which they neatly conclude with a "Retraction" in place of an Afterword or Authors' Note. They begin by asking, "all who have given to this fiction their money and their time that if in some measure it has pleased them, they give thanks with us for Geoffrey Chaucer. May his soul rest in peace" (221). The authors also align themselves with the medieval practice of appropriating and revising stories, invoking Chaucerian authority: "Where we have knowingly falsified, we beg indulgence for following the example of our Poet, who seldom permitted bothersome fact to deter him from a diverting tale" (222). And they offer a final fleeting reference to Chaucer's poetry, this time from *Troilus and Criseyde*: "And so both makers of this little book take their leave, beseeching you to pray for us, as for all pilgrims and story-tellers on the road to Holy Truth" (222). The Clancys seek to honor Chaucer by aligning their novel more closely with the concerns of medievalism than with the conventions of crime fiction.

Hardboiled Chaucer: Duane Crowley

Duane Crowley's *Riddle Me a Murder* (1986) is a stark departure from the Clancys' gentle homage. Crowley's novel is not only an unusually early example of medieval crime fiction, it also appears to be the first to feature Chaucer as detective-protagonist. Crowley sets himself an ambitious agenda, framing his narrative with a description of an elderly Chaucer, in the late 1390s, visited by his old enemy, William Courtenay, Archbishop of Canterbury.[5] Courtenay has discovered a secret that will cause political chaos; namely, that Henry Bolingbroke is Chaucer's illegitimate son. Courtenay not only despises Chaucer for insults and political opposition in the previous decades, he also blames the poet for the harm that his vernacular writing continues to impose upon the realm: "'This "English" you've foisted upon us has made the rulers of our country one with the dullest swineherd'" (Crowley 2). The Archbishop threatens Chaucer with revealing his secret—forcing Henry to forfeit his Lancaster inheritance and sullying John of Gaunt's first wife Blanche's reputation—unless Chaucer renounces his poetry. Courtenay's plan is to use Chaucer's own words to obliterate both himself and his writing from the pages of history: "'I'll see your filth purged from the realm before I die and you will be my instrument. You'll publish a retraction of your pernicious books, label them the snare of Satan that they are and ask the forgiveness of our most merciful God for writing them'" (Crowley 2). After Courtenay departs, Chaucer mulls over his quandary and begins to reminisce about events that occurred more than thirty years before, in the mid–1360s, at a time when Chaucer was a young squire, in the service of the Duchess of Lancaster, and already in love with Philippa Roet. One of Blanche's ladies-in-waiting—and Gaunt's most recent mistress—is poisoned and Chaucer must discover the perpetrator before (then) Canon Courtenay can accuse the Duke and gain ascendancy over the powerful house of Lancaster.

The young woman's death is, however, merely an excuse for Crowley's exploration of chivalry, violence and class tensions. Crowley underscores his novel with a deep sense of radicalism, in keeping with the novel's mid–1980s context, and his overarching concern is to dismantle the facade of honor behind which chivalry conceals its violence. As Forni perceptively observes, "chivalry is shown to be a sham, the same violence differentiated only by class and locution: mounted knights on a policing mission and marauding Genoese brigands are all butchers" (68–69). Crowley casts Chaucer as a hardboiled detective, navigating the mean medieval streets of England and Italy, and often expressing the customary despair and cynicism generated by the corruption that he continually encounters and which taints most of the characters. Forni describes Crowley's Chaucer as "protodemocratic" (69): early in the novel, Chaucer chides his friend, Hugh le Hunt, for his cavalier opinion of the serfs tied to his brother's estate, saying, "'They smile and bow when you ride by but have you ever thought of the plodding days they must pass before they die—dull days little different from those of the oxen they follow behind'" (Crowley 19). Chaucer's voice is that of the trans-historical poet that readers frequently imagine speaks social truth across the centuries. Throughout the novel, however, Crowley also endeavors to depict the poet's "zest for living" in order to counteract the rather melancholy assessment of his own, late-twentieth century moment, as he forlornly muses in his Afterword: "Some historians have found in this 14th century, a loss of nerve that they compare to our own. It may be so but there is no flinching from life in Geoffrey Chaucer or in those he loved" (230).

As far as the detective narrative is concerned, Crowley, like the Clancys, allows Chaucer to discover the truth, but then silences him through the excuse of political expediency so that he may not reveal the perpetrator. The novel ends with a gloomy sense of justice not served, which is magnified by Chaucer's capitulation to the demands of feudalism when he agrees, at John of Gaunt's request, to marry Philippa (who is pregnant by the latter), thereby saving the face of the Duke's cast-off mistress. Crowley attempts to soften this homosocial transaction by tracing the development throughout the novel of Chaucer and Philippa's love for each other, but their feelings cannot displace the unpalatable misogyny of this trafficking of women between the two men that has its mirror in Chaucer's brief affair with Blanche. Both Philippa and Katherine Roet function as amalgams of the idealized lady of courtly love convention and the *femme fatale* of the hardboiled tradition.

Crowley concludes his novel with an idealization of Chaucer himself, common practice for authors who reimagine famous literary figures. Chaucer composes the retraction of his poetry that Courtenay demands in return for his silence; however, the poet writes with confidence that "Those who loved and understood his work would know that what he was about to write was satirical cant. The others wouldn't matter" (Crowley 228). Crowley thereby suggests that he is one of those who "understands" Chaucer's poetry and invites his readers to join him in this ostensibly exclusive group.

New Age Chaucer: Mary Devlin

In another contrasting depiction of the medieval poet, Mary Devlin has published two novels featuring Chaucer as a detective. *Murder on the Can-*

terbury Pilgrimage (2000), as its title suggests, conforms to the strand of Chaucerian mystery fiction in which a fictionalized Chaucer interacts with his own characters on the way to Canterbury. In this example, Devlin has added some extra pilgrims, including tavern owner Agatha Willard, her ex-professor husband Robert, and a beautiful young gypsy named Sophia. Agatha and Robert are close friends of Chaucer's and, having surveyed the group and agreed to Harry Bailey's story-telling competition, Agatha turns to her husband and says, "'Do you know who would really enjoy being here? Telling stories—observing this motley collection of human creatures? Geoffrey!'" (Devlin, *Murder on the Canterbury Pilgrimage* 11). Accordingly, Robert sends an urgent message to Aldgate, asking Chaucer to join them. Chaucer leaves his duties at the customs house to his gaggle of lieutenants and sets out with the group from the Tabard Inn. He is delighted with the variety of pilgrims and expresses his joy, worth quoting in full, with an enthusiasm that Devlin conveys with an overabundance of exclamation marks:

> A wave of exhilaration passed through Chaucer. "What a fascinating cross-section of humanity we have here!" he cried. "The men range from the lowest dregs of society—like that disgusting summoner—to a group of obnoxious guildsmen to a learned professor like yourself, Robert, all the way to our handsome knight and squire! And the women! We have spring, or the dawn, in that lovely little nun and in the gypsy with whom young Simon [the squire] is so infatuated! We have summer, or the day, in you, my dear Agatha, and for autumn, or evening, Madame Eglantine! No winters of course … but a fine group nonetheless! How interesting this is all going to be! Thank you so much, dear friends, for inviting me!" [Devlin, *Murder on the Canterbury Pilgrimage* 20].

The pilgrimage is certainly "interesting" and Chaucer listens attentively to the travelers' stories, composing his own *Tales* in his head, which he writes down each evening. Like the Clancys, Devlin punctuates her narrative with snatches of the pilgrims' portraits from the *General Prologue*, described by Chaucer as he observes each person. Chaucer also includes a description of the lovely Sophia and the opening few lines of *The Gipsy's Tale*, a racy story of ancient Egypt with which Sophia has shocked the pilgrims.

Stopping for the night at an inn only twenty-five miles from London, however, Agatha shakes Chaucer awake to inform him that poor Sophia has been murdered. The pilgrims must remain at the inn until Chaucer discovers the murderer; in order to do so, he eventually requests the help of his "dear friend," John of Gaunt. Chaucer feels Sophia's death deeply and he is determined that she shall not be forgotten. He therefore continues with his *Gipsy's Tale*, bringing the myth of Isis and Osiris to life and realizing that this tale "was a masterpiece": "*No matter how great the other tales told here will be,* [Chaucer] reflected, *my retelling of them will never match this one. Many gen-*

erations to follow, perhaps even into the next millennium, will still be fascinated with Sophia" (Devlin, *Murder on the Canterbury Pilgrimage* 119, emphasis in original).

Devlin describes herself as "quite well known in the fields of astrology and New Age thought" (*Murder on the Canterbury Pilgrimage* 243). This interest emerges in her novels through Chaucer's habit of regularly casting astrological charts and observing the night sky with his astrolabe. Improbably, Chaucer shares this interest with the King of England, although the former's discretion suggests that he comprehends the inherent risks in such practices: "Even at so young an age, King Richard was a devout worshipper of the arts, both creative and occult. The latter was an interest Chaucer shared with only a few..." (Devlin, *Murder on the Canterbury Pilgrimage* 14). Before setting out on his pilgrimage to Canterbury, Chaucer draws up an astrological chart filled with ominous predictions for his journey. Rather than heed its warning, however, Chaucer's innate curiosity overcomes his common sense.

In Devlin's second novel, *The Legend of Good Women* (2003), Chaucer is asked by the young Earl of Sussex, William Taggart, to investigate the fraudulent activities of one of his manor's stewards, who the earl believes is embezzling funds. Chaucer travels to West Sussex to see for himself and, while he is there, the body of the steward is discovered in the forest. Chaucer uses his astrolabe to read the night sky and make a horoscope to help him discover the murderer. By comparing his horoscope with another cast sixteen years earlier, he postulates that the same person who recently killed the steward also murdered the young Earl's uncle, who had disappeared in London and was thought to be a victim of the plague. From the evidence of these two horoscopes, Chaucer assures William, "Your uncle did not die of plague. He was murdered" (Devlin, *Legend of Good Women* 93). Unfortunately, the horoscopes do not reveal the identity of the murderer and so Chaucer must deploy traditional investigative methods to discover the perpetrator. Once again, John of Gaunt is an imposing presence in this novel, lurking in the background and suspiciously interested in the progress of Chaucer's investigation. Chaucer and Gaunt remain on intimate terms, although Devlin does stretch the credulity of her readers by having Chaucer refer to the intimidating duke as "Johnny."

Forni suggests that Devlin's primary interest is in recreating a Chaucer "made in the New Age author's own image" and describes Devlin's work as an example of the "congenial communion" with Chaucer that Trigg identifies in the ease with which "writers and critics can 'speak' and write in Chaucer's place and in Chaucer's voice" (67–68). Devlin certainly embraces the opportunity to play with Chaucer's poetic voice, interspersing her own Middle

English verse with the poet's. She also describes Chaucer's life in idealized terms, especially his marriage to Philippa: "Yes, [Chaucer] had been fortunate. He had been married for nearly twenty years to someone whom he considered the most beautiful and wonderful in the world, and they had three children of whom he was very proud" (Devlin, *Legend of Good Women* 100). Moreover, Chaucer's job at the Customs House "had been tailored so that he rarely had to put in an appearance," leaving him ample time to work on his "poetry, history and astrology" (Devlin, *Legend of Good Women* 100). As Paul Strohm has recently demonstrated in his biography of a monumental year in the poet's life, Chaucer's role with the Customs office was a real one, involving regular attendance and scrutiny (*The Poet's Tale* 7), and so Devlin's attempt to reframe Chaucer's job as allowing for so much free time does not quite convince. Additionally, Devlin's Chaucer solves mysteries due to an overdeveloped sense of curiosity rather than any perceivable desire to see justice served (although this latter trait is apparent in Chaucer's sympathy for the victims of crime). In this way Devlin participates in the popular, even clichéd, positioning of Chaucer as exemplary observer and scribe of the human condition, which she somewhat unconvincingly expands into a more interventionist concern with the affairs of others.

Youthful Chaucer: Tim Shaw

A Death in Catte Street is Tim Shaw's first novel, published in 2013 and intended as part of a series, although there has not yet been a second book. Shaw has identified a six-year gap in Chaucer's official records, beginning in 1361. Taking advantage of this biographical lacuna, Shaw sets his novel in October 1360, estimating that the poet was at that time just nineteen years old. Shaw has studied medieval history and offers detailed notes at the end of the novel to provide historical context, including two medieval recipes for the "fig tartlettes" that Chaucer's mother makes at one stage. Shaw employs the common framing device of an elderly Chaucer, towards the end of his life, musing upon his past experiences as a page attached to Prince Lionel's household. Lionel was Edward III's third son and married to Elizabeth de Burgh, the Countess of Ulster, whom Chaucer also served.

At this time, Chaucer has returned from the war in France "in order to transport several letters royal from King Edward and his sons" (Shaw ch. 1, loc. 53). That duty having been discharged, Chaucer finds himself escorting several young ladies from Queen Philippa's household to the London port markets, having imparted news to the queen about her husband and sons. While at the port, the group encounters a shipload of ransomed English soldiers disembarking, being welcomed and blessed on the dock by the Bishop of London. Among the bystanders, Chaucer observes three, prosperous merchants, "dressed richly in the Italian fashion of the day" (Shaw ch. 1, loc. 84). Chaucer notices something odd about the group and it takes him a little while to work out that the three men are not making "the customary obeisance" whenever the bishop mentioned the name of Jesus Christ in his prayers (Shaw ch. 1, loc. 92). Chaucer is curious, but unconcerned, realizing that "London was large enough that [he] could have wandered the streets for a fortnight and never seen them again. And [Chaucer] cared little about heresy, if heretics they were" (Shaw ch. 1, loc. 92). But Chaucer does have cause to recall this scene because not long afterwards, one of the merchants is discovered dead, at the bottom of the cellar stairs, in a house in Catte Street. It turns out that the man was Jewish and Chaucer, like many of the detectives discussed in Chapter Five, must overcome his innate prejudice in order to seek the reasons behind the man's murder.

Shaw's Chaucer is young, ambitious, flirtatious, and endearingly sure of his own talents and opinions. This is a naïve Chaucer, who misreads the dynamics of the group of household knights into which he attempts to inveigle his way and, while his intelligence and keen observational skills lead him to the solution, as the case progresses Chaucer learns just as much about himself: "I felt a very different person from the young man who had visited Thames Street such a short time ago" (Shaw ch. 7, loc. 831). Similarly, when Chaucer's conscience threatens his social standing at court, he recognizes the conflict within him: "My desire to do what was right by the poor old man was at odds with a smooth path to social advancement" (Shaw ch. 9, loc. 1003). Shaw also cannot resist depicting Chaucer's development as a poet. At one stage, he is asked to recite some poetry for the queen and her ladies that he has learned while traveling in Europe. He "gave them something from Machaut" that is so well received, he risks reciting some of his own work. Shaw notes that the subsequent song his character performs is from a medieval manuscript attributed to "Ch," which could contain some of Chaucer's early work (Shaw notes, loc. 2722). There are, moreover, the seeds for Chaucer's *Book of the Duchess* and the *House of Fame*; the latter is a particularly amusing recasting of the famous dream sequence in which Chaucer is scooped up by an eagle as "part of an anxiety dream brought on by alcohol and recent events" (Shaw notes, loc. 2722).

The novels discussed in this section all contribute to the ongoing reinvention of Chaucer and his poetry that has been a consistent feature of literary culture since the author's death in 1400. These novels vary greatly in style and substance, but they all participate in the translation of both Chaucer and his *Canterbury Tales*, especially, into a fictional form that undeniably reaches a new audience. Moreover, that audience is comprised of a much broader swathe of social strata than the small section of the population that had access to Chaucer's poetry in his own time and for a century or more afterwards. Following the exemplar of Eco's *The Name of the Rose*, these authors—with mixed results—exploit the possibilities of offering several interpretative layers that appeal to multiple audiences. For example, aficionados of crime or historical fiction may enjoy reading a detective narrative located in a medieval setting, while readers familiar with Chaucer will perhaps find that the subtle (and not so subtle) allusions to his poetry and his fourteenth-century life provide a richer historical context that buttresses the crime fiction formula. One of the pleasures that nearly all scholars of medieval literature or history experience is to have a student, colleague, friend or new acquaintance ask them about the Middle Ages because they have encountered premodern culture through a product of contemporary medievalism. These examples of medieval crime fiction effectively reimagine the historical person of Chaucer in order to perform exactly this type of cultural work.

"*Chaucers Wordes unto Adam, his Owne Scriveyn*": Garry O'Connor

British author and former theater director Garry O'Connor has written an unusual medieval crime fiction novel featuring Chaucer's regular scribe, Adam Scriven, as a discontented copyist tasked with completing the last of the poet's *Canterbury Tales*. In *Chaucer's Triumph: A Novel* (2007), O'Connor describes John of Gaunt's funeral procession as it travels from Leicester to London in March 1399. Katherine Swynford, recently married to the Duke, and Geoffrey Chaucer accompany Gaunt's body. O'Connor structures the novel nominally as a murder mystery—unexplained deaths plague the progress of the cortège's journey—but "O'Connor's larger concerns are the conjunction of sexual immorality and political instability and the paradox of poetic genius arising from the lurid imagination of a licentious reprobate" (Forni 73). While Forni's assessment is strongly worded, it is true that *Chaucer's Triumph* revels in the salacious details of the sexual exploits of its characters, in particular, John of Gaunt and Chaucer.

Over the five days it takes the cortège to arrive at St. Paul's, Adam is determined to unearth the truth behind a twenty-year-old scandal: in 1380, a woman called Cecilia Chaumpaigne released Chaucer from all future legal actions in relation to "de raptu meo" [of my rape] (Harley 78).[6] Two other men were also released by Chaumpaigne, one of who agreed to pay her ten pounds the following Michaelmas. Scholars have pointed out that *raptus* could mean abduction, as well as rape, and many have clung to this semantic distinction, suggesting that Cecilia accused Chaucer in an act of retaliation after a love affair gone awry. However, since the 1990s, feminist scholars have contested the sanitizing of Chaucer's biography and dismantled the argument that the author of such works as *Troilus and Criseyde* and the *Canterbury Tales* could never have committed the unspeakable act of rape.

O'Connor clearly agrees with the latter position and he voices this opinion through his disgruntled scribe, Adam, who wonders at the bleakness of the final tale Chaucer has asked him to copy—the *Parson's Tale*. As Adam observes, "It was not so much a tale as a sermon, and a frightening and apocalyptic one at that, full of guilt, remorse, and the profession of virtue" (G. O'Connor 12). To Adam, Chaucer appears "more and more morbidly pre-occupied with remorse," but he refrains from asking the poet what is troubling him because he also "knew how secretive he was, and had ever been, in talking directly of his own life and feelings" (G. O'Connor 11–12). Instead, as Adam gradually discovers the shocking exploits of the people he serves, he begins to comprehend a deeper meaning buried in the poetry that he has copied for Chaucer over three decades.

Scriven attempts to reconstruct the complicated entanglements between Katherine Swynford, Philippa Chaucer, John of Gaunt and his first wife Blanche, and Chaucer himself. O'Connor's narrative is similarly complicated by multiple points of view and irregular switches between different events in the past and present. It is narrated in the first person, primarily in the voices of Adam and Chaucer, although it also includes interjections from Philippa, Katherine, John of Gaunt and Sir Hugh Swynford, Katherine's first husband. Adam even has the opportunity to copy and recount the series of confessions that the Duke of Lancaster made to the famous English chronicler, Brother Thomas Walsingham of St. Alban's. O'Connor matches his complex narrative style with allegations and suggestions that similarly confuse the reader's understanding of history: John of Gaunt is Thomas Chaucer's father (a common rumor and favorite scenario for historical novelists); Katherine de Roet is forced to marry Sir Hugh Swynford after he attempts to rape her, an attempt forestalled by the intervention of Chaucer and Blanche; and Adam Scriven is Swynford's illegitimate son—among other intriguing, if far-fetched, suggestions. But the crux of the novel concerns Chaucer's guilt or otherwise regarding Cecilia Chaumpaigne's alleged *raptus*. Adam endures a traumatic journey from Leicester to London, obsessed with the revelations about the despicable behavior of the nobility he has served all of his life, as well as attempting to come to terms with the confronting truth about his own parentage. Chaucer's customary evasiveness finally drives Adam to hysteria, as he himself recounts, "I could contain myself no longer. I burst out. I howled. 'It's you!!! You, master!! YOU WILL NOT OWN UP TO RAPING CECILIA CHAUMPAIGNE!!!'" (G. O'Connor 212, emphasis [!] in original). Ultimately, however, as Forni notes, "O'Connor himself is unable to untangle the ostensible enigma" and, albeit reluctantly, "tends to mitigate the raptus" (75).

While Forni admits that O'Connor's Chaucer "is quite different from the detective hero found in most Chaucerian mystery fiction," she nevertheless retains this descriptor for the poet. However, it is Adam Scriven who seems to fit the detective role more securely in that he discovers a mystery to solve and undertakes an investigation following a traditional process that includes interviewing witnesses and pursuing evidence. Chaucer, as he does in the novels of Westerson, Robb and Holsinger (all discussed below), remains a little removed from Adam's search for knowledge, even disappearing from the narrative on certain occasions, such as the moment when King Richard greets the procession just outside London. More significantly, Chaucer seems precluded as detective because he already knows the answers to the questions Adam seeks. He is the omniscient presence that structures the novel through reference to his poetry and the life O'Connor imagines for him.

O'Connor's fascination with Chaucer's guilt or innocence in the Chaumpaigne case has continued: in November 2014 he adapted *Chaucer's Triumph* into a play called *De Raptu Meo: Geoffrey Chaucer on Trial for Rape*, staged at London's Inner Temple. According to one reviewer, the audience participated as the jury, deciding at the end of the play whether the poet was guilty or innocent: "And once we had pronounced the defendant Not Guilty, it was revealed that on the first performance the night before, he was found Guilty. Which denotes, at least, a remarkable achievement of balance" (Purves). According to Stephen Tomlin, the actor who played Adam Scriven, earlier in the year Sir Derek Jacobi—well known for his portrayal of Brother Cadfael in the television adaptation of Ellis Peters' series—performed the role of Chaucer in a "rehearsed reading" of the play (Tomlin). This confluence of medievalist connections is surprisingly common and always entertaining to observe.

Chaucer on the Periphery: Jeri Westerson and Candace Robb

Medieval crime fiction authors who depict the second half of the fourteenth century can rarely resist including Chaucer as a character. He is often fondly and amusingly portrayed and this section considers some examples of medieval crime fiction where Chaucer is not the detective *per se*, but features as a significant character who sometimes functions as a medieval Watson. For both Jeri Westerson and Candace Robb, Chaucer turns out to be an old acquaintance of their fictional investigators, Crispin Guest and Owen Archer, respectively.

As discussed in Chapter Two, Jeri Westerson's disgraced knight, Crispin Guest, is a medieval exemplar of the hardboiled detective type. Crispin is endearingly reckless and brash, stumbling through his investigations with a show of bravado, impressive knife-wielding skills and a penchant for quoting Aristotelian maxims. After one such outburst from Crispin, the character Chaucer asks, "'Are you still quoting that philosopher? I thought you would have grown out of that by now'" (Westerson, *Blood Lance* 155). In *Troubled Bones* (2011), Crispin must leave London to escape the repercussions of an unwise tavern scuffle with a courtier and so he accepts a commission from the Archbishop of Canterbury to circumvent a threat to one of England's most famous relics, the bones of St. Thomas à Becket. While in Canterbury, Crispin encounters Chaucer and a band of pilgrims loosely based upon the poet's *Canterbury Tales* and including the Prioress, the Wife of Bath, the Franklin, the Pardoner, the Summoner, the Miller and Harry Bailey, among others.

Crispin and Chaucer, it seems, became close friends while serving the Duke of Lancaster, John of Gaunt, although their meeting in Canterbury is the first between the pair since Crispin's banishment from court eight or so years previously. While Crispin resigns himself to Chaucer's presence with a marked lack of enthusiasm, Chaucer presses the former knight for details of his life as "The celebrated 'Tracker,'" remarking, "'There's a poem in that, I'll warrant. Like a modern-day Robin Hood.'" Crispin, however, has little respect for Chaucer's writerly activities, warning him, "'Put me in one of your poems and you're a dead man,' he growled" (Westerson, *Troubled Bones* 18). Later, Chaucer continues to pester Crispin about his adopted profession, not quite believing that he truly makes a living by investigating crime: "'I suppose ... I just thought being this Tracker ... I thought it might be a metaphor.' [Crispin] snorted. 'Metaphor. Only *you* would think such'" (Westerson, *Troubled Bones* 76, emphasis in original). Eventually, once Chaucer points out that his cases seem better suited to sheriffs, Crispin offers a wonderful definition of the medieval hardboiled detective: "'Consider me a *private* sheriff, if you will'" (Westerson, *Troubled Bones* 78, emphasis in original).

In this particular case, Crispin is woefully inadequate in his mission to protect the saint's bones and, having fallen asleep while guarding the tomb, awakens to discover the bones missing and the Prioress murdered. And then Chaucer is arrested for this murder and accused of killing one of the cathedral's monks. William Courtenay, a historical figure who was Archbishop of Canterbury in 1385, when this novel is set, welcomes the opportunity to imprison Chaucer for both murder and heresy because he is vehemently opposed to Chaucer's patron, John of Gaunt (as discussed above, Courtenay also features as Chaucer's enemy in Duane Crowley's *Riddle Me a Murder*). Crispin has very little time to prove Chaucer's innocence before Courtenay enacts his plan to discredit the duke by, startlingly, executing "Lancaster's pet," as Crispin describes Chaucer (Westerson, *Troubled Bones* 263).

Chaucer also makes an appearance in Westerson's next novel, *Blood Lance* (2012), which concerns yet another famous relic, the spear of Longinus. Indeed, the number of mystical relics that Crispin encounters throughout the series is significant enough to make the reader question, along with Crispin's apprentice, Jack, "'Why, sir, if you hate dealing with relics so much, were you in such a hurry to do this task?'" (Westerson, *Troubled Bones* 2). The answer, of course, is the conventional straitened circumstances that force many private eyes to undertake unpalatable jobs in order to eke out a living. In *Blood Lance*, Chaucer attends the so-called Wonderful Parliament of 1386 as the member for Kent and entangles Crispin in the political maneuvering between the appellant lords and the soon-to-be-impeached Chancellor of England, Michael de la Pole. Chaucer is also searching for the relic and attempts to hire Crispin to assist him. Crispin, however, is deeply offended, chastising the poet: "'Don't. Don't sound like those cursed dogs I must deal with every day. Twisted men with a vile purpose. For God's sake, Geoffrey! Don't sound like them'" (Westerson, *Blood Lance* 155). Crispin has never reconciled himself to his disgraced status as a tracker-for-hire, despite his undoubted proficiency for his new occupation. His humiliation and self-disgust lurk just below the surface and inevitably erupt during encounters with associates from his previous life at court, such as Chaucer.

According to one Afterword, Westerson "grew up with *The Canterbury Tales*" and believes in the theory that "some [of Chaucer's pilgrims] might be based on actual individuals" (Westerson, *Troubled Bones* 286, 285). Furthermore, she claims that her pilgrims' "descriptions come directly from the text, with some added help from the Ellsmere [*sic*] Manuscript with its extraordinary illustrations of all the characters" (Westerson, *Troubled Bones* 285). Westerson's enthusiasm for Chaucer and his pilgrims shines through her writing and makes any critique of the several inaccuracies seem churlish indeed. Of particular joy is the author's portrayal of "Alyson," the Wife of Bath. Alyson is as clever, sympathetic and voluptuous as readers familiar with her *Prologue* and *Tale* would expect. Alyson prepares the Prioress's body for burial and offers pragmatic sympathy to the traumatized young nun who witnessed the murder. Moreover, in an entirely predictable sequence, Alyson seduces Crispin with her "gat-toothed grin" and they spend a night together. As Crispin departs the next morning, he concludes that "'Bath must be a very accommodating city'" (Westerson, *Troubled Bones* 151).

However, Westerson's depiction of the Canterbury pilgrims offers one false note that is difficult to ignore. She assigns her pilgrims names that bear little resemblance to their monikers in the *Canterbury Tales*, despite the author's assurance that she has sourced her information "directly from the text" (*Troubled Bones* 285). Westerson calls the Miller, for example, "Edwin Gough," which seems unrelated to Chaucer's "Robyn" (*General Prologue* I.3129). Both the Summoner and the Pardoner are deeply unpleasant characters, as is to be expected, involved in their own nefarious trade in relics. Westerson names the Summoner "Maufesour" and while this name does not appear in Chaucer's works, Dave Postles, in his investigation into how names developed throughout the period 1100 to 1350, records a man named "John Maufesour" who was hanged for theft and murder in Wakefield (114). Loosely translating to "wrong-doer," this appellation seems entirely appropriate.

However, the connotations of the Pardoner's name, "Peter Chaunticleer,"[7] are less straightforward. Westerson claims in her Afterword that she "just assumed school kids in 1960s Los Angeles all knew the story of Chaunticleer" (*Troubled Bones* 286), having gained her own knowledge from a children's version of the *Canterbury Tales*. It appears that Westerson has conflated the *Nun's Priest's Tale* and the markedly more somber *Pardoner's Tale*, although Chaucer's rollicking barnyard romp is more likely to be included in a children's book than the latter. Naming her Pardoner after the iconic rooster strikes a discordant note each time "Chaunticleer" appears and does distract from this particular narrative thread. It is, of course, entirely likely that only those with a detailed understanding of Chaucer's poetry may succumb to this trivial irritation and this level of nitpicking is rather ungracious. Nevertheless, the names of the pilgrims in Joseph and Gertrude Clancy's *Death is a Pilgrim* and in Mary Devlin's novels, described earlier, do not rankle at all, indicating that it is possible to change or adapt Chaucer's work without destabilizing the recreation of the poet's fourteenth-century context.

In *Troubled Bones* and *Blood Lance*, Westerson demonstrates the two most common ways of depicting Chaucer in medieval crime fiction. The earlier novel brings the Canterbury pilgrims to life, having them interact with their creator and allowing Westerson to speculate how real people may have inspired the poet's characters. *Blood Lance* embeds Chaucer in the political context of the late fourteenth century, where his poetry is incidental to his broader concern with serving his patron, John of Gaunt. Both strategies are effective and illustrate the enduring interest in both Chaucer himself and his medieval world.

Chaucer also appears as a secondary character throughout Candace Robb's successful Owen Archer series. In her third novel, *The Nun's Tale* (1993), Archer is reluctantly investigating a young woman's claim to be a resurrected nun, buried the year before, on behalf of the Archbishop of York. He must travel through the northern towns of Beverley, Leeds and Scarborough and encounters Geoffrey Chaucer, working as a spy for John of Gaunt, the Duke of Lancaster. Specifically, Chaucer had been sent to Navarre to intercept "five Englishmen of renown" who, due to "misguided chivalry," were planning to participate in a war between Castile and Navarre, against the wishes of King Edward—as Owen pointedly notes, "'A dangerous mission for a poet'" (Robb, *Nun's Tale* 189). Chaucer succeeded in finding four of the five men, but the fifth has disappeared and both Chaucer and Lancaster believe that the man Owen is searching for will lead them to this missing man. Owen's first impression of Chaucer is a combination of irritation and interest, considering him to be "A complex little man" (Robb, *Nun's Tale* 188). It seems extremely unlikely that Chaucer undertook such dangerous missions as described in the novel, but Robb, like all medieval crime fiction authors, seeks and researches periods in Chaucer's life that are poorly documented. In this case, she points out in her Afterword that "The extent of Chaucer's espionage work is unknown" and that "For Chaucer's mission to Navarre, I use Donald R. Howard's interpretation of a safe conduct preserved in the archives in Pamplona" (*Nun's Tale* 352).

While Chaucer also appears briefly in Robb's *A Vigil of Spies* (2008), the poet makes his most significant appearance in *A Gift of Sanctuary* (1998). In March 1370, Archer is traveling to Wales on a commission from John of Gaunt to recruit more archers from the Marcher lords for a planned attack on French soil in the summer. Archer is accompanied by his father-in-law, Sir Robert D'Arby, and Brother Michaelo, a monk from the abbey in York. Both of these men are on a pilgrimage to St. David's shrine in the town named for the saint in order to perform penance and seek forgiveness for past sins. Chaucer joins them, ostensibly sent by Gaunt to survey and report back on the garrisoning of the duke's Welsh castles. King Edward III, concerned about a rumored invasion by France, has ordered all coastal castles to be prepared to repel an attack. Chaucer may also be traveling to Wales in order to observe Archer's reaction to his long-awaited return to his native land. Sir Robert warns Owen that "Master Chaucer has watched you closely since Carreg Cennen" and fears that Archer's growing remembrance of the family and land that he left behind fifteen years earlier may confuse his loyalties (Robb, *Gift of Sanctuary* 26). Chaucer, however, is soon reassured about Archer's commitment to England's cause. Both men are distracted from their primary assignments by a series of disturbing incidents, including the murder of an unknown pilgrim and the theft of a large amount of gold. Owen is increasingly irritated by Chaucer's interference in his investigation; for example, on his way to question Roger Aylward, who was injured in the theft, Owen discovers that Chaucer has been there first:

> So that was how Geoffrey had won the man's friendship—by playing the bard. Owen would admire his ingenuity if he were not so angry. What was Geoffrey thinking, to come here and question the Duke's receiver? What did he know of the cunning necessary for such things? Well, he knew something, Owen could not deny it [Robb, *Gift of Sanctuary* 170].

Robb's Chaucer is the diplomatic spy that many modern critics and authors wish him to be. He is also the canny observer of the human condition that readers enjoy most in his poetry. Robb indulges in a popular convention by having other characters view Chaucer with suspicion. For example, Brother Michaelo "found [Chaucer] insufferable, smugly self-important, and imagined the man wooing new acquaintances at court with tales in which all the world came off as fools but himself" (Robb, *Gift of Sanctuary* 336). The famous Welsh bard, Dafydd ap Gwilym, also appears throughout the novel and Robb enjoys contrasting the styles of the two poets. Dafydd's writing features love and nature as dominant themes, and is deeply personal, as opposed to Chaucer's more removed, observational style.[8] At the end of the novel, Robb summarizes her interpretation of the two medieval poets: "Dafydd laughs at himself; Geoffrey laughs at mankind [*sic*]" (Robb, *Gift of Sanctuary* 369). Chaucer appears in Robb's novel as a precursor to the poet he will become—John of Gaunt's duchess, Blanche, has only recently died and Chaucer is musing over his elegy to her—and not as a medieval detective in the strictest sense. While he undoubtedly assists Archer in this role (indeed, he insists on accompanying the captain when the investigation demands a change in their plans), Robb prefers to showcase Chaucer's abilities as a public servant and spy, for which there is historical evidence, rather than reimagine him as a (potentially anachronistic) detective.

Gower's Dark Matter

Bruce Holsinger has written two novels (so far) featuring the late-fourteenth-century poet, John Gower. A contemporary of Chaucer's, Gower's poetry is largely unknown to those who are not specialists in the literature of the Middle Ages. Holsinger is a well-regarded professor of medieval studies at the University of Virginia and translates his expertise into a convincing portrayal of the social, political and literary landscape of the late fourteenth century. Academic specialists embarking upon fictional enterprises often produce wonderfully rich, multi-layered novels, where the narrative's backdrop is impeccably detailed. The exemplar of this undertaking in medieval crime fiction is, of course, Eco's *The Name of the Rose*, which maintains its status as both a pre-eminent crime novel and a masterful instance of postmodern historiographic metafiction. Holsinger's novels are similarly impressive in their recreation of late-medieval life in London, Greenwich and Calais.

At the most obvious level, Holsinger's *A Burnable Book* (2014) and *The Invention of Fire* (2015) are crime novels, each depicting multiple murders and requiring their detective, Gower, to discover the who, what and why pertaining to each crime. But Holsinger is just as concerned with weaving an intricate tapestry of medieval life and exploring the artistic process of creating poetry. Regarding the latter, Holsinger's characterization of the complicated, affectionate and prickly relationship between Gower and Chaucer is entertainingly successful. Gower is one of few contemporary figures named in Chaucer's poetry, most famously at the end of *Troilus and Criseyde* where he dedicates his epic poem to "O moral Gower, this book I directe / To the…" (V.1856–57). Capitalizing on Gower's comparative obscurity, Holsinger imagines a relationship between the two men based upon a regular exchange of poetic verses, Chaucerian obscurantism and Gower's not-insignificant inferiority complex.

Holsinger emphasizes his interest in the artistic process by subjecting his own creative experience to some rigorous scrutiny in several articles and interviews. In one article, Holsinger describes the anxiety of facing the "devoted readers of historical fiction" who "can be wonderfully fanatical" and quick "to lob charges of anachronism, sentimentalism, presentism, and any other –ism ready to hand" ("Stretching the Truth" 35). In addition to the "surprising challenge" of confronting the significant gaps in his knowledge of the historical period that he has studied and taught for decades, Holsinger also had to relinquish his instinct for what he calls "the disciplinary protocols of literary criticism," ingrained in him since graduate school, and instead "embrace a mode of written expression and a form of thought that have been trained out of our critical souls" ("Stretching the Truth" 36–37). This is a perceptive assessment of the transition from "professional" academic to "amateur" historical fiction author, and perhaps explains the self-conscious anxiety that Holsinger's Gower feels regarding the quality of his poetry—particularly in comparison to Chaucer's.

In terms of medieval crime fiction, Holsinger's Middle Ages expertise overshadows the crime narrative in his first novel, *A Burnable Book*. It turns out that Gower is not a very good detective. Holsinger introduces Gower as "a seller of suspicion, a purveyor of foibles and the hidden things of private life" (*Burnable Book* 18). In other words, Gower trades in secrets and his financial security relies upon the exchange of favors that forms the currency of any medieval court. Gower prides himself on his skill at obtaining information and he is not above deploying tactics such as blackmail or bribery to further his interests. In *The Invention of Fire*, Ralph Strode—another historical figure Chaucer mentions in his poetry—explains why Gower is best suited to the investigative process: "'That is why I have come to you. For your cunning ways with coin, your affinity with the rats, the devious beauty of your craft. And for your devotion to the right way, much as you like to hide your benevolent flame under a bushel of deceit'" (20).

In *A Burnable Book*, Chaucer seeks Gower's assistance to discover the whereabouts of the eponymous object and Gower follows an investigative path that keeps him frustratingly one step behind the manuscript's location. Gower demonstrates leaps of intuition and moments of impressive ratiocination, but when he pursues these leads he often dramatically announces the existence of the book in order to shock information out of someone who already knows more about it than Gower does himself. Of course, the unsuccessful detective is an important subgenre of crime fiction, especially in postmodern narratives favored by writers such as Jorge Luis Borges. However, unlike Eco's William of Baskerville, who castigates himself for "failing" as a detective because he followed an incorrect path of reasoning despite discovering the murderer, Gower's ratiocination is sound; it is simply a few steps behind everyone else's. Holsinger's second novel, *The Invention of Fire*, is much more compelling as a detective narrative. In this book, Gower maintains a tight hold over all the threads of evidence and manages to restrain his tendency to reveal his knowledge at every opportunity.

Holsinger's depiction of Chaucer also changes between his two novels. In *A Burnable Book*, Chaucer is elusive, enigmatic and largely absent from daily London life. He is a shadowy figure who manipulates Gower to suit his own purposes, and there is a sense throughout the book that Chaucer is either the detective pursuing the real investigation behind the scenes, or the perpetrator of the crimes.[9] Chaucer is unpleasantly condescending towards Gower about his abilities as both a poet and a purveyor of secrets. In *The Invention of Fire*, on the other hand, Chaucer appears more frequently and contributes substantially to the progression of Gower's investigation in a partnership that is markedly more equitable.

The overwhelming success of Holsinger's novels, however, lies in his recreation of fourteenth-century London. The city is indispensable to both narratives, at times aiding or obscuring Gower's investigations. Holsinger's London echoes the decay and corruption of the modern city of hardboiled convention, while anchored firmly in its medieval context through snatches of descriptive prose redolent of fourteenth-century poetry. For example, Gower commences his search for the identities of sixteen murdered men discovered in the public privy by visiting London's famous portals: "The gates of London are so many mouths of hell, Chaucer once observed, swallowing the sinful by the dozen, commingling them in the rich urban gruel of waste, crime, lust, and vice that flows down every lane…. To know the gates of London is to know the truest pathways to the city's soul" (Holsinger, *Invention of Fire* 22). Here Holsinger simultaneously captures the futility of the private detective's individual fight against streets teeming with corruption and suggests that fourteenth-century poets such as Chaucer and Gower were aware of the growing city's depravity. Gower loves London, although he does live outside the city precincts in the grounds of St. Mary Overy's Church in Southwark. Chaucer gently mocks Gower's reluctance to leave London's environs, having to insist repeatedly that Gower visit him in Greenwich, just a few miles away. In a letter accompanying some poetry, Chaucer writes to Gower:

> We also appeal to your great courtesy in asking that you delay no longer in visiting us in Greenwich, home to many a shrew, and scoundrels aplenty. A man of your habits and skills would feel quite at home in these village precincts. Leave aside your dark matter for a few days, John. London can surely spare your lurking presence [Holsinger, *The Invention of Fire* 91].

Chaucer's missive has its desired effect, pricking Gower's conscience and prompting a visit to Kent where Chaucer arranges for him to interview a gaoler and observe a crime scene, deep in the forest, both of which turn out to be crucial to his investigation.

In his reimagining of Gower, Holsinger offers an intriguingly complex portrait of a relatively unknown medieval poet. The crime fiction genre provides an effective platform for this purpose, as well as for Holsinger's overarching concern with depicting late-fourteenth-century London. Gower, in these novels, is vastly more entertaining than readers might expect based solely upon his own poetry. Holsinger magnifies the political acumen that may be glimpsed in Gower's works—most obviously in his rededication of *Confessio Amantis* to Henry IV after Richard II's deposition—and takes advantage of the mystery of Gower's profession to imagine him as a trader in secrets; an apposite occupation for a medieval detective. Holsinger also garners sympathy for a man with a slightly sanctimonious reputation through his sensitive description of Gower's increasing blindness.

As suggested earlier, medieval crime fiction featuring Chaucer may foster a broader audience for medieval literature itself, and Holsinger similarly participates in this project. David M. Perry, writing in the *Chronicle of Higher Education*, describes *A Burnable Book* as "clearly a form of academic public engagement" (1). He goes on to cite recent debates surrounding the role of such engagement and "the nature of the modern public intellectual," suggesting that "Novels, culturally accepted as serious works, provide an interesting case study in how scholars can reach a wider audience" (1). Furthermore, Perry concludes that novels by academics such as Holsinger, "based on deep research and scholarly expertise, have the potential to reach people on a scale that is unthinkable for more overtly academic publications" (1). This statement alludes to the blurring of the line between so-called "professional" and "amateur" readers that Carolyn Dinshaw has most recently illustrated; in particular, Dinshaw uncovers the symbiotic relationship between amateur and academic readers that informs contemporary interpretations of medieval texts (*How Soon is Now?*). The cultural work that Holsinger's medievalism performs is to translate his medieval studies expertise for an amateur audience, whose members will, Perry hopes, "end up in our classrooms, ready to learn more" (1).

Idealized Leonardo

Leonardo da Vinci's multifaceted genius across the fields of painting, sculpture, anatomy, mathematics and mechanics, combined with his commensurate talent for observation and investigation, make him irresistible to several authors, who enthusiastically repackage him into a detective. Almost without exception, these novels depict an idealized Leonardo, seemingly without fault.

Diane A.S. Stuckart's three novels realize this glorification project through her narrator, a young apprentice attached to Leonardo's workshop in Milan during the early 1480s. Stuckart, a successful author of historical romances, emphasizes the relationships between her characters and allows her main protagonist to respond to deeply felt emotions that are not necessarily conducive to the impartiality required when functioning as a detective. "Dino," like the other apprentices, absolutely adores the "Master," as they call Leonardo, and tries desperately hard to please him. "Dino" is especially anxious to succeed because "he" is actually Delfina della Fazia, a girl who has disguised herself as a boy in order to be accepted as an apprentice. "Dino" becomes a favorite of Leonardo's over the course of the first book in the series, *The Queen's Gambit* (2008), in which the Duke of Milan, Ludovico Sforza, commands Leonardo to construct a chessboard for a live game using members of the Duke's court. Inevitably, someone is murdered during the match and Sforza assigns Leonardo the role of discovering the perpetrator. Leonardo avails himself of "Dino's" excellent observational skills and the novel plays out in a manner reminiscent of a police procedural, in which Leonardo acts as the experienced, somewhat cynical, older cop, while "Dino" is his enthusiastic junior partner tasked with doing all the legwork.

"Dino's" real identity is ironically mirrored in the series' second novel, *Portrait of a Lady* (2009), whereupon Leonardo orders "Dino" to go "undercover" and masquerade as a lady-in-waiting for the Duke's cousin and ward, Contessa Caterina de Sasina. Delfina, of course, has no trouble with this assignment and becomes the contessa's trusted confidante. The third book in the trilogy, *A Bolt from the Blue* (2010), explores Leonardo's abiding interest in the possibility of human flight, within the context of simmering tensions between the Duke of Milan and his neighbor, the Duke of Pontalba. Leonardo successfully builds a prototype of a flying machine, with the help of "Dino's" father, a talented cabinetmaker summoned to Milan by the artist. When one of the other apprentices is murdered, "Dino" and Leonardo must once again investigate the crime, as well as orchestrate the rescue of the Duchess of Pontalba from her abusive husband and prevent the slaughter of the remaining apprentices by the vindictive Duke.

Stuckart's novels idolize Leonardo to a distracting extent. In *Portrait of a Lady*, the murderer, having just confessed to the crimes, attacks Leonardo. "Dino" watches in horror, but it seems that in addition to his creative genius, Leonardo is also handy with a sword: "A man with normal reflexes would have been impaled on that first strike, but Leonardo was no normal man. Moving with the swift grace of his namesake lion, he twisted out of the way in time to deflect [the] blade with his own" (Stuckart, *Portrait of a Lady* 294). However, at the end of this novel, "Dino" deserts Leonardo in grief and anger over the latter's handling of the final confrontation with the murder suspect, accusing the painter of being unable to love or to mourn and departing with an emotional, "'Find another apprentice to do your bidding, to spy for you and follow you about in the night. I cannot bear to look upon you ever again'" (Stuckart, *Portrait of a Lady* 308). Eventually, however, "Dino" returns to the workshop, apologizes to Leonardo and resumes "his" apprenticeship.

In *A Bolt from the Blue*, "Dino's" true identity is revealed by Delfina's irate mother who, having followed her husband to Milan, is horrified to discover that her daughter has been dressing like a boy and living in such close proximity to several young men. Delfina fears Leonardo's reaction, but, of course, the painter had known the truth "Almost from the start" (Stuckart, *Bolt from the Blue* 305). Leonardo's explanation for retaining Delfina as his apprentice conforms to a common desire in contemporary popular culture to appropriate icons such as Leonardo, Chaucer or Dante for the "modern" world, perpetuating the belief that they are somehow transhistorical. Stuckart's incarnation of the great artist displays a decidedly feminist outlook when he explains to Delfina that he accepted her because

> "your eagerness pleased me, and your talent with the brush was far greater than most of the boys I'd taken on. It did not seem fair that you should be denied the training you sought, simply because you were the wrong sex. And so I decided that if you did not tell, I would not ask" [Stuckart, *Bolt from the Blue* 306].

The other apprentices, once over their shock, demonstrate a similarly enlightened attitude towards the young woman who has lived among them and Stuckart describes Delfina's necessary departure from Leonardo's workshop in touchingly regretful terms that plainly acknowledge the gender-biased injustice of the situation.

A contrasting series featuring Leonardo da Vinci chooses to capitalize on other imagined characteristics of the great inventor. Martin Woodhouse and Robert Ross collaborated in the mid-seventies to write a trilogy featuring Leonardo as a Cold War spy; indeed, the synopsis for the third novel, *The Medici Hawks* (1978) describes him as "the 'James Bond' of Renaissance Italy." Woodhouse and Ross emphasize Leonardo's towering intellect and privilege his mechanical innovations. In the first novel, *The Medici Guns*, published in 1974, Leonardo assists Lorenzo Medici, ruler of Florence, to recapture the fortress city of Castelmonte by devising a new way to deploy the Duke's cannons. Leonardo spends a significant period experimenting in the environs of the Medicis' Florentine mansions, to the condescending skepticism of the so-called "doctors" (of the university) who come to observe his mechanical machinations. Woodhouse and Ross regard Leonardo's intellect as vastly superior to everyone he encounters. The next two novels, *The Medici Emerald* (1976) and *The Medici Hawks* conform to the spy thriller format that the two authors prefer; while strictly not mystery fiction, in that there is not a case to be solved, but rather a dangerous situation to overcome, these are nevertheless intriguing, early examples of medieval crime fiction that speak to their Cold War context and also participate in the idealization of Leonardo project.

Spanish author Javier Sierra's successful novel, *The Secret Supper*, was published in 2004 and translated into English in 2006. A *New York Times* bestseller, Sierra's novel has also been published in thirty-five countries. Sierra's Leonardo is intent on embedding symbols from a lost testament of the disciple St. John in his magnificent "Last Supper" fresco. He is opposed by the Church, especially Pope Alexander VI (Rodrigo Borgia), because the so-called "Secret Supper" that John supposedly had with Christ in heaven before returning to Earth to write his last testament threatens the Church's interventionist status and presages the Reformation, as one dying monk is horrified to realize:

> "I know what you're after, Leonardo. You came to Catholic Milan full of extravagant notions. Your friends Botticelli, Raphael, Ficino filled your head with vainglorious ideas about God. And now you want to give the world the formula for speaking directly to Him, without intermediaries and without the Church" [Sierra 297].

This is precisely what Sierra's proto-Lutheran Leonardo desires, and Sierra neatly manipulates the fame of the "Last Supper" fresco, as well as its fragility, by recasting it as a dissemination tool for "the secret": the artists Leonardo invited to copy it ensure its fame travels throughout the world, while Leonardo's painting technique, *a secco*, was "never intended to be long-lasting" (Sierra 298).[10]

Grumpy Dante

Professor of Italian literature, Giulio Leoni, lives in Rome and writes a medieval crime fiction series featuring fourteenth-century poet Dante Alighieri. Leoni has written five novels to date, of which three have been translated into English. The most striking characteristic of Leoni's novels is the far from idealized depiction of the famous writer. Dante is a prior of Florence and a bad-tempered bully who demonstrates unsettlingly misogynistic tendencies. But, as *Independent* reviewer, Barry Forshaw, comments, "[Un]like the customary modern figure clashing with a medieval age, Dante is presented as a man of his time, obsessed with the religious protocol of his high office, bullying his inferiors and disapproving of female sexuality" ("Third Heaven"). Another reviewer, Frank Wilson, notes that "Unlike most modern fictional sleuths, with their proletarian bona fides, Dante hasn't a democratic bone in his body. He's a snob, both intellectually and socially. In fact, he's a misanthropic crank sorely in need of anger management" (F. Wilson). For example, in one scene in *The*

Kingdom of Light (2005), Dante watches in disgust as two gangs supporting rival Florentine political factions engage in a riotous brawl through the streets. Unable to stop them, he rants from the sidelines:

> "This shameful rabble was unleashed like an irresistible flood within our walls. It came from the four corners of Tuscany.... It spilled into our streets after overflowing from the sewers in which it first sheltered, taking over the land that our fathers spilled their blood to redeem from barbarism. Florence now looks like a maddened horse" [Leoni 91].

Both of these critics, and others, perceive the effectiveness of Leoni's rendering of Dante as a man of his time; the author eschews the more common practice of making his detective a modern interloper to a medieval world with the intention of translating that foreign landscape for a twenty-first-century reader. In so doing, Leoni also avoids the double temptation of over-idealizing his famous poet-sleuth or rehearsing the fantasy that famous writers such as Dante, Chaucer or Shakespeare transcend time in order to appear contemporary in whatever period they or their works appear.

Dante's companion while watching the riot is the (fictional) philosopher Arrigo da Jesi, Dante's one-time teacher in Paris. The pair discusses Dante's investigation of a recent murder, as well as some philosophical theories about the "rabble," when they are interrupted by one of the rioters urinating down upon the square from a higher vantage point. Furious, Dante scrabbles around for a stone and hurls it at the man, striking him on the forehead. Arrigo is astonished, crying, "'Heavens above, Prior!' … 'A throw of biblical dimensions! You Florentines should have David on your coins, rather than the lily'" (Leoni 95).

Leoni's Dante is obsessed with composing his magnum opus, *The Divine Comedy*. At the end of *The Kingdom of Light*, while demonstrating the mechanics of the devices Frederick the Great had commissioned in order to prove that light has its own motion, his first thought is his own poetry:

> The image of the glory of the heavens, that image that he had sought for so long, was there now, in front of him, the Comedy was finally about to find its epilogue. "This was written by God in the nature of the boundless splendour, this my words will represent upon parchment, this men will read for their ultimate edification!" [Leoni 378].

This obsession with the thoughts contained in his head makes Dante irritable and peremptory, earlier snapping at a group of monks, "'Do as I say, and have no fear. I am the Prior of Florence and there is a logic to my actions. Nothing of what you see contravenes the rules of your order'" (Leoni 365–66). But what this characterization of Dante also achieves is a more amusingly believable rendition of a literary genius that does not suffer from the idealization that undermines the generally preferred portrayal of Leonardo, as demonstrated above.

Heartbroken Machiavelli

Derek Wilson's favorite historical period is the sixteenth century; in particular, he is interested in the impact of the Reformation because he believes it is "the single most important development in the last 1000 years of western history. Everyone, from rulers to 'ordinary folk,' was caught up in the massive cultural, political and social changes that came out of that ideological conflict" (D. Wilson, "Derek Wilson"). This interest has led to a series of crime novels set in London in the mid–sixteenth century and featuring the goldsmith, Thomas Treviot, as the detective-protagonist.[11] But Wilson has also written one novel featuring Niccolò Machiavelli as a young man in Florence, before his rise through the political ranks. This is apparently Wilson's only foray into medieval crime fiction and he follows Eco's premise of framing his narrative with a contemporary account of the discovery of the fictional "Escobaldi Papers," that "since their discovery four years ago caused a ferment of excitement in the world of Renaissance scholarship" (*Swarm of Heaven* 10). The papers purport to be autobiographical and describe, in his own words, traumatic events in Machiavelli's early life, before he achieves his political ambitions. Indeed, Wilson suggests that the events described in these "papers" contributed significantly to the trajectory of the young Florentine's future career.

The novel begins with the wedding between Machiavelli and the beautiful daughter of a local fur trader, Baccia Vernacci. Florence is in turmoil and the political background to these opening scenes is the imminent demise of Piero de Medici's tyrannical hold over the city and the rise of the puritanical monk Girolamo Savonarola. There is also an invasion of the northern duchy of Milan by Charles VIII of France, with whom Savonarola achieves a truce to support the Florentine Republic, allowing Charles to pass through on his way to the kingdom of Naples. In the middle of the upheaval of the French forces entering the city, Machiavelli's wife Baccia is discovered strangled. The young man is crazed with grief and believes the killer to be a lustful Dominican monk who had earlier impressed upon Baccia and her cousins the importance of chastity, even in marriage.

Machiavelli sets off to Rome after Fra Roberto, who has been sent to the mother house by Savonarola, in which city the young man is pressed into the service of Cesare Borgia to be a spy within a Turkish delegation to Rome. Meanwhile, Charles VIII has also arrived in Rome and Borgia orchestrates a delicate diplomatic balancing act within which Machiavelli eventually plays a pivotal role. In this way, Machiavelli's personal vendetta becomes a second frame within the fiction of the newly discovered "Escobaldi Papers" for Wilson's primary objective of exploring the political machinations of this extraordinary period of Italian history. At the end of the novel, Machiavelli, "a little older and more than a little wiser" (D. Wilson, *Swarm of Heaven* 187), returns to Florence, where he identifies poor Baccia's murderer, and hopes to commence "a quiet life of study" (D. Wilson, *Swarm of Heaven* 188). But, in the end, he is peremptorily summoned back to Rome by Cesare, much to his disgust, and his famous career is launched.

"Holmes and Holmes": Machiavelli and Leonardo

Michael Ennis has combined the forensic skills of Leonardo da Vinci with Machiavelli's expertise in the study of human behavior and psychology to imagine a scenario in which the two collaborate to solve what Ennis suggests is a historical crime. At the end of 1502 (just outside the temporal parameters of this book, but impossible not to include), Ennis takes advantage of the fact that both Leonardo and Machiavelli were in the service of Cesare Borgia in the remote fortress of Imola, and later were working together in Florence. His novel, *The Malice of Fortune* (2012), achieved the *New York Times*' bestseller list, enjoying a range of positive reviews. The premise is intriguing in that Ennis claims to have found the "truth" regarding the crime his novel describes "between the lines of *The Prince*," Machiavelli's political masterpiece. Ennis, more than most, emphasizes the authenticity of his historical research, insisting that "The following narrative is based entirely on actual events. All of the major characters are historical figures, and all of them do exactly what the archival evidence tells us they did, exactly where and when they did it" (1).

Despite Ennis's extensive "Author's Note" supporting this prefatory epigraph, it is a bold claim; terms such as "exactly" are troublesome for historians, especially since more than one perspective regarding the same event is now commonly accepted, as is the acknowledgment that both memory and the historical record should be viewed with suspicion. Moreover, Ennis's claim to historical accuracy is immediately undermined by the attachment of a crime narrative that he anachronistically describes in terms of modern fiction. Nevertheless, Ennis's novel does achieve a historical authenticity that is not disrupted by the modern forensic practices undertaken by Leonardo and Niccolò's joint investigation into a series of murders.

It is an irresistible premise to think of the two intellectual giants combining their talents in order to seek justice for murdered peasant women, and to consider them "Holmes and Holmes" as opposed to detective and assistant. This doubling of the detective-genius character does, however, produce insufferable instances of shared secret knowledge between the two masters for the "assistants" who trail behind them. In just one example, a pot of unguent is discovered at a murder scene and "Messer Niccolò" directs the narrator of this part of the novel to

> "Allow the maestro to smell it. He will recognize the scent." ... Both Messer Niccolo [*sic*] and Maestro Leonardo had sniffed their fingertips after running them across the flesh of that poor, butchered woman. And now I understood Leonardo's apparent indifference to this discover; he had already known what he would smell in that pot [Ennis 71].

"Holmes and Holmes," though, fail to inform anyone else and maddeningly maintain their extra-sensory-perception-esque private conversation.

Where Are the Women of the Middle Ages?

What is strikingly and disturbingly obvious in this chapter is the absence of female medieval detectives who are also historical figures. This is a puzzling situation, especially when, as noted in the introduction, historical crime fiction of other periods embraces the opportunity to reimagine women such as Jane Austen or Elizabeth I as detectives. There are three exceptions to this unspoken medieval crime fiction rule, although each one presents its own complications to the generic form.

Jeremy Potter's *Death in the Forest* (1977) is an early example of medieval crime fiction and is discussed in more detail in Chapter One. The novel features Edith, known as the "Rose of Romsey," who endeavors to discover the murderer of one of William the Conqueror's sons during a visit to the New Forest abbey in which she has been ensconced by her royal Scottish family. Edith eventually becomes Matilda, queen to Henry I, and her role in discovering who had murdered her husband's brother, Lord Richard, is hampered by the obfuscations of her aunt, the abbess, her priest and the men who surround her and control her fate. Potter is effusive in his praise for Edith's rule, "acclaimed as wise and just and merciful" (loc. 2861), but she remains deceived as to the true murderer and is less a medieval detective and more a central character around whom Potter can weave his historical speculation.

G.M. Dyrek has also selected a woman from history as her medieval detective. In this case, it is the German mystic, Hildegard of Bingen. Dyrek has written two novels featuring Hildegard and her amanuensis, Volmar (also a historical figure), that are aimed at a young adult audience. The historical Hildegard is rightly venerated as a woman of extraordinary intelligence and astonishing celebrity throughout her own lifetime for her writing on the cosmology of the universe, natural history, and the interpretation of scripture, as well as beautiful hymns and chants that are still performed and recorded today. Hildegard also experienced visions and dispensed prophecies. Dyrek chooses the early period of her life for her mysteries, and the young nun's visions certainly prove a useful tool for aiding her investigations with Volmar into both murder and the power of holy relics. Included here because of the dearth of female historical figures, Dyrek's novels are perhaps a little too reliant upon supernatural intervention to be classified strictly as crime fiction. Her target audience of twelve years and above is also unusual; there are no other medieval crime fiction novels included in this book that target a young adult readership.

Roberta Gellis, author of the Magdalene la Bâtarde series, discussed in Chapter Four, has also written a single novel featuring Lucrezia Borgia as a medieval detective. *Lucrezia Borgia and the Mother of Poisons* (2003) attempts to salvage Lucrezia's dubious historical reputation through this account of her third marriage to Alfonso d'Este of Ferrara. Lucrezia is happy to escape Rome where her father, Pope Alexander VI, and her brother, Cesare Borgia, have been nothing but detrimental to her reputation and peace of mind:

> Marriage to Alfonso had promised freedom, freedom from the sickening rumors about her, freedom from being dangled like a ripe fruit in front of those who desire her father's favor, freedom from Cesare's dangerous notions of how she could be used to forward his purposes [Gellis, *Lucrezia Borgia* 15].

Lucrezia is happy in Ferrara, despite her husband's animosity; the latter was forced into the marriage by the greed of his father, the Duke of Ferrara. But the murder of Bianca, one of her ladies-in-waiting and also Alfonso's mistress, shatters that happiness and threatens Lucrezia's security because she is accused of poisoning Bianca. Lucrezia is left with no choice but to discover the murderer for herself. Conforming to rehabilitation conventions, Gellis depicts Lucrezia as an intelligent, resourceful woman attempting to transcend both the restrictions of her historical context and the dangerous intrigues of her powerful family. However, Lucrezia is not completely devoid of the talent for Borgian machinations: recognizing and appreciating the cleverness of her maid, Lucia, Lucrezia sends her among the courtiers to act as a spy: "'Because you are a maid, no one sees you. No one thinks that you hear and see. Will you hear and see for me, Lucia?'" (Gellis, *Lucrezia Borgia* 20).

Lucrezia is undeniably appealing and Gellis successfully garners the reader's sympathy for her impossible plight. She throws herself into discovering the perpetrators behind Bianca's murder, and the subsequent murder of Bianca's latest lover, which occupies her focus to such an extent that she is shocked when reminded of her importance to the politics of Ferrara: "She raised her startled eyes to his, realizing how her concentration on the murder had warped her point of view. To her, Bianca's and Palagio's death [*sic*] were of paramount importance, but to Duke Ercole, it would be political considerations that came first, and she was still the daughter of the Pope and the sister of Cesare Borgia" (Gellis, *Lucrezia Borgia* 311). Lucrezia discovers the murderer and the motivation, placing herself in some danger in the process, before explaining her solution to a room full of Ferraran nobles, including Alfonso and the Duke. While this scene conforms to the presentation of evidence by conventional detectives, Lucrezia is annoyed by the masculine energy in the room, "angry ... at those who sat around gaping at her as if she were a clever beast trained to do tricks" (Gellis, *Lucrezia Borgia* 332). After she has finished her explanation, she requests permission to return to her room, sarcastically stating, "'I will leave you to explain to each other what kind of accidents allowed a silly woman to first discover the truth that *doubtless* you would have found in another hour or two'" (Gellis, *Lucrezia Borgia* 332, emphasis in original). But Lucrezia has won the Duke's admiration; he assures her that he has not thought her silly for some time, while her husband, Alfonso, accompanies her to her room with a somewhat ambiguous request that Lucrezia not allow her cleverness to put herself in danger again, indicating a possible affection for her after all.

Authors of medieval crime have embraced the recent trend of casting historical figures as detectives, deriving pleasure from intertwining a crime narrative with the biography of people such as Chaucer, Gower, da Vinci and Dante. Historical fiction universally depicts people from history because to do so contributes to its main purpose, which is, according to Georg Lukács, to offer a faithful portrayal of the social and political mores of the time the novelist wishes to recreate (42). There is an additional benefit in accessing an established narrative in the life stories of famous historical figures, especially if those figures are also infamously entertaining. But there are also dangers in manipulating the biographies of well-known people because being too manipulative of the historical record could irreparably undermine the novel's authenticity effect.

While historical figures are to be found in almost all examples of medieval crime fiction series and novels, most often on the periphery, authors who choose to bring those figures to the center of their narratives incorporate both the biography and the extant writing or work they undertook. For Chaucer, authors such as Philip Gooden enjoy speculating about the poet's possible activities as a spy for Edward III, traveling across Italy and France on the crown's behalf and gathering material for his own poetry. Other writers, such as Mary Devlin or Joseph and Gertrude Clancy, imagine Chaucer as embedded within his poetry, choosing to believe his assertion that he did travel to Canterbury with a mixed group of pilgrims drawn from a range of medieval social estates. Giulio Leoni also seeks inspiration for Dante's great works in the responsibilities of his daily life as a prior of Florence. Roberta Gellis uses her historical crime novel to rehabilitate the awful reputation that the historical record applies to Lucrezia Borgia, while Bruce Holsinger brings Chaucer's contemporary, John Gower, to the center of his narratives in a reversal of the traditional privileging of Chaucer's poetry over Gower's by literary critics.

What appears constant across the range of medieval crime fiction novels depicting historical figures as detectives is the desire to find new meaning in past events, people and their actions through the application of a crime narrative. This intermingling of historical record with modern genre fiction offers the chance to interrogate the motivation or inspiration behind both words and actions, explaining strange gaps in a person's life, and burnishing an already mighty reputation.

Conclusion

In recent decades, the boundary between "literary" and "popular" texts has become increasingly blurred. Literary critics and cultural theorists examine genres such as romance and science fiction, television series and cinema, fan fiction and massive multi-player online games for what they reveal about their particular social, cultural and political moments. It used to be customary to draw a sharp distinction between "amateur" and "professional" readers: the first group read with keen pleasure and an eye for detail; while the second wrote fine-grained or wide-ranging analytical criticism of literary texts. But this distinction barely holds; and in the case of both detective fiction and medievalism, these genres not only speak to the contexts in which they were made, but are also endlessly flexible in offering different experiences for readers.

Ironically, one of literary criticism's traditionally more conservative disciplines, medieval studies, has been at the forefront of bridging this gap between "professional" and "amateur" readers through its increasingly influential sibling discipline, medievalism studies. Umberto Eco's assertion that the Middle Ages never really went away is a commonplace now, as is his famous taxonomy of the "ten little Middle Ages" that offer us a choice between the Middle Ages that we "need." It is undeniable that each subsequent century has found its own way to reimagine, recreate or reinvent some aspect or other of the medieval period: rehearsing medieval texts in the sixteenth century; parodying those same texts in the seventeenth century; producing new editions of Chaucer in the eighteenth century; nostalgically recreating medieval culture in the nineteenth century; and the twentieth and twenty-first century's love affair with depicting the Middle Ages on screen. Medievalism studies recognizes that these recreations say more about the contexts that produced them than they do about the historical period they purportedly describe. This recognition allows scholars to avoid the trap of simply pointing out what makes a book, film, artwork or electronic game "medieval"—an early habit that has now, thankfully, dissipated. Medievalism is both an academic and a popular practice and medieval crime fiction similarly reaches into both the past and the present, and across historical and popular modes.

In generic terms, medieval crime fiction straddles the intersection of the historical novel, crime fiction and medievalist fictions. Chapter One of this book broadly sketched the parameters that shape medieval crime fiction, noting the curious absence of any sustained discussion of this genre by critics in either crime fiction or medievalism studies. Medieval crime fiction's beginnings lie firmly in the second half of the twentieth century and while Ellis Peters and Umberto Eco are rightly regarded as the originators of this specific form of historical novel, there are examples that predate these two. Edward Frankland's 1955 novel, *The Murders at Crossby*, is the author's paen to his beloved Cumbrian countryside and its Nordic heritage, as well as appearing to be the earliest example of a murder mystery set in the Middle Ages.

Eco's *The Name of the Rose* is the one medieval crime fiction novel that retains sustained interest from literary critics, as much for its deft deployment of postmodern irony and medieval semiotics as its contribution to crime fiction. Eco more often sees what he calls "moderns" acting "medievally" than vice versa—a medievalist point of view that characterizes both Eco's novels and his academic focus. *The Name of the Rose* and Eco himself continue to influence medievalism studies. Most recently, Louise D'Arcens has used the novel's description of a lost Aristotelian treatise on laughter to frame her analysis of *Comic Medievalism* (2014); while the journal *postmedieval* published a special issue called "After Eco: Novel Medievalisms" (2016) which grounded its studies of medievalist historical fiction on Eco's work. Ellis Peters' Brother Cadfael series has not received anywhere near the same critical focus, although compared to other examples of medieval crime fiction, the small amount that does exist appears more significant. While not often analyzed from a literary criticism perspective, it is notable how often the Brother Cadfael series is cited by reviewers of new medieval crime fiction as the standard to which these novels should aspire. Peters' novels remain in print, more than forty years after the first one was published, and if critical studies of crime fiction mention any historical crime subgenres at all—let alone medievalist incarnations—it is always the Brother Cadfael series.

Clearly, Peters and Eco demonstrate very different forms of medievalism in their recreation of two specific moments in the history of the Middle Ages, separated by a continent and two hundred-odd years. But it is that difference, anchored by the shared deployment of crime fiction conventions and a firm, self-conscious grasp of their historical periods, that reveals the myriad possibilities inherent in medieval crime fiction; possibilities that more than one hundred and fifty authors have perceived and developed in the decades since the genre's inception. Eco and Peters also share the extremely rare experience of having seen their medieval crime fiction novels adapted to film and television. Of all the many hundreds of novels that comprise this genre, there is only one other example: Booker Prize-shortlisted *Morality Play* (1995) by Barry Unsworth was significantly altered and made into a 2003 film called *The Reckoning*.

Chapter Two examined medieval detectives who occupy secular roles that buttress or disguise investigative activities. Many medieval crime fiction authors follow the patterns of medieval romance and gravitate towards the knight (in various incarnations) as an ideal premodern type to suit the conventions of a detective narrative. These detective-knights are ex-crusaders, ex-Templars, current Templars, coroners, spies and warriors who have fallen on hard times. There are, however, other secular occupations that coalesce well with the demands of being a detective, including lawyers, booksellers, apothecaries, doctors, clerks and scribes. Moreover, these secular sleuths conform closely to contemporary crime fiction conventions. It is impossible to ignore the parallels between the "soiled knight" traversing the "mean streets" of the corrupt city that Raymond Chandler invokes in his depiction of the hardboiled private eye and the actual knights who stalk the mostly unpaved but equally corrupt thoroughfares of the Middle Ages. Chandler introduces Philip Marlowe in a burst of medievalist allusion and his character is still praised as the original incarnation of an essentially chivalric ethos that Chandler repackages for an American public jaded by war and depression.

The hardboiled detectives of medieval crime fiction also perform a more complicated function. In addition to combatting their own systems of corruption and crime, they must translate the Middle Ages for their modern audiences. Despite contemporary popular culture's love affair with medievalism, the Middle Ages largely remain shrouded in misinterpretation. The social, economic and political inequality of the feudal structure adds to the challenge of seeking justice for each person, regardless of wealth or status. Medieval detectives, like their modern hardboiled counterparts, frequently deploy violence in their investigations, with the important distinction that, in certain circumstances such as trial by battle, physical prowess can determine the innocence or guilt of a suspected criminal. The literary detective's methodological process of evidence gathering and intellectual reasoning is abandoned in favor of a haphazard and risky test of arms. But the medieval detective's success in all these physical and detective encounters reassures the reader that a familiar figure of justice might have traversed the mean streets of the Middle Ages.

In Chapter Three, the medieval constraints that confronted Chapter

Two's secular detectives become rather more restrictive through the imposition of the religious life. Residing in the cloistered world of a monastery, priory or abbey necessitates following strict rules that inevitably preclude much contact with the outside world. While secular characters such as knights, doctors, booksellers or clerks invariably demonstrate strong religious beliefs, they are more able to question those beliefs without the risk of triggering a crisis of faith that is highly incompatible with the staunch vocation that most members of religious orders experience. As such, medieval detectives who are bishops, priests, monks, priors, or brothers appear to tread more carefully around issues such as the possibility of divine or diabolical intervention in a crime, wary of inadvertently denying such interpretations in a way that suggests heresy. Many authors cannot resist allowing their medieval religious detectives to experience the occasional moment of doubt; however, these moments are most often fleeting, or directed towards the activities of the Church hierarchy, or an uncharitable interpretation of sacred texts such as the bible.

In another historical challenge, being enclosed in a monastery from childhood or young adulthood is not conducive to developing the skills or experience required by detectives, medieval or otherwise. Consequently, many authors allow their medieval detectives to choose religion later in life, after experiencing the wider world in some form or other. Additionally, religious detectives tend to occupy positions within their establishment that offer the greatest contact with the outside world, such as infirmarians, hostelers, cellarers or supervisors of large and dispersed landholdings. Brother Cadfael's varied past combines extremely well with his role as herbalist for his monastery, while E.M.A. Allison's portrayal of Brother Barnabas's almost complete incapacity as an investigator, having been sent to his abbey at the age of eight, illustrates the incompatibility of the cloistered life and the detective role. On the other hand, those religious orders whose primary function is militant, such as the Knights Hospitallers or Knights Templar, seem ideally placed to produce medieval detectives who can balance religious devotion with combat skills and worldly experience. Maureen Ash's Bascot de Marins achieves this balance perfectly: his crusading past, long years in Saracen captivity, and his successful recovery from an existential crisis of faith all suggest that he may indeed be the ideal medieval religious detective—with the obvious exception of Brother Cadfael, who emerges from this study as the once and future detective-monk.

The female medieval detectives who featured in Chapter Four occupy a literary space structured by two traditionally patriarchal cultural fields: medieval studies and crime fiction. However, over the past several decades there has been a surge of compelling and important feminist scholarship and literature that has challenged, appropriated and dismantled those rather old-fashioned notions. Critics have long pointed out that women have featured in crime fiction since the nineteenth century and there are now just as many female sleuths, police officers, forensic scientists, spies and private detectives as there are male characters in contemporary crime fiction. Feminist medieval studies has been similarly successful at retrieving women's voices from the historical record and challenging the entrenched patriarchy of feudalism, as well as troubling the traditionally male-dominated discipline that studies the Middle Ages. Feminist medieval studies not only recovers the neglected writing and history of marginalized groups such as women, children, the poor and the illiterate; it also reexamines canonical authors such as Chaucer, the *Gawain*-poet, Malory, Augustine, Abelard, and many others, through a gender-neutral or feminist framework that generates new perspectives for their work.

But these productive interventions, both scholarly and creative, do not necessarily mean that female detectives negotiating the Middle Ages find their medieval landscape any more forgiving. Almost without exception, these women must rely on men to assist in the gathering of evidence, apprehending the perpetrators and facilitating movement in the world outside their home or cloister. Medieval crime fiction novels featuring female detectives are also the most likely to veer towards romance and to explore supernatural themes such as miraculous intervention or pagan rituals. As such, several of these authors come perilously close to contravening the conventions of the crime fiction genre they invoke.

While these female characters are intelligent, observant, witty, and as independent as their medieval context allows, there nevertheless appears to be a certain reluctance to embrace the belief that women in the Middle Ages were not necessarily the oppressed group of medieval studies' tradition. In other words, the perception that premodernity was a "dark age" for women persists in these criminographical examples of contemporary medievalism. Reimagining a feminist medieval landscape may well be a scenario that poses too much danger to the authenticity of the premodern world that medieval crime fiction privileges above all else.

Chapter Five acknowledged race as a fraught topic in medieval and medievalism studies both because of the way different ethnicities and religions are portrayed in the texts they examine and revere, as well as for the way medieval symbols can be appropriated and deployed in the service of contemporary fascist and racist organizations. European medieval texts almost always depict the Jewish religion, culture and people as the monstrous other to Christianity. Hypocritically, the broader political and economic context surrounding the production of these texts meant that Jewish traders were tolerated for their usefulness as political pawns and moneylenders. As such, Jewish communities across Europe found themselves occupying a precariously liminal space, constrained by fickle protection from monarchs, variable community support for assimilation and overt hostility from the local and broader Christian church. Jewish people also lived under the constant threat that any unexplained crime—particularly murder—would spark a conflagration of violence that often ended in devastating pogroms.

Many of the authors in this book engage with the "Jewish question" at one stage or another throughout their series. While Caroline Roe is the only author to feature a Jewish detective, there are other examples of detectives with Jewish heritage, such as Sharan Newman's Catherine LeVendeur and Ariana Franklin's Adelia Aguilar, as well as characters such as Jewish doctors and merchants who engage with medieval detectives. But what characterizes all of the Jewish people in medieval crime fiction, regardless of period, location or crime, is their unwaveringly positive depiction. There appears to be an unspoken agreement among medieval crime fiction authors that Jewish people are not to be cast as the villain, nor is the Jewish religion to be shown in any way other than tolerant, reasonable and misunderstood by outsiders. This insistence appears anchored in a contemporary desire to rewrite the historical record through fictional accounts of cordial Jewish-Christian relations: upstanding Jewish citizens who contribute usefully to medieval society and Christian seekers of justice—medieval detectives—who are not blinded by racial prejudice; at least, not by the end of their investigation. Roe's series featuring Isaac of Girona is an exception to this rule: she has superstitious, intolerant and murderous Jewish characters in her novels—but her strongly positive Jewish detective despairs at their failings in the same way a Christian detective critiques his or her own community's faults.

What strikingly emerges from Chapter Six's study of medieval crime fiction authors who cast historical figures as premodern sleuths is the reverence in which they hold their protagonists. Leonardo da Vinci, in particular, is treated with adoration by Diane A.S. Stuckart and Javier Sierra, and while Giulio Leoni offers a rather irascible portrait of Dante Alighieri, he nevertheless lauds Dante's poetry and his dedication to his beloved Florence.

However, the many incarnations of Geoffrey Chaucer form by far the most numerous examples of this significant subset of medieval crime fiction. Chaucer's biographical elasticity is evident in the varied ways he performs as a detective: while all the authors capitalize on his reputation as an acute observer of the human condition to ensure a successful investigative process, there is a wide range of Chaucerian versions on offer. Tim Shaw and Philip Gooden present the young, enthusiastic, carefree squire with an eye for a pretty lady-in-waiting, on the brink of realizing his genius for the written word. Garry O'Connor and Duane Crowley, on the other hand, depict an older, wiser, but vastly more cynical and jaded figure, adept at political maneuverings, skirting the rules, and demonstrating questionable ethics that recall the world-weary private eye of hardboiled crime fiction convention. Jeri Westerson and Candace Robb focus on Chaucer's unwavering loyalty to John of Gaunt, while Mary Devlin and the Clancys prefer to harness his mystical and diplomatic skills.

The convergence of popular medievalism and medieval studies is an ideal framework in which to locate crime fiction featuring historical figures such as Chaucer, Gower, Leonardo or Dante. Anecdotally, university teachers describe numerous examples of students choosing subjects in medieval studies because of past exposure to medievalist cultural products such as movies, online gaming or fantasy novels. Medieval scholars such as Bruce Holsinger and Giulio Leoni therefore participate in what David M. Perry has termed "academic public engagement" by translating their specialist knowledge into a cultural product that engages a much broader audience (1). This is medievalism at its most effective: a reimagining of the Middle Ages that not only recreates an authentic medieval world, but also assigns that world the task of introducing a new audience to the medieval literature and art of these cultural icons.

Medieval crime fiction continues to expand at a rate that evinces its consistent popularity and relevance to an audience of knowledgeable readers. This book, in the first instance, has endeavored to survey a neglected form of popular fiction that, despite the number of authors and sustained presence in the marketplace since the later-twentieth century, has been largely ignored by literary and cultural critics of medievalism, crime fiction and medieval literature. Medieval crime fiction speaks to contemporary demands for cultural products that provide temporary relief from troubling current events in a form that is recognizable and yet different enough to offer an escapist landscape. But that landscape must also offer its own intelligible order and that is where medievalism and crime fiction triumphantly combine to create a narrative safe haven, although not one without its own range of contemporarily relevant questions and critiques.

This remarkable genre embraces the variety of crime fiction and the romance of medievalism, and vice versa. Its detectives span the crime fiction spectrum, including the existential and metaphysical "failures" of Eco's William of Baskerville and John Fuller's Abbot, who make the most of their postmodern moment. The valiant, jaded, good-with-a-sword knights and crusaders are numerous but share a common desire to dispense justice in a manner that owes as much to medieval chivalric romance as to contemporary hardboiled detective conventions. The women of medieval crime fiction are not only princesses, prioresses and nuns, but also physicians, lawyers and apothecaries, united in their attempt to navigate the feudal patriarchy that thwarts their search for truth. Medieval detectives are found across Europe, from Ireland in 500, to Germany in 1100, to Rome in 1500, and everywhere and when in between. The poets of the Middle Ages make an appearance: Chaucer and Dante apply their understanding of the human condition to solving crime as well as to creating timeless verse; Leonardo and Machiavelli's skills with mechanics and politics penetrate mysteries other than those recorded by history. Even more, medieval crime fiction's establishment as a genre is entrenched enough to generate its own self-referential intertextuality. Priscilla Royal's medieval crime fiction series opens with a preface explaining the historical background to her novel and notes that Matilda "was no shrinking violet when it came to war and fought for the throne against her cousin, Stephen, during Ellis Peters' Brother Cadfael period" (*Wine of Violence* Foreword). Royal is able to orient her readers not through reference to traditional forms of periodization, but rather through what may be called "medieval crime fiction time."

Crime fiction has always offered a sense of social order restored and justice achieved—particularly in its golden-age form—while medievalism's appeal, at least since the Pre-Raphaelite movement of the nineteenth century, lies in the depiction of a simpler life free from rapid and overwhelming technological change; overlain, of course, by the romance of knights undertaking their quests for justice and women who are perhaps not as oppressed as history would have us believe. This is what medievalism offers to crime fiction, the opportunity to escape from the scientific imperatives of contemporary crime drama. But the Middle Ages, by and large, did not provide the romantic life of courtly love convention or Arthurian romance. As Eco noted long ago, postmodern irony affords the contemporary reader the benefit of critical distance: we love the Middle Ages, but we know we do not want to return there.

Medieval crime fiction, successfully and positively, evades this dilemma by inserting a modern interloper into the landscape of the premodern world whose function is not only to seek justice and restore order to a medieval society that we fear may contain no justice at all, but also to translate that "foreign country" intelligently and valuably for our modern sensibilities. In other words, the medieval detective can be disgusted by the offensive smells, rotten food, and appalling sewerage systems that probably would not have affected a "local" because that detective is actually a cypher for the twenty-first century time traveler. The detective traverses the Middle Ages armed with the aforementioned critical distance that allows him or her to navigate potentially restrictive systems such as feudalism and religious hierarchies while still adhering to the conventions of a literary detective. Medieval crime fiction perfectly encapsulates and combines contemporary popular culture's desire both to reimagine the Middle Ages and to witness the restoration of a society fractured by crime.

Appendix:
Authors, with Characters and Settings

Authors of medieval crime fiction current as of September 2018. An asterisk indicates inclusion in this book.

*E.M.A. Allison	Brother Barnabas, 1397, Yorkshire, England
Timothy J. Armstrong	Brothers Wilfridus and Thomas, 1235, Canterbury, England
*Maureen Ash	Sir Bascot de Marins, 1200s, Lincoln, England
	Estrid, 1080s, Rochester, England
Cherith Baldry	Gwyneth and Hereward, 1190s, Glastonbury, England
Andrew Barlow	Hopkin ap Griffith ap Rhys, 1410s, Wales, England and France
Charles Barnitz	Hring, 780s, Northumbria, England
Simon Beaufort	Sir Geoffrey Mappestone, 1100s, Herefordshire, England
J.M.C. Blair	Merlin, 500s, Carlisle, England
*David Bland	Father Martin, 1157, London, England
*Barbara Cherne	Giuditta, 1494, Florence, Italy
*Gertrude Clancy and Joseph P. Clancy	Geoffrey Chaucer, 1387, Rochester, England
*Alys Clare	Abbess Helewise and Sir Josse d'Acquin, 1190s–1210s, Kent, England
*Cassandra Clark	Prioress Hildegard, 1380s, York, England
David Coles and Jack Everett	Abbot Rutilius and acolyte William, 1200s, France
*Alfredo Colitto	Mondino de 'Liuzzi, 1310s, Bologna, Italy
*Sara Conway	Lord Godwin, 1220s, Hexham, England
*Mary Ellen Cooper	Avisa Baglatoni and Bernardo, 1490s, Bologna, Italy
*Duane Crowley	Geoffrey Chaucer, 1370s, London, England
*Mary Devlin	Geoffrey Chaucer, 1380s, England
*Paul C. Doherty	Templar series, 1095 and 1152, Jerusalem and England
	Hugh Corbett, 1280s-1300s, London, England
	Mathilde of Westminster, 1300s, London, England
	Brother Athelstan, 1370s, Southwark, England
	Matthew Jankyn, 1410s, London, England
	Kathryn Swinbrooke, 1470s, Canterbury, England
	Wars of the Roses Trilogy, 1400s, England

*Denise Domning	Sir Faucon de Ramis, 1190s, Warwickshire, England
*G.M. Dyrek	Hildegard of Bingen, 1100s, Germany
*Umberto Eco	William of Baskerville, 1327, northern Italy
Clayton Emery	Robin Hood and Maid Marian, 1100s, Sherwood Forest, England
*Michael Ennis	Niccolò Machiavelli and Leonardo da Vinci, 1502, Imola, Italy
Elizabeth Eyre	Sigismondo, 1400s, Italy
Robert Farrington	Henry Morane, 1480s, England
Marina Fiorato	Luciana Vetra, 1482, Florence, Italy
*Odelia Floris	Rowena Walden, 1430s, southwest England
*Edward Frankland	Norse settlers, 940s, Westmorland, England
*Ariana Franklin	Adelia Aguilar, 1170s, England, Italy
*Margaret Frazer	Dame Frevisse, 1430–50s, Oxfordshire, England
	Bishop Pecock, 1430–60s, Oxford, England
	Joliffe, 1430s, England
*Philip Freeman	Sister Deirdre, 500s, Ireland
*John Fuller	Vane, 1300s (?), Wales
*Stephen Gaspar	Brother Thomas, 900s, northern Italy
	Sir Jean-Marc de Montpellier, 1300s, Paris, France
*Barbara Reichmuth Geisler	Dame Averilla, 1130s, Shaftesbury, England
*Roberta Gellis	Magdalene la Bâtarde, 1140s, Southwark, England
	Lucrezia Borgia, 1502, Ferrara, Italy
*Philip Gooden (Philippa Morgan)	Geoffrey Chaucer, 1359, 1370s, France, Italy, England
*Alan Gordon	Feste / Theophilos, 1200s, France, Italy
*Susanna Gregory	Matthew Bartholomew, 1350s, Cambridge, England
Claudia Gross	Konrad Steiner, 1413, Cologne, Germany
John Hall	Martin Byd, 1450, Lincolnshire, England
Sylvian Hamilton	Sir Richard Straccan, 1210s, England
*C.B. Hanley	Edwin Weaver, 1210s, Lincoln, England
Indrek Hargla	Melchior, 1410s, Tallinn, Estonia
*Cora Harrison	Mara, 1500s, the Burren, Ireland
*Sarah Hawkswood	Serjeant Catchpoll and Lord Bradecote, 1140s, Worcestershire, England
*Ned Hayes	Mear, 1377, northeast England
Tony Hays	Malgwyn ap Cuneglas, 500s (Arthurian), Carlisle, Glastonbury, England
*Judith Koll Healey	Alais Capet, 1200s, France and England
Jane Heritage	Marcello D'Estari, 1281, Venice, Italy
George Herman	Leonardo da Vinci and Niccolo da Pavia, 1490s, Milan, Italy
Domini Highsmith	Father Simeon de Beverley, 1180s, Yorkshire, England
Sheri Holman	Friar Felix Fabri, 1483, Germany and Mount Sinai
*Bruce Holsinger	John Gower, 1380s, London, England
*Howard of Warwick	Brother Hermitage, 1060s, England and Normandy
Eric Jager	Guillaume de Tignonville, 1407, Paris, France
*Andrea H. Japp	Agnès de Souarcy, 1300s, Normandy, France
*Michael Jecks	Sir Baldwin Furnshill and Simon Puttock, 1300s, Devon, England (The Templar series)
*Martin Jensen	Halfdan and Winston, 1010s, Oxford, England
*Catherine Jinks	Various, 1300s, South of France
J. Robert Kennedy	Sir Marcus de Rancourt, 1280s, Paris and environs, France

*Bernard Knight	Sir John de Wolfe, 1190s, Exeter, England
Adriana Koulias	Sir Andre and Christian de St. Armand, 1254, Pyrenees, France
*Giulio Leoni	Dante Alighieri, 1300s, Florence, Italy
*Joyce Lionarons	Matthew Cordwainer, 1270s, York, England
*Karen Maitland	Various
*Jay Margrave	Priedeux, 1390s, northwest England
*Edward Marston	Sir Ralph Delchard and Gervase Bret, 1080s, England
K.E. Martin	Francis Cranley, 1470s, Yorkshire, England
*Robin Maxwell	Nell Caxton, 1480s, London, England
*Susan McDuffie	Muirteach MacPhee, 1370s, Inner Hebrides, Scotland
*Pat McIntosh	Gil Cunningham, 1490s, Glasgow, Scotland
Austin McKinley	Nick Gauntlet, 1208, "Calomel," Yorkshire, England
*The Medieval Murderers	Various
Viviane Moore	Chevalier Galeran de Lesneven, 1140s, Brittany and Normandy, France
Ian Morson	William Falconer, 1260s, Oxford, England
*Toni Mount	Sebastian Foxley, 1470s, London, England
*Sharan Newman	Catherine LeVendeur, 1140s, Paris, France
*Chris Nickson	John Carpenter, 1360s, Chesterfield, England
*Garry O'Connor	Adam Scriven, 1399, England
*Sharon Penman	Justin de Quincy, 1190s, England and France
*David Penny	Thomas Berrington, 1480s, Gharnatah (Granada), Spain
*Ellis Peters	Brother Cadfael, 1140s, Shrewsbury, England
*Jeremy Potter	Edith (Matilda), 1100, Romsey, England
*E.M. Powell	Sir Benedict Palmer, 1170s, England and Ireland
	Aelred Barling and Hugo Stanton, 1170s, York, England
*Candace Robb	Margaret Kerr, 1290s, Edinburgh, Scotland
	Owen Archer, 1360s, York, England
	Kate Clifford, 1399, York, England
*Caroline Roe	Isaac, 1350s, Girona, Spain
*Priscilla Royal	Prioress Eleanor, 1270s, East Anglia, England
John R. Sack	Brother Conrad, 1200s, Italy
Frank Schätzing	Jacob, 1200s, Cologne, Germany
*Kate Sedley	Roger Chapman, 1470s, Bristol, England
*Tim Shaw	Geoffrey Chaucer, 1360, London, England
*Javier Sierra	Leonardo da Vinci, 1497, Milan, Italy
*Keith Souter	Sir Richard Lee, 1322, Wakefield, England
	Sir Giles Beeston, 1485, Wakefield, England
Keith Souter (as Clay More)	Thomas Smythe, 1320, Warwickshire, England
*Mel Starr	Hugh de Singleton, 1360s, Oxfordshire, England
*C.J. Stevermer	Nicholas Coffin, 1501, Rome, Italy
*Diane A.S. Stuckart	Leonardo da Vinci, 1480s, Milan, Italy
*Ann Swinfen	Nicholas Elyot, 1350s, Oxford, England
S.D. Sykes	Oswald de Lacy, 1350s, Kent, England
J.R. Tomlin	Sir Law Kintour, 1420s, Perth, Scotland
*Peter Tremayne	Sister Fidelma, 660s, Ireland and England
*Barry Unsworth	Nicholas Barber, 1380s, northern England
*Jason Vail	Sir Stephen Attebrook, 1260s, Ludlow, England
Pip Vaughan-Hughes	Brother Petroc, 1230s, Devon, England
*Jeri Westerson	Crispin Guest, 1380s, London, England

Stephen Wheeler	Brother Walter, 1200s, Suffolk, England
*Derek Wilson	Niccolò Machiavelli, 1492, Florence and Milan, Italy
Joan Wolf	Hugh de Leon, 1140, Lincoln, England
*Sarah Woodbury	Gareth and Gwen, 1140s, Wales
*Martin Woodhouse and Robert Ross	Leonardo da Vinci, 1470s, Florence, Italy

Chapter Notes

Introduction

1. I have cited this favorite example previously in "Medievalism, the Detective," pp. 161–62.

2. There are very few surveys of historical crime fiction. In Browne and Kreiser's edited collection, *The Detective as Historian* (2000), over one-third of the critical essays examine novels set in the Middle Ages, more than any other period. In Burgess and Vassilakos's bibliographic volume, *Murder in Retrospect* (2005), medieval Britain and Ireland again dominate, representing one in six of all settings. Joerg O. Fichte cites an older study (1997) that "quotes sales people as saying that mysteries set in medieval England generate the most interest and sell more than any other detective fiction" (54). Most recently, Barry Forshaw has issued a Pocket Essentials guide to *Historical Noir* (2018) that lists novels set in the ancient world through to the 1970s and includes brief interviews with selected authors. In 2018, there are more than one hundred and fifty authors who have written detective stories set in the European Middle Ages. See the Appendix for a listing of medieval crime fiction authors, writing in or translated into English, as of September 2018.

3. For a recent consideration of the productive combination of science fiction and medievalism, see Kears and Paz, eds., *Medieval Science Fiction*.

4. The earliest example of medieval crime fiction appears to be Edward Frankland's little-known, *Murders at Crossby* (1955), discussed in Chapter One. There were, however, some other examples of early historical fiction that predated Christie's novel, although these are short stories rather than novels. In America, Melville Davisson Post's long-running series featuring "Uncle Abner" in mid-nineteenth century Virginia was published between 1911 and 1928, while Lillian

de la Torre's short story series depicted Samuel Johnson and James Boswell as eighteenth-century detectives (the first of these was published in 1943).

5. See, for example, French author Frédéric Lenormand, who has written close to twenty Judge Dee ("juge Ti") novels since 2004 that have not yet been translated into English; Chinese author Lin Qianyu whose *Detective Dee: Mystery of the Phantom Flame* (translation) was made into a 2010 Chinese film; and Chinese-American author Zhu Xiao Di's *Tales of Judge Dee* (2006).

6. This remains the case even when compared to historical crime novels featuring the other two most popular centuries: the sixteenth and the nineteenth (see Browne and Kreiser; Burgess and Vassilakos).

7. Martin Woodhouse and Robert Ross also preceded Peters and Eco with their mid-1970s trilogy featuring Leonardo da Vinci as "the James Bond of Renaissance Italy." This series is briefly discussed in Chapter Six.

Chapter One

1. Medieval literature abounds with what would now be described generically as crime fiction. Indeed, most medieval romance involves a transgression that the hero (and sometimes the heroine) must rectify, usually through the structure of a quest rather than an investigative process, although these two frameworks are remarkably similar. Famous medieval texts that could be described "crime fiction" include *The Tale of Gamelyn*, *Havelok*, *King Horn*, *Bevis of Hamtoun*, among others.

2. Lukács's analysis remains the standard framework for discussions of historical fiction, whether they approach the field from postmodernist or feminist or other theoretical positions.

See, as one recent example, Melanie Micir, "The Impossible Miss Woolf: Kate Atkinson and the Feminist Modernist Historical Novel," for a reconsideration of Atkinson's "postmodern metafiction" in the context of Lukács's and Fredric Jameson's theories of the historical novel.

3. Feminist criticism has claimed more recently that Scott's fiction was heavily influenced by women's historical fiction such as the novels by Anglo-Irish Maria Edgeworth, a contemporary and friend of Scott's (Curthoys and Docker 68). It is also important to recognize the significance of the Gothic novels of the late eighteenth century to the development of what is understood to constitute the historical novel today.

4. Scott's novel may be the first medieval historical novel, if one excludes the Gothic novels of Horace Walpole, Ann Radcliffe, and other writers of the late eighteenth century.

5. Medieval anti-Semitism is explored by many medieval crime fiction authors with the ostensible objective of reversing the entrenched prejudice of the period. Their success or otherwise is discussed in detail in Chapter Five.

6. For a helpful account of the history of crime fiction literary criticism, see Pyrhönen, "Criticism."

7. See, most recently, Knight's *Towards Sherlock Holmes* (2017) and his *Australian Crime Fiction: A 200-Year History* (forthcoming).

8. For feminist approaches to crime fiction, see Chapter Four. Other notable subgeneric criticism includes *Crime Fiction in the City: Capital Crimes*, edited by Lucy Andrew and Catherine Phelps (2013); *Italian Crime Fiction*, edited by Giuliana Pieri (2011); and *A Counter-History of Crime Fiction*, by Maurizio Ascari (2007).

9. The second half of this phrase is Linda Hutcheon's and refers to "those well-known and popular novels which are both intensely self-reflexive and yet paradoxically also lay claim to historical events and personages" (*Poetics* 5).

10. Throughout this book, I concur with Knight's insistence upon the usefulness of synopses, particularly for affording an overall sense of the variety inherent in a genre that is not well-studied. See Knight's *Secrets of Crime Fiction Classics*, which also contains a comprehensive summary and analysis of *The Name of the Rose* (169–79).

11. The other "little Middle Ages" described by Eco are: the barbaric age; the Middle Ages of Romanticism; of neo-Thomism, the return to the philosophies of Saint Thomas Aquinas; of decadentism; of philological reconstruction; of tradition; and, finally, the expectation of the millennium.

12. Biographical information comes from Margaret Lewis's 1994 literary biography, *Edith Pargeter: Ellis Peters*.

13. There are many reviews; for a representative sample of the series' general reception, see the comments contained on *IMDb*, www.imdb.com/title/tt0108717/reviews.

14. The prize was known as the "Ellis Peters Historical Dagger" from 1999 to 2005 and then the "Ellis Peters Historical Award" up until 2013. The award is now sponsored by Endeavour Press (Forshaw, *Historical Noir* 11).

15. Puzzlingly, there is an entrenched habit of categorizing C.J. Sansom's Shardlake series as "medieval" when it is, in fact, firmly situated in the Early Modern world of Henry VIII.

16. Agatha Christie's *Death Comes as the End*, set in Ancient Egypt and published in 1945, appears to be the first full-length novel that combined a mystery or crime narrative with historical fiction and is an important originary text for historical crime fiction more broadly. Martin Woodhouse and Robert Ross were also early adopters of the medieval crime fiction formula, writing a trilogy in the mid-seventies featuring Leonardo da Vinci as a "cold war spy." These novels are discussed in Chapter Six.

Chapter Two

1. This is the American term, signifying a "tough egg," and these two expressions are often used interchangeably.

2. See Durham, *Down These Mean Streets a Man Must Go*; Holden, "The Case of Raymond Chandler's Fiction as Romance"; and Knight, *Secrets of Crime Fiction Classics*.

3. Bishop William and Lord Graistan are characters from Domning's romance series, *The Graistan Chronicles* (1994 to 1997).

4. Vail has written a book about medieval and early modern daggers, *Medieval and Renaissance Dagger Combat* (2006), and this interest in the mechanics of medieval martial practices informs his novels. There are long and detailed descriptions of the battles that Stephen fights and these passages take precedence over his investigative procedures.

5. The biographical note that appears in all of her novels begins "Candace Robb studied for a Ph.D. in Medieval and Anglo-Saxon literature and has continued to read and research medieval history and literature ever since" (*A Spy for the Redeemer* i).

6. Robb has also written series featuring female protagonists Margaret Kerr and Kate Clif-

ford, as well as historical novels about Alice Perrers and Joan of Kent.

7. However, there has recently been a greater recognition among scholars for the important role that so-called "amateurs" play in our engagement with the medieval past: see Carolyn Dinshaw's *How Soon Is Now?* for a methodological approach to the future of amateur and expert interaction.

8. See, in particular, Stearns and Stearns for an older, influential essay that argues for the separation of individual and group emotional experience from the "collective emotional standards of a society" (813).

9. Barbara Rosenwein made an early challenge to what she terms the "grand narrative" approach to the history of emotions inherited from Elias, Huizinga and others; she calls this approach the "hydraulic" model and she argues that it is no longer tenable (834). See also W. Reddy and McNamer.

10. There is a longer discussion of autopsy and its heretical implications in Chapter Three with regard to John Fuller's *Flying to Nowhere*.

Chapter Three

1. There does not appear to be any Islamic religious detectives (such as Imams), although there are a small number of devout Muslim detectives. This chapter focuses on medieval detectives within the Christian faith; see Chapter Five for Jewish characters.

2. For example, Philip Grosset's helpful website, *Clerical Detectives* lists a bewildering number of detectives "with a significant church or religious background." As well as alphabetically, Grosset also divides his subjects into categories, including the amusing "A beginners' [*sic*] guide to detective nuns (of whom there are too many, particularly medieval ones)" (Grosset).

3. For good overviews see, for example, Riddy, "Women"; Duffy, *Voices*; and Edden, "Devotional Life."

4. See Roach and Simpson's "Introduction" to their edited collection *Heresy and the Making of European Culture* for a good historiography of medieval heresy scholarship, which they demonstrate expanded significantly in the years after the Second World War (3). See also Moore's excellent *The War on Heresy*. For more particular studies, see Cameron on Waldensians; Strohm, *England's Empty Throne*, Somerset, et al., and Hudson on Lollardy; and, as an example of the more recent challenges to the existence of heretical movements, see Pegg on the Cathars.

5. Fraser's primary example is the extremely successful first season of the *True Detective* series created by HBO, broadcast in 2014.

6. The Abbot's autopsy practice recalls the significant interest that premodern investigations into the functions of the human body hold for authors of medieval crime fiction. See the several examples described in Chapter Two.

7. Eco was a professor of semiotics when *The Name of the Rose* was published, while Fuller was a Fellow at Magdalen College, Oxford.

8. Even without the knowledge of Fuller's occupation as a poet, it is difficult not to associate this name with Geoffrey Chaucer.

9. This small gland serves an endocrine function, producing melatonin, and is located in the center of the brain. The Greek doctor Galen (c. 130–c. 210) first described the pineal gland and speculated as to its function. Fuller's Abbot consults Arabic scholar Avicenna's (980–1037) variant on Galen that incorporated the psychological distinctions found in Aristotle's *On the Soul*. By the time of René Descartes (1596–1650), much more was understood about human anatomy, and the philosopher demonstrated a keen interest. Descartes discussed the pineal gland in numerous letters, his first book, the *Treatise of Man* (1637) and his last, *The Passions of the Soul* (1649). Descartes believed (incorrectly, even according to the evidence available in his own time) that the gland was suspended among the ventricles, full of animal spirits conveyed by numerous small arteries and that it is full of an air-like substance ("Descartes and the Pineal Gland").

10. According to Park, from 1299 Italian doctors were regularly performing anatomical dissection and by the early fourteenth century, the University of Bologna "had introduced the practice of dissecting human corpses into the study and teaching of anatomy, for the first time since the early Hellenistic period" (114).

11. For example, *Pascali's Island* (1980) is located in Greece in 1908, also achieving the Booker Prize shortlist. Arguably Unsworth's best novel, *Sacred Hunger* (1992) follows the fortunes of those aboard a mid-eighteenth-century slave ship and won the 1992 Booker Prize jointly with Michael Ondaatje's *The English Patient*. *The Song of the Kings* (2002) considers the events of the Trojan War, focusing in particular upon the sacrifice of Agamemnon's daughter Iphigenia.

12. *The Advocate* features a medieval lawyer rather than a cleric as a detective, although Haydock categorizes the character as such.

13. Nicolaa (or Nicholaa) de la Haye remains

relatively unknown and deplorably absent from most histories of the Battle of Lincoln. More details about her extraordinary life can be found in Sharon Bennett Connolly's recent book, *Heroines of the Medieval World*; and Louise J. Wilkinson's *Women in Thirteenth-Century Lincolnshire*, esp. pp. 13ff. For contemporary accounts of the Battle of Lincoln, see the Anglo-Norman biographical poem, *The History of William Marshal* in which Nicolaa appears as "the good lady of the castle—may God preserve her, body and soul—who was doing her utmost to defend it" (199); and the vivid account in Roger of Wendover's Latin *Flowers of History*, in which Nicolaa is not mentioned.

14. Ann Swinfen's fourteenth-century bookseller, Nicholas Elyot, expresses a similar doubt about the existence of God in the wake of the devastating Black Plague, as does Roger the Chapman, Kate Sedley's medieval detective, a hundred or so years later (see Chapter Two).

15. It is, one hopes, overly cautious to point out that at no stage in human history was there a widespread belief that the Earth is flat.

16. Not discussed here, but worth noting, is medieval crime fiction's over-representation (compared to other periods) in anthologies of historical crime fiction, such as the several editions of *The Mammoth Book of Historical Crime Fiction*, edited by Mike Ashley, and *Murder through the Ages*, edited by Maxim Jakubowski. In 2000, Martin H. Greenberg and John Helfers edited an anthology dedicated exclusively to crime in the Middle Ages, *Murder Most Medieval: Noble Tales of Ignoble Demises*.

Chapter Four

1. There are some excellent studies of women and crime fiction, particularly from the 1990s. See, for example, M. Reddy, "Feminist Counter-Tradition" and *Sisters in Crime*; Munt, *Murder by the Book?*; as well as the helpful essays in Irons's collection, *Feminism in Women's Detective Fiction*, among many others.

2. Cheri L. Ross cites Kathleen Gregory Klein's example of Harlan P. Halsey's 1882 novel, *The Lady Detective*, which features Kate Goelet. Kate, despite being a successful detective, plans to retire as soon as she has earned enough money, an intention that Klein interprets as her "detecting persona mask[ing] her true status as a potential wife" (qtd. in Ross 85, note 10).

3. For a detailed analysis of James's novel, see Horsley 253–58.

4. See also Reddy, "Women Detectives" 201.

According to Megan Casey, a librarian and moderator of the Goodreads lesbian mystery study group, by 2015 there were over one thousand lesbian mystery titles penned by two hundred and fifty authors (Casey).

5. See, in particular, Dinshaw and Wallace, eds. *Cambridge Companion to Medieval Women's Writing*; Lochrie, *Margery Kempe*; Farmer and Pasternack, eds., *Gender and Difference*; Brabant, ed. *Politics, Gender, and Genre*; and Dinshaw, *Chaucer's Sexual Poetics*.

6. Tremayne, like Paul C. Doherty and Michael Jecks, is a prolific writer: the first of the Sister Fidelma novels appeared in 1994. The most recent is *Night of the Lightbringer* (2017) and there are twenty-seven books between these two.

7. For a comprehensive account of the Society's activities, publications and Peter Tremayne, see www.sisterfidelma.com.

8. When Franklin died, she left a manuscript which has been completed and published by her daughter, Samantha Norman. However, *The Winter Siege* (2014) is set earlier than Franklin's series, in the turbulence of the mid-twelfth-century civil war between Stephen and Matilda. Norman is also, it seems, writing a fifth and final Mistress of the Art of Death novel.

9. Catherine's father is a Christian who has converted from Judaism and a key feature of Catherine's modernity is her acceptance of this and of her father's extended Jewish family. This tolerance is explored in more detail in Chapter Five.

10. There are currently eight novels in the Aelf Fen series, set in the fens of East Anglia during the time of William the Conqueror's son, William Rufus. These books are described as "medieval mysteries" and they feature Lassair, a mystic and apprentice healer, who relies a little too much upon her "gift" for healing and her prophetic "sight" to be included in this survey. While there are undoubtedly similar mystical or supernatural elements embedded in Clare's Hawkenlye series, as discussed above, Helewise and Josse do not possess paranormal powers themselves.

11. Gellis has also written a novel featuring Lucrezia Borgia as a detective, *Lucrezia Borgia and the Mother of Poisons* (2003), discussed in Chapter Six.

Chapter Five

1. See, for example, Pavlac, ed., *Game of Thrones versus History: Written in Blood*; Holsinger, *Neomedievalism, Neoconservatism,*

and the War on Terror; Elliott, *Medievalism, Politics and Mass Media*; and Livingston, "Racism, Medievalism, and the White Supremacists of Charlottesville."

2. There is also an overview contained in Cord Whitaker's special issue of the journal, *postmedieval*, "Making Race Matter in the Middle Ages." Whitaker's introduction traces the developing interest in race in the Middle Ages, noting the impact of Thomas Hahn's 2001 edited edition of the *Journal of Medieval and Early Modern Studies*, "Race and Ethnicity in the Middle Ages."

3. Rose cites the period with the greatest frequency of blood libel accusations as between 1870 and 1935 (11).

4. This incident, among others in North America, is recounted in Perry and Schweitzer, pp. 43–44.

5. See Rubin, "Making a Martyr," for a concise account of the case.

6. This account is a summary of Langmuir's excellent research into the affair ("Knight's Tale" 459–82).

7. As Westerson explains in her Afterword, these deaths are based on the horrific deeds of Gilles de Rais, a fifteenth-century French baron who is said to have murdered hundreds of children in a similar manner (*Demon's Parchment* 301).

8. In Jewish folklore, the *golem* is a mythological creature constructed out of clay or stone. Often created in order to protect the Jewish people, in various versions of the myth, the *golem* becomes unruly, violent or liable to interpret instructions literally, with unintended consequences, and leading to rampages (Kalso).

9. See Chapter Two for a discussion of the way "Julian" also destabilizes Crispin's inherent homophobia.

10. Henry III was still only 13 in 1220 and so royal authority rested with the regents. The first of these, William Marshal—England's most famous knight—had died the year before.

Chapter Six

1. Even a cursory search reveals an abundance of this investigative language applied to the historian's task, used particularly to encourage students and amateurs into the field. See, for example, "Historians are Detectives" and "History Detectives: Special Investigations."

2. Most relevant to this discussion about crime fiction are P. D. James's disappointing sequel to *Pride and Prejudice, Death Comes to Pemberley* (2011), and Carrie Bebris's Mr. & Mrs. Darcy Mysteries series.

3. The *Life-Records* have a somewhat controversial history and certain items continue to face productive challenges from scholars such as Thomas H. Bestul, who provides an excellent summary of the collection's development as well as investigating "the unequivocal statement that Chaucer lived at 177 Upper Thames Street" (1).

4. Citations of Chaucer's poetry refer to *The Riverside Chaucer*, Larry D. Benson (gen. ed.) and note fragment or book and line number.

5. Courtenay appears in several medieval crime fiction novels as an antagonist to Richard II, John of Gaunt and, in this case, Chaucer himself.

6. There are several accounts of this case, from various different perspectives: see Harley, "Geoffrey Chaucer, Cecilia Chaumpaigne, and Alice Perrers" and Cannon, "Raptus in the Chaumpaigne Release."

7. Rather like Chaucer himself, Westerson is inconsistent with her spelling of the Pardoner's name: he is introduced as "Chaunticleer," although by the end of the book he is "Chanticleer" (*Troubled Bones* 272).

8. See the excellent online resource prepared by the Welsh Department at Swansea University: www.dafyddapgwilym.net. See also medieval crime fiction author Joseph P. Clancy's translations of Dafydd's poetry.

9. This portrait of Chaucer recalls Jay Margrave's depiction of the poet in his *The Gawain Quest* (2007), in which the detective character, Priedeux, describes Chaucer as "quiet, self-effacing, and [he] usually vanished when Priedeux strode into the presence of his lord [John of Gaunt]" (10). Despite this unassuming demeanor, Margrave's Chaucer wields considerable influence and manipulates other characters and events to suit Gaunt's purposes.

10. Worth noting is George Herman, who is fully on board with an idealized Leonardo and whose depiction has the maestro perpetually speaking "softly." In his six novels, Herman assigns an assistant to Leonardo, Niccolo da Pavia, a dwarf with a (possibly anachronistic) photographic memory.

11. Wilson is a prolific author, with several crime series set in various periods, as well as numerous popular history books with a focus on the Reformation and the Elizabethan period. The most recent is *The Queen and the Heretic* (2018), a dual biography of Catherine Parr and Anne Askew.

Works Cited

Adams, Tracy. "Crossing Generic Boundaries: The Clever Courtly Lady." *Essays in Medieval Studies*, vol. 21, 2004, pp. 81–96. *Project Muse*, doi: 10.1353/ems.2005.0002.

Allison, E.M.A. *Through the Valley of Death*. 1983. iUniverse, 2011.

Andrew, Lucy, and Catherine Phelps, eds. *Crime Fiction in the City: Capital Crimes*. U of Wales P, 2013.

Ascari, Maurizio. *A Counter-History of Crime Fiction*. Palgrave Macmillan, 2007.

Ash, Maureen. *The Alehouse Murders*. Berkley, 2007.

_____. *The Canterbury Murders*. Kindle ed., InterMix Books, 2013.

_____. *Death of a Squire*. Berkley, 2008.

_____. *A Plague of Poison*. Berkley, 2009.

Ashley, Mike, ed. *The Mammoth Book of Historical Detectives*. Carroll & Graf Publishers, Inc., 1995.

Ashton, Gail, and Daniel T. Kline, eds. *Medieval Afterlives in Popular Culture*. Palgrave Macmillan, 2012.

Bale, Anthony. "Afterword: Violence, Memory and the Traumatic Middle Ages." *Christians and Jews in Angevin England: The York Massacre of 1190, Narratives and Contexts*, edited by Sarah Rees Jones and Sethina Watson, Boydell & Brewer, 2013, pp. 294–304.

_____. *Feeling Persecuted: Christians, Jews and Images of Violence in the Middle Ages*. Reaktion Books, 2010.

_____. *The Jew in the Medieval Book: English Antisemitisms, 1350–1500*. Cambridge UP, 2006. Cambridge Studies in Medieval Literature.

Barkey, Karen, and Ira Katznelson. "States, Regimes, and Decisions: Why Jews Were Expelled from Medieval England and France." *Theory and Society*, vol. 40, no. 5, 2011, pp. 475–503. *JSTOR*, www.jstor.org/stable/41475705.

Benjamin, Walter. "On Some Motifs in Baudelaire." *Illuminations*, translated by Hannah Arendt, Harcourt, Brace & World, 1968, pp. 157–202.

Bestul, Thomas H. "Did Chaucer Live at 177 Upper Thames Street?: The *Chaucer Life-Records* and the Site of Chaucer's London Home." *The Chaucer Review*, vol. 43, no. 1, 2008, pp. 1–15. *Project Muse*, doi.org/10.1353/cr.0.0006.

Bidisha. "Master of the Medieval Mystery." *The Guardian*, 11 June 2009, www.theguardian.com/commentisfree/2009/jun/11/medieval-mystery-cadfael.

Bitel, Lisa M. "*Celtic Women: Women in Celtic Society and Literature*. by Peter Berresford Ellis. (Review)." *The Historian*, vol. 60, no. 2, 1998, pp. 427–27.

Bland, David. *Father Martin and the Hermitage Mystery*. Janus Publishing Company, 2005.

Boccardi, Mariadele. "Barry Unworth's *Morality Play*: Narrative, Detection, History." *postmedieval*, vol. 7, no. 2, 2016, pp. 204–13.

Bodden, M.C. *Language as the Site of Revolt in Medieval and Early Modern England: Speaking as a Woman*. Palgrave Macmillan, 2011. The New Middle Ages.

Bondanella, Peter. *Umberto Eco and the Open Text. Semiotics, Fiction, Popular Culture*. Cambridge UP, 1997.

"*Bone of Contention* (Review)." *Publishers Weekly*, 25 Nov. 2002, www.publishersweekly.com/978-0-7653-0019-5.

Boyarin, Adrienne Williams, ed. and trans. *Miracles of the Virgin in Middle English*. Broadview, 2015.

Brabant, Margaret, ed. *Politics, Gender, and*

Genre: The Political Thought of Christine De Pizan. Westview Press, 1992.

Brodey, Lisette. "Chat with Michael Jecks." *Lisette's Writers' Chateau,* 20 October 2013, http://lisettebrodey.com/chat-michael-jecks/.

Browne, Ray B., and Lawrence A. Kreiser, Jr., eds. *The Detective as Historian: History and Art in Historical Crime Fiction.* Bowling Green State UP, 2000.

Burgess, Michael, and Jill H. Vassilakos. *Murder in Retrospect: A Selective Guide to Historical Mystery Fiction.* Libraries Unlimited, 2005.

Burns, Mary F. "Review: The *Great Revolt: A Brother Athelstan Medieval Mystery.*" *The Historical Novels Review,* no. 77, Aug. 2016. *Historical Novel Society,* historicalnovelsociety.org/reviews/the-great-revolt-a-brother-athelstan-medieval-mystery/.

Burroway, Janet. "The Great Pretenders." *The New York Times,* 12 Nov. 1995, www.nytimes.com/1995/11/12/books/the-great-pretenders.html.

Calabrese, Michael. "Performing the Prioress: 'Conscience' and Responsibility in Studies of Chaucer's Prioress's Tale." *Texas Studies in Literature and Language,* vol. 44, no. 1, 2002, pp. 66–91.

Cameron, Euan. *Waldenses: Rejections of Holy Church in Medieval Europe.* Blackwell, 2001.

Cannon, Christopher. "Raptus in the Chaumpaigne Release and a Newly Discovered Document Concerning the Life of Geoffrey Chaucer." *Speculum,* vol. 68, no. 1, 1993, pp. 74–94.

Capozzi, Rocco, ed. *Reading Eco: An Anthology.* Indiana UP, 1997.

Casey, Megan. "Megan Casey Writes About the Top 20 Lesbian Mystery Novels." *The Lesbrary,* 18 Mar. 2015, lesbrary.com/2015/03/18/megan-casey-writes-about-the-top-20-lesbian-mystery-novels/.

"Chains of Folly." *Kirkus Reviews,* 20 May 2010, www.kirkusreviews.com/book-reviews/roberta-gellis/chains-of-folly/.

Chambers, Robert. *Parody: The Art That Plays with Art.* Peter Lang, 2010. Studies in Literary Criticism and Theory 21.

Chandler, Raymond. *The Big Sleep.* 1939. First Vintage Crime, 1992.

———. "The Simple Art of Murder." *The Simple Art of Murder,* Houghton Mifflin, 1950. *University of Texas,* www.en.utexas.edu/amlit/amlitprivate/scans/chandlerart.html.

Chaucer, Geoffrey. *The Riverside Chaucer.* Edited by Larry D. Benson (gen. ed.), 3rd ed., Houghton Mifflin, 1987.

Cherne, Barbara. *Bella Donna.* Daniel & Daniel, 2001.

Christian, Edwin Ernest, and Blake Lindsay. "The Habit of Detection: The Medieval Monk as Detective in the Novels of Ellis Peters." *Studies in Medievalism,* vol. iv, 1992, pp. 276–89.

Clancy, Gertrude, and Joseph Clancy. *Death Is a Pilgrim: A Canterbury Tale.* Northgate Books, 1993.

Clare, Alys. *Girl in a Red Tunic.* Hodder, 2005.

———. *The Joys of My Life.* Severn House, 2008.

———. *A Shadowed Evil.* Severn House, 2015.

———. *The Tavern in the Morning.* St. Martin's Minotaur, 2000.

Clark, Cassandra. *Hangman Blind.* Minotaur Books, 2008.

———. *A Parliament of Spies.* Allison & Busby, 2012.

Coakley, Joan. "Susanna Gregory: Doctor Matthew Bartholomew, Master of Medicine and Detection." Browne and Kreiser, eds., pp. 85–94.

Cohen, Jeffrey J. "The Flow of Blood in Medieval Norwich." *Speculum,* vol. 79, no. 1, 2004, pp. 26–65. *JSTOR,* www.jstor.org/stable/20462793.

Cohen, Michael. "The Hounding of Baskerville: Allusion and Apocalypse in Eco's *The Name of the Rose.*" Inge, ed., pp. 65–76.

Connolly, Sharon Bennett. *Heroines of the Medieval World.* Amberley Publishing, 2017.

Conway, Sara. *Murder on Good Friday.* Cumberland House, 2001.

Cooper, Helen. *The English Romance in Time: Transforming Motifs from Geoffrey of Monmouth to the Death of Shakespeare.* Oxford UP, 2004.

Cooper, M.E. *Key Confrontations.* Padlock Mystery Press, 2002.

———. *Key Deceptions.* Padlock Mystery Press, 2000.

Crowley, Duane. *Riddle Me a Murder.* Blue Boar Press, 1986.

Curthoys, Ann, and John Docker. *Is History Fiction?* U of Michigan P, 2005.

Cusack, Carole M. "Fiction, Feminism and the 'Celtic Church': The Sister Fidelma Novels of Peter Tremayne." *Celts in Legend and Reality: Papers from the Sixth Australian Conference of Celtic Studies July*

2007, edited by Pamela O'Neill, The Medieval and Early Modern Centre at The University of Sydney, 2010, pp. 315–42.

_____. "Scarlet and Black: Non-Mainstream Religion as 'Other' in Detective Fiction." *The Buddha of Suburbia: Proceedings of the Eighth Australian and International Religion, Literature and Arts Conference 2004*, RLA Press, 2005, pp. 159–74. *Sydney EScholarship Repository,* hdl.handle.net/2123/1252.

D'Arcens, Louise. *Comic Medievalism.* D.S. Brewer, 2014.

_____. "Mirthful Faces in *The Name of the Rose.*" *postmedieval: A Journal of Medieval Cultural Studies,* vol. 8, no. 1, 2017, pp. 51–66.

D'Arcens, Louise, ed. *The Cambridge Companion to Medievalism.* Cambridge UP, 2016.

de Lauretis, Teresa. "Gaudy Rose: Eco and Narcissism." *Reading Eco: An Anthology,* edited by Rocco Capozzi, Indiana UP, 1997, pp. 239–55.

DelFattore, Joan. "Eco's Conflation of Theology and Detection in *The Name of the Rose.*" Inge, ed., pp. 77–89.

"Descartes and the Pineal Gland." *Stanford Encyclopaedia of Philosophy,* 25 Apr. 2005, revised 18 Sept. 2013, plato.stanford.edu/entries/pineal-gland/.

Devlin, Mary. *The Legend of Good Women.* Writers Club Press, 2003.

_____. *Murder on the Canterbury Pilgrimage.* Writers Club Press, 2000.

Dinshaw, Carolyn. *Chaucer's Sexual Poetics.* U of Wisconsin P, 1989.

_____. *How Soon Is Now? Medieval Texts, Amateur Readers, and the Queerness of Time.* Duke UP, 2012.

Dinshaw, Carolyn, and David Wallace, eds. *The Cambridge Companion to Medieval Women's Writing.* Cambridge UP, 2003.

Disch, Thomas M. "Looking for the Seat of the Soul." *The Washington Post,* 4 Mar. 1984, www.washingtonpost.com/archive/entertainment/books/1984/03/04/looking-for-the-seat-of-the-soul/eb524c75-bbb6-4147-aa94-3e6c54b4082f/.

Doherty, Paul C. *The Angel of Death.* Headline, 1989.

_____. *The Assassin in the Greenwood.* Headline, 1993.

_____. *Crown in Darkness.* Headline, 1988.

_____. *The Devil's Domain.* Headline, 1999.

_____. *The Great Revolt.* Severn House, 2016.

_____. *The Herald of Hell.* Severn House, 2015.

_____. *The House of the Red Slayer.* Headline, 1992.

_____. *The Nightingale Gallery.* Headline, 1991.

_____. *A Pilgrimage to Murder.* Severn House, 2016.

_____. *Satan in St. Mary's.* R. Hale, 1986.

_____. *The Song of a Dark Angel.* Headline, 1994.

_____. *The Straw Men.* Severn House, 2012.

Domning, Denise. *Season of the Fox.* CreateSpace Independent Publishing, 2015.

_____. *Season of the Raven.* CreateSpace Independent Publishing, 2014.

Duffy, Eamon. *The Voices of Morebath: Reformation and Rebellion in an English Village.* Yale UP, 2001.

Durham, Philip. *Down These Mean Streets a Man Must Go: Raymond Chandler's Knight.* U of North Carolina P, 1963.

Dyer, Gary R. "*Ivanhoe,* Chivalry and the Murder of Mary Ashford." *Criticism,* vol. 39, no. 3, 1997, pp. 383–409. *Expanded Academic ASAP,* http://find.galegroup.com. mate.lib.unimelb.edu.au.

Dyrek, G.M. *The Seer and the Scribe: Spear of Destiny.* Luminis Books, 2011.

Eco, Umberto. *The Name of the Rose.* 1983. Translated by William Weaver, Vintage, 2004.

_____. "Reflections on the *Name of the Rose.*" *Encounter,* vol. 64, no. 4, 1985, pp. 7–19.

_____. *Travels in Hyperreality: Essays.* Translated by William Weaver, Brace Harcourt Jovanovich, 1986.

Edden, Valerie. "The Devotional Life of the Laity in the Late Middle Ages." *Approaching Medieval English Anchoritic and Mystical Texts,* edited by Edden, et al., D.S. Brewer, 2005, pp. 35–49.

Elam, Diane. "P.S. 'I Love You': Umberto Eco and The Romance of the Reader." *Umberto Eco's Alternative: The Politics of Culture and the Ambiguities of Interpretation,* edited by Norma Bouchard and Veronica Pravadelli, Peter Lang, 1998, pp. 186–207.

Elliott, Andrew B.R. *Medievalism, Politics and Mass Media: Appropriating the Middle Ages in the Twenty-First Century.* D.S. Brewer, 2017.

Ellis, Peter Berresford. *Celt and Saxon: The Struggle for Britain, AD 410–937.* Constable, 1993.

_____. *Celtic Women: Women in Celtic Society and Literature*. Constable, 1995.

Ely, Peter B. "Detective and Priest: The Paradoxes of Simenon's Maigret." *Christianity and Literature*, vol. 59, no. 3, 2010, pp. 453–77. *Literature Resource Center*, https://ezp.lib.unimelb.edu.au/login?url=https://search-ebscohost-com.ezp.lib.unimelb.edu.au/login.aspx?direct=true&db=edsglr&AN=edsgcl.228428449&site=eds-live&scope=site.

Emery, Elizabeth, and Richard Utz, eds. *Medievalism: Key Critical Terms*. D.S. Brewer, 2014.

Ennis, Michael. *The Malice of Fortune*. Anchor Books, 2012.

Evans, James Allan. "*Celt and Roman: The Celts in Italy* (Book Review)." *Canadian Journal of History*, vol. 35, no. 3, 2000, pp. 521–22.

Evans, Michael. "'My Fiction Is the Natural Outgrowth of My Fascination with the Times': An Interview with Candace Robb." *Medievally Speaking*, 26 Jan. 2015, http://medievallyspeaking.blogspot.com.au/search?q=candace+robb.

Farmer, Sharon, and Carol Braun Pasternack, eds. *Gender and Difference in the Middle Ages*. U of Minnesota P, 2003. Medieval Cultures 32.

Farronato, Cristina. *Eco's Chaosmos: From the Middle Ages to Postmodernity*. U of Toronto P, 2003.

Faulkner, Peter. "'The Paths of Virtue and Early English': F.J. Furnivall and Victorian Medievalism." *From Medieval to Medievalism*, edited by John Simons, Macmillan, 1992, pp. 144–58.

Ferrante, Joan. *To the Glory of Her Sex: Women's Roles in the Composition of Medieval Texts*. Indiana UP, 1997.

Fichte, Joerg O. "Crime Fiction Set in the Middle Ages: Historical Novel and Detective Story." *ZAA*, vol. 53, no. 1, 2005, pp. 53–70.

Finke, Laurie A., and Martin B. Shichtman. *Cinematic Illuminations: The Middle Ages on Film*. Johns Hopkins UP, 2010.

Ford, Judy Ann. "Umberto Eco: The *Name of the Rose*." Browne and Kreiser, eds., pp. 95–110.

Forni, Kathleen. *Chaucer's Afterlife: Adaptations in Recent Popular Culture*. McFarland, 2013.

Forshaw, Barry. "Editor's Introduction." *Detective*, edited by Forshaw, Intellect, 2016, pp. 7–13. Crime Uncovered Series.

_____. *Historical Noir: The Pocket Essential Guide to Fiction, Film & TV*. Pocket Essentials, 2018.

_____. "The Third Heaven Conspiracy by Giulio Leoni, Trans Anne Milano Appel." *Independent*, 31 Jan. 2007, www.independent.co.uk/arts-entertainment/books/reviews/the-third-heaven-conspiracy-by-giulio-leoni-trans-anne-milano-appel-434447.html.

Frankland, Edward. *The Murders at Crossby*. Dent, 1955.

Frankland, Helga. "Dr Helga Frankland's Account of the Family Association with Ravenstonedale." *Ravenstonedale*, Feb. 2005, www.ravenstonedale.org/kk/frankland.htm.

Franklin, Ariana. *The Assassin's Prayer*. Bantam Press, 2010.

_____. *Mistress of the Art of Death*. Bantam Press, 2007.

Fraser, Giles. "Are Modern Detectives the New Priests?" *The Guardian*, 11 July 2014, www.theguardian.com/commentisfree/belief/2014/jul/11/modern-detectives-new-priests.

Frazer, Margaret. *The Apostate's Tale*. Berkley, 2008.

_____. *The Bishop's Tale*. Berkley, 1994.

_____. *The Clerk's Tale*. Berkley, 2002.

_____. *The Novice's Tale*. Berkley, 1992.

_____. *The Sempster's Tale*. Berkley, 2006.

_____. *The Servant's Tale*. Berkley, 1993.

_____. *The Traitor's Tale*. Berkley, 2007.

Freeman, Philip. *Sacrifice*. Pegasus, 2015.

_____. *Saint Brigid's Bones*. Pegasus, 2014.

Fuller, John. *Flying to Nowhere*. 1983. George Braziller, 1984.

Ganim, John M. "Chaucer and the Noise of the People." *Exemplaria*, vol. 2, no. 1, 1990, pp. 71–88.

Garrett, George. "The Historical Novel Today: Two Instances." *The Sewanee Review*, vol. 104, no. 3, 1996, pp. 456–60. *JSTOR*, www.jstor.org.ezp.lib.unimelb.edu.au/stable/27547238.

Gaspar, Stephen. *To Know Evil*. Pemberley Press, 2009.

Gaylord, Alan T. "O Rare Ellis Peters: Two Rules for Medieval Murder." *Studies in Medievalism*, vol. xx, 2011, pp. 129–46. *JSTOR*, www.jstor.org/stable/10.7722/j.ctt81hp7.12.

Geisler, Barbara Reichmuth. *Graven Images.* Lost Coast Press, 2004.

———. *Other Gods.* Lost Coast Press, 2002.

Gellis, Roberta. *Lucrezia Borgia and the Mother of Poisons.* Forge Books, 2003.

———. *A Mortal Bane.* 1999. Kindle ed., Belgrave House, 2012.

Gelly, Lorraine. "Review: A *Poultice for a Healer.*" *The Historical Novels Review,* no. 27, Feb. 2004. *Historical Novel Society,* https://historicalnovelsociety.org/reviews/a-poultice-for-a-healer/.

George, Kaye. *Death in the Time of Ice.* Untreed Reads, 2014.

The Germersheim Group. "Murderous Intersections: Genre, Time, Place and Gender in Ellis Peters's Cadfael Mysteries." English Department Seminar, U of Mainz (Winter 1996/97), 2006, www.fask.uni-mainz.de/inst/iaa/peters.pdf.

Gooden, Philip. *Chaucer and the Doctor of Physic.* 2006. Albert Bridge Books, 2013.

———. *Chaucer and the House of Fame.* 2004. Albert Bridge Books, 2013.

———. *Chaucer and the Legend of Good Women.* 2005. Albert Bridge Books, 2013.

———. *Chaucer and the Vintry Ward Death.* Albert Bridge Books, 2013.

Green, Anna Katharine. *That Affair Next Door and Lost Man's Lane.* 1897. Duke UP, 2003.

Greenberg, Martin H., and John Helfers, eds. *Murder Most Medieval: Noble Tales of Ignoble Demises.* Cumberland House Publishing, 2000.

Gregory, Susanna. *A Bone of Contention,* St. Martin's Press, 1997.

———. *A Plague on Both Your Houses,* Time Warner Books, 1996.

Grosset, Philip. *Clerical Detectives.* www.detecs.org/intro.html.

Hallissy, Margaret. "Reading the Plans: The Architectural Drawings in Umberto Eco's *The Name of the Rose.*" *Critique,* vol. 42, no. 3, 2001, pp. 271–86.

Hamilton, Charles D. "*Celt and Roman: The Celts in Italy.*" *History: Reviews of New Books,* vol. 27, no. 3, 1999, pp. 134–35.

Harley, Marta Powell. "Geoffrey Chaucer, Cecilia Chaumpaigne, and Alice Perrers: A Closer Look." *The Chaucer Review,* vol. 28, no. 1, 1993, pp. 78–82.

Harrison, Cora. *My Lady Judge.* Minotaur, 2007.

Haydock, Nickolas A. *Movie Medievalism: The Imaginary Middle Ages.* McFarland, 2008.

Healey, Judith Koll. *The Canterbury Papers.* William Morrow, 2004.

Heng, Geraldine. "Pleasure, Resistance, and a Feminist Aesthetics of Reading." *The Cambridge Companion to Feminist Literary Theory,* edited by Ellen Rooney, Cambridge UP, 2006, pp. 53–72.

Hernandez, Erika. "Review of *The Reckoning.*" *About Film,* Mar. 2004, www.aboutfilm.com/movies/r/reckoning.htm.

"Historians Are Detectives." *Smithsonian's History Explorer,* 19 Nov. 2008, https://historyexplorer.si.edu/resource/historians-are-detectives.

"History Detectives: Special Investigations." *PBS,* www.pbs.org/opb/historydetectives/educators/.

The History of William Marshal. Translated by Nigel Bryant, The Boydell Press, 2016.

Holden, Jonathan. "The Case of Raymond Chandler's Fiction as Romance." *Kansas Quarterly,* vol. 10, no. 4, 1978, pp. 41–47.

Holquist, Michael. "Whodunit and Other Questions: Metaphysical Detective Stories in Postwar Fiction." 1971–72. Most and Stowe, eds., pp. 148–74.

Holsinger, Bruce. *A Burnable Book.* William Morrow, 2014.

———. *The Invention of Fire.* William Morrow, 2016.

———. *Neomedievalism, Neoconservatism, and the War on Terror.* Prickly Paradigm, 2007.

———. "Stretching the Truth: A Scholar Tries His Hand." *Humanities,* vol. 35, no. 6, 2014, pp. 34–38. *Art Full Text (H.W. Wilson),* ezp.lib.unimelb.edu.au/login?url=https://search-ebscohost-com.ezp.lib.unimelb.edu.au/login.aspx?direct=true&db=aft&AN=99285645&site=eds-live&scope=site.

Holsinger, Bruce, and Stephanie Trigg. "Editors' Introduction: Novel Medievalisms." *postmedieval: A Journal of Medieval Cultural Studies,* vol. 7, no. 2, 2016, pp. 175–80.

Horsley, Lee. *Twentieth-Century Crime Fiction.* Oxford UP, 2005.

Howard, H. Wendell. "The World of Brother Cadfael." *Logos: A Journal of Catholic Thought & Culture,* vol. 11, no. 1, 2008, pp. 149–62.

Howard of Warwick. *The Heretics of De'Ath.* Kindle ed., 2010.

_____. *Howard of Warwick.* howardofwarwick.com/.

Hsy, Jonathan, and Julie Orlemanski. "Race and Medieval Studies: A Partial Bibliography." *postmedieval: A Journal of Medieval Cultural Studies,* vol. 8, no. 4, 2017, pp. 500–31.

Hudson, Anne. *The Premature Reformation: Wycliffite Texts and Lollard History.* Clarendon Press, 1988.

Hutcheon, Linda. *A Poetics of Postmodernism. History, Theory, Fiction.* Routledge, 1988.

_____. *The Politics of Postmodernism.* Routledge, 1989.

_____. "The Power of Postmodern Irony." *Genre, Trope, Gender,* edited by Barry Rutland, Carleton UP, 1996, pp. 35–49.

Inge, M. Thomas, ed. *Naming the Rose: Essays of Eco's The Name of the Rose.* UP of Mississippi, 1988.

"The Inquisitor (Mystery)." *Kirkus Reviews,* no. 18, 2002, p. 1355. EBSCO*Host,* ezp.lib.unimelb.edu.au/login?url=https://search-ebscohost-com.ezp.lib.unimelb.edu.au/login.aspx?direct=true&db=edsgao&AN=edsgcl.92527293&site=eds-live&scope=site.

Irons, Glenwood, ed. *Feminism in Women's Detective Fiction.* U of Toronto P, 1995. *JSTOR,* www.jstor.org.ezp.lib.unimelb.edu.au/stable/10.3138/j.ctt1287pdb.

Jakubowski, Maxim, ed. *Murder through the Ages.* Headline, 2000.

Jameson, Fredric. *The Antinomies of Realism.* Verso, 2013.

Japp, Andrea H. *The Breath of the Rose.* Translated by Lorenza Garcia, Gallic Books, 2009.

_____. *The Divine Blood.* Translated by Lorenza Garcia, Gallic Books, 2009.

_____. *The Season of the Beast.* Translated by Lorenza Garcia, Gallic Books, 2008.

Jecks, Michael. *The Last Templar.* Headline, 1995.

_____. *The Templar's Penance.* Headline, 2003.

_____. "Who Are the Medieval Murderers?" www.michaeljecks.co.uk/medievalmurder/index.html.

Jinks, Catherine. *The Inquisitor.* MacMillan, 1999.

_____. *The Notary.* MacMillan, 2000.

_____. *The Secret Familiar.* Allen & Unwin, 2006.

Johnsen, Rosemary Erickson. *Contemporary Feminist Historical Crime Fiction.* Palgrave Macmillan, 2006.

Johnson, Hannah R. *Blood Libel: The Ritual Murder Accusation at the Limit of Jewish History.* U of Michigan P, 2012.

Johnson, Julie Christine. *In Another Life.* Sourcebooks, 2016.

Joseph, Alison. "Reason and Redemption: The Detective in the Secular Age." *Detective,* edited by Barry Forshaw, Intellect, 2016, pp. 190–99. Crime Uncovered Series.

Kaler, Anne K., ed. *Cordially Yours, Brother Cadfael.* Bowling Green State U Popular P, 1998.

Kalso, Reed. "Golem (Jewish Folklore)." *Salem Press Encyclopedia,* 2017. EBSCO*Host,* ezp.lib.unimelb.edu.au/login?url=https://search-ebscohost-com.ezp.lib.unimelb.edu.au/login.aspx?direct=true&db=ers&AN=87322327&site=eds-live&scope=site.

Kears, Carl, and James Paz, eds. *Medieval Science Fiction.* Boydell & Brewer, 2016.

Knight, Bernard. *Crowner's Quest.* Pocket Books, 1999.

_____. *Figure of Hate.* Pocket Books, 2005.

Knight, Stephen. *Crime Fiction 1800–2000: Detection, Death, Diversity.* Palgrave Macmillan, 2004.

_____. *Form and Ideology in Crime Fiction.* Palgrave Macmillan, 1980.

_____. *Secrets of Crime Fiction Classics: Detecting the Delights of 21 Enduring Stories.* McFarland, 2015.

Kristeva, Julia. *Murder in Byzantium,* Columbia UP, 2006.

Lake, Lori L. "The Lesbian Detective Novel." *Crimespree Magazine,* no. 10, 2006, www.lorillake.com/lesbiandetective.html.

Langmuir, Gavin I. "The Knight's Tale of Young Hugh of Lincoln." *Speculum,* vol. 47, no. 3, 1972, pp. 459–82. *JSTOR,* www.jstor.org/stable/2856155.

_____. "Thomas of Monmouth: Detector of Ritual Murder." *Speculum,* vol. 59, no. 4, 1984, pp. 820–46.

Leoni, Giulio. *The Kingdom of Light.* Translated by Shaun Whiteside, Vintage Books, 2010.

Lewis, Margaret. *Edith Pargeter: Ellis Peters.* Dufour, 1994.

Lindley, Arthur. "The Ahistoricism of Medieval Film." *Screening the Past,* no. 3, 1998, www.latrobe.edu.au/screeningthepast/firstrelease/fir598/ALfr3a.htm.

Lionarons, Joyce. *Blood Libel.* Kindle ed., n.p., 2018.

Lipton, Sara. "The Words That Killed Medieval Jews." *The New York Times,* 11 Dec. 2015, www.nytimes.com/2015/12/13/opinion/the-words-that-killed-medieval-jews.html.

Livingstone, Josephine. "Racism, Medievalism, and the White Supremacists of Charlottesville." *The New Republic,* 16 Aug. 2017, newrepublic.com/article/144320/racism-medievalism-white-supremacists-char
lottesville.

Lochrie, Karma. *Margery Kempe and Translations of the Flesh.* U of Pennsylvania P, 1991.

Luehrs, Christiane W., and Robert B. Luehrs. "Peter Tremayne: Sister Fidelma and the Triumph of Truth." Browne and Kreiser, eds., pp. 45–59.

Lukács, Georg. *The Historical Novel.* 1937. Translated by Hannah and Stanley Mitchell, Merlin Press, 1962.

Makinen, Merja. *Feminist Popular Fiction.* Palgrave Macmillan, 2001.

Marcus, Laura. "Detection and Literary Fiction." Priestman, ed., pp. 245–67.

Margrave, Jay. *The Gawain Quest.* Goldenford, 2007.

Martín, Jorge Hernández. *Readers and Labyrinths: Detective Fiction in Borges, Bustos Domecq, and Eco.* Garland, 1995.

Martínez Alfaro, María Jesús. "Mystery and Performance in Barry Unsworth's *Morality Play.*" *Miscelánea: A Journal of English and American Studies,* vol. 24, 2001, pp. 79–92, www.miscelaneajournal.net/archive/index.
php?option=com_content&task=view&id=
25&Itemid=48#art5.

Matthews, David. *Medievalism: A Critical History.* Boydell & Brewer, 2015.

Maxwell, Robin. *To the Tower Born: A Novel of the Lost Princes.* Harper, 2006.

McArthur, Colin. "*Braveheart* and the Scottish Aesthetic Dementia." *Screening the Past: Film and the Representation of History,* edited by Tony Barta, Praeger, 1998, pp. 167–87.

McCarthy, Conor, ed. *Love, Sex and Marriage in the Middle Ages: A Sourcebook.* eBook ed., Taylor and Francis, 2013.

McCulloh, John M. "Jewish Ritual Murder: William of Norwich, Thomas of Monmouth, and the Early Dissemination of the Myth." *Speculum,* vol. 72, no. 3, 1997, pp. 698–740.

McDuffie, Susan. *A Mass for the Dead.* Kindle ed., Five Star, 2006.

_____. *The Study of Murder.* Kindle ed., Five Star, 2013.

McIntosh, Pat. *The Harper's Quine.* Kindle ed., Constable, 2004.

_____. *The Nicholas Feast.* Constable, 2005.

_____. *The Stolen Voice.* Constable, 2009.

McKendry, Anne. "Medievalism, the Detective, and the Quest for Whodunnit." *The Middle Ages in Popular Culture: Medievalism and Genre,* edited by Helen Young, Cambria Press, 2015, pp. 155–77.

McNamer, Sarah. *Affective Meditation and the Invention of Medieval Compassion.* U of Pennsylvania P, 2010.

The Medieval Murderers. *House of Shadows.* Simon & Schuster, 2007.

_____. *The Tainted Relic.* Simon & Schuster, 2005.

Meek, Edward L., Theron M. Westervest, and David N. Eldridge. "P.C. Doherty: Hugh Corbett, Secret-Agent and Problem-Solver." Kreisner and Browne, eds., pp.76–84.

Mendelson, Edward. "More Murder in the Monastery." *New York Times,* 4 Mar. 1984, p. BR9. *ProQuest Historical Newspapers,* search.proquest.com.ezp.lib.unimelb.edu.
au/docview/122345687?accountid=12372.

Merriam-Webster. "Ratiocination." www.merriam-webster.com.

Micir, Melanie. "The Impossible Miss Woolf: Kate Atkinson and the Feminist Modernist Historical Novel." *Modern Language Quarterly,* vol. 78, no. 4, 2017, pp. 517–39.

Moore, R.I. *The War on Heresy.* Harvard UP, 2012. *JSTOR,* www.jstor.org.ezp.lib.unimelb.
edu.au/stable/j.ctt2jbv6x.

Morillo, John, and Wade Newhouse. "History, Romance, and the Sublime Sound of Truth in *Ivanhoe.*" *Studies in the Novel,* vol. 32, no. 3, 2000, pp. 267–95. *Expanded Academic ASAP,* http://find.galegroup.com.mate.lib.
unimelb.edu.au.

"*A Mortal Bane* (Review)." *Kirkus Reviews,* 20 May 2010, www.kirkusreviews.com/book-reviews/roberta-gellis/a-mortal-bane/.

Mortensen, Annabelle. "*Jane and the Waterloo Map: Being a Jane Austen Mystery.*" *Library Journal,* vol. 140, no. 20, 2015, p. 80.

Most, Glenn W., and William W. Stowe, eds. *The Poetics of Murder: Detective Fiction and Literary Theory.* Harcourt Brace Jovanovich, 1983.

Munt, Sally. *Murder by the Book? Feminism and the Crime Novel.* Routledge, 1994.

Neufeld, Christine. "*The Reckoning: Law and Order* on a Medieval Stage." *The Journal of the Midwest Modern Language Association,* vol. 40, no. 1, 2007, pp. 1–10. *JSTOR*, www.jstor.org/stable/20464205.

Newman, Sharan. *Death Comes as Epiphany*. Forge, 1993.

_____. *The Difficult Saint*. Bella Rosa Books, 1999.

_____. *Heresy*. Forge, 2002.

_____. *The Outcast Dove*. Forge, 2003.

_____. *Strong as Death*. Bella Rosa Books, 1996.

_____. *The Wandering Arm*. Tom Doherty Associates, 1995.

_____. *The Witch in the Well*. Forge, 2004.

Nokes, David. "Putting on Corruption." *Times Literary Supplement* (London), 13 May 1983, p. 480, find.galegroup.com.ezp.lib.unimelb.edu.au/tlsh/infomark.do?&source=gale&prodId=TLSH&userGroupName=unimelb&tabID=T003&docPage=article&searchType=AdvancedSearchForm&docId=EX1200441125&type=multipage&contentSet=LTO&version=1.0.

O'Connor, Garry. *Chaucer's Triumph*. Petrak Press, 2007.

O'Connor, John J. "Brother Cadfael on the Case." *The New York Times*, 12 Jan. 1995, www.nytimes.com/1995/01/12/arts/television-review-brother-cadfael-on-the-case.html.

Paden, William D. "I Learned It at the Movies: Teaching Medieval Film." *Studies in Medievalism*, vol. xiii, 2004, pp. 79–98.

Park, Katharine. "The Life of the Corpse: Division and Dissection in Late Medieval Europe." *Journal of the History of Medicine and Allied Sciences*, vol. 50, no. 1, 1995, pp. 111–32. *JSTOR*, www.jstor.org.ezp.lib.unimelb.edu.au/stable/24623559.

Pavlac, Brian A., ed. *Game of Thrones Versus History: Written in Blood*. Wiley & Sons, 2017.

Pegg, Mark Gregory. *A Most Holy War: The Albigensian Crusade and the Battle for Christendom*. Oxford UP, 2008. *ProQuest Ebrary*, site.ebrary.com/lib/unimelb/reader.action?docID=10212187.

Penman, Sharon. *The Prince of Darkness*. Berkley, 2005.

_____. *The Queen's Man*. Ballantine Books, 1996.

Penny, David. *The Red Hill*. n.p., 2014.

Pepper, Andrew. "Black Crime Fiction." Priestman, ed., pp. 209–26.

Perry, David M. "Fictionalizing Your Scholar-ship." *Chronicle of Higher Education*, vol. 61, no. 7, 2014, p. 1. *Academic Search Complete*, ezp.lib.unimelb.edu.au/login?url=https://search-ebscohost-com.ezp.lib.unimelb.edu.au/login.aspx?direct=true&db=a9h&AN=98907381&site=eds-live&scope=site.

Perry, Marvin, and Frederick M. Schweitzer. *Antisemitism: Myth and Hate from Antiquity to the Present*. Palgrave Macmillan, 2002.

"A Personal Devil: A Magdalene La Batarde Mystery (Review)." *Publishers Weekly*, 1 Jan. 2001, www.publishersweekly.com/978-0-312-86998-4.

Peters, Ellis. *Brother Cadfael's Penance*. Time Warner, 1994.

_____. *Dead Man's Ransom*. 1984. Time Warner, 1994.

_____. *A Morbid Taste for Bones*. 1977. Time Warner, 1996.

_____. *The Virgin in the Ice*. 1982. Warner, 1995.

Picker, Lenny. "Spending Hours Pondering How to Murder Someone." *Publishers Weekly*, vol. 261, no. 48, 24 Nov. 2014, p. 52. *Education Research Complete*, ezp.lib.unimelb.edu.au/login?url=https://search-ebscohost-com.ezp.lib.unimelb.edu.au/login.aspx?direct=true&db=ehh&AN=99644720&site=eds-live&scope=site.

Pieri, Giuliana, ed. *Italian Crime Fiction*. U of Wales P, 2011.

Pitcher, John A. *Chaucer's Feminine Subjects: Figures of Desire In* The Canterbury Tales. Palgrave Macmillan, 2012.

Porter, Dennis. "The Private Eye." Priestman, ed., pp. 95–113.

_____. *The Pursuit of Crime: Art and Ideology in Detective Fiction*. Yale UP, 1981.

Postles, Dave. *Naming the People of England, c. 1100–1350*. Cambridge Scholars P, 2006.

Potter, Jeremy. *Death in the Forest*. 1977. eBook ed., Bloomsbury, 2011.

_____. "Richard III'S Historians: Adverse and Favourable Views (1991)." *Richard III Society—American Branch*, n.d., www.r3.org/on-line-library-text-essays/jeremy-potter-richard-iiis-historians-adverse-and-favourable-views/.

Powell, E.M. *The Blood of the Fifth Knight*. Thomas & Mercer, 2015.

_____. *The Fifth Knight*. Thomas & Mercer, 2012.

_____. *The King's Justice*. Thomas & Mercer, 2018.

_____. *The Lord of Ireland.* Thomas & Mercer, 2016.

Priestman, Martin, ed. *The Cambridge Companion to Crime Fiction.* Cambridge UP, 2003.

Pugh, Tison. "Chaucer in Contemporary Mystery Novels: A Case Study in Genre Fiction, Low-Cultural Allusions, and the Pleasure of Derivative Forms." *The Journal of Popular Culture,* vol. 46, no. 2, 2013, pp. 411–32.

Pugh, Tison, and Angela Jane Weisl. *Medievalisms: Making the Past in the Present.* Routledge, 2013.

Purves, Libby. "De Raptu Meo at the Inner Temple." *TheatreCat: Libby Purves Reviews,* 9 Nov. 2014, theatrecat.com/2014/11/09/de-raptu-meo-at-the-inner-temple/.

Pyrhönen, Heta. "Criticism and Theory." *A Companion to Crime Fiction,* edited by Charles J. Rzepka, and Lee Horsley, Wiley-Blackwell, 2010, pp. 43–56.

_____. *Mayhem and Murder: Narrative and Moral Problems in the Detective Story.* U of Toronto P, 1999.

_____. *Murder from an Academic Angle: An Introduction to the Study of the Detective Narrative.* Camden House, 1994.

Reddy, Maureen T. "The Feminist Counter-Tradition in Crime: Cross, Grafton, Paretsky and Wilson." *The Cunning Craft: Original Essays on Detective Fiction and Contemporary Literary Theory,* edited by Ronald G. Walker, and June M. Frazer, Western Illinois UP, 1990, pp. 174–87.

_____. *Sisters in Crime: Feminism and the Crime Novel.* Continuum, 1988.

_____. "Women Detectives." Priestman, ed., pp. 191–207.

Reddy, William M. *The Navigation of Feeling: A Framework for the History of Emotions.* Cambridge UP, 2001.

Richter, David H. "The Mirrored World: Form and Ideology in Umberto Eco's *The Name of the Rose.*" Capozzi, ed., pp. 256–75.

Riddy, Felicity. "'Women Talking About the Things of God': A Late Medieval Subculture." *Women and Literature in Britain, 1150–1500,* edited by Carol M. Meale, 2nd ed., Cambridge UP, 1996, pp. 104–27.

Rielly, Edward J., and David Robert Wooten, eds. *The Sister Fidelma Mysteries: Essays on the Historical Novels of Peter Tremayne.* McFarland, 2012.

Roach, Andrew P., and James R. Simpson, eds.

Heresy and the Making of European Culture: Medieval and Modern Perspectives. Ashgate, 2013.

Robb, Candace. *The Apothecary Rose.* St. Martin's Paperbacks, 1993.

_____. *A Gift of Sanctuary.* St. Martin's Paperbacks, 1998.

_____. *The Nun's Tale.* St. Martin's Paperbacks, 1995.

_____. *A Spy for the Redeemer.* St. Martin's Paperbacks, 1999.

_____. *A Vigil of Spies.* St. Martin's Paperbacks, 2008.

Roe, Caroline. *Consolation for an Exile.* Berkley, 2004.

_____. *Cure for a Charlatan.* Berkley, 1999.

_____. *A Poultice for a Healer.* Berkley, 2003.

_____. *Remedy for Treason.* Berkley, 1998.

Roger of Wendover. *Flowers of History.* Translated by J.A. Giles, vol. 2, London, Henry G. Bohn, 1849.

Rose, E.M. *The Murder of William of Norwich: The Origins of the Blood Libel in Medieval Europe.* Oxford UP, 2015.

Rosenwein, Barbara H. "Worrying About Emotions in History." *The American Historical Review,* vol. 107, no. 3, 2002, pp. 821–45.

Ross, Cheri L. "The First Feminist Detective: Anna Katharine Green's Amelia Butterworth." *Journal of Popular Culture,* vol. 25, no. 2, 1991, pp. 77–86. *ProQuest,* ezp.lib. unimelb.edu.au/login?url=https://search-ebscohost-com.ezp.lib.unimelb.edu.au/login. aspx?direct=true&db=ahl&AN=9201200709 &site=eds-live&scope=site.

Rowley, Tom. "Richard III Burial: Five Centuries On, the Last Medieval King Finally Gains Honour in Death." *The Telegraph* (London), 23 Mar. 2015, www.telegraph.co. uk/news/earth/environment/archaeology/ 11489187/Richard-III-burial-five-centuries-on-the-last-medieval-king-finally-gains-honour-in-death.html.

Royal, Priscilla. *Covenant with Hell.* Poisoned Pen Press, 2013.

_____. *The Sanctity of Hate.* Poisoned Pen Press, 2012.

_____. *Satan's Lullaby.* Poisoned Pen Press, 2015.

_____. *Sorrow Without End.* Poisoned Pen Press, 2006.

_____. *Wine of Violence.* Poisoned Pen Press, 2003.

Rozett, Martha Tuck. "Constructing a World:

How Postmodern Historical Fiction Reimagines the Past." *Clio,* vol. 25, no. 2, 1996, pp. 145–65. *Expanded Academic ASAP,* http://find.galegroup.com.mate.lib.unimelb.edu.au.

Rubin, Miri. "Making a Martyr: William of Nowich and the Jews." *History Today,* vol. 60, no. 6, 2010, pp. 49–54.

Russell, Richard Rankin. "The Dramatic Conversion of Nicholas Barber in Barry Unsworth's *Morality Play.*" *Renascence,* vol. 58, no. 3, 2006, pp. 221–39. *Literature Resource Center,* ezp.lib.unimelb.edu.au/login?url=https://search-ebscohost-com.ezp.lib.unimelb.edu.au/login.aspx?direct=true&db=edsglr&AN=edsgcl.147747963&site=eds-live&scope=site.

Rzepka, Charles J. *Detective Fiction.* Polity, 2005.

Scaggs, John. *Crime Fiction.* Routledge, 2005.

Scott, A.O. "Film Review: Seeking Human Truths Through the Stage." *The New York Times,* 5 Mar. 2004, www.nytimes.com/2004/03/05/movies/film-review-seeking-human-truths-through-the-stage.html?_r=0.

Scott, Walter. *Ivanhoe.* 1819. Edinburgh UP, 1998.

Sedley, Kate. *The Saint John's Fern.* Headline, 1999.

_____. *The Three Kings of Cologne.* Severn House, 2007.

Shaw, Tim. *A Death in Catte Street.* Kindle ed., Smashwords, 2013.

Sieg, Katrin. "Women in the Fortress Europe: Feminist Crime Fiction as Antifascist Performative." *Differences: A Journal of Feminist Cultural Studies,* vol. 16, no. 2, 2005, pp. 138–66. *Humanities International Complete,* ezp.lib.unimelb.edu.au/login?url=https://search-ebscohost-com.ezp.lib.unimelb.edu.au/login.aspx?direct=true&db=hlh&AN=17844034&site=eds-live&scope=site.

Sierra, Javier. *The Secret Supper.* Translated by Alberto Manguel, Washington Square Press, 2006.

Simmons, Clare A., ed. *Medievalism and the Quest for the "Real" Middle Ages.* Frank Cass, 2001.

Sir Gawain and the Green Knight. Edited by J.R.R. Tolkien, and E.V. Gordon. 2nd ed., edited by Norman Davis, Clarendon Press, 1967.

Somerset, Fiona, et al., eds. *Lollards and Their Influence in Late Medieval England.* Boydell Press, 2003.

Songer, Marcia J. "The Ultimate Penance of Brother Cadfael." *Clues: A Journal of Detection,* vol. 23, no. 4, 2005, pp. 63–68. *Humanities International Complete,* ezp.lib.unimelb.edu.au/login?url=https://search-ebscohost-com.ezp.lib.unimelb.edu.au/login.aspx?direct=true&db=hlh&AN=22465948&site=eds-live&scope=site.

Souter, Keith. *The Fool's Folly.* Robert Hale, 2009.

Stanbury, Sarah. "Medieval Studies." *Encyclopedia of Feminist Literary Theory,* edited by Elizabeth Kowaleski-Wallace, Taylor & Francis, 2009, pp. 364–66.

Starr, Mel. *The Abbot's Agreement.* Lion Hudson, 2014.

_____. *Ashes to Ashes.* Kregel Publications, 2015.

_____. *A Trail of Ink.* Lion Hudson, 2010.

_____. *The Unquiet Bones.* Lion Hudson, 2008.

Stearns, Peter N., and Carol Z. Stearns. "Emotionology: Clarifying the History of Emotions and Emotional Standards." *The American Historical Review,* vol. 90, no. 4, 1985, pp. 813–36.

Stevermer, C.J. *The Alchemist.* Ace Charter, 1980.

Strohm, Paul. *England's Empty Throne: Usurpation and the Language of Legitimation, 1399–1422.* Yale UP, 1998.

_____. *The Poet's Tale: Chaucer and the Year That Made the* Canterbury Tales. Profile Books, 2014.

Stuckart, Diane A.S. *A Bolt from the Blue.* Berkley, 2010.

_____. *Portrait of a Lady.* Berkley, 2009.

_____. *The Queen's Gambit.* Berkley, 2008.

Swett, Katharine W. "Assessing Patriarchies: Continuity and Change for European Women." *Journal of Women's History,* vol. 11, no. 2, 1999, pp. 224–35. *Project MUSE,* doi: 10.1353/jowh.1999.0014.

Swinfen, Ann. *The Bookseller's Tale.* Shakenoak Press, 2016.

_____. *The Novice's Tale.* Shakenoak Press, 2016.

Thomas of Monmouth. *The Life and Passion of William of Norwich.* Translated and edited by Miri Rubin, Penguin, 2014.

Tomlin, Stephen. "2014 Archive." *Stephen Tomlin,* stevetomlin.co.uk/index.php/2014-blog/.

Tremayne, Peter. *Absolution by Murder.* Headline, 1994.

_____. *The Devil's Seal.* Headline, 2014.

_____. *The Haunted Abbot.* Headline, 2002.

Trigg, Stephanie. *Congenial Souls: Reading Chaucer from Medieval to Postmodern.* Minnesota UP, 2002.

_____. "Medievalism and Convergence Culture: Researching the Middle Ages for Fiction and Film." *Parergon,* vol. 25, no. 2, 2008, pp. 99–118. *Project Muse,* doi:10.1353/pgn.0.0060.

Unsworth, Barry. *Morality Play.* Penguin, 1995.

Vail, Jason. *Bad Money.* Hawk Publishing, 2016.

_____. *Medieval and Renaissance Dagger Combat.* Paladin Press, 2006.

_____. *Saint Milburga's Bones.* Hawk Publishing, 2015.

Vaughan, David. "Edith Pargeter: An English Novelist in Prague." *Radio Praha in English,* 1 Oct. 2011, www.radio.cz/en/section/books/edith-pargeter-an-english-novelist-in-prague.

Vickers, Anita. "Stephanie Barron: (Re)Inventing Jane Austen as Detective." Browne and Kreiser, eds., pp. 213–21.

Wallace, Diana. "'History to the Defeated': Women Writers and the Historical Novel in the Thirties." *Critical Survey,* vol. 15, no. 2, 2003, pp. 76–94. *Expanded Academic ASAP,* http://find.galegroup.com.mate.lib.unimelb.edu.au.

Westerson, Jeri. *Blood Lance.* Minotaur Books, 2012.

_____. *The Demon's Parchment.* Minotaur Books, 2010.

_____. *Troubled Bones.* Minotaur Books, 2011.

The Westminster Chronicle 1381–1394. Edited and translated by L.C. Hector, and Barbara F. Harvey, Clarendon, 1982.

Whitaker, Cord, ed. "Making Race Matter in the Middle Ages." Special Journal Issue. *postmedieval: A Journal of Medieval Cultural Studies,* vol. 6, no. 1, 2015.

White, Hayden. "Introduction: Historical Fiction, Fictional History, and Historical Reality." *Rethinking History,* vol. 9, no. 2–3, 2005, pp. 147–57.

Whiteman, Robin. *Brother Cadfael's Book of Days: The Material and Spiritual Wisdom of a Medieval Crusader-Monk.* Headline, 2000.

_____. *Brother Cadfael's Herb Garden: An Illustrated Companion to Medieval Plants and Their Uses.* Little, Brown, 1996.

_____. *The Cadfael Companion: The World of Brother Cadfael.* Mysterious P, 1995.

Wilkinson, Louise J. *Women in Thirteenth-Century Lincolnshire.* The Boydell Press, 2007.

Willis, Connie. *Doomsday Book.* Bantam Spectra, 1992.

Wilson, Derek. "Derek Wilson: Historian of Fact, Faith, Fiction & Fantasy." www.derek-wilson.com/index.php.

_____. *The Swarm of Heaven.* Allison & Busby, 1999.

Wilson, Frank. "The Mosaic Crimes by Giulio Leoni." *The Philadelphia Inquirer,* 5 Apr. 2007. *Popmatters,* www.popmatters.com/review/the-mosaic-crimes-by-giulio-leoni/.

Woodhouse, Martin, and Robert Ross. *The Medici Emerald.* Coronet Books, 1976.

_____. *The Medici Guns.* Coronet Books, 1974.

_____. *The Medici Hawks.* Coronet Books, 1978.

Wren-Lewis, John. "Adam, Eve and Agatha Christie: Detective Stories as Post-Darwinian Myths of Original Sin." *Australian Religion Studies Review,* vol. 6, no. 1, 1993, pp. 20–24. openjournals.library.usyd.edu.au/index.php/arsr/issue/view/671.

Young, Helen. "Place and Time: Medievalism and Making Race." *The Year's Work in Medievalism.* Special Issue: Medievalism Now, vol. 28, 2013, pp. 2–6, pwp.gatech.edu/wp-content/uploads/sites/491/2016/09/28-Young.pdf.

Zamora, Lois Parkinson. "Apocalyptic Visions and Visionaries in *The Name of the Rose.*" Inge, ed., pp. 31–47.

Index